Chartered Institute of Housing

ing Costs:

to Housing Benefit

2021-22

Sam Lister and Martin Ward

D1343908

Shelter

Guide to Housing Benefit
Peter McGurk and Nick Raynsford, 1982-88
Martin Ward and John Zebedee, 1988-90

Guide to Housing Benefit and Community Charge Benefit
Martin Ward and John Zebedee, 1990-93

Guide to Housing Benefit and Council Tax Benefit
John Zebedee and Martin Ward, 1993-2003
John Zebedee, Martin Ward and Sam Lister, 2003-12
Sam Lister and Martin Ward, 2012-13

Guide to Housing Benefit and Council Tax Rebates
Sam Lister and Martin Ward, 2013-14

Guide to Housing Benefit
Sam Lister and Martin Ward, 2014-17

Help with Housing Costs: Guide to Housing Benefit
Sam Lister and Martin Ward, 2015-22

Sam Lister is policy and practice officer at the Chartered Institute of Housing
(email: *sam.lister@cih.org*) and a founding director of Worcester Citizens Advice Bureau
and Whabac. He has specialised in housing benefit and social security since 1993.

Martin Ward is an independent consultant and trainer on housing and benefit related
matters (e-mail: *mward@knowledgeflow.org.uk*). He has provided consultancy services
and training for several national organisations as well as many local authorities and
large and small housing providers across the UK since 1982.

ISBN 978-1-9993510-5-2

Edited and typeset by Davies Communications
(www.daviescomms.com)

Printed by MBA Group Ltd

Chartered Institute of Housing

The Chartered Institute of Housing (CIH) is the independent voice for housing and the home of professional standards. Our goal is simple – to support housing professionals to create a future in which everyone has a place to call home. We passionately believe in the life-changing impact of the work of housing professionals and our purpose is to provide everyone involved in housing with the advice, support and knowledge they need to make a difference every day.

CIH was granted a Royal Charter in 1984. We are a registered charity and the professional body for the housing sector.

> Chartered Institute of Housing
> Suites 5 and 6
> First Floor, Rowan House
> Westwood Way
> Coventry
> CV4 8HS
>
> Telephone: 024 7685 1700
>
> E-mail: *customer.services@cih.org*
>
> Website: *www.cih.org*

Shelter

Shelter helps over a million people a year struggling with bad housing or homelessness – and we campaign to prevent it in the first place.

We're here so no-one has to fight bad housing or homelessness on their own.

Please support us at *shelter.org.uk*

For more information about Shelter, please contact:

> 88 Old Street
> London
> EC1V 9HU
>
> Telephone: 0300 330 1234
>
> Website: *shelter.org.uk*

For help with your housing problems, phone Shelter's free housing advice helpline on 0808 800 4444 (open from 8am to 8pm on Mondays to Fridays and from 8am to 5pm on weekends: calls are free from UK landlines and main mobile networks) or visit *shelter.org.uk/advice*

Contents

Preface

This guide explains the rules about housing benefit as they apply from 1st April 2021, using the information available on that date.

We welcome comments and criticisms on the contents of our guide and make every effort to ensure it is accurate. However, the only statement of the law is found in the relevant Acts, regulations, orders and rules (chapter 1).

This guide has been written with the help and encouragement of many other people. Much material remains as written by John Zebedee. This year we thank the following in particular:

Linda Davies and Peter Singer (editing and production), Richard Stanier (Shelter) and John Zebedee as well as staff from the Department for Work and Pensions. Their help has been essential to the production of this guide.

Sam Lister and Martin Ward

April 2021

List of tables

Abbreviations

The principal abbreviations used in the guide are given below.

CTB	Council tax benefit
CTC	Child tax credit
CTR	Council tax rebate
DHP	Discretionary Housing Payment
DLA	Disability living allowance
DFC	The Department for Communities in Northern Ireland
DMG	Decision makers' guide: staff guide
DWP	The Department for Work and Pensions in Great Britain
EP	Extended payment
ESA	Employment and support allowance (including ESA(C) and ESA(IR))
ESA(C)	Contributory employment and support allowance
ESA(IR)	Income-related employment and support allowance
GB	England, Scotland and Wales
GLHA	The DWP guidance local housing allowance
GM	The DWP HB/CTB Guidance Manual
HB	Housing benefit
HMRC	Her Majesty's Revenue and Customs
HMCTS	Her Majesty's Courts and Tribunals Service
IB	Incapacity benefit
IS	Income support
JSA	Jobseeker's allowance (including JSA(C) & JSA(IB))
JSA(C)	Contribution-based jobseeker's allowance
JSA(IB)	Income-based jobseeker's allowance
MHCLG	Ministry of Housing, Communities and Local Government
NI	Northern Ireland
NIHE	The Northern Ireland Housing Executive
OG	The DWP HB/CTB Overpayments Guide
PIP	Personal independence payment
SDA	Severe disablement allowance
SI	Statutory instrument
SMI	Support for Mortgage Interest
SPC	State pension credit (including guarantee credit and savings credit)
SR	Statutory rules (Northern Ireland)
SSI	Scottish Statutory Instrument
UC	Universal credit
UK	England, Scotland, Wales and Northern Ireland
WTC	Working tax credit

Key to footnotes

Each reference applies to Great Britain only unless otherwise stated.
If prefixed by 'NI' (e.g. NIAA) it applies to Northern Ireland only.

AA	The Social Security Administration Act 1992 [section number]
AC	Appeal Cases, published by The Incorporated Council of Law Reporting for England and Wales, London
All ER	All England Law Reports, published by Butterworths
art	Article number
BC	Borough Council
BMLR	Butterworths Medico-Legal Reports
CA	Court of Appeal for England and Wales
C&P87	The Social Security (Claims and Payments) Regulations 1987, SI No 1968
CBA	The Social Security Contributions and Benefits Act 1992 [section number]
CC	City Council
ChD	High Court (England and Wales) Chancery Division
COD	Crown Office Digest, published by Sweet & Maxwell
CPR	The Housing Benefit and Council Tax Benefit (Consequential Provisions) Regulations 2006, SI No 217 [regulation number]
CPSA	The Child Support, Pensions and Social Security Act 2000 [section number]
CS	Court of Session, Scotland
DAR	The Housing Benefit and Council Tax Benefit (Decisions and Appeals) Regulations 2001, SI No 1002 [regulation number]
DAR99	The Social Security and Child Support (Decisions and Appeals) Regulations 1999, SI No 991 [regulation number]
DC	District Council
DFA	The Discretionary Financial Assistance Regulations 2001, SI No 1167 [regulation number]
ECJ	European Court of Justice
EWCA Civ	Court of Appeal Civil Division for England & Wales (neutral citation)
EWHC Admin	High Court for England & Wales, Administrative Court (neutral citation)

FTPR	The Tribunal Procedure (First-tier Tribunal) (Social Entitlement Chamber) Rules 2008, SI No 2685 [rule number]
HB	The Housing Benefit Regulations 2006, SI No 213 [regulation number]
HB66+	The Housing Benefit (Persons who have attained the age for state pension credit) Regulations 2006, SI No 214 [regulation number]
HBRB	Housing Benefit Review Board
HC (Admin)	High Court for England and Wales, Administrative Court
HL	House of Lords
HLR	Housing Law Reports, published by Sweet & Maxwell
LBC	London Borough Council
MBC	Metropolitan Borough Council
NIAA	The Social Security Administration (Northern Ireland) Act 1992 [section number]
NICBA	The Social Security Contributions and Benefits (Northern Ireland) Act 1992 [section number]
NIC&P87	The Social Security (Claims and Payments) Regulations (Northern Ireland) 1987, NISR No 465
NICPR	The Housing Benefit (Consequential Provisions) Regulations (Northern Ireland) 2006, SR No 407 [regulation number]
NICPSA	The Child Support, Pensions and Social Security Act (Northern Ireland) 2000 [section number]
NIDAR	The Housing Benefit (Decisions and Appeals) Regulations (Northern Ireland) 2001, SR No 213 [regulation number]
NIDAR99	The Social Security and Child Support (Decisions and Appeals) Regulations (Northern Ireland) 1999, SR No 162 [regulation number]
NIDFA	The Discretionary Financial Assistance Regulations (Northern Ireland) 2001, SR No 216 [regulation number]
NIED	The Housing Benefit (Executive Determinations) Regulations (Northern Ireland) 2008, SR No 100 [regulation number]
NIHB	The Housing Benefit Regulations (Northern Ireland) 2006, SR No 405 [regulation number]
NIHB66+	The Housing Benefit (Persons who have attained the age for state pension credit) Regulations (Northern Ireland) 2006, SR No 406 [regulation number]
NIPC	The State Pension Credit Regulations (Northern Ireland) 2003, NISR No 28

NISPCA	The State Pension Credit Act (Northern Ireland) 2002
NISR	Statutory Rules of Northern Ireland (equivalent to Statutory Instruments in GB)
NISSCPR	The Social Security Commissioners (Procedure) Regulations (Northern Ireland) 1999, SR No 225 [regulation number]
NIWRO	The Welfare Reform (Northern Ireland) Order 2015, SI 2015 No 2006
NIUCTP	The Universal Credit (Transitional Provisions) Regulations (Northern Ireland) 2016, NISR No 226
PC	The State Pension Credit Regulations 2002, SI No 1792
QBD	High Court (England and Wales) Queens Bench Division
reg	regulation [regulation number]
ROO	In England and Wales, The Rent Officers (Housing Benefit Functions) Order 1997, SI 1984; in Scotland, The Rent Officers (Housing Benefit Functions) (Scotland) Order 1997, SI 1995 [in both cases followed by article number or schedule and paragraph number]
sch	Schedule
SI	Statutory Instrument [year and reference number]
SLT	Scots Law Times, published by W. Green, Edinburgh
SO	The Income Related Benefits (Subsidy to Authorities) Order 1998, SI No 562
SPCA	The State Pension Credit Act 2002
SR	Statutory rules [year and reference number (apply to NI only)]
SSWP	Secretary of State for Work and Pensions
TCEA	Tribunals, Courts and Enforcement Act 2007 [section number]
UCTP	Universal Credit (Transitional Provisions) Regulations 2014, SI No 1230 [regulation number]
UKHL	House of Lords, UK case (neutral citation)
UKSC	Supreme Court (neutral citation)
UTPR	The Tribunal Procedure (Upper Tribunal) Rules 2008, SI No 2698 [rule number]
WLR	Weekly Law Reports, published by The Incorporated Council of Law Reporting for England and Wales, London
WRA	The Welfare Reform Act 2012

What you can claim

	Working age	Pension age
Renters		
Rent payments	UC	HB
Service charge payments	UC	HB
Renters in supported or temporary accommodation		
Rent payments	HB	HB
Service charge payments	HB	HB
Owners		
Owner occupier payments	SMI	SMI
Service charge payments	UC	SPC
Shared owners		
Owner occupier payments	SMI	SMI
Rent payments	UC	HB
Service charge payments	UC	HB
All		
Living costs	UC	SPC
Council tax (Great Britain)	CTR	CTR
Rates (Northern Ireland)	RR	RR
Other help	DHPs etc	DHPs etc

Universal credit (UC)	volume 1
Housing benefit (HB)	volume 2
Support for mortgage interest (SMI)	volume 1
State pension credit (SPC)	volume 2
Council tax rebate (CTR)	volume 1
Rate rebate (RR)	volume 1
Discretionary housing payments (DHPs)	volume 2

Chapter 1 **Introduction**

- ■ Summary of HB and how it is changing: see paras 1.2-14.
- ■ Using this guide, the law and guidance: see paras 1.15-21.
- ■ Universal credit and council tax rebate summary: see paras 1.22-35.

1.1 Welcome to this guide, which describes housing benefit (HB) throughout the UK. The guide is used by people claiming HB, advisers, landlords, benefit administrators and appeal tribunals. It gives the rules from April 2021. Table 1.1 summarises the main terminology.

The HB scheme

1.2 HB can help you pay your rent. Chapters 2 and 3 give the details about who is eligible and this depends partly on your age (paras 1.3-4). Over three million people get HB (table 1.2).

Pension age claims

1.3 Anyone over pension age can make a claim for HB, and if you are already on HB you can continue to receive it. Pension age is now 66 for everyone.

Working age claims

1.4 Working age means under pension age. If you are working age you can only make a claim for HB if you live in supported or temporary accommodation (table 2.3). If you live in any other kind of accommodation, UC can help with your rent: see *Help With Housing Costs Volume 1: Universal Credit and Council Tax Rebates*. If you are already on HB you can continue to receive it until you transfer to UC (para 1.22).

Table 1.1 **HB terminology**

Housing benefit

In this guide, housing benefit means any kind of HB for rent.

Rent rebate and rent allowance

A rent rebate means HB (as a reduction in rent) for a council tenant or NIHE tenant. A rent allowance means HB (as a cash payment) for anyone else.

Tenant and landlord/agent

A tenant includes any kind of rent-payer (for example a licensee). Your landlord or agent is the person your rent is due to.

Social renter and private renter

If you rent from the council, the NIHE or a housing association you are usually a social renter. If you rent from any other landlord you are usually a private renter.

Eligible rent

Your eligible rent is the amount of rent HB can meet.

Local housing allowance

LHAs are the main way of working out eligible rent for private renters.

Family

Your HB is based on your circumstances and those of the following members of your family:

- your partner if you are in a couple (or partners in a polygamous marriage); and/or
- each child or young person you or your partner are responsible for.

Single person

You are a single person if you do not have a partner. HB law uses 'lone parent' if you have at least one child or young person or 'single claimant' if you don't.

Couple

You are a couple if you are two people who are married or in a civil partnership or living together as a couple. HB law uses 'couple' whether or not you have children or young persons.

Polygamous marriage

You have a polygamous marriage if you (or your husband or wife) are married to more than one person under the law of a country that permits this.

Child and young person

A child is someone under the age of 16. A young person is someone aged 16 to 19 who is in, or has recently left, secondary education or approved training.

Claimant and partner

If you are in a couple or polygamous marriage, only one of you is the claimant. The other one (or each of the others) is your partner.

Pension age and working age claims

Pension age is 66 for everyone. You have a pension age claim if you are single and aged 66 or over, or a couple and both of you are. You have a working age claim if you are single and under 66, or a couple and at least one of you is.

Benefit week

HB is calculated on a weekly basis. Each weekly period begins on a Monday and ends at midnight on the following Sunday night. This is called a benefit week.

Maximum HB and applicable amount

The calculation of your HB is based on your income and capital, your maximum HB and your applicable amount. Your maximum HB is your eligible rent minus any non-dependant contributions. Your applicable amount is made up of the personal allowances, premiums and components you qualify for.

Non-dependants

A non-dependant is an adult who lives with you but who isn't in your family. If you have one or more non-dependants they may be expected to contribute towards your rent.

Table 1.2 **Key HB statistics**

HB claims in Great Britain on 1st August 2020

Number of cases	3,045,794

Of which:

In receipt of passport benefit	63.9%
Claimants aged 65+	38.1%
Local authority tenants	30.6%
Housing association tenants	44.8%
Private tenant LHA cases	20.6%
Private tenant non-LHA cases	4.0%

■ Source: DWP, Single Housing Benefit Extract (SHBE).

The amount of your HB

1.5 HB helps you pay your rent. How much you get depends on your financial and other circumstances (paras 1.6-7) and your eligible rent (para 1.8). Chapter 6 gives the calculation.

1.6 You get maximum HB if you are on a passport benefit (para 1.7). If you aren't on a passport benefit, your HB is based on:

    (a) your income and capital: see chapters 13 to 15; and

    (b) your 'applicable amount' – this reflects your basic living needs: see chapters 4 and 12.

In either case, your HB can be reduced if you have one or more non-dependants – these are adults who live with you and are expected to contribute (paras 4.26-32).

The passport benefits

1.7 The 'passport benefits' are:

    (a) the guarantee credit of state pension credit (SPC) (chapter 22);

    (b) universal credit (UC) in supported or temporary accommodation (para 2.13);

    (c) income-based jobseeker's allowance (JSA(IB));

    (d) income-related employment and support allowance (ESA(IR)); and

    (e) income support (IS).

These help you meet basic living needs other than your rent (such as food and heating).

Your eligible rent

1.8   Your eligible rent is the figure used in calculating your HB:

(a) in most social sector lettings, your eligible rent equals the rent payable on your home (reduced in certain cases if the home is larger than you need), apart from any charges included in the rent for particular services which HB cannot meet (paras 8.57-74);

(b) in most private sector lettings, your eligible rent is a fixed 'local housing allowance' figure depending on where you live and the size of accommodation you need.

Chapters 7-11 give the details.

How to get HB

1.9   To get HB you make a claim to the authority that administers HB for your area (para 1.13). We call this 'your council'. If you are a couple, your claim includes both of you. See chapter 16 for how to claim.

1.10   If a council owns properties outside its area, the tenants there claim HB from their landlord council. And if your council contracts out its administration of HB to another council, or group of councils, or a private company, you may have to claim HB from them.

1.11   You can usually claim council tax rebate (in Great Britain) or rate rebates (in Northern Ireland) at the same time as HB.

HB payments and appeals

1.12   HB is a weekly benefit based on 'benefit weeks' which begin each Monday. If you are a council (or NIHE) tenant it is paid as a rebate to your rent account. If you are a private tenant it is usually paid fortnightly or four weekly, or in some cases to your landlord. If you are overpaid you may have to repay it. If you think your HB is wrong (or you have been refused HB), you can ask your council (or NIHE) to reconsider it and appeal to an independent tribunal. See chapters 18-20.

Authorities that administer HB

1.13   HB is administered (along with CTR or rate rebates) by:

(a) district or borough councils (called housing authorities) in parts of England with two layers of local government;

(b) unitary or London councils in other parts of England;

(c) Welsh county or county borough councils;

(d) Scottish local councils;

(e) the Northern Ireland Housing Executive.

Non-unitary county councils in England don't administer HB but in some cases receive HB claims on behalf of district or borough councils.

Who administers other benefits

1.14   The DWP in Great Britain and DFC in Northern Ireland administer most other state benefits, including UC (para 1.22), SPC (chapter 22) and the passport benefits. But HMRC administers tax credits, child benefit and guardian's allowance.

Using this guide

1.15   The HB rules in this guide apply from April 2021 and recent changes are in table 1.3. The next edition will give the rules from April 2022.

HB and other benefit figures

1.16   The HB figures in this guide apply from:

(a) Monday 5th April 2021 if your rent is due weekly or in multiples of weeks; or

(b) Thursday 1st April 2021 in all other cases.

The figures for most other benefits (appendix 2) apply from week commencing Monday 5th April, but affect your HB from 1st or 5th April (para 17.37).

Abbreviations and footnotes

1.17   The tables at the front of this guide give:

(a) a list of the abbreviations used in the text; and

(b) a key to the abbreviations used in the footnotes.

The footnotes throughout this guide refer to the law governing HB. All the references are to the law as amended.

Law and guidance

HB law

1.18   The law governing the HB scheme is in the Social Security Contributions and Benefits Act 1992, the Social Security Administration Act 1992 and their Northern Ireland equivalents. The regulations and orders giving the details of the scheme are listed in Appendix 1 (along with other Acts of Parliament). These are called statutory instruments in Great Britain (SIs) and statutory rules (NISRs) in Northern Ireland. The main ones are the Housing Benefit Regulations 2006, the Housing Benefit (Persons who have attained the qualifying age for state pension credit) Regulations 2006, and their Northern Ireland equivalents. See also paras 20.22-24.

1.13   AA 134(1),(1A),(1B),(2),(5), 139(1),(2), 191; NIAA 126(2),(3)

1.16   AA 150(10); NIAA 132(1); HB 79(3); HB66+ 59(3); NIHB 77(5); NIHB66+ 57(5)

DWP guidance

1.19   The DWP publishes guidance on HB for councils in Great Britain including:

(a)   Housing Benefit and Council Tax Benefit Guidance Manual (GM);

(b)   Local Housing Allowance Guidance Manual and Good Practice Guide;

(c)   HB Overpayments Guide (OG);

(d)   Subsidy Guidance Manual;

(e)   Guidance on Discretionary Housing Payments;

(f)   circulars in the 'A' series (about adjudication and operations);

(g)   circulars in the 'S' series (about subsidy matters);

(h)   circulars in the 'U' series (about urgent matters); and

(i)   LA Welfare Direct bulletins (on general matters – replacing the HB general information bulletins).

In NI the DFC provides the Housing Benefit Decision Makers Guide. Its HB Memos provide further guidance.

Case law

1.20   Case law refers to the body of principles established by judges while deciding cases in courts of record such as the Upper Tribunal. These set a precedent and are binding on local authority decision makers and First-tier Tribunals. The cases referred to in this guide are about HB, or other benefit law which is relevant because of its similarities with HB law. Generally speaking, case law from one part of the UK is regarded as binding in other parts of the UK.

Obtaining the law and guidance

1.21   The Acts, regulations, government guidance and case law are available online [www].

Universal credit summary

1.22   UC can help working age claimants meet basic living needs (such as food and heating), rent and childcare costs. It is replacing the legacy benefits, which are:

(a)   working age HB (except in supported or temporary accommodation);

(a)   the passport benefits JSA(IB), ESA(IR) and IS;

(a)   the tax credits CTC and WTC.

For full details see volume 1.

1.22   GB law: www.legislation.gov.uk
        NI law: www.communities-ni.gov.uk/services/law-relating-social-security (Northern Ireland)
        Guidance: www.gov.uk/guidance/housing-benefit-information-guidance-and-good-practice-for-local-authority-staff
        www.gov.uk/government/collections/local-housing-allowance-information-for local-authorities
        GB case law before January 2016: www.tinyurl.com/UKUT-decisions-pre2016
        GB case law from January 2016: https://www.gov.uk/administrative-appeals-tribunal-decisions
        NI guidance: https://tinyurl.com/HB-NI-Guidance
        NI case law: www.communities-ni.gov.uk/services/northern-ireland-digest-case-law

Who can get UC

1.23   The main conditions for UC are:

(a) you must be working age (under 66);

(b) you must not be an excluded student;

(c) you must not be an excluded migrant, under 18 years old, prisoner, hospital detainee or member of a religious order – but prisoners can continue getting UC for their rent payments during their first six months in prison;

(d) you must in most cases be present in the UK;

(e) your capital (combined if you are a couple) must not be over £16,000;

(f) your income (combined if you are a couple) must be low enough.

1.24   If you are single you must meet all the conditions in para 1.23. If you are a couple, you get UC as a couple if you both meet them all or only one of you meets conditions (a) or (b), but you can get UC as a single person if only one of you meets conditions (c) or (d).

UC claims and payments

1.25   You claim UC from the DWP in Great Britain or DFC in Northern Ireland. It is awarded for 'assessment periods' of one month (normally beginning on the same day of each month) and is paid in arrears. Most changes in your circumstances take effect from the beginning of the assessment period they occur in.

Migrating to UC

1.26   Transferring from legacy benefits to UC is called 'migration'. See paras 17.19-24 for the date your HB ends.

1.27   'Natural migration' is when you transfer to UC without having received a migration notice from the DWP. This occurs when your circumstances change in a way that ends one or more of your legacy benefits. For example, your HB ends if you move to a new area (table 17.3(d),(e)). The law stops you from claiming that benefit again, so you can only replace your lost income by claiming UC instead – which ends all your other legacy benefits.

1.28   'Managed migration' is when you transfer to UC because you have received a migration notice advising you to claim UC. The DWP is currently running a pilot scheme of up to 10,000 cases and plans then to have a full scheme of all remaining cases.

1.27   UCTP 5(1), 6(1), 7(2), 8(2),(2A); NIUCTP 3(1), 4(1), 5(2), 6(2),(2A)

1.28   UCTP 44-46; NIUCTP 45-47

Transitional protection

1.29   If you transfer to UC due to natural or managed migration (other than when you become a couple: para 17.24) you get a two-week run-on of HB and/or JSA(IB)/ESA(IR)/IS. This overlaps with the beginning of your UC (para 17.20). People who are worse off on UC than on legacy benefits can also get a transitional element in their UC. This applies to:

(a)   anyone who transfers due to managed migration; and

(b)   severely disabled people (para 1.30) who transfer due to natural migration.

Severely disabled people

1.30   Since 27th January 2021, severely disabled people can make a claim for UC, (in other words, para 1.22 applies). But if you transfer to UC as part of natural migration, you can only get a UC transitional element if you were getting a severe disability premium in your JSA(IB)/ESA(IR)/IS. Getting that premium in your HB is not enough by itself, though in this case you may be able to get discretionary help from the DWP or your council (para 23.1-2).

CTR summary

1.31   In Great Britain many people get council tax rebates (CTR) at the same time as HB and most councils have one claim form covering both benefits (para 16.10).

1.32   Paras 1.33-35 summarise the main CTR rules if you don't get UC. And for these (non-UC) cases appendix 3 gives equivalent CTR footnotes for chapters 12-15. For full details about CTR, including how to calculate it if you get UC, see volume 1 chapters 16 and 17.

Calculating main CTR

1.33   'Main CTR' is the most common kind of CTR. Except as described in para 1.34:

(a)   your weekly main CTR equals your weekly council tax minus:

 ■   amounts for non-dependants, and

 ■   20% of your excess income;

(b)   your, capital income and excess income are assessed for main CTR in the same way as for HB (chapters 13-15);

(c)   non-dependant contributions are much lower in CTR than in HB;

(d)   applicable amounts are sometimes different (para 1.34).

1.29   UCTP 8A, 8B; NIUCTP 6A, 6B

1.30   UCTP 4A; SI 2019/1152 regs 1(5), 7; NIUCTP 2B; NISR 2019/152 regs 1(5), 6

CTR applicable amounts

1.34   The differences from HB are as follows:

(a) the personal allowances (table 12.1) are higher in CTR for children and young persons in Scotland and for working age adults in Wales (volume 1 appendix 2);

(b) the lower rate personal allowance (para 12.8) only applies in CTR if you are single, aged under 18, not a lone parent, and not on the main phase of ESA;

(c) the two-child limit (para 12.10) doesn't apply to CTR in Scotland and Wales;

(d) the family premium (para 12.24) continues to apply in Wales;

(e) the transitional addition if you transfer onto ESA (para 12.50) no longer applies to CTR in Wales.

Local CTR for working age claims in England

1.35   In England, local councils can devise their own schemes for working age CTR. These sometimes:

(a) use different figures for applicable amounts and non-dependant contributions;

(b) assess income and capital differently;

(c) deduct up to 35% (rather than 20%) of excess income;

(d) have a completely different method of calculation.

Your local council should tell you how its own local scheme works.

Table 1.3 **Summary of HB changes from April 2020**

15th July 2020 SI 2020/618 NISR 2020/108	Grenfell Tower Payments, National Emergencies Trust, Child Migrants Trust and new style ESA special payments (to compensate for DWP errors) are disregarded. Definition of 'postgraduate loan' widened (ADM 18/20).
24th Aug 2020 SI 2020/683 NISR 2020/149	Certain third country (non-EEA) nationals who are the family member of a 'person from Northern Ireland' (whether currently resident in Northern Ireland or not) can acquire a right to reside and therefore entitlement to UC.
6th Oct 2020	Raising of state pension age complete. Pension age now 66 for men and women (para 2.4). No further raises expected until 2024 (when it is expected to rise gradually from 66 to 68).
9th Nov 2020 SI 2020/989	New Scottish social security benefits introduced. The new lump sum payments 'Young Carer Grant' and 'Winter Heating Assistance' are disregarded as capital. 'Short-term Assistance' is disregarded as income in working age and pension age HB and 'Scottish Child Payment' is disregarded in pension age HB (because it does fall within the definition of income). See also Welfare Direct Bulletin 11/20.
12th Nov 2020 SI 2020/1156 SI 2020/1201 SI 2021/476 NISR 2020/227 NISR 2020/242 NISR 2021/105	Coronavirus measure relating prisoners on temporary release that was due to expire on 12th November is extended until 12th May 2021 (see below) and from 12th May to 31st August 2021 in cases where the DWP deems it necessary due to coronavirus.
25th Nov 2020 SI 2020/655 NISR 2020/119	New UC run on for claimants transferring to SPC on reaching 66. UC award that overlaps HB/SPC is disregarded as income. In mixed age couples the elder member can claim SPC/HB as a single person on reaching pension age even if some other exclusion applies.
31st Dec 2020/ 1st Jan 2021 SI 2020/1209 SI 2020/1279 SI 2020/1309 SI 2020/1372	End of Brexit transition period ('Implementation Period'). EEA nationals who enter the UK on or after 1 January 2021 are now subject to immigration control. Those who entered the UK before then can use their EEA rights during the 'grace period' until 30th June 2021 – the deadline to apply to the EU settlement scheme (EUSS). From 1st July 2021, EEA nationals can only use their EEA rights if they applied to the EUSS on or before the deadline.

27th Jan 2021 SI 2019/1152 NISR 2019/152	Severe disability gateway condition for migration to UC ends. Severely disabled working age claimants must now claim UC instead of HB and other legacy benefits. Former JSA(IB)/ESA(IR)/IS claimants with a severe disability premium who migrate naturally to UC qualify for a transitional element (para 1.29). See also A11/2020.
1st Apr 2021 SI 2021/188 NISR 2021/70	Personal allowance for new pension age claimants no longer includes the savings credit uplift and is now the same rate as the guarantee credit element of SPC (tables 12.1, 22.1). Change reflects the abolition of savings credit for new claims from April 2016 (para 22.8).
6th Apr 2021 SI 2020/1519 NISR 2021/14	LHA rates frozen during 2021-22 at their April 2020 levels.
6th Apr 2021 SI 2020/371 SI 2021/162 NISR 2020/53 NISR 2021/82	Benefits up-rating based on previous September consumer prices index of 0.5 per cent. The extra £20 per week in the additional earned income disregard (para 14.68) introduced in April 2020 due to coronavirus ends.
12th May 2021 31st Aug 2021	Coronavirus-related temporary measure, allowing prisoners on temporary release to claim HB, expires. (See also 12th November entry.)
30th Jun 2021/ 1st July 2021	EU settlement scheme closes. EEA nationals who have not registered by 30th June 2021 lose their EEA rights on 1st July and their immigration status changes to an overstayer. (See also entry above for 31st December 2020/1st January 2021.)

Planned changes

2021 – Jun 2024	'Managed migration' of claimants on legacy benefits onto UC on an area-by-area basis resumes, with transitional protection against losses. Claimants living in supported or temporary accommodation continue to get HB.
2023-24	New exemptions to the LHA shared accommodation rate (para 9.20) to be introduced covering rough sleepers aged 16-24, care leavers up to the age of 25, and victims of domestic abuse and human trafficking (HM Treasury, Budget Red Book 2020, paras 1.190, 2.20).
2024 or later	The transfer of pension age claimants from HB to SPC, with SPC meeting housing costs in a similar way to UC (called 'housing credit').

Chapter 2 **Who can get HB**

- Basic rules for pension age and working age HB: see paras 2.1-12.
- Supported or temporary accommodation: see paras 2.13-20.
- Migrants and recent arrivals, care leavers, students and trainees: see paras 2.21-33.

Basic rules

2.1　　To get HB, you must make a valid claim (chapter 16) and meet the conditions in table 2.1.

2.2　　The rules about this depend on whether you are:

(a) pension age – this means 66 or over; or

(b) working age – this means under 66.

Table 2.2 shows whether you get pension age or working age HB.

2.3　　The rules also depend on whether you live in:

(a) supported or temporary accommodation – this means any accommodation in table 2.3; or

(b) general accommodation – this means any other accommodation.

Table 2.1 **Basic and financial conditions for HB**

(a) You occupy the dwelling as your home (chapter 3).

(b) You are liable to make payments there (paras 5.2-14).

(c) The payments are not for a contrived or excluded letting (paras 5.15-35).

(d) The payments count as 'rent' for HB purposes (table 7.1).

(e) If you are a migrant, care leaver or student you must be in an eligible group (paras 2.21-33).

(f) Your capital (apart from disregarded capital) is not over £16,000 (paras 15.2-4).

(g) Your income and any non-dependant deductions are not too high for you to qualify (paras 6.2-7).

(h) For working age HB only, you must live in supported or temporary accommodation or have claimed under earlier rules (paras 2.6-7).

T2.1　　AA 1(1),(1A),(1B); CBA 130(1),(4), 134(1),(4); NIAA 1(1),(1A),(1B); NICBA 129(1), 130(1),(3)

Table 2.2 **Pension age or working age HB**

Single person

(a)	Aged 66 or over	Pension age HB
(b)	Under 66	Working age HB

Couple

(c)	Both aged 66 or over	Pension age HB
(d)	Both under 66	Working age HB
(e)	Mixed ages (para 2.11)	Working age HB

Partners in a polygamous marriage

(f)	All aged 66 or over	Pension age HB
(g)	All under 66	Working age HB
(h)	Mixed ages (para 2.12)	Working age HB

Pension age HB

2.4 Pension age HB is for single people aged 66 or over and couples if you are both aged 66 or over (table 2.2). You can make a claim for pension age HB whether you live in general, supported or temporary accommodation.

2.5 Pension age HB is usually more generous than working age HB because:

(a) you can get pension age HB if you live in any kind of accommodation that meets the conditions in table 2.1(a)-(d);

(b) there is no cap to the total benefits you can get in a week (table 6.4);

(c) there are no size criteria for social tenants (para 8.11 and table 8.1);

(d) the HB personal allowances are higher (table 12.1);

(e) more kinds of income and capital are disregarded (tables 13.6, 14.5 and 15.1);

(f)   you can have more capital before it affects your HB (para 15.5);

(g) backdating for three months is automatic (16.36).

Working age HB

2.6 Working age HB is for single people under 66 and couples if at least one of you is under 66 (table 2.2). You can only make a claim for working age HB if you live in supported or temporary accommodation (table 2.3).

T2.2	HB 5; HB66+ 5; NIHB 5; NIHB66+ 5; SI 2019/37; NISR 2019/2
2.4	HB 5; HB66+ 5; SI 2019/37; NIHB 5; NIHB66+5; NISR 2019/2
2.6	UCTP 5(2)(a), 6(8); NIUCTP 3(2)(a), 4(8)

2.7 You can no longer make a claim for working age HB in general accommodation; instead, you can get UC towards your housing costs. Most people now on working age HB claimed under rules that applied before the introduction of UC (para 1.22).

If you are currently on HB

2.8 If you are currently getting pension age or working age HB (whenever you claimed) your HB ends if:

    (a) you stop meeting the conditions in table 2.1; or

    (b) you move to an area where HB is administered by a different council (table 17.3(d)).

2.9 For working age HB the following also apply:

    (a) if you live in general accommodation your HB ends if you claim UC (paras 1.26-29); or

    (b) if you live in supported or temporary accommodation and are on UC as well as HB, your HB ends if you move to general accommodation.

Severely disabled people

2.10 Since 27th January 2021, the rules about claiming HB/UC are the same for severely disabled people as they are for other claimants (paras 1.22-30).

Mixed age claims

2.11 You are a mixed age couple if one of you is aged 66 or over and one under 66. You can get:

    (a) working age HB if you (the claimant) are aged 66 or over and your partner can't get UC because of being an excluded migrant, under 18 years old, prisoner, hospital detainee, member of a religious order or absent from the UK (paras 1.23-24);

    (b) pension age HB if you (the claimant) reached pension age before 15th May 2019 and have been on HB or SPC or both since before that date;

    (c) working age HB in all other cases.

In case (a), you get HB as though you were a single person (circular A9/2019); but in cases (b) and (c), you get HB as a couple in the normal way.

2.12 The rules in para 2.11 also apply if you are in a mixed age polygamous marriage. Alternatively, the two of you who were married earliest can get pension age HB as a couple, and the other(s) can get pension age or working age HB as a single person.

2.7   UCTP 5(1); NIUCTP 3(1)

2.8   AA 130(1); HB 79(1),(8); HB66+ 59(1),(8); NIAA 129(1); NIHB 77(1),(10); NIHB66+57(1),(10)

2.9   UCTP 7(2),(5), 8(2A),(3); NIUCTP 5(2),(5), 6(2),(3)

2.10   SI 2019/1152 reg 7; NISR 2019/152 reg 6

2.11-12 HB 5; HB66+ 5; SI 2019/37 art 7(2), SI 2019/935; NIHB 5; NIHB66+5; NISR 2019/2 art 7(2); NISR 2019/107

Table 2.3 **Supported or temporary accommodation**

For supported accommodation see (a) to (e); for temporary accommodation see (f).

(a) Exempt accommodation

- You rent from a not-for-profit landlord; and
- you are provided with care, support or supervision by your landlord, or by someone else on your landlord's behalf (table 10.1).

(b) General supported accommodation

- You rent from a not-for-profit landlord; and
- you are provided with care, support or supervision by your landlord, or by someone else (this needn't be on your landlord's behalf); and
- you were admitted to the accommodation to meet a need for this.

(c) Domestic violence refuges

- You rent from a not-for-profit landlord or from a council that administers HB (para 1.13); and
- the building you live in (or relevant part of it) is wholly or mainly used as non-permanent accommodation for people who have left their home as a result of domestic violence; and
- the accommodation is provided to you for that reason.

(d) Local authority hostels

- The building you live in is owned or managed by an authority which administers HB (para 1.13); and
- it provides non-self-contained domestic accommodation with meals or adequate food-preparation facilities (and is not a care home or independent hospital); and
- you are provided with care, support or supervision by your landlord, or by someone else (this needn't be on your landlord's behalf).

(e) Resettlement accommodation

- You live in a hostel for homeless people; and
- the hostel received a resettlement grant under section 30 of the Jobseekers Act 1995 in the past (these grants are no longer awarded).

(f) Temporary accommodation

- You rent from a council that administers HB (para 1.13) or from a registered housing association (para 7.14); and
- the accommodation was provided to you because you were homeless or to prevent you from becoming homeless (para 21.33).

Notes:

'Not-for-profit landlord', means:

- a housing association, registered or unregistered (para 7.13); or

> - a registered charity;
> - a voluntary organisation (para 7.21); or
> - an English county council that doesn't administer HB.
>
> 'Care, support or supervision': see table 10.1.
>
> Domestic violence is defined as including 'controlling or coercive behaviour, violence, or psychological, physical, sexual, emotional, financial or other abuse, regardless of the gender or sexuality of the victim'.
>
> Resettlement accommodation is also exempt accommodation.

Supported or temporary accommodation

2.13   Table 2.3 gives all the kinds of supported or temporary accommodation (STA). Your landlord should normally be able to tell you if your home is included.

Getting HB for your housing costs in STA

2.14   If you live in supported or temporary accommodation, you can get HB whether you have a pension age or working age claim. The only exception is that if you were getting UC on temporary accommodation before 10th April 2018 (when the rules changed), you can continue to get UC until your rent goes up or down.

Eligible rent in STA

2.15   Eligible rent in supported or temporary accommodation is worked out as follows in both working age and pension age HB:

(a) for exempt and resettlement accommodation (table 2.3(a),(e)) the 'old scheme' rules apply (paras 10.9-22);

(b) in other cases (table 2.3(b)-(d),(f)) the rules for social or private renters apply in the same way and with the same exceptions as for other renters (chapters 8 and 9).

Getting benefit on two homes in STA

2.16   The following rules apply when you are liable for housing costs on two homes:

(a) if both are supported or temporary accommodation, you can get HB on both in any of the situations in para 3.39;

(b) if only one is supported or temporary accommodation, you can get HB on that one and UC towards your housing costs on the other, but only if you are absent due to fear of violence (para 3.16).

T2.3(a)-(e)   HB 2(1) definitions: 'hostel', 'housing association', 'voluntary organisation', 75H; NIHB 2(1), 73F

T2.3(f)   UC sch 1 para 3B; Housing Act 1996 part 7; Housing (Scotland) Act 1987 part 2; NIUC sch 1 para 4A

2.13   UCTP 2(1) – 'specified accommodation', 'temporary accommodation'; NIUCTP 2(1)

2.14   UCTP 5(2)(a), 6(8), 7(5)(4), 8(3); NIUCTP 3(2)(a), 4(8), 5(5)(a), 6(3); SI 2018/65 reg 8(2); NISR 2018/92 reg 10(1)

2.16(a)   HB 7(6)(a)-(e); HB66+ 7(6)(a)-(e); UCTP 6(8), 7(5), 8(3); NIHB 7(6)(a)-(e); NIHB66+ 7(6)(a)-(e); NIUCTP 4(8), 5(5), 6(3)

2.16(b)   HB 7(6)(a); HB66+ 7(6)(a); UC sch 3 para 6; UCTP 6(8), 7(5), 8(3);
NIHB 7(6)(a); NIHB66+ 7(6)(a); NIUC sch 3 para 5; NIUCTP 4(8), 5(5), 6(3)

The benefit cap in STA

2.17   When the benefit cap is calculated in HB (table 6.4) or UC (volume 1 chapter 9):

(a) HB on supported or temporary accommodation isn't included in the benefit caps;

(b) HB on general accommodation is included in the HB benefit cap, but not the UC one;

(c) UC for housing costs on general accommodation is included in the UC benefit cap, but not the HB one.

Two homes and the benefit cap in STA

2.18   If you qualify for benefit on two homes, para 2.17 applies separately to each of them. For example, if one is supported accommodation, (a) applies to that one; and if the other is general accommodation, (b) or (c) applies to that one. If you qualify for HB on two homes (and neither is supported accommodation), the DWP advises that any benefit cap reduction should be apportioned between them pro rata (A15/2013).

Decisions and appeals about STA

2.19   Decisions about whether your home is supported or temporary accommodation are made by your council. If you are working age and claiming UC, the DWP follows the council's decision [www].

2.20   If you disagree with the council's decision, you can ask the council to reconsider and appeal to a tribunal using the HB appeals procedure (chapter 20).

Migrants, care leavers, students and trainees

2.21   This section explains which migrants, recent arrivals, care leavers, students and trainees can get HB.

Migrants and recent arrivals

2.22   If you are a migrant or have recently arrived in the UK, you can only get HB if you are in one of the eligible groups in table 2.4. These apply to both pension age and working age HB. Further details are in volume 1 chapters 20 and 21.

Care leavers

2.23   If you are a care leaver (para 2.24), you can only get HB if:

(a) you are aged 18 or over; or

(b) you have at some time had a successful family placement (para 2.25); or

(c) your partner is a care leaver but you are not.

2.17-18 HB 75C(2)(a), 75F(1)(g), 75H; UC sch1 paras 3A, 3B; NIHB 73C(2)(a), 73F(1)(g), 73H; NIUC sch 1 paras 4, 4A
            DWP OPerational Guidance (2020) specified accommodation (version 6.0) https://tinyurl.com/OG-specified-accom-2020

2.22   Immigration and Asylum Act 1999 s115; HB 10; HB66+ 10; NIHB 10; NIHB66+ 10; SI 2000/636 reg 2(1), sch paras 2-4;
            NISR 2000/71 reg 2(1), sch paras 2-4; SI 2020/1209 regs 3, 11

2.23-24 Children Act 1989 sch 2 para 19B; Children (Leaving Care) Act 2000 s6; Children (Leaving Care) Act (Northern Ireland) 2002 s6;
            SI 2001/2874 (E); SSI 2004/747 (S); SI 2001/289, SI 2004/1732 (W); NISR 2005/221

Table 2.4 **Migrants and recent arrivals: eligible groups**

(a) You are a national of the Common Travel Area (CTA) and you:

- ■   are habitually resident in the CTA; or
- ■   are present in the UK as a result of your deportation, removal or expulsion from another country.

(b) You entered the UK before 1st January 2021 and you are a national of any other EEA country and you:

- ■   are a worker or self-employed, or retain that status while out of work; or
- ■   are a family member of one of the above; or
- ■   are habitually resident in the CTA and either you have been granted settled status under the EU settlement scheme or you have a right to reside other than as a jobseeker.

But your HB ends on 1st July 2021 unless you made an application to the EU settlement scheme before then.

(c) You are a national of any other country and you have:

- ■   leave to be in the UK which allows you to have 'recourse to public funds', and are habitually resident in the CTA; or
- ■   leave to be in the UK as a national of Turkey or North Macedonia, and are habitually resident in the CTA; or
- ■   refugee status following an application you made for asylum; or
- ■   humanitarian protection, discretionary leave, or leave under the 'Destitution Domestic Violence Concession'.

Notes

- ■   The CTA means the UK (England, Scotland, Wales and Northern Ireland), the Republic of Ireland, the Channel Islands and the Isle of Man.
- ■   The EEA means (apart from Ireland) Austria, Belgium, Bulgaria, Cyprus, Czech Republic, Denmark, Estonia, Finland, France, Germany, Greece, Hungary, Iceland, Italy, Latvia, Lichtenstein, Lithuania, Luxembourg, Malta, Netherlands, Norway, Poland, Portugal, Romania, Slovakia, Slovenia, Spain, Sweden and Switzerland.

2.24 You are a care leaver if:

(a) you were in care ('looked after by a local authority') for one or more periods beginning after you reached 14 (in Scotland, following a children's hearing);

(b) one of these periods continued past your 16th birthday; and

(c) the periods totalled at least 13 weeks, or (except in Scotland) would have done apart from the fact that on your 16th birthday you were in hospital or detained in an institution under a court order.

But periods of up to four weeks aren't counted towards the 13 weeks if you spent them in respite care and returned at the end to the care of your parent(s) or the person with parental responsibility for you.

2.25 A successful family placement means one that was arranged by social services and:

(a) in England, Wales or Northern Ireland, was with a family, lasted for a continuous period of at least six months (whether or not it began while you were in care or afterwards) and didn't end as a result of breaking down;

(b) in Scotland, was with a member of your family aged 18 or over, or with the person who was looking after you before you went into care.

Students

2.26 The general rule is that:

(a) full-time students (para 2.31) can get HB if you are in any of the eligible groups in table 2.5; and

(b) all part-time students can get HB.

2.27 But there are some differences if you rent from an educational establishment (e.g. you live in a hall of residence). In this case, during your period of study (para 2.32):

(a) full-time students can get HB if you are in any of the eligible groups in table 2.5; and

(b) part-time students can get HB if you are in groups (c) to (k) in that table.

During your summer vacation, para 2.26 applies.

Students with two homes

2.28 If you have term-time accommodation that is different from your normal home:

(a) single students can get HB only on one of these (para 3.24); but

(b) couples may be able to get HB on both (para 3.25).

2.25   SSI 2004/747; NISR 2005/324 reg 2(2)

2.26-28 CBA 130(1)(a), 137(2)(i); HB 2(1) definitions 7(6)(b), 8(1), 53(1) definitions, 54, 56, 57(4), 58; HB66+ 2(1), 7(6)(b), 8(1); NICBA 129(1)(a), 133(2)(i); NIHB 2(1), 7(6)(b), 8(1), 50(1), 51, 53, 54(4), 55; NIHB66+ 2(1), 7(6)(b), 8(1)

Table 2.5 **Students: eligible groups**

Paras 2.26-27 explain when these apply to full-time and part-time students.

(a) You are on UC in supported or temporary accommodation (table 2.3).

(b) You are on JSA(IB)/ESA(IR)/IS in any accommodation.

(c) You are under 21 and your course is not above A levels, Scottish Highers and equivalent qualifications or you are aged 21 and you are continuing on such a course.

(d) You are responsible for one or more children or young persons (para 4.14).

(e) You are single and have a foster child placed with you.

(f) You qualify for a severe disability premium (para 12.25) or disability premium (para 12.37).

(g) You have been accepted for ESA purposes as having limited capacity for work for at least 28 weeks (ignoring gaps of up to 12 weeks).

(h) You have a UK grant that includes an amount for deafness.

(i) You had an agreed absence from your studies due to sickness or providing care and less than one year has passed since the absence ended, but you haven't yet resumed your studies and can't get a grant or student loan.

(j) You are claiming pension age HB (table 2.2).

(k) Your partner is a student but you aren't.

Student terminology

2.29   You are a student if you are 'attending or undertaking a course of study at an educational establishment'. This could be a university, college, school or any other establishment used for the purpose of training, education or instruction (GM C2 annex A para C2.04).

2.30   You count as a student from when your course begins to when it ends, or you abandon it or are dismissed from it. This includes:

(a) all term-times and vacations within the course (but not the vacations after it ends, or between two different courses);

(b) all periods of work experience in a sandwich course; and

(c) absences while you remain registered with your educational establishment (for example, because you are sick or caring for someone, or for other personal reasons): O'Connor v Chief Adjudication Officer.

2.31   Your educational establishment tells you whether your course is full-time or part-time, and the council normally accepts this. In many cases 'full-time' means more than 16 hours per week. There is further DWP guidance (GM chapter 2 annex A) and online.

2.29-32 HB 2(1) definitions, 53(1) definitions; NIHB 2(1), 50(1)
        O'Connor v Chief Adjudication Officer [1999] EWCA Civ 884 1 FLR 1200

2.32   Your period of study means term-times and short vacations, but not your long summer vacation. If you don't have a summer vacation but are expected to study for at least 45 weeks a year (this applies to many postgraduates and student nurses), your period of study is the whole year.

Trainees

2.33   If you are a trainee on a government sponsored or government approved training course:

(a)   you don't count as a student, so you only have to meet the conditions in table 2.1 to be eligible for HB;

(b)   but if you rent accommodation away from your normal home, in order to be nearer your course, the rules in paras 3.24-25 apply to you.

2.33   HB 7(18) definition: 'training course'; HB66+ 7(18); NIHB 7(18); NIHB66+ 7(18)

Chapter 3 **Occupying your home**

Your home

3.1　The general rule is that you can only get HB on accommodation in the UK which you normally occupy as your home (paras 3.2-4). But there are also rules about absences from home, moving home and getting HB on two homes (paras 3.5-42).

Types of accommodation

3.2　Your home (or 'dwelling') can be any residential accommodation whether or not it is self-contained. This includes a house, flat, mobile home, houseboat, or room in someone else's home or in a hostel. It also includes somewhere converted, such as when two flats have been knocked together to form a single home (R(H) 5/09; CH/1895/2008). It doesn't include business premises or somewhere used only for a holiday.

Your normal home

3.3　Whether you normally occupy accommodation as your home is decided in your and your family's particular circumstances (CH/2521/2002). It means more than paying housing costs or having the right to live there: it means being physically present – though exceptions can arise (R(H) 9/05). If you have more than one home (in the UK or abroad), only one can be your normal home. This is decided on the facts, including how much time you and your family spend in each of them.

Short-term accommodation

3.4　Your home can be somewhere short-term, e.g. if you move a lot or are staying in a hostel or refuge. But it must be a 'home' in the ordinary sense, and this doesn't normally include night shelters where you have no right to live during the day ([2013] UKUT 65 (AAC)).

3.1　CBA 130(1)(a); NICBA 129(1)(a)

3.2　CBA 137(1) definition: 'dwelling'; NICBA 133(1)

3.3　HB 7(1),(2); HB66+ 7(1),(2); NIHB 7(1),(2); NIHB66+ 7(1),(2)

Absences from home

3.5   This section explains when you can get HB during an absence from home. If you are in a couple and your partner is absent, see paras 4.23-25.

Temporary absences

3.6   You can get HB on your normal home during an absence if:

(a) you intend to return (para 3.8);

(b) your expected absence is unlikely to exceed, or substantially exceed, the time limit (para 3.10);

(c) your actual absence hasn't yet reached the time limit (para 3.11);

(d) you remain liable for rent on your normal home; and

(e) the part you normally occupy hasn't been rented out (by you or your landlord) to someone else.

Different rules apply if your home is being repaired or you are trying out a care home (paras 3.13, 3.20).

3.7   If you don't meet the conditions at the outset, your HB ends on the day before you go away. If you stop meeting them while you are away (including when your intentions change or events cause them to change), your HB ends on the day before that (CH/1237/2004).

Intending to return

3.8   Whether and when you intend to return to your normal home is decided by your own intentions rather than what a relative or official intends for you. Your intentions can depend on the outcome of events, for example:

(a) if you are absent due to fear of violence, you need only intend to return when it becomes safe to do so (para 3.15);

(b) if you are trying out a care home, you need only intend to return if the care home doesn't suit you (para 3.20).

But your return must be possible within the time limit. Wanting to return is not enough if your return is in fact impossible (CSHB/405/2005).

Time limits

3.9   Table 3.1 gives the time limits for temporary absences. They apply to:

(a) your expected absence (unless you are trying out a care home: para 3.20); and

(b) your actual absence (in all cases).

3.6   HB 7(11)-(13),(14)-(17),(18) definition: 'main dwelling'; HB66+ 7(11)-(13),(14)-(17);
         NIHB 7(11)-(13),(14)-(17),(18); NIHB66+ 7(11)-(13),(14)-(17),(18)

Table 3.1 **Time limits for HB during an absence**

Reason for your absence	Time limit
(a) You are a patient in hospital or a similar institution.	UK absences 52 weeks
(b) You are receiving medical treatment or medically approved care or convalescence.	Absences abroad 26 weeks
(c) Your partner or child is receiving medical treatment or medically approved convalescence.	
(d) You fear violence (para 3.14).	
(e) You are receiving care in a care home other than during a trial period (para 3.19).	UK absences 52 weeks
(f) You are providing medically approved care to someone.	Absences abroad four weeks
(g) You are caring for a child whose parent/guardian is away from their home to receive medical treatment or medically approved care.	
(h) You are studying or training (para 3.23).	
(i) You are on remand or on bail (para 3.26).	
(j) You are having a trial period in a care home (para 3.20).	UK absences 13 weeks
(k) You are temporarily absent for other reasons (on holiday, working, serving a sentence, etc).	Absences abroad four weeks
(l) You are outside the UK as a mariner, continental shelf worker or member of HM armed forces.	26 weeks
(m) A member of your family (para 4.2) or close relative of your family (para 5.18) has died outside the UK and you can't return within four weeks.	Eight weeks

Note: For these purposes, Great Britain counts as 'abroad' in Northern Ireland, and vice versa.

Examples: Working away from home

1. Mordred gets HB on a privately rented flat. He gets a contract to work for one term as a cleaner at a school. It is too far for him to commute and he stays rent-free with a friend for the whole of the term.

- He can get HB on his flat because his absence is unlikely to be longer than 13 weeks (table 3.1(k)), but his new income is taken into account.

2. Mordred (who still qualifies for HB) gets a year's contract to work at the school. He goes back to his flat for each of the school holidays.

T3.1   HB 7(11)-(18) definition: 'main dwelling'; HB66+ 7(11)-(18); NIHB 7(11)-(18); NIHB66+ 7(11)-(18)

> ■   He can continue to get HB on his flat because each absence is less than 13 weeks (table 3.1(k)).
>
> **3.** Mordred then gets a permanent contract at the school. He keeps his flat on but removes most of his possessions from it and stops going back in the holidays.
>
> ■   He stops qualifying for HB on his flat because his absence is now likely to be longer than 13 weeks. Even if he returns occasionally to the flat, it is unlikely to count as his normal home so he can't get HB there (para 3.1).

Your expected absence

3.10   Your expected absence must be:

(a)   unlikely to exceed the time limit in table 3.1; or

(b)   in exceptional circumstances (except in cases (j) to (m) in the table), unlikely to substantially exceed it.

For UK absences with a time limit of 52 weeks, the DWP advises that 15 months is not 'substantially' longer, and that 'exceptional circumstances' can include unanticipated events such as a relapse in hospital (GM A3.532).

Your actual absence

3.11   Your actual absence can never exceed the time limit. If it reaches the time limit, your HB stops. You can't get working age HB again (except on supported or temporary accommodation), but you can get pension age HB (on any accommodation) when you return to your normal home or have a new home.

Counting the time limits

3.12   The time limits apply to absences that are continuous (R v Penwith DC ex parte Burt). The day you go away counts as a day of absence, but the day you return does not ([2019] UKUT 28 (AAC)). And so long as you return for at least 24 hours, going away again starts a new absence with a new time limit (GM A3.460).

> ### Examples: A long stay in hospital
>
> **1.** Michaela gets HB on her rented home. She has a serious accident and her doctors expect her to be in hospital for between nine and 15 months.
>
> ■   She can get HB because her expected absence is unlikely to substantially exceed 52 weeks (para 3.10)
>
> **2.** Michaela leaves hospital after 13 months and returns home.
>
> ■   She can get HB for the first 52 weeks of her absence in hospital (para 3.11).
>
> ■   If Michaela was in a couple and her partner was the HB claimant, HB could be awarded throughout Michaela's absence (paras 4.23-25).

3.12   R v Penwith DC HBRB ex p Burt 26/02/90 QBD 22 HLR 292

Repairs to your normal home

3.13 When you move somewhere temporary because of repairs to your normal home, you can get HB on:

(a) your temporary home if:

  ■ you don't pay rent on your normal home (e.g. you live there with relatives or friends or own it), or

  ■ the rent on your normal home has stopped;

(b) your normal home in any other case (if you rent it).

Fear of violence

3.14 For HB purposes, you have a fear of violence if you fear violence towards yourself or a member of your family (para 4.2) either:

(a) in your normal home (whoever it would be from); or

(b) outside your normal home from a person who was a member of your family but no longer is, for example a former partner.

The DWP says you are normally expected to have reported the matter to the police or another reputable body (GM A3.549). But no violence needs actually to have occurred so long as your fear of it is 'reasonably held' (CH/1237/2004).

Moving out temporarily

3.15 If you leave your normal home due to a fear of violence and intend to return to it, you can get HB for up to 52 weeks on:

(a) your normal home (para 3.3); or

(b) the place you are staying (GM A3.630); or

(c) both of these if you are liable for rent on both (para 3.39) and it is reasonable to award HB on both.

Intending to return when it is safe to do so is normally sufficient.

3.16 But if you claim UC because the place you are staying is in a different council's area (table 17.3), you can get:

(a) UC on one or both homes for up to 12 months; or

(b) HB on one home if it is supported or temporary accommodation (table 2.3) and/or UC on the other for up to 12 months.

3.13   HB 7(4); HB66+ 7(4); NIHB 7(4); NIHB66+ 7(4)

3.14   HB 7(6)(a),(16)(c)(x); HB66+ 7(6)(a),(16)(c)(x); NIHB 7(6)(a),(16)(c)(x); NIHB66+ 7(6)(a),(16)(c)(x)

3.15-16 HB 7(6)(a),(16)(c)(x),(17); HB66+ 7(6)(a),(16)(c)(x),(17); NIHB 7(6)(a),(16)(c)(x),(17); NIHB66+ 7(6)(a),(16)(c)(x),(17)

Moving out permanently

3.17   If you leave your home due to a fear of violence and don't intend to return, you can get:

(a)   HB on your old home for up to four weeks (para 3.36); and/or

(b)   HB on your new home in the ordinary way.

Examples: Fear of violence

1. Morgana gets HB on her council flat. Her partner lives with her and he begins to threaten her with violence. She goes to stay in a refuge, but she intends to return to her flat and has got her parents to tell her ex-partner to leave.

- She can get HB for up to 52 weeks on her flat because she intends to return. She can also get HB on the refuge (para 3.15).

2. After four months in the refuge, Morgana goes to stay with her parents. She still intends to return to her flat and her solicitor has written to her ex-partner instructing him to leave. A month after that she decides she won't return to her flat.

- She can continue to get HB on her flat until she decides not to return to it (paras 3.10-12).

Care homes

3.18   The following rules apply to care homes, and also to independent (non-NHS) hospitals and Abbeyfield Homes.

Moving temporarily to a care home

3.19   If you are being cared for in a care home and intend to return to your normal home, you can get HB on your normal home for up to 52 weeks (table 3.1). For example, you could be staying in the care home for a period of respite care.

Trying out a care home

3.20   If you are trying out a care home to see if it suits you, you can get HB on your normal home:

(a)   for up to 13 weeks while you are still considering whether to stay; and

(b)   for up to four weeks if and when you do decide to stay (R(H) 4/06) (para 3.36).

You can try out more than one care home and the 13 weeks starts again for each one, but only until you have been absent from your normal home for 52 weeks overall.

3.17   HB 7(1),(2),(6)(d),(7),(10); HB66+ 7(1),(2),(6)(d),(7),(10); NIHB 7(1),(2),(6)(d),(7),(10); NIHB66+ 7(1),(2),(6)(d),(7),(10)

3.18   HB 7(18) definition: 'residential accommodation'; HB66+ 7(18); NIHB 7(18); NIHB66+ 7(18)

3.20   HB 2(1) definitions: 'care home', 'independent hospital', 7(11),(12),(18); HB66+ 2(1), 7(11),(12),(18); NIHB 2(1), 7(11),(12),(18); NIHB66+ 2(1), 7(11),(12),(18)

Moving permanently to a care home

3.21   If you move to a care home and don't intend to return to your normal home, you can get HB on your normal home for up to four weeks (para 3.36).

Leaving a care home

3.22   If you are waiting to leave a care home, you can get HB on your normal home for up to four weeks (para 3.35). This can include a new home you have never yet lived in.

Examples: A care home

1. Betella gets HB on a rented house. She goes into a care home for a six-week trial period.

- She can get HB on her normal home throughout the trial period (para 3.20)

2. At the end of the trial period, Betella decides to stay in the care home and gives notice to her old landlord.

- She can get HB on her old home during the notice period for up to four weeks (para 3.20).

Students

3.23   The following rules apply to students who are in an eligible group (table 2.5), and also to trainees on a government sponsored or approved training scheme.

Single students

3.24   When you are a single student renting term-time accommodation away from your normal home:

(a)   if you pay rent on your normal home, you can get HB there for up to 52 weeks while you are staying in your term-time accommodation (para 3.6), but you can't get HB on your term-time accommodation;

(b)   if you don't pay rent or a mortgage on your normal home (e.g. it is a relative's home), you can get HB on your term-time accommodation (but during the summer vacation your HB stops during absences of more than a week);

(c)   if you pay a mortgage on your normal home, you can't get HB on either home.

However, (b) only applies to pension age HB, because you can no longer make a claim for working age HB (para 2.6) and UC has no equivalent rule.

3.21   HB 7(7),(8)(c)(iii); HB66+ 7(7),(8)(c)(iii); NIHB 7(7),(8)(c)(iii); NIHB66+ 7(7),(8)(c)(iii)

3.22   HB 7(7),(10); HB66+ 7(7),(10); NIHB 7(7),(10); NIHB66+ 7(7),(10)

3.23   HB 2(1) definitions, 7(18) definition 'training course', 53(1) definitions; HB66+ 7(18); NIHB 2(1), 7(18), 50(1); NIHB66+ 7(18)
          O'Connor v Chief Adjudication Officer [1999] EWCA Civ 884 1 FLR 1200

3.24   HB 7(1),(3),(16)(iv),(viii),(17), 55; HB66+ 7(1),(3),(16)(iv),(viii),(17);
          NIHB 7(1),(3),(16)(iv),(viii),(17), 52; NIHB66+ 7(1),(3),(16)(iv),(viii),(17)

Student couples

3.25   When you are a couple and at least one of you is a student:

(a)   you can get HB on two homes (para 3.39) if this is reasonable and occupying both is unavoidable (e.g. because one of you is studying in one area and the other is studying or working in another);

(b)   otherwise you can get HB on one home in the same way as described in para 3.24.

Prisoners

Remand and bail

3.26   You can get HB on your normal home for up to 52 weeks (para 3.6) while you are:

(a)   a prisoner on remand; or

(b)   bailed to live away from your normal home – for example in a bail hostel or relative's home.

Serving a sentence

3.27   If you are serving a custodial sentence in prison, you can get HB on your normal home:

(a)   for up to 13 weeks if your overall absence is unlikely to exceed 13 weeks; or

(b)   for up to four weeks from when you left your normal home (para 3.36).

You are likely to meet the time limit in (a) if you have a fixed term sentence of up to six months (which is 13 weeks after remission) or ten months (if you qualify for home detention curfew). But if you are detained in hospital only (b) applies. For DWP guidance see GM A3.485-518.

Parole and temporary release

3.28   If you are released on parole (licence) you can get HB in the ordinary way. The same also applies to prisoners on temporary release until 12th May 2021 regardless of the reason (HB A8/2020). This has been extended from 12th May 2021 to 31st August 2021, but only in cases where the DWP decides it is necessary due to coronavirus (for example where the release has been approved by the Ministry of Justice, as part of the response to reduce the spread of coronavirus within prisons). But from 1st September 2021, prisoners on temporary release count as still being in prison, so you can only get HB as described in para 3.27.

3.25   HB 7(6)(b); HB66+ 7(6)(b); NIHB 7(6)(b); NIHB66+ 7(6)(b)

3.26   HB 7(16)(c)(i),(16A),(17); HB66+ 7(16)(c)(i),(16A),(17); NIHB 7(16)(c)(i),(16A),(17); NIHB66+ 7(16)(c)(i),(16A),(17)

3.27   HB 7(7),(13); HB66+ 7(7),(13); NIHB 7(7),(13); NIHB66+ 7(7),(13)

3.28   HB 7(14),(15); HB66+ 7(14),(15); SI 2020/409 regs 5, 6; SI 2021/476 reg 4; NIHB 7(14),(15); NIHB66+ 7(14),(15); NISR 2020/63 regs 5, 6; NISR 2021/105 reg

> **Examples: Remand and conviction**
>
> **1.** Gabriel gets HB on a rented flat. He is arrested and sent to prison on remand.
>
> - He can get HB for up to 52 weeks (para 3.26).
>
> **2.** Gabriel is found guilty and given a prison sentence of one year.
>
> - His total absence from home is now likely to be six months after remission. So his HB ends when he is sentenced (para 3.27).
>
> - If Gabriel was in a couple and his partner was the HB claimant, HB could be awarded throughout Gabriel's absence (paras 4.23-25).

Moving home

3.29   When you move home your HB changes on the date of your move to take account of your new housing costs, unless you move to a different council area, in which case you need to claim HB or UC (table 17.3). But in some cases, you can get HB for up to four weeks before moving in or after moving out (paras 3.31-38).

The date of your move

3.30   The date of your move means the day you physically transfer from one home to another, along with any family members who are moving with you, though there can be exceptions if your move is delayed at the last moment (R (H) 9/05). It doesn't mean the date on the letting agreement (if different) or the day you start getting your new home ready (R (H) 9/05; CH/1911/2006). If you have more than one home, it means the date your normal home changes.

Waiting for adaptations for a disability

3.31   You can get HB on a new home for up to four weeks before the date you move into it if:

(a)   your liability for rent there has begun;

(b)   you are waiting for it to be adapted to meet your disability needs or those of a member of your family (para 4.2); and

(c)   your delay in moving is necessary and reasonable.

The adaptations can include furnishing, carpeting and redecorating as well as changes to your new home's fabric or structure (R (Mahmoudi) v Lewisham LBC).

3.32   You can get HB on both your old and new home for up to four weeks before the date of your move if:

(a)   you are liable for rent on both of them; and

(b)   you meet the other conditions in para 3.31.

3.29   HB 79(2A)(a); HB66+ 59(2A)(a); NIHB 77(3)(a); NIHB66+ 57(3)(a)

3.31   HB 7(8)(c)(i); HB66+ 7(8)(c)(i); NIHB 7(8)(c)(i); NIHB66+ 7(8)(c)(i);
         R (Mahmoudi) v Lewisham [2014] EWCA 284 www.bailii.org/ew//cases/EWCA/Civ/2014/284.html

3.32   HB 7(6)(e); HB66+ 7(6)(e); NIHB 7(6)(e); NIHB66+ 7(6)(e)

Waiting for local welfare assistance

3.33   You can get HB on a new home for up to four weeks before the date you move in if:

(a)   your liability for rent there has begun;

(b)   you are waiting for local welfare assistance (para 23.35) to help with the move or setting up home;

(c)   you (or your partner):

  ■   are over 66, or

  ■   qualify for a disability premium (paras 12.37-39), or

  ■   have limited capability for work or for work-related activity (para 12.47), or

  ■   have a child under 6, or

  ■   have a child or young person who qualifies for a disabled child premium (para 12.22); and

(d)   your delay in moving is reasonable.

3.34   You can't get HB on your old home at the same time. So, if you are liable for rent on both your old and new homes, you can get HB on whichever counts as your normal home.

Waiting to leave hospital or a care home

3.35   You can get HB on a new home for up to four weeks before the date you move into it if:

(a)   your liability for rent there has begun;

(b)   you are waiting to leave hospital or a care home (para 3.18); and

(c)   your delay in moving is reasonable.

Unavoidable liability for rent

3.36   You can get HB on your old home for up to four weeks from the date you move out of it if:

(a)   you continue to be liable for rent there;

(b)   your liability could not reasonably have been avoided (para 3.38); and

(c)   either:

  ■   you have moved into somewhere new – this can include hospital, a care home, or prison, even though you can't get HB on these (GM A3.688 example 3), or

  ■   you left your old home due to fear of violence (para 3.14) and don't yet have a new address or don't want to say where it is.

3.33   HB 7(8)(c)(ii); HB66+ 7(8)(c)(ii); NIHB 7(8)(c)(ii); NIHB66+ 7(8)(c)(ii)

3.35   HB 7(8)(c)(iii),(18); HB66+ 7(8)(c)(iii),(18); NIHB 7(8)(c)(iii),(18); NIHB66+ 7(8)(c)(iii),(18)

3.36   HB 7(7),(10); HB66+ 7(7),(10); NIHB 7(7),(10); NIHB66+ 7(7),(10)

3.37   You can get HB on your old home as well as your current home for up to four weeks from the date of your move if:

(a) you are liable for rent on both of them; and

(b) your liability on both could not reasonably have been avoided (para 3.38).

This is sometimes called the 'overlapping HB rule'. It doesn't apply when you move out for repairs to be done (para 3.13).

3.38   Whether your liability for rent could reasonably have been avoided is decided on the facts and any alternatives that were open to you (CH/4546/2002), such as whether and when you gave notice to your landlord. Your situation doesn't have to be 'exceptional' (though DWP advice wrongly says it should be: GM A3.682).

Example: Unavoidable liability (overlapping HB)

Barnaby gets HB on a private rented flat. He is offered a housing association house in the same area and has to take up the tenancy there on the following Monday. He gives notice to his old landlord and is liable for rent on both homes for the overlap period.

■   He can get HB on both homes during the overlap for up to four weeks (para 3.37).

Two homes

3.39   You can get HB on two homes when:

(a) you have a large family (para 3.41); or

(b) you are absent from your normal home due to fear of violence (para 3.14); or

(c) are a couple and one or both of you are a student or a trainee (para 3.25); or

(d)   you are waiting for adaptations for a disability (para 3.32); or

(e) you are unavoidably liable for rent on both homes (para 3.37).

3.40   In any other case you can only get HB on your normal home (paras 3.3-4). If you start or stop qualifying on two homes, your HB changes on the exact day.

Large families

3.41   You can get HB on two homes (with no time limit) if your council or another housing authority has housed you in both, or arranged for you to be housed in both, due to the size of your family (para 4.2). The DWP advises that both homes must be provided but not necessarily owned by the council, and would normally be next to each other or within a few streets of each other (GM A3.660).

3.37   HB 7(6)(d); HB66+ 7(6)(d); NIHB 7(6)(d); NIHB66+ 7(6)(d)

3.39   HB 7(6); HB66+ 7(6); NIHB 7(6); NIHB66+ 7(6)

3.41   HB 7(6)(c); HB66+ 7(6)(c); NIHB 7(6)(c); NIHB66+ 7(6)(c)

Calculating HB on two homes

3.42   When you qualify for HB on two homes:

(a)   the two eligible rents are added together; but

(b)   deductions for excess income and non-dependants are only made once (paras 6.2, 6.6).

This applies even if the two homes are in different council areas ([2013] UKUT 5 (AAC)). For the benefit cap see paras 2.17-18.

Chapter 4 **The people in your home**

- ■ Your family, couples, children and young persons: see paras 4.2-19.
- ■ Household membership: see paras 4.20-25.
- ■ Non-dependants: see paras 4.26-32.
- ■ Carers, lodgers, joint tenants and others: see paras 4.33-50.

4.1 This chapter explains how the people in your home affect your HB. They are divided into:

(a) you and your family; and

(b) other people, including foster children, non-dependants, carers, lodgers and joint tenants.

Your family

4.2 For HB purposes, your 'family' does not always mean the same as in day-to-day life. It means only the following members of your household:

(a) your partner if you are in a couple (or partners in a polygamous marriage); and/or

(b) each child or young person you or your partner are responsible for.

Table 1.1 gives a summary of family and other terminology.

4.3 You and the members of your family are included when the council decides your applicable amount (para 12.2) and the size of accommodation you need (para 11.10). And your partner's income and capital is included with yours (paras 13.2 and 15.2).

Examples: Families and other occupiers

1. Laurel and Oliver are a married couple who rent their home. They have two daughters aged 15 and 21 living with them, a foster son aged 14, and a lodger who rents a room from them. Laurel claims HB.

Laurel is the claimant, with Oliver as her partner. Oliver and the younger daughter are the members of Laurel's family (para 4.2). The older daughter is Laurel's non-dependant (para 4.26). Their foster son and lodger are not included in their family and are not non-dependants (table 4.3).

2. Stanley and Hardeep are living together as a couple and rent their home. Hardeep's son aged 7 lives with them and so does Hardeep's adult sister. Stanley claims HB.

Stanley is the claimant, with Hardeep as his partner. Hardeep and his son are the members of Stanley's family. Hardeep's sister is Stanley's non-dependant.

Couples

4.4　　This section explains who counts as a couple. If you are in a couple your partner is a member of your family (paras 4.2-3). If you are in a polygamous marriage (table 1.1) you don't count as a couple but your partners are included in the same way.

4.5　　You are a couple for HB purposes if you are two people who are:

(a)　married or in a civil partnership; or

(b)　living together as though you were married or in a civil partnership (paras 4.8-12).

You must also be members of the same household (paras 4.20-22) – whether you are married/civil partners (CIS/72/1994) or living together ([2004] UKUT 17 (AAC)). If your partner is temporarily absent see paras 4.23-25.

4.6　　If your relationship has ended, you are no longer a couple if you now maintain separate households. In deciding this, your shared understanding that your relationship has ended and your actual living arrangements are more important than whether you still share responsibilities and financial arrangements (CIS/72/1994), but by itself a shared understanding may not be enough if you are still married/civil partners (CIS/2900/1998).

4.7　　Someone who no longer counts as your partner (paras 4.5 and 4.25) is not included in your applicable amount. Their income and capital is not included with yours, but income you receive from them is counted as maintenance (table 13.6). If they still live in your dwelling they fall within one of the other descriptions in this chapter (for example they might be your joint tenant or a non-dependant) and the effect on your HB follows from that.

Living together as a couple

4.8　　The law doesn't give a fixed definition of:

(a)　living together as though you were a married couple, or

(b)　living together as though you were civil partners;

except to say that these are decided in the same way.

4.9　　The decision about this is made by looking at:

(a)　your purpose in living together (Crake and Butterworth v the Supplementary Benefits Commission); and

(b)　(if your purpose is unclear) your relationship and living arrangements.

For example, living together for 'care, companionship and mutual convenience' doesn't necessarily mean you are a couple (R(SB) 35/85). The later sections of this chapter illustrate the other ways in which two people can live in the same dwelling.

4.10　　What matters is your relationship as a whole (R(SB) 7/81), taking account of the following factors (Crake case; [2013] UKUT 505 (AAC); [2019] UKUT 312 (AAC)):

(a)　whether you share the same household;

(b)　the emotional element of your relationship;

4.5　　CBA 137(1) definition: 'couple'; NICBA 133(1); HB 2(1) definition: 'couple'; HB66+ 2(1); NIHB 2(1); NIHB66+ 2(1)

4.8　　CBA 137(1) definition: 'couple', (1A); NICBA 133(1),(1A)

4.9　　Crake and Butterworth v SBC 21/07/80 QBD [1982] All ER 498

(c)   whether you publicly acknowledge you are a couple;

(d)   the stability of your relationship;

(e)   your financial arrangements;

(f)   whether you have a sexual relationship;

(g)   whether you share responsibility for a child.

4.11   The factors in para 4.10 can have different importance in different situations. None of them is conclusive by itself (GM C1 annex A para A1.02) unless you do not share a household (paras 4.20-24). But (b) and (c) were emphasised in [2014] UKUT 17 (AAC), which held that a 'committed loving relationship must be established and publicly acknowledged' (since marriage and civil partnership are a public commitment). In that case the parties' denial that they had an emotional relationship 'itself seriously undermined the notion that there is such a relationship'.

4.12   Detailed advice about living together cases is in volume 3 ch 11 of the DWP Decision Maker's Guide [www]. Guidance on the questions councils should ask is in GM C1 annex A paras A1.07-10.

DWP decisions about couples

4.13   If you have claimed a passport benefit (para 1.7) the council is likely to accept the DWP's decision about whether you are a couple. But:

(a)   if the DWP decided you are in a couple, the council must make its own decision about this if you say the DWP is wrong (R(H) 9/04);

(b)   if the DWP awarded you a passport benefit on the basis that you aren't in a couple, the council should accept this unless it has evidence of fraud which the DWP is unaware of and hasn't considered (CH/4014/2007).

Children and young persons

4.14   This section explains who counts as a child or young person and when they are included in your family.

4.15   A 'child' means someone who is aged under 16.

4.16   A 'young person' means someone who meets all the following conditions:

(a)   they are aged 16 or more but under 20;

(b)   they meet the conditions for child benefit to be paid for them (table 4.1) – in practice it is almost always enough if child benefit is actually being paid for them;

(c)   they are not a care leaver aged 16 or 17 (paras 2.23-25); and

(d)   they are not themself on JSA(IB), ESA(IR), IS or UC.

4.12   www.gov.uk/government/publications/decision-makers-guide-vol-3-subjects-common-to-all-benefits-staff-guide

4.15   CBA 137(1) definition: 'child'; NICBA 133(1); HB 2(1) definition: 'child'; HB66+ 2(1); NIHB 2(1); NIHB66+ 2(1)

4.16   HB 19; HB66+ 19; NIHB 17; NIHB66+ 17

4.17 A child or young person is included in your family (paras 4.2-3) if:

(a) you or your partner are responsible for them – in other words they normally live with you (paras 4.18-19); and

(b) they do not fall within any of the exceptions in table 4.2.

They must also be a member of your household (paras 4.20-22) – but this is usually the case if they meet the above conditions. If a child or young person is temporarily absent, see paras 4.23-25.

Responsibility for a child or young person

4.18 You are 'responsible' for a child or young person if they are 'normally living' with you. This is usually straightforward. For example they could be your son or daughter, adopted by you, a step-child, a grandchild, or any other child or young person (whether related to you or not); so long as they normally live with you.

4.19 Each child or young person can only be the responsibility of one person (or one couple) at any one time. This is the person they 'normally' live with, whether or not that person gets child benefit for them. But if this is unclear, or they spend equal time in different households (e.g. when parents have separated), they are the responsibility of:

(a) the person who gets child benefit for them; or

(b) if no-one gets child benefit, the person who has claimed it for them; or

(c) if no-one has claimed it (or more than one person has), the person who has 'primary responsibility' for them. Deciding this may mean looking at a wide range of factors and so may not depend on who they spend most time with ([2018] UKUT 44 (AAC)).

See table 4.2(e) for children and young persons who do not normally live with you.

Table 4.1 **Who is a young person**

Someone aged 16 or more but under 20 is a 'young person' (para 4.16) during any or all of the following periods (the periods in which child benefit can be paid for them):

(a) Until the 31st August following their 16th birthday (in all cases, whether or not they are in education, training or work).

(b) While they are undertaking a course of education which:

- is not above GCE A level or equivalent (national standard level 3) [www]; and
- takes up more than 12 hours per week on average during term-time of tuition, practical work, supervised study or taking examinations; and
- they began before their 19th birthday.

(c) While they are between two courses which meet the above conditions. But this only applies if they are enrolled on and actually start the second course.

4.17   CBA 137(1) definition: 'family'; NICBA 133(1)

4.18   HB 20(1); HB66+ 20(1); NIHB 18(1); NIHB66+ 18(1)

4.19   HB 20(2),(3); HB66+ 20(2),(3); NIHB 18(2),(3); NIHB66+ 18(2),(3)

(d) While they are undertaking approved training which is not provided under an employment contract. This includes many kinds of employment preparation course etc [www].

(e) From when they leave the above education or training until the last day of August, November, February or May, whichever comes first. This is called the 'child benefit terminal date'.

(f) If they are aged 16 or 17, from when they leave the above education or training until the end of the 20th whole week after that. This is called the 'child benefit extension period'. But it only applies if:

■ they are not in remunerative work; and

■ they are registered for work, education or training with the Careers Service or Connexions Service; and

■ an application is made, within three months of the end of the education or training, for child benefit to continue during this period.

For exceptions, see para 4.16 and table 4.2.

Table 4.2 **Children and young persons who are not included in your family**

The following are not included in your family (para 4.17), your applicable amount (para 12.2), or the 'size criteria' (the size of accommodation you need: paras 11.10 and 11.13).

Fostering and adoption

Fostering is also called 'boarding out' or 'kinship care'.

(a) A child or young person who is placed with you or your partner as a foster child or prior to adoption.

■ But they can affect the size criteria (paras 11.21-22).

■ And they are included in your family, your applicable amount and the size criteria when you actually adopt them – if they normally live with you (paras 4.17-19).

(b) A child or young person who is placed with someone else as a foster child or prior to adoption.

T4.1   HB 19; HB66+ 19; NIHB 17; NIHB66+ 17
       https//www.gov.uk/what-different-qualification-levels-mean
       www.hmrc.gov.uk/manuals/ccmmanual/ccm18035.htm

T4.2(a) HB 21(3),(6); HB66+ 21(3),(6); NIHB 19(3),(6); NIHB66+ 19(3),(6)

T4.2(b) HB 21(4)(b),(c); HB66+ 21(4)(b)(c); NIHB 19(4)(b),(c); NIHB66+ 19(4)(b)(c)

Local authority care

This is also called 'being looked after by a local authority'.

(c) A child or young person who is in local authority care and is not living with you.

   ▪ But they are included in your family, your applicable amount and the size criteria in any benefit week in which they live with you for part or all of that week, if it is reasonable to do so – e.g. if they are visiting you under local authority supervision (GM paras C1.120, C1.150).

Living with you but not a young person

(d) Someone aged 16 or more who lives with you but doesn't count (or no longer counts) as a young person (para 4.16 and table 4.1).

   ▪ But they usually count as a non-dependant (para 4.26).

   ▪ And they are included in the size criteria (para 11.10(b),(e)).

Not normally living with you

(e) A child or young person who doesn't live with you, or doesn't normally live with you (para 4.19), even if they spend some time with you.*

   ▪ But they are included in your family, your applicable amount and the size criteria if they are only temporarily absent (para 4.24).

   ▪ And if they normally live with another occupier of your dwelling, see paras 4.32, 4.39, 4.46 and 4.48-49.

* Exclusion from applicable amount: [2013] UKUT 642 (AAC), [2014] UKUT 223 (AAC);
  from social sector size criteria: [2015] UKUT 34 (AAC);
  from private sector size criteria: R v Swale HBRB ex parte Marchant, [2010] UKUT 208 (AAC).

Household membership

4.20   Someone can only be included in your family if you are members of the same 'household' (paras 4.5 and 4.17). Other HB rules also refer to household membership (e.g. about joint tenants: para 4.45).

4.21   Rather than being defined in the law, a household has its ordinary meaning. It means a domestic arrangement involving two or more people who live together as a unit (R(IS) 1/99), even when they have a reasonable level of independence and self-sufficiency (R(SB) 8/85). It requires a settled course of daily living rather than visits from time to time (R(F) 2/81). And a person can't be a member of two or more households at the same time (R(SB) 8/85).

T4.2(c)   HB 21(4)(a),(5),(6); HB66+ 21(4)(a),(5),(6); NIHB 19(4)(a),(5),(6); NIHB66+19(4)(a),(5),(6)

T4.2(d)   HB 19; HB66+ 19; NIHB 17; NIHB66+ 17

T4.2(e)   HB 20; HB66+ 20; NIHB 18; NIHB66+ 18

T4.2(*)   R v Swale HBRB ex p Marchant 9/11/99 CA 32 HLR 856

4.20   CBA 137(1) definition: 'family'; NICBA 133(1)

4.22   You are not members of the same household if you have:

(a) separate homes in different dwellings (R(SB) 4/83); or

(b) separate households within the same dwelling (CIS/072/1994).

So if you keep your eating, cooking, food storage, finances (including paying your housing costs), living space and family life separate, you are unlikely to be members of the same household.

Absences of family members

4.23   Paras 4.24-25 explain the rules about absences of family members. Different rules apply if you (the claimant) are absent from your home (para 3.5) or a non-dependant is (para 4.31).

4.24   A partner, child or young person who is temporarily living away from you continues to be included in your household and in your family. So they are included in your applicable amount, and normally included when the council decides the size of accommodation you need (paras 11.10-11). They could be on holiday, working or looking for work, studying or training (e.g. a child/young person at boarding school or a partner taking a course), in hospital or receiving or providing care, in prison, and so on.

4.25   But they stop being included if:

(a) they don't intend to resume living with you (this is usually looked at in the same way as in para 3.8); or

(b) their absence is likely to be longer than 52 weeks, unless there are exceptional circumstances and it is unlikely to be substantially longer than this.

'Exceptional circumstances' includes being in hospital and other situations where they have no control over the length of their absence. 'Substantially' longer than 52 weeks is likely to mean longer than 15 months (GM para A3.532).

Non-dependants

4.26   A 'non-dependant' is someone who:

(a) normally resides with you (paras 4.29-31); and

(b) does not fall within any of the exceptions in table 4.3.

For example, an adult daughter, son, relative or friend is usually a non-dependant if they live with you on a non-commercial basis. (See also paras 4.41 and 4.47 for special cases.)

4.27   If you have one or more non-dependants you may get less HB – this is called a non-dependant deduction (para 6.9 and tables 6.2 and 6.3). Non-dependants are not included in your applicable amount, but they are included when the council decides the size of accommodation you need (para 11.10).

4.28   Non-dependants can't get HB themselves (para 5.3). But they may be able to get HB if they take over paying your rent because you aren't paying it (paras 5.11-12).

4.24   HB 21(1); HB66+ 21(1); NIHB 19(1); NIHB66+ 19(1)

4.25   HB 21(2); HB66+ 21(2); NIHB 19(2); NIHB66+ 19(2)

4.26   HB 3; HB66+ 3; NIHB 3; NIHB66+ 3

Normally residing with you

4.29   Someone is only a non-dependant if they 'normally reside' with you (or you 'normally reside' with them). Paras 4.30-31 give the two parts to this rule.

4.30   They must actually share some accommodation with you. Sharing just a bathroom, toilet or communal area is not enough. They must share accommodation beyond that, e.g. a kitchen or living room. (Communal areas mean halls, corridors, stairways, etc: para 8.43.) A person may 'reside' in two places but can't 'normally reside' in more than one; so if a non-dependant resides elsewhere, they can't 'normally reside' with you ([2018] UKUT 75 (AAC)).

4.31   You must also have the sort of relationship that means you 'normally reside' with each other in the ordinary sense (Khadim v Brent LBC). For example:

   (a) a temporary visitor is not a non-dependant (CH/4004/2004), unless and until residing with you becomes the normal arrangement (CH/3935/2007);

   (b) a longer absence usually means someone stops counting as a non-dependant (e.g. moving to a care home), but a shorter temporary absence does not (e.g. a holiday).

Some absences always mean there is no non-dependant deduction (table 6.2).

If a non-dependant has a family of their own

4.32   If your non-dependant has their own family, each of them counts as your non-dependant (paras 4.27-28) if they normally reside with you. But:

   (a) there is only one deduction for a non-dependant couple instead of two (para 6.18);

   (b) there is no deduction for any non-dependants aged under 18 (or for many others: para 6.11 and table 6.2);

   (c) a non-dependant's child or young person counts as a member of your own family (instead of being a non-dependant) if they meet the conditions for this (paras 4.14-19).

Example: Three generations living together

- Gloria's daughter aged 15 lives with her, as does the daughter's baby. Gloria gets child benefit for them both. The council decides that Gloria is responsible for them both, and includes both in Gloria's family (and thus in her applicable amount).

- Later, (after leaving school) the daughter claims income support for herself. The council decides that the daughter and baby now form a separate family, and so excludes them from Gloria's family (and applicable amount).

In both cases, the daughter and baby are included in deciding the size of accommodation Gloria needs. In the second situation the daughter and baby are Gloria's non-dependants (paras 4.26 and 4.32).

4.29   HB 3(1); HB66+ 3(1); NIHB 3(1); NIHB66+ 3(1)

4.30   HB 3(4), sch 1 para 8; HB66+ 3(4), sch 1 para 8; NIHB 3(4), sch 1 para 8; NIHB66+ 3(4), sch 1 para 8

Table 4.3 **People who are not your non-dependants**

None of the following count as your non-dependants (para 4.26):

(a) Members of your family (paras 4.2-25).

(b) Children and young persons who are a foster child, placed for adoption, or in local authority care (table 4.2(a)-(c)).

(c) Carers you pay a voluntary or charitable organisation for (para 4.33).

(d) Lodgers of yours (paras 4.36-41).

(e) Joint tenants of yours (paras 4.42-47).

(f) Separate tenants of your landlord (para 4.48).

(g) Your landlord (para 4.49).

(h) People who normally reside with someone in (d) to (g) (see the paras referred to above).

(i) Anyone else who doesn't normally reside with you (paras 4.29-31).

Other people in your home

Carers provided by a charitable or voluntary organisation

4.33 A carer who lives in your home doesn't count as a non-dependant if:

(a) they are living with you to look after you or your partner;

(b) they are employed or engaged by a charitable or voluntary organisation (not a public or local authority); and

(c) the organisation makes a charge to you or your partner for this.

No deduction is made from your HB for them. But if your dwelling is their home, they are included when the council decides the size of accommodation you need (para 11.10(e)).

Other carers

4.34 Any other carer who lives in your home falls within one of the other descriptions in this chapter, and the effect on your HB follows from that. For example they could be your family member, non-dependant, joint tenant, landlord, etc. If you employ them see para 4.50.

T4.3(a) HB 3(2)(a),(b); HB66+ 3(2)(a),(b); NIHB 3(2)(a),(b); NIHB66+ 3(2)(a),(b)

T4.3(b) HB 3(2)(c); HB66+ 3(2)(c); NIHB 3(2)(c); NIHB66+ 3(2)(c)

T4.3(c) HB 3(2)(f); HB66+ 3(2)(f); NIHB 3(2)(f); NIHB66+ 3(2)(f)

T4.3(d) HB 3(2)(e)(i); HB66+ 3(2)(e)(i); NIHB 3(2)(e)(i); NIHB66+ 3(2)(e)(i)

T4.3(e) HB 3(2)(d); HB66+ 3(2)(d); NIHB 3(2)(d); NIHB66+ 3(2)(d)

T4.3(f) HB 3(1),(4); HB66+ 3(1),(4); NIHB 3(1),(4); NIHB66+ 3(1),(4)

T4.3(g) HB 3(2)(e)(ii); HB66+ 3(2)(e)(ii); NIHB 3(2)(e)(ii); NIHB66+ 3(2)(e)(ii)

T4.3(h) HB 3(1),(2)(e)(iii); HB66+ 3(1),(2)(e)(iii); NIHB 3(2)(e)(iii); NIHB66+ 3(2)(e)(iii)

T4.3(i) HB 3(1); HB66+ 3(1); NIHB 3(1); NIHB66+ 3(1)

4.33 HB 3(2)(f); HB66+ 3(2)(f); NIHB 3(2)(f); NIHB66+ 3(2)(f)

4.35   If you or your partner have overnight care from one or more carers who don't live in your home, this can affect the size of accommodation you need (paras 11.25-33). But no deduction is made from your HB for them.

Lodgers

4.36   A lodger is someone who is liable to pay you or your partner rent, on a commercial basis, in order to live in your home. (We use 'lodger' in this guide because HB law doesn't have a straightforward term for this.) The following rules apply separately for each lodger you have.

4.37   The HB rules divide lodgers into two kinds:

(a)   lodgers whose rent includes meals (para 4.38), sometimes called boarders; and

(b)   lodgers whose rent doesn't include meals, sometimes called sub-tenants.

In either case, they might have people who normally reside with them rather than with you (e.g. their family members or non-dependants).

4.38   A lodger's rent counts as including meals if:

(a)   'at least some meals' are provided as part of the letting agreement between you (e.g. breakfast every day is enough);

(b)   they are cooked or prepared by you or someone else, but not by the lodger or a member of their family; and

(c)   they are cooked/prepared and consumed in your home or in associated premises.

4.39   Your lodger, and the people who normally reside with them, affect your HB as follows:

(a)   part of the rent you receive from them counts as your income, and the way this is done means you are usually better off if you provide meals than if you don't (table 13.7);

(b)   they are included when the council decides the size of accommodation you need (para 11.10(c),(e));

(c)   they are not included in your applicable amount; and

(d)   they are not your non-dependants (table 4.3).

The lodger can make their own claim for HB and – if they do – the people who reside with them are taken into account in their claim.

4.37   HB sch 5 paras 22,42; HB66+ sch 5 paras 9,10; NIHB sch 6 paras 23,44; NIHB66+ sch 6 paras 10,11

4.38   HB sch 5 para 42(2); HB66+ 2(1) definition: 'board and lodging accommodation'; NIHB sch 6 para 44(2); NIHB66+ 2(1)

Example: A claimant whose lodger also claims HB

Fred rents his home from a commercial landlord. It has three bedrooms and he rents (sub-lets) two of these to Barney, one for Barney and one for Barney's son Dino, aged 8. Fred is working and is on HB. Barney is on JSA(IB) and is also on HB.

Fred's HB

Fred is the claimant, Barney is his lodger (para 4.36), and Dino is Barney's child. So Fred is a single claimant. The rent Barney pays is taken into account as Fred's income (table 13.7). The LHA figure for a three-bedroom dwelling is used to calculate Fred's HB, because Barney and Dino live in his dwelling as his home (para 11.10), as well as Fred.

Barney's HB

Barney is the claimant, Dino is his child, and Fred is his landlord. So Barney is a lone parent. The LHA figure for a two-bedroom dwelling is used to calculate Barney's HB (paras 9.16-17), because just he and his son are taken into account.

Distinguishing lodgers from non-dependants

4.40   The difference between lodgers and non-dependants is that:

(a) a lodger has a commercial relationship with you, and is liable to make payments which usually count as 'rent' in the HB sense (table 7.1);

(b) a non-dependant doesn't have a commercial relationship with you, whether or not they contribute towards your housing costs.

Even if a non-dependant has exclusive occupation (e.g. of their bedroom) this doesn't make them a lodger, because there are 'many examples… of family arrangements and acts of friendship or generosity not… giving rise to a tenancy even when exclusive occupation is given' ([2012] UKUT 114 (AAC)).

When a lodger counts as a non-dependant

4.41   A lodger who has a 'contrived' or other letting for which HB can't be paid (paras 5.15-35) counts instead as a non-dependant. For example if you rent out part of your home to a close relative (para 5.18) they count as a non-dependant not a lodger.

Joint tenants

4.42   A joint tenant is someone who is jointly liable to pay the rent on your home. They could be jointly liable with you, your partner, or both of you. The following rules apply separately for each joint tenant you have.

4.41   HB 3(3); HB66+ 3(3); NIHB 3(3); NIHB66+ 3(3)

4.42   HB 3(2)(d); HB66+ 3(2)(d); NIHB 3(2)(d); NIHB66+ 3(2)(d)

4.43   The HB rules divide joint tenants into two kinds:

(a) joint tenants who are a member of your family, e.g. your partner or a young person; and

(b) joint tenants who aren't a member of your family, e.g. a relation or friend who jointly rents your home as your house-sharer or flat-sharer.

Joint tenants who are a member of your family

4.44   A joint tenant who is a member of your family is just included in your family, and the effect on your HB follows from that (paras 4.2-3).

Joint tenants who are not a member of your family

4.45   A joint tenant who is not a member of your family might:

(a) share your household (paras 4.20-22); or

(b) maintain a separate household from you.

In either case, they might have people who normally reside with them rather than with you (e.g. their family members or non-dependants).

4.46   The joint tenant, and the people who normally reside with them, affect your HB as follows:

(a) they affect what your share of the eligible rent on your home is (paras 8.6, 9.7-8 and table 10.5);

(b) they are included when the council decides the size of accommodation you need (paras 8.16, 9.17, 10.13, 10.53 and 11.10) as follows:

■   in social sector, exempt accommodation and rent referral cases, this applies whether they share your household or maintain a separate household, but

■   in private sector (LHA) cases, this applies only if they share your household (para 9.7);

(c) they are not included in your applicable amount;

(d) they are not your non-dependants (table 4.3) – except in the case of a non-dependant who normally resides with both you and your joint tenant (para 6.19).

The joint tenant can make their own claim for HB and – if they do – the people who reside with them are taken into account in their claim. For examples see chapters 7 to 10.

When a joint tenant counts as a non-dependant

4.47   A joint tenant who has a 'contrived' or other letting for which HB can't be paid (paras 5.15-16) counts instead as a non-dependant. For example if you and a friend are renting from a resident landlord who is the friend's close relative (para 5.18) the friend counts as either your or your landlord's non-dependant, depending on who they normally reside with (paras 4.29-31).

4.47   HB3(3); HB66+ 3(3); NIHB 3(3); NIHB66+ 3(3)

Separate tenants of your landlord

4.48   If you live in a dwelling which is rented out in separate lettings, the other tenants aren't included when the council decides the size of accommodation you need, and don't affect the amount of your HB in any way. The same applies to people who normally reside with them rather than with you (e.g. their family members or non-dependants).

Resident landlords

4.49   If you have a resident landlord, they aren't included when the council decides the size of accommodation you need, and don't affect the amount of your HB in any way. The same applies to people who normally reside with them rather than with you (e.g. their family members, non-dependants or any other member of their household).

Employees

4.50   If you employ someone who lives in your dwelling as their home (e.g. a nanny, an au pair, or a carer who does not fall within para 4.33):

(a)   they are included when the council decides the size of accommodation you need (para 11.10(e));

(b)   they may count as a non-dependant (paras 4.26-32), but in practice they usually don't unless they work for you free of charge (GM para C1.185);

(c)   they don't affect your HB in any other way.

4.48   HB 3(1),(4); HB66+ 3(1),(4); NIHB 3(1),(4); NIHB66+ 3(1),(4)

4.49   HB 3(2)(e)(ii),(iii); HB66+ 3(2)(e)(ii),(iii); NIHB 3(2)(e)(ii),(iii); NIHB66+ 3(2)(e)(ii),(iii)

Chapter 5 **Liability for rent**

- ■ What liability is: see paras 5.1-8.
- ■ Treating you as liable when you are not: see paras 5.9-14.
- ■ Contrived and other excluded lettings: see paras 5.15-35.

What liability is

5.1   You can only get HB if you are:

(a) liable to pay rent for your home – in other words, you have a legal obligation or duty to pay (paras 5.2-8); or

(b) treated as liable to pay rent (paras 5.9-14).

5.2   Chapter 7 explains which payments count as 'rent' for HB purposes. But even if you are liable for rent, you can't get HB if your letting arrangements mean that you have an excluded letting (paras 5.15-35)

The nature of liability

5.3   Liability for rent arises under a tenancy, but for HB includes any kind of 'periodical payments' made in return for the right to occupy a dwelling. There is no requirement for a written agreement (GM A3.50): word of mouth alone may be sufficient: R v Poole BC ex p Ross. The landlord normally has a sufficient legal interest in the dwelling to grant you the letting, but circumstances can arise where a landlord does not have such an interest but nevertheless can still create a liability upon which HB is payable (CH/2959/2006).

5.4   Most landlords would expect to end the agreement if a tenant does not pay and large arrears may suggest that there is no genuine liability: CH/1849/2007. But the fact that there has been no payment of the rent 'even for an extensive period, does not of itself mean there is no legal liability': [2010] UKUT 43 AAC; and nor is this necessarily implied by the fact that the rent actually changing hands is less than the rent on the tenancy agreement.

5.5   It is not possible in law for you to grant a tenancy to yourself: Rye v Rye; neither can liability arise under a tenancy 'granted' to you if you already have the right to occupy that dwelling. For example, if you are one of a couple and are joint owners of a property and your partner leaves, your partner cannot 'grant' a tenancy to you as the remaining occupier.

People who are unable to act

5.6   If you are unable to act, or are aged under 18, you may have someone appointed to act for you (paras 16.5-7). If you don't and are incapable of understanding the agreement you

---

5.1   CBA 130(1)(a); NICBA 129(1)(a); HB 8(1)(a); NIHB 8(1)(a); NIHB66+ 8(1)(a)

5.3   R v Poole BC ex p Ross, QBD 05/05/95 28 HLR 351

5.5   Rye v Rye [1962] A.C. 496

are entering (lack capacity), this can make the agreement void under Scottish law following a 'transaction by transaction approach' to deciding legal capacity: [2012] AACR 20; but does not do so in the rest of the UK: CH/2121/2006 and [2012] UKUT 12 (AAC).

Unlawful lettings

5.7   Sub-tenancies created in breach of a clause in the head lease not to sublet or assign the tenancy do not prevent the assignment or sub-letting from being valid between the head tenant and sub-tenant: Governors of Peabody Donation Fund v Higgins (not a HB case). Such lettings are unlawful rather than illegal and expose the head tenant to eviction for breach of the agreement. Given that there is a legal liability for rent it seems that these lettings are eligible for HB, unless it is also a letting to which paras 5.15-35 apply.

Illegal lettings

5.8   An illegal letting is one in which its creation would necessarily involve committing a criminal offence. An example is where a landlord lets a dwelling knowing it to be in contravention of a Housing Act prohibition order. In contrast to unlawful contracts, illegal contracts are generally not binding and so would not be eligible for HB. Where a letting was not illegal when it was created (e.g. prior to a prohibition order) it seems likely that it remains binding until the end of the next rental period.

Treating you as liable when you are not

5.9   If you fit one of the descriptions below (paras 5.10-14) you may be eligible for HB even though you are not liable for rent etc (so long as you meet the other conditions: table 2.1). The law says that you are 'treated as liable to make payments'.

You are the liable person's partner

5.10   If you are in a couple (or in a polygamous marriage) and only your partner is liable for rent, the council should treat you as liable to make payments. For example, if your partner is the liable person and you are not liable for rent because your name is not on the tenancy agreement, you can nevertheless be treated as liable and therefore eligible for HB.

Former partners and others when the liable person is not paying the rent

5.11   If the liable person is not paying the rent, the council should treat you as liable if you have to make payments in order to continue living in the home and you are:

(a) the liable person's former partner (current partners are covered instead by the rule in para 5.10); or

(b) someone else the council considers it reasonable to treat as liable. An example might be a son or daughter left in occupation where the tenant is now living in a care home or independent hospital.

5.7   Governors of the Peabody Donation Fund v Higgins 20/06/83 CA (1983) 1 WLR 1091, 10 HLR 82

5.10   HB 8(1)(b); HB66+ 8(1)(b); NIHB 8(1)(b); NIHB66+ 8(1)(b)

5.11   HB 8(1)(c); HB66+ 8(1)(c); NIHB 8(1)(c); NIHB66+ 8(1)(c)

Examples: Treated as liable to pay rent

Megan has been deserted by her partner Ffion. Although Megan is not the tenant, the landlord will allow her to remain in the property if she continues to pay the rent. The council should treat Megan as liable if her former partner is not paying.

Logan is the father of a council tenant. He takes over responsibility for paying the rent while his son is working abroad. Logan should be treated as liable to make payments if it is reasonable to do so.

5.12   This rule helps someone who could perhaps arrange to become the tenant (but who has not done so) remain in their home. It can be used if the liable person has been absent for too long to get HB (table 3.1), or has left permanently, and a partner or other person remains. The liable person need not be an individual; they could be a company or other body (R(H) 5/05) – including, presumably, the executors of a deceased tenant. If you claim under this rule you still need to meet the requirements relating to national insurance numbers (para 16.26): [2013] UKUT 321 (AAC). The test of reasonableness does not apply to you if you are a former partner of the liable person: for you, the rule is automatic. For anyone else claiming under this rule, the test of reasonableness applies. In particular, if the only reason the liable person is not paying is that they are excluded from HB (paras 5.15-35) then it may not be reasonable to award HB to you (CSHB/606/2005).

When your rent is waived in return for work you do on the home

5.13   If your rent is waived by your landlord the council should still treat you as liable – but only:

(a)   if the waiver is reasonable compensation for reasonable repairs or redecoration work actually carried out by you; and

(b)   for up to eight weeks in respect of any one waiver of liability.

Rent already paid or varied

5.14   If you have already paid your rent wholly or partly in advance you are nonetheless treated as liable for it over the period it is due. If your rent liability is varied during that period, you are treated as liable for the revised amount due.

Contrived and other excluded lettings

5.15   The rest of this chapter describes the circumstances in which you cannot get HB, even though you are in fact liable for rent. The law does this by saying that you are treated as not liable to make payments. The term 'contrived' does not appear in HB legislation but it is commonly used for the lettings described in para 5.35.

5.13   HB 8(1)(d); HB66+ 8(1)(d); NIHB 8(1)(d); NIHB66+ 8(1)(d)

5.14   HB 8(2); HB66+ 8(2); NIHB 8(2); NIHB66+ 8(2)

Non-commercial agreements

5.16   You are not eligible for HB if the agreement under which you occupy the accommodation is not on a commercial basis. In reaching its decision the authority must consider whether the agreement contains terms which are not legally enforceable. The regulations do not define what constitutes a commercial basis and how each case should be decided but this has been considered by the courts and tribunals. Table 5.1 provides a summary of the case law and guidance.

Landlord is a close relative residing in the dwelling

5.17   If your landlord is your or your partner's 'close relative' (para 5.18), and the landlord also resides in the dwelling (para 5.20), you are not eligible for HB.

5.18   A 'close relative' is:

  (a)   a parent, step-parent or parent-in-law; or

  (b)   a brother or sister; or

  (c)   a son, son-in-law, daughter, daughter-in-law, step-son, step-daughter; or

  (d)   a partner of any of the above.

5.19   The terms 'brother' and 'sister' include 'half-brothers' and 'half-sisters' ([2016] UKUT 517 (AAC)), but not 'step-brothers' or 'step-sisters'.

5.20   For your landlord to count as 'residing in' the same dwelling as you (para 5.17), it is not necessary to share all the accommodation, merely some essential living accommodation: CH/542/2006. Similarly, if you have exclusive possession of one room in a house, this does not mean that the landlord is not residing with you: CH/3656/2004. Despite the slight difference of wording, the definition of 'residing with' (para 4.29) also applies here (GM A3.238).

Renting a former joint home from an ex-partner

5.21   If you separate from your partner and your liability is to your former partner for accommodation that you both occupied when you were together then you are treated as not liable and thus not eligible for HB. This rule also applies if your liability is to your partner's former partner and is in respect of accommodation they both occupied before they separated.

5.22   The rule applies if the informal shared living arrangements changed but the dwelling overall did not, for example, if you are a tenant and you form a relationship with your landlord but then revert to being a tenant. This exclusion does not constitute discrimination under the Human Rights Act: R (Painter) v Carmarthenshire County Council HBRB and [2011] UKUT 301 (AAC).

5.16   HB 9(1)(a),(2); HB66+ 9(1)(a),(2); NIHB 9(1)(a),(2); NIHB66+ 9(1)(a),(2)

5.17   HB 9(1)(b); HB66+ 9(1)(b); NIHB 9(1)(b); NIHB66+ 9(1)(b)

5.18   HB 2(1) definition: 'close relative'; HB66+ 2(1); NIHB 2(1); NIHB66+ 2(1)

5.21   HB 9(1)(c); HB66+ 9(1)(c); NIHB 9(1)(c); NIHB66+ 9(1)(c)

5.22   R (Painter) v Carmarthenshire County Council HBRB & Anor [2001] EWHC Admin 308 04/05/01
        www.bailii.org/ew/cases/EWHC/Admin/2001/308.html

Responsibility for your landlord's child

5.23 You are not eligible for HB if you, or your partner, are responsible for the landlord's child (i.e. someone under the age of 16). See paras 4.18-19 for responsibility for a child.

5.24 This rule is likely to apply if your landlord is the parent or adoptive parent of a child in your family. It has been found not to be contrary to the Human Rights Act: R v Secretary of State for Social Security, ex parte Tucker.

Certain trusts

5.25 A trust is an arrangement whereby the legal ownership (title) of property is separated from its benefits (such as the right to live in it or get an income from it). The title is held by the trustees who ensure that its benefits are delivered for use by someone else, 'the beneficiary'.

5.26 You are not eligible for HB if your landlord is a trustee of a trust of which one of the following is a trustee or a beneficiary:

(a) you or your partner;

(b) your or your partner's close relative (para 5.18) if the close relative 'resides with' you (para 4.29); or

(c) your former partner or your partner's former partner.

'Beneficiary' here means someone who could benefit from the trust by occupying the property in question: [2009] UKUT 7 (AAC). This disentitlement does not apply however where you are able to satisfy the council that the liability was not intended to be a means of taking advantage of the HB scheme.

5.27 You are not eligible for HB if your landlord is a trustee of a trust of which your child or your partner's child is a beneficiary. Unlike in the previous paragraph, this rule has no exception.

Renting from a company of which you are a director or an employee

5.28 You are not eligible for HB if your landlord is a company of which one of the following is a director or an employee:

(a) you or your partner;

(b) your or your partner's close relative (para 5.18) if the close relative 'resides with' (para 4.29) you; or

(c) your former partner or your partner's former partner.

This disentitlement does not apply however where you are able to satisfy the council that the liability was not intended to be a means of taking advantage of the HB scheme. Note also that this rule does not apply if you are employed by a company and rent from a director of the company (since a director is not the company itself).

5.23   HB 9(1)(d); HB66+ 9(1)(d); NIHB 9(1)(d); NIHB66+ 9(1)(d)

5.24   R v Secretary of State for Social Security, ex p Tucker 08/11/01 [2001] EWCA Civ 1646
        www.bailii.org/ew/cases/EWCA/Civ/2001/1646.html

5.26   HB 9(1)(e),(3); HB66+ 9(1)(e),(3); NIHB 9(1)(e),(3); NIHB66+ 9(1)(e),(3)

5.27   HB 9(1)(f); HB66+ 9(1)(f); NIHB 9(1)(f); NIHB66+ 9(1)(f)

5.28   HB 9(1)(e),(3); HB66+ 9(1)(e),(3); NIHB 9(1)(e),(3); NIHB66+ 9(1)(e),(3)

5.29   The DWP advises (GM para A3.271) that a 'company' means a registered company. This can be checked online with Companies House for any part of the UK [www].

Former non-dependants

5.30   You are not eligible for HB if:

(a) you were, at any time before the creation of the liability, a non-dependant (para 4.26) of someone who resided in the dwelling; and

(b) that person continues to reside in the dwelling.

This disentitlement does not apply however where you are able to satisfy the council that the liability was not intended to be a means of taking advantage of the HB scheme.

Former owners (sale and rent back or mortgage rescue)

5.31   You are not eligible for HB if:

(a) you or your partner previously owned the dwelling (including owning it on a long lease: table 7.2); and

(b) owned it within the last five years (even if you subsequently moved out and then back in: CH/3698/2008).

This disentitlement does not apply however where you are able to satisfy the council that you or your partner could not have continued to live in the dwelling without giving up ownership. Good advice on this is given in DWP circular HB/CTB A5/2009.

5.32   Whether you could have remained in the dwelling is a practical test based on fact – and in exceptional cases this can include your perceptions if the stress of the situation you were in forced a quick sale: R(H) 6/07; [2018] UKUT 322 (AAC). The council is entitled to examine why you gave up ownership and what other options you might have had, such as getting work to finance the mortgage, taking in a tenant, etc: CH/1586/2004. You are not expected to act irresponsibly (e.g. using a credit card to pay mortgage arrears): CH/2340/2008. You may have had no real choice if a mortgage lender would have sought possession and a housing association used a mortgage rescue scheme to buy the property and rent it back to you (GM A3.282-286).

Tied accommodation

5.33   You are not eligible for HB if your or your partner's occupation of the dwelling is a condition of employment by the landlord. The DWP advises (GM A3.291) that this test should not be taken to mean 'as a result of the employment'. A retired employee, for example, may continue to live in previously tied accommodation but this would no longer be as a condition of employment by the landlord, and so this rule would not prevent eligibility for HB.

5.29   www.gov.uk/get-information-about-a-company

5.30   HB 9(1)(g),(3); HB66+ 9(1)(g),(3); NIHB 9(1)(g),(3); NIHB66+ 9(1)(g),(3)

5.31   HB 9(1)(h),(ha); HB66+ 9(1)(h),(ha); NIHB 9(1)(h),(ha); NIHB66+ 9(1)(h),(ha)

5.33   HB 9(1)(i); HB66+ 9(1)(i); NIHB 9(1)(i); NIHB66+ 9(1)(i)

Members of religious orders

5.34   You are not eligible for HB if you are a member of a religious order and are fully maintained by it (apart from any payments you make for your accommodation). This applies for example to monks or nuns in enclosed orders. The DWP (GM A3.257) points out that members of religious communities (as opposed to religious orders) are often eligible for HB since they frequently do paid work or retain their own possessions.

Contrived liability

5.35   You are not eligible for HB if the authority is satisfied that your liability 'was created to take advantage of the HB scheme' (usually called a 'contrived' tenancy). The regulations do not describe what constitutes a contrived tenancy, but this has been considered by the courts and tribunals. Table 5.1 provides a summary of the case law and further guidance can be found in GM paragraphs A3.310-319.

Table 5.1 **Commerciality and contrivance**

Commerciality

(a) *What makes a letting commercial:* The primary consideration is about what was agreed between you and your landlord rather than what in fact happens, and claiming towards your housing costs can be evidence that the agreement is commercial ([2020] UKUT 240 (AAC)). Not only the financial arrangements between you and your landlord but all the terms of your agreement should be taken into account (R v Sutton LBC ex parte Partridge). Each case must be considered on its individual facts and is a matter of judgment (R(H) 1/03). The arrangements between you should be 'arms length' (R v Sheffield HBRB ex part Smith). It is their true factual basis which matters.

(b) *Personal and religious considerations:* If your letting is in fact commercial, friendliness and kindness between you and your landlord does not make it non-commercial (R v Poole BC ex parte Ross, CH/4854/2003, [2009] UKUT 13 AAC). If your letting is non-commercial, the fact that it was drawn up in a way that meets your religious beliefs does not make it commercial (R(H) 8/04).

(c) *Lettings between family members:* A letting between family members may or may not be commercial. The family arrangement is not decisive by itself. If the letting enables a disabled family member to be cared for more easily, this is not decisive by itself. Each case depends on its individual circumstances (CH/296/2004, CH/1096/2008, CH/2491/2007).

5.34   HB 9(1)(j); HB66+ 9(1)(j); NIHB 9(1)(j); NIHB66+ 9(1)(j)

5.35   HB 9(1)(l); HB66+ 9(1)(l); NIHB 9(1)(l); NIHB66+ 9(1)(l)

T5.1   R v Sutton LBC ex p Partridge 04/11/94 QBD 28 HLR 315; R v Sheffield HBRB ex p Smith 08/12/94 QBD 28 HLR 36; R (Ross) v Poole BC ex parte Ross 05/05/95 QBD 28 HLR 351; R (Simpson) v Solihull HBRB 03/12/93 QBD 26 HLR 370; R (Keegan) v Sutton HBRB 15/05/92 QBD 27 HLR 92; R (Baragrove Properties) v Manchester CC 15/03/91 QBD 23 HLR 337

(d) *If the circumstances of your letting change:* If your letting was commercial when it began, it can become non-commercial if there is an identifiable reason for this (CH/3497/2005).

Contrivance

(e) *What makes a letting contrived:* You must be liable for rent but the liability must have been contrived as a way of gaining UC. The word 'contrived' implies abuse of the UC scheme (CH/39/2007). There must be evidence of this (R v Solihull HBRB ex parte Simpson), and the circumstances and intentions of both you and your landlord should be taken into account (R v Sutton HBRB ex parte Keegan).

(f) *No liability vs contrived liability:* These are separate considerations and should not be confused (CSHB/718/2002). If your landlord is unlikely to evict you if you do not pay, this can be evidence that you are not liable (para 5.4) or that your liability is contrived (Solihull case).

(g) *Lettings between family members:* If your landlord is a relation of yours (e.g. your parent) this does not by itself mean your letting is contrived (Solihull case). But see table 5.1(c) and 5.17 for other rules which may affect you.

(h) *Lettings to people on low incomes:* If you cannot afford your rent, this is not evidence that your letting is contrived (Solihull case). And there is no objection to landlords letting to people on low incomes in order to make a profit unless their charges and profits show abuse (CH/39/2007, R v Manchester CC ex parte Baragrove Properties).

Chapter 6 **Calculating HB**

- How HB is calculated: see paras 6.1-8.
- Non-dependant deductions: see paras 6.9-20.
- The HB benefit cap: see paras 6.21-33.
- Converting figures to weekly amounts: see paras 6.34-38.

How to calculate HB

6.1   This chapter explains how much HB you qualify for. To calculate this, work through the steps in paras 6.2-8.

Maximum benefit

6.2   The starting point for all HB calculations is your weekly 'maximum benefit'. This is:

(a) your weekly eligible rent;

(b) minus any non-dependant deductions which apply.

See chapter 7-11 for how your eligible rent is worked out. Paras 6.9-20 give the amounts of the non-dependant deductions and explain when they apply.

People on a passport benefit

6.3   If you are on a passport benefit (table 6.1) you qualify for maximum benefit (para 6.2).

Table 6.1 **Passport benefits**

You are 'on a passport benefit' if you are:

(a) on the guarantee credit of SPC (or have 'underlying entitlement' to between 1p and 9p of guarantee credit);

(b) on UC in supported or temporary accommodation (para 2.13);

(c) on JSA(IB), ESA(IR) or IS;

(d) entitled to JSA(IB) or ESA(IR) but not receiving it because of a sanction.

6.2   CBA 130(1),(3), 130A; NICBA 129(1),(3), 129A; HB 70; HB66+ 50; NIHB 68; NIHB66+ 48

6.3   CBA 130(3)(a), NICBA 129(3)(a); HB 2(3),(3A),(3B), sch 5 paras 4,5, sch 6 paras 5,6; HB66+ 2(3),(3A), 26; NIHB 2(3),(3A),(3B), sch 6 paras 4,5, sch 7 paras 5,6; NIHB66+ 2(3),(3A), 24

T6.1   CBA 130(1),(3)(a),130A; NICBA 129(1),(3)(a),129A; HB 2(3),(3A),(3B) sch 5 paras 4,5, sch 6 paras 5,6; HB66+ 2(3),(3A), 26; NIHB 2(3),(3A) sch 6 paras 4,5, sch 7 paras 5,6; NIHB66+ 2(3),(3A), 24

People not on a passport benefit

6.4   If you aren't on a passport benefit (table 6.1):

(a)   your HB is based on your income and applicable amount, as described in paras 6.5-6;

(b)   but you don't qualify for HB if your capital is over £16,000.

See chapters 12-15 for how applicable amounts, income and capital are assessed.

Income and excess income

6.5   If you have no income, or your income is less than or equal to your applicable amount, you qualify for maximum benefit (para 6.2).

6.6   If your income is more than your applicable amount, the difference between the two is called 'excess income'. You qualify for:

(a)   maximum benefit (para 6.2); minus

(b)   a percentage of this excess income.

The percentage – also called a 'taper' – is 65%.

Minimum benefit

6.7   If the amount of HB calculated as above is less than the 'minimum benefit' figure of 50p per week, then it is not awarded.

Other calculation rules

6.8   The amount of HB can be reduced to recover an overpayment (para 19.40) or, in cases of fraud, reduce your award for a fixed period (para 19.71) and/or to recover an administrative penalty (para 19.74). For working age claims, HB is also subject to a benefit cap (para 6.21).

Non-dependant deductions

6.9   This section explains the deductions that are made if you have one or more non-dependants. The deductions are made from your eligible rent in the calculation of your HB (para 6.2). They can be described as the amount your non-dependants are expected to contribute towards your rent.

6.10   A non-dependant is usually an adult son, daughter, other relative or friend who lives with you on a non-commercial basis: for details see paras 4.26-32.

6.4   CBA 130(3), 134(1); NICBA 129(3), 130(1); HB 43; HB66+ 28; NIHB 40; NIHB66+ 26

6.5   CBA 130(3)(a); NICBA 129(3)(a)

6.6   CBA 130(3)(b); NICBA 129(3)(b); HB 71; HB66+ 51; NIHB 69; NIHB66+ 49

6.7   HB 75; HB66+ 56; NIHB 73; NIHB66+ 54

6.10   HB 3; HB66+ 3; NIHB 3; NIHB66+ 3

When a deduction is made

6.11   Unless any of the exceptions in table 6.2 applies:

(a) one deduction is made for each non-dependant you have;

(b) but if two non-dependants are a couple, one deduction is made between them (para 6.18).

There are further rules if you are a joint tenant (para 6.19) or pension age (para 6.20).

The amount of the deduction

6.12   The amounts of the deductions are in table 6.3. These vary depending on whether your non-dependant is working at least 16 hours per week and (if they are) on their gross income (paras 6.14-17).

Assuming the amount of the deduction

6.13   If you don't provide evidence of your non-dependant's circumstances, the council could make an assumption about which deduction applies. It mustn't make an assumption that is unlikely to reflect the non-dependant's actual circumstances (CH/48/2006), but otherwise it could make the highest deduction if they are working at least 16 hours per week. If you then provide evidence showing a lower deduction applies, the council must award you arrears of HB (but see paras 17.13-15 if you delay doing this).

Working at least 16 hours per week

6.14   The rules about working at least 16 hours per week (which the law calls 'remunerative work') apply to non-dependants in the same way as they apply to you (the claimant): for the details see paras 14.69-72. For example, a non-dependant on maternity, paternity, adoption or sick leave doesn't count as working at least 16 hours per week (para 14.72).

Gross income

6.15   When a non-dependant's income is taken into account (table 6.3), the following are wholly disregarded:

(a) PIP;

(b) DLA;

(c) attendance allowance, or constant attendance allowance paid with an industrial injury or war disablement pension; and

(d) payments from (or originally derived from) the government-sponsored trust funds listed in para 15.42.

6.11   HB 74(1)-(3); HB66+ 55(1)-(3); NIHB 72(1)-(3); NIHB66+ 53(1)-(3)

6.12-13 HB 74(1),(2); HB66+ 55(1),(2); NIHB 72(1),(2); NIHB66+ 53(1),(2)

6.14   HB 2(1) definition: 'remunerative work', 6; HB66+ 2(1),6; NIHB 2(1),6; NIHB66+ 2(1),6

6.15   HB 2(1) definition: 'attendance allowance', 74(9); HB66+ 2(1), 55(10); NIHB 2(1), 72(9); NIHB66+ 2(1), 53(10)

Table 6.2 **No non-dependant deductions**

Your circumstances:

No deductions are made for any non-dependants you have if you or your partner are:

- (a) getting the daily living component of PIP;
- (b) getting the care component of DLA;
- (c) getting attendance allowance, or constant attendance allowance paid with an industrial injury or war disablement pension;
- (d) getting an armed forces independence payment; or
- (e) severely sight-impaired, blind or have recently regained sight (para 12.54).

But (a)-(c) don't apply if the benefits mentioned cease – e.g. when you/your partner have been in hospital for four weeks.

Your non-dependant's circumstances:

In any other case, there is no deduction for any single non-dependant who is, or any non-dependant couple who are both:

- (f) on state pension credit;
- (g) aged under 18;
- (h) aged under 25 and:
  - ■ on JSA(IB),
  - ■ on the assessment phase of ESA(IR),
  - ■ on IS, or
  - ■ on UC without any earned income;
- (i) a full-time student (paras 2.26-32) – unless you or your partner are are under 66, it is the student's summer vacation, and the student is working at least 16 hours per week;
- (j) getting a government training allowance as a youth trainee;
- (k) a member of the armed forces (regular or reserve) who is away on operations;
- (l) a patient who has been in hospital or similar institution for more than 52 weeks (ignoring breaks of up to four weeks);
- (m) a prisoner, whether sentenced, on remand or bail; or
- (n) a temporary resident or visitor or anyone whose normal home is elsewhere.

T6.2   HB 2(1), definition: 'attendance allowance', 74(6)-(8),(10); HB66+ 2(1), 55(6)-(9);
        NIHB 2(1), 3(2), 72(7),(8),(10); NIHB66+ 2(1), 3(2), 53(7)-(9)

Examples: Calculating HB

Claimant on a passport benefit

A claimant is on a passport benefit (table 6.1). She has no non-dependants. Her eligible rent is £105.00 per week.

Claimants on a passport benefit get maximum benefit – which equals their eligible rent.

Eligible rent equals weekly HB	£105.00

Claimant not on a passport benefit

A couple are not on any of the passport benefits. They have no non-dependants. Their joint weekly income exceeds their applicable amount by £20.00. Their eligible rent is £130.00 per week.

Claimants with excess income get maximum benefit minus a percentage of their excess income.

Eligible rent	£130.00
minus 65% of excess income (65% x £20.00)	£13.00
equals weekly HB	£117.00

Claimant on ESA(IR) with working non-dependant

A claimant is on ESA(IR). Her eligible rent is £120.00 per week. Her 26-year-old son lives with her. He earns £500 per week gross for a 35-hour week.

Claimants on ESA(IR) get maximum benefit, which in this case involves a non-dependant deduction. The son works at least 16 hours per week and the level of his gross income means the highest deduction applies in HB (table 6.3).

Eligible rent	£120.00
minus non-dependant deduction	£102.85
equals weekly HB	£17.15

Claimant on ESA(IR) with non-dependant on JSA(C)

The son in the previous example loses his job and starts receiving JSA(C).

The calculation is as above, except that now the lowest deduction applies in HB (table 6.3).

Eligible rent	£120.00
minus non-dependant deduction	£15.95
equals weekly HB	£104.05

Table 6.3 **Weekly non-dependant deductions: 2020-21**

HB for rent

If the non-dependant works at least 16 hours per week and has gross weekly income of:

- at least £469   £102.85
- at least £377 but under £469   £93.70
- at least £283 but under £377   £82.30
- at least £217 but under £283   £50.30
- at least £149 but under £217   £36.65
- under £149   £15.95

    Any other non-dependant (regardless of income level)   £15.95

Notes:

- See paras 6.14-17 for how to assess income and table 6.2 for exceptions.
- For comparison, the UC deduction (weekly equivalent) is £17.43 in all cases.

6.16   Apart from that, HB law says that the non-dependant's 'normal weekly gross income' is taken into account, without giving a list of what to include. In practice the council is likely to include:

(a)   employed earnings (before tax, national insurance, etc have been deducted);

(b)   self-employed net profit (after the deduction of reasonable expenses but before tax, national insurance, etc have been deducted);

(c)   social security benefits, pensions and credits (except those in para 6.15);

(d)   state, occupational and private pensions;

(e)   rental income;

(f)   maintenance;

(g)   charitable and voluntary income; and

(h)   interest on savings.

6.17   Because the 'normal' amount of gross weekly income is taken into account, short-term variations are likely to be ignored, but longer-term changes are taken into account. For example, a non-dependant who is a school assistant could count as working at least 16 hours per week throughout the year (see para 14.70(c)) but changes in their income may mean different levels of non-dependant deduction in term-times and holidays.

T6.3   HB 74(1),(2); HB66+ 55(1),(2); NIHB 72(1),(2); NIHB66+ 53(1),(2); SI 2021/162 regs 24(3), 25(3)

6.16   HB 74(1),(2); HB66+ 55(1),(2); NIHB 72(1),(2); NIHB66+ 53(1),(2)

Non-dependant couples

6.18   If you have non-dependants who are a couple (or a polygamous marriage) only one deduction is made for them. This is the higher (or highest) of the amounts that would have applied if they were single. For the gross income limits in table 6.3, each of them is treated as having the gross income of both (or all) of them.

Example: A non-dependant couple

A claimant in Great Britain has two non-dependants, Nick and Pat, who are a couple. Nick works for 30 hours per week and has gross earnings of £300 per week. Pat works for 12 hours and has gross earnings of £200 per week.

If they were single, there would be two deductions, £82.30 for Nick and £15.95 for Pat (table 6.3).

Because they are a couple, there is only one deduction. Their combined gross income is £500 per week, so the deduction is £102.85 (table 6.3 and para 6.18).

Non-dependant of joint tenants

6.19   The following applies if you are a joint tenant of your home (with someone other than your partner), and there is also a non-dependant living there. If the non-dependant normally resides (para 4.29) with:

  (a)   only you (and your family), the whole non-dependant deduction is made from your HB;

  (b)   only your joint tenant (or more than one joint tenant), no non-dependant deduction is made from your HB;

  (c)   both you and your joint tenant (or more than one joint tenant), each of you gets a share of the non-dependant deduction.

The share mentioned in (c) need not be equal: the council should take into account the number of joint tenants concerned and the proportion of rent each of you pays (paras 8.6-7, 9.7-8 and table 10.5).

Delayed non-dependant deductions for pension age claims

6.20   The following rule applies if:

  (a)   you or your partner are over 66; and

  (b)   a non-dependant moves in, or there is any change in a non-dependant's circumstances which causes an increase in the amount of the deduction.

In these cases the change relating to the deduction is not implemented until the day 26 weeks after the change actually occurred; or if that is not a Monday, it is implemented from the following Monday. But the non-dependant is taken into account straight away for other purposes such as the size criteria in chapter 11.

6.18   HB 74(3),(4); HB66+ 55(3),(4); NIHB 72(3),(4); NIHB66+ 53(3),(4)

6.19   HB 74(5); HB66+ 55(5); NIHB 72(5); NIHB66+ 53(5)

6.20   HB66+ 59(10)-(13); NIHB66+ 57(12)-(15)

The HB benefit cap

6.21   The 'benefit cap' sets a limit on the amount of HB and other welfare benefits working age claimants can receive. This section explains when and how it applies.

6.22   If your HB is reduced because of the benefit cap, you may be able to get help from discretionary housing payments (para 23.8) and/or in Northern Ireland from welfare supplementary payments (para 23.23). The Supreme Court has decided that the benefit cap does not discriminate unlawfully: R (SG and others) v SSWP; R (DA and others) v SSWP.

When the benefit cap applies

6.23   The benefit cap only applies to working age claims (table 2.2). But the council/NIHE doesn't have to apply the benefit cap or reduce your HB unless and until it receives notice from the DWP/DFC (para 6.31).

The amount of the benefit cap

6.24   The amount of the benefit cap is as follows:

(a)   for single claimants

■   £296.35 per week (£15,410 per year) in Greater London,

■   £257.69 per week (£13,400 per year) elsewhere;

(b)   for lone parents and couples:

■   £442.31 per week (£23,000 per year) in Greater London,

■   £384.62 per week (£20,000 per year) elsewhere.

6.25   If you are in a polygamous marriage (table 1.1), the benefit cap applies to the two of you who were married earliest as though you were a couple. It doesn't apply to the others.

The amount of the HB reduction

6.26   Table 6.4 explains how the reduction in your HB is calculated. As the table shows, the calculation can't reduce your HB to below 50p per week.

Exceptions

6.27   Table 6.5 and paras 6.29-30 give the situations in which the benefit cap does not apply.

Supported and temporary accommodation

6.28   If you live in supported or temporary accommodation (table 2.3) and are on UC, the HB benefit cap doesn't apply at all (table 6.5). If you aren't on UC the amount of your HB is excluded from the benefit cap calculation (table 6.4). See also paras 2.13-20.

6.22-23   WRA 96-97; HB 75A-75H; SI 2012/2994; NIWRO 101; NIHB 73A-73H; NISR 2016/55;
          R (SG and others) v SSWP UKSC (2015) www.bailii.org/uk/cases/UKSC/2015/16.html
          R (DA and others) v SSWP UKSC (2019) www.bailii.org/uk/cases/UK/2019/21.html

6.24-25   HB 75CA, 75G definition: 'relevant amount'; NIHB 73CA, 73G; SI 2016/909; NISR 2016/375

6.26   HB 75G definition: 'couple'; NIHB 73G

6.27   HB 75D(2); NIHB 73D(2)

6.28   HB 75C(2)(a), 75F(1)(g), 75H; NIHB 73C(2)(a), 73F(1)(g), 73H

The 39 week grace period after leaving work

6.29   The HB benefit cap does not apply during the 39 weeks beginning with the day after your or your partner's last day of work if the following conditions are met (para 6.30). The DWP calls this time limited exception a 'grace period'. If you are a couple, either you or your partner must meet all the conditions; and if you each meet all the conditions from different dates, both grace periods apply.

Table 6.4 **Calculating HB benefit cap reductions**

For each benefit week (para 16.49):

(a)   Add together your and your partner's entitlement in that week to:

- HB, except in supported or temporary accommodation (para 6.28);
- JSA, ESA and IS;
- child benefit, child tax credit and maternity allowance;
- severe disablement allowance;
- widowed mother's/parent's allowance; and
- widow's pension and bereavement allowance.

(b)   If the total exceeds the benefit cap (paras 6.24-25), your HB is reduced by the amount of the excess.

(c)   But your HB can't be reduced below 50p per week.

Notes:

- Use the weekly amount of any benefit before any reductions are made for recovering overpayments, administrative penalties, third party deductions or sanctions. In practice, the DWP's/DFC's Benefit Cap Calculation Team provides the council/NIHE with the figures (HB A15/2013 paras 12 onwards).

- Paras 2.17-18 give the benefit cap rules if you live in supported or temporary accommodation or get HB on two homes.

Example: The HB benefit cap

A claimant and her children are renting their home in London (it isn't supported accommodation). Before the benefit cap is applied, she qualifies for:

HB	£240.00 per week
Other benefits in table 6.5	£220.00 per week

Because the total of £460.00 per week exceeds the benefit cap of £442.31 per week (para 6.24), her HB is reduced by the difference (£17.69 per week) to £222.31 per week.

6.29-30 HB 75E(1),(3)-(5); NIHB 73E(1),(3)-(5)

T6.4   WRA 96(10) definition: 'welfare benefit'; NIWRO 101(7); HB 75A, 75C, 75D, 75G definition: 'reference period'; NIHB 73A, 73C, 73D, 73G

Table 6.5 **Exceptions to the HB benefit cap**

The HB benefit cap doesn't apply in any of the following circumstances:

(a) You, your partner or a child or young person in your family are getting:

- PIP,
- DLA,
- attendance allowance or constant attendance allowance paid with an industrial injury pension (you or your partner only), or
- a war disablement or war bereavement pension (para 13.16) (you or your partner only);

or are entitled to them but not receiving them because of being in a hospital or care home.

(b) You, your partner or a child or young person in your family are getting:

- carer's allowance,
- guardian's allowance, or
- working tax credit (you or your partner only);

or are entitled to them but not receiving them (e.g. as in para 12.31).

(c) You or your partner are getting:

- main phase ESA with a support component,
- industrial injuries disablement benefit, or
- universal credit.

(d) You have a pension age HB claim (table 2.2).

(e) During an extended payment of HB (para 17.32).

(f) During the 39 week 'grace period' after leaving work (para 6.29).

Note:

In practice, the DWP's/DFC's Benefit Cap Calculation Team is expected to notify the council/NIHE when these exceptions apply, apart from those relating to war pensions (HB A15/2013 paras 23 and 52).

T6.5   HB 2(1), definition: 'attendance allowance', 75E,75F; NIHB 2(1), 73E,73F; SI 2016/909; NISR 2016/375

6.30   The conditions are that you/your partner:

(a) have ceased work; and

(b) for at least 50 of the 52 weeks before the last day of work, were engaged in work for which payment was made or expected, and were not entitled to JSA, ESA or IS.

For these purposes, being on maternity, paternity or adoption leave, or getting statutory sick pay, counts as being in work.

Applying, changing and ending benefit cap reductions

6.31   In any particular case, the council need not apply the benefit cap or change the amount of any reduction until it receives notification from the DWP's/DFC's Benefit Cap Calculation Team. The council may however do either of these on its own initiative if it has the relevant information and evidence to do so. If the benefit cap stops applying to you, the council might delay removing it until it receives notice from the DWP/DFC, but must then award you arrears of HB (para 6.32).

When benefit cap reductions take effect

6.32   A benefit cap reduction can apply from the beginning of your HB claim. It can also start, change or end during your award of HB, and when it:

(a) starts or increases, HB changes from the date the council makes the decision to do so (this prevents overpayments of HB occurring as a result of a reduction);

(b) reduces or ends, HB changes from the date entitlement to the relevant welfare benefit (table 6.5) changed (so you get your resulting arrears of HB).

6.33   Claims wrongly decided as to a reduction may be corrected at any time. So if the council wrongly applied a benefit cap to you, you are entitled to arrears of HB no matter how far back they go. If you consider the council got the calculation wrong, you can ask for a reconsideration (para 20.37) or appeal (para 20.41).

Conversion to weekly amounts

Rent and service charges

6.34   Whenever a weekly figure is needed for rent, the following rules apply. The same rules apply to service charges:

(a) for rent due in multiples of weeks, divide by the number of weeks it covers;

(b) for rent due calendar monthly, multiply by 12 then divide by 52 to find the weekly figure;

(c) for rent due daily, multiply by seven to find the weekly figure.

6.31   HB 75B; NIHB 73B

6.32-33 DAR 4(7H), 7(2)(r), 8(14F); NIDAR 4(6E), 7(2)(m), 8(14A)

6.34   HB 80; HB66+ 61; NIHB 78; NIHB66+ 59

Rent-free periods

6.35   No HB is awarded during rent-free periods. HB is awarded only for periods in which rent is due (and if a rent-free period begins or ends part way through a benefit week, the eligible rent that week is calculated on a daily basis).

6.36   During the periods in which rent is due, the calculation factors (i.e. applicable amount, income and any non-dependant deductions) are adjusted as follows:

  (a) if rent is expressed on a weekly basis: multiply the calculation factors by 52 or 53, then divide by the number of weeks when rent is due in that year;

  (b) if rent is not expressed on a weekly basis: multiply the calculation factors by 365 or 366, then divide by the number of days when rent is due in that year.

Income

6.37   Whenever a weekly income figure is needed, the following rules apply:

  (a) for an amount relating to a multiple of weeks, divide by the number of weeks it covers;

  (b) for an amount relating to a calendar month, multiply by 12 then divide by 52;

  (c) for an amount relating to a year, there are two rules. For working age claims, divide the annual amount by 365 or 366 then multiply by seven. For pension age claims, simply divide the annual amount by 52;

  (d) for income relating to a self-employed person's assessment period (para 14.30), divide the amount by the number of days in the assessment period, then multiply by seven;

  (e) for an amount relating to any other period longer than a week, divide the amount by the number of days it covers, then multiply by seven;

  (f) for an amount relating to a period less than a week, that is the weekly amount.

Rounding

6.38   The council may 'if appropriate' round any amount involved in the calculation of HB to the nearest penny, halfpennies being rounded upwards.

6.35   HB 81(1),(2),(3); HB66+ 62(1),(2),(3); NIHB 79(1),(2),(3); NIHB66+ 60(1),(2),(3)

6.37   HB 33; HB66+ 33; NIHB 30; NIHB66+ 31(a)

6.38   HB 80(8); HB66+ 61(7); NIHB 78(8); NIHB66+ 59(7)

Chapter 7 **Which eligible rent rules**

- ■ The payments HB can meet: see paras 7.2-4.
- ■ The different kinds of eligible rent and the meaning of 'landlord': see paras 7.5-9.
- ■ Eligible rent and landlord type: see paras 7.10-22.
- ■ Eligible rent: special kinds of accommodation: see paras 7.23-34.
- ■ Eligible rent: old claims and tenancies: see paras 7.35-43.
- ■ Rent restrictions – protected groups: see paras 7.44-58.

7.1 Your eligible rent is the starting point in the calculation of your HB (para 6.2). So the higher it is, the more HB you get. This chapter explains the different ways of working out eligible rent and the rules that determine which one of these applies to your claim. It also describes how your eligible rent can be restricted (e.g. if your rent is high), how you can get temporary protection from this, and the general rules about what is counted as rent for HB. Chapters 8-11 give the detailed rules about how eligible rent is worked out for each particular eligible rent category.

The payments HB can meet

Meaning of 'rent'

7.2 For HB purposes all the payments in table 7.1 count as 'rent' whether or not they count as rent in landlord and tenant law. In this guide 'tenant' means any kind of rent-payer.

'Actual rent' and 'rent'

7.3 Your:

(a) 'actual rent' means the total of all payments in table 7.1 which you are liable to pay on your home (including any charges that HB can't cover);

(b) 'referred rent' is the figure (including meals) the council passes to the rent officer in rent referral cases. It means your 'actual rent' after any deductions for ineligible services (other than meals) that the council is responsible for valuing (table 8.3);

(c) 'eligible rent' means the (often lower) figure used in calculating your HB (para 7.5) and if you are a joint tenant (para 4.42) your HB may be based on your share of the rent (paras 8.6, 9.7, 10.10, 11.16 and table 10.5).

7.2   HB 2(1) definition: 'rent'; HB66+ 2(1); NIHB 2(1); NIHB66+ 2(1)

7.3   HB 12(1)(a)-(j),114A(3)(f),(4) Old 12(1)(a)-(j); HB66+ 12(1)(a)-(j), 95A(3)(f),(4) Old 12(1)(a)-(j);
       NIHB 13(1)(a)-(h), Old 13(1)(a)-(h); NIHB66+ 13(1)(a)-(h), Old 13(1)(a)-(h)

Table 7.1 **Payments that count as rent for HB purposes**

(a) Rent payable under a tenancy agreement.

(b) Rent payable under a shared ownership (also called equity sharing) tenancy but not mortgage payments.

(c) Board and lodging payments (i.e. a licence fee and a charge for meals).

(d) Licence fees and payments for 'use and occupation'.

(e) Rent payable to a co-operative ('co-op') if you have no more than a nominal equity share in the co-op (GM A4.170-172).

(f) Payments under a rental purchase scheme – where you pay instalments to purchase your home over a fixed period, but your landlord remains the owner until you make the final payment (GM A4.140).

(g) In Scotland, payments in respect of a croft and the land it is on or relates to.

(h) 'Mesne profits' (in Scotland 'violent profits') payable after your tenancy or right to occupy is terminated.

(i) Site charges for a caravan or mobile home (whether or not you own it) as well as rent (if you don't own it).

(j) Mooring charges and berthing fees for a houseboat (whether or not you own it) as well as rent (if you don't own it) – the payments can include a continuous cruiser licence ([2020] UKUT 158 (AAC)); and a houseboat includes a narrow boat 'fitted out as a dwelling suitable for permanent residence' (R(H) 9/08).

(k) Service charges you have to pay as a condition of occupying your home (paras 8.33-35).

(l) Contributions towards maintenance and essential services in a charitable almshouse provided by a housing association (para 7.13) in Great Britain.

Notes: For exceptions see table 7.2. For limits on your eligible rent and for when service charges are (or aren't) included in it, see chapters 8-11.

Payments that don't count as rent

7.4 Table 7.2 lists the payments that don't count as 'rent' for HB purposes (or can't be met by HB for other reasons). You may be able to get help from universal credit, pension credit or a DWP loan with some of these: see chapter 22 and volume 1 chapters 6 and 8.

T7.1   HB 12(1)(a)-(j), Old 12(1)(a)-(j); HB66+ 12(1)(a)-(j), Old 12(1)(a)-(j);
             NIHB 13(1)(a)-(h), Old 13(1)(a)-(h); NIHB66+ 13(1)(a)-(h), Old 13(1)(a)-(h)

7.4   CBA 130(1)(a),(2)(b); NICBA 129(1),(2); HB 7(1),(5), 9(1)(k),(4), 11(2), 12(2); HB66+ 7(1),(5), 9(1)(k),(4), 11(2), 12(2);
             NIHB 7(1),(5), 9(1)(k),(4), 11(2), 13(2); NIHB66+ 7(1),(5), 9(1)(k),(4), 11(2), 13(2)

Table 7.2 **Payments that aren't rent for HB purposes**

(a) Mortgage and all other payments on a home you and/or your partner own, even if you only have the right to sell it with the consent of other joint owners (but HB can meet rent and service charges for a shared ownership tenancy, and see notes).

(b) Payments on a long lease ('long tenancy') which was for more than 21 years when it was first granted, and which meets the legal formalities for a lease (R(H) 3/07).

(c) Payments under a co-ownership scheme – where you are entitled to a payment related to the value of your home when your membership of the scheme ends.

(d) Payments under a hire purchase or credit sale agreement (e.g. to buy a mobile home or furniture) or under a conditional sale agreement (unless it is for land).

(e) Payments on many Crown and government department tenancies, except where the landlord is the Duchy of Cornwall or Lancaster, or where the dwelling is managed by the Crown Estate Commissioners (GM A3.217-18).

(f) Payments for a tent or its pitch.

(g) Payments on some night shelters (para 3.4).

(h) Payments on bail and probation hostels ('approved premises') – for prisoners on remand and former prisoners.

(i) Payments on care homes and independent hospitals (see notes).

Notes:

If you claim guarantee credit you can get help with service charge payments for (a) and (b) and for payments (c)-(f): see table 22.3. You may also be able to get DWP loan payments for your mortgage interest or similar home loan: see volume 2 chapters 6 and 8.

In HB law, payments (a) to (e) are excluded because they don't count as 'rent', and payments (f) to (i) because you are treated as either not being in occupation or liable to pay rent (para 5.1). For other exclusions from HB, see chapter 2.

'Independent hospital' means a non-NHS hospital that is regulated by the Care Quality Commission in England; Healthcare Improvement Scotland in Scotland; Healthcare Inspectorate Wales in Wales; and the Regulation and Quality Improvement Authority in Northern Ireland.

The different kinds of eligible rent

7.5 It is your 'eligible rent' rather than your actual rent that is used to calculate your HB (para 7.3) but there are several different kinds and each one calculates the eligible rent figure in a different way. The method used for each kind is described in chapters 8 to 10.

T7.2(a)-(e) CBA 130(2)(b); NICBA 129,(2); HB 2(1): definition 'Crown tenant', 12(2), Old 12(2); HB66+ 2(1),12(2), Old 12(2); NIHB 13(2), Old 13(2); NIHB66+ 13(2), Old 13(2)

T7.2(f) HB 11(2); HB66+ 11(2); NIHB 11(2); NIHN60+ 11(2)

T7.2(g)-(h) CBA 130(1)(a); NICBA 129(1)(a); HB 7(1),(5); HB66+ 7(1),(5); NIHB 7(1),(5); NIHB66+ 7(1),(5)

T7.2(i) CBA 130(2); NICBA 129(2); HB 2(1),9(1)(k),(4); HB66+ 9(1)(k),(4); NIHB 2(1),9(1)(k),(4); NIHB66+ 9(1)(k),(4)

7.6   There are four main ways of calculating eligible rent. These are:

(a)   the 'social renter' rules (chapter 8);

   ■   without the social renter size criteria,

   ■   with the social renter size criteria;

(b)   the 'private renter' rules (chapter 9) – also known as the 'local housing allowance';

(c)   the 'rent referral' rules (chapter 10); or

(d)   'old scheme' rules (chapter 10).

Only one of these can apply to your claim for any given period (they are mutually exclusive) and if you fall in more than one category then the one lowest down the list usually takes precedence: see paras 7.10-43.

7.7   The names in para 7.6 are also used in chapters 8 to 10. These terms are not used in the law (see paras 8.9, 9.4 and 10.39) but are often used by benefits staff.

7.8   The way your eligible rent is calculated largely depends on:

(a)   who your landlord is (e.g. council, housing association, private) (paras 7.10-22);

(b)   the type of accommodation you occupy (e.g. shared ownership, hostel, temporary) (paras 7.23-34); and

(c)   the date of your claim or tenancy agreement (paras 7.35-43).

Landlords and managing agents

7.9   Your 'landlord' means the person you have a legal liability to pay rent to. This means your immediate landlord and not, for example, the head landlord (owner) or your landlord's managing agent. For example:

(a)   if your legal liability to pay rent is to a housing association, then it is your landlord even it has leased the property from a private landlord;

(b)   if your legal liability to pay rent is to a private landlord, it is your landlord even if a housing association manages your tenancy on its behalf;

(c)   if your liability to pay rent is to the council, it is your landlord even if the council manages its homes through a separate company (typically an 'arms-length management organisation' or 'tenant management organisation': ALMO/TMO);

(d)   if you are a lodger your landlord is the person your rent is due to (e.g. if you are a lodger of a council tenant your landlord is the tenant, not the council).

It is your 'landlord' type that usually determines how your eligible rent is worked out (para 7.10), but if you live in a hostel it can be either your landlord or your managing agent (paras 7.28-29).

7.6   HB 11(1)(a)-(d),12B,12BA,12C,12D,Old 12; HB66+ 11(1)(a)-(d),12B,12C,12D,Old 12; NIHB 11(1)(a)-(b),13A,13AA,13B,13C,Old 13; NIHB66+ 11(1)(a)-(b),13A,13B,13C,Old 13

7.9   HB 2(1) definition: 'hostel', 12(1), Old 12(1); HB66+ 2(1), 12(1), Old 12(1); NIHB 2(1), 13(1), Old 13(1); NIHB66+ 2(1), 13(1), Old 13(1)

Eligible rent and landlord type

7.10 The rules that determine how your eligible rent is worked out mainly depend on the type of landlord you have (e.g. social, private). This section sets out the different types of landlord (paras 7.11-22) and how this affects which eligible rent rules apply to you (para 7.6).

Local authority and NIHE tenants

7.11 If your landlord (para 7.9) is the council you claim HB from, your HB is paid as a rent rebate (para 18.4) and your eligible rent is worked out as a social renter (chapter 8): there are no exceptions. (The LHA, rent referral and old scheme rules only apply to rent allowance claims.) If your landlord is an English county council that doesn't administer HB, see paras 7.18-19.

Former local authority/NIHE ('stock transfer') tenants

7.12 Where your tenancy started with the council/NIHE but was transferred to a new landlord following a vote (a 'stock transfer') your eligible rent is worked out as follows:

(a) if your new landlord is a registered housing association (para 7.14), according to the rules for that type of landlord (para 7.16);

(b) if (a) does not apply, using the social renter rules without the size criteria (paras 8.9-16) if:

   ▪ your rent is reasonable (or isn't but hasn't been increased since the transfer), or

   ▪ you have a registered rent or other similar old tenancy (paras 7.39-43); or

(c) in any other case, using the LHA rules (or rent referral rules if table 9.1 applies).

Housing associations

7.13 A 'housing association' means a society, body of trustees or company:

(a) whose objects or powers include the power to provide, manage, construct or improve housing; and

(b) which doesn't trade for profit or, if it does, is limited by its constitution not to pay a dividend.

7.14 A 'registered housing association' is a 'housing association' (para 7.13) that is registered with the appropriate national regulator which is:

(a) in England, with the Regulator of Social Housing;

(b) in Scotland, with the Scottish Housing Regulator;

(c) in Wales, with the Welsh Government;

(d) in Northern Ireland, with the Department for Communities.

7.11 AA134(1A), NIAA 126(1)(b); HB 12B(1),12BA,A13(1),(2); HB66+ 12B(1); NIHB 13A(1),13AA,A14(1),(2), NIHB66+ 13A(1)

7.12 HB 12B(1), A13(1),(2); 13C(5)(c), 14(2)(b), sch 2 para 11; HB66+ 12B(1), 13C(5)(c), 14(2)(b), sch 2 para 11; NIHB 13A(1), A14(1),(2), 14C(5)(c), 15(3)(b), sch 3 para 5; NIHB66+ 13A(1), 14C(5)(c), 15(3)(b), sch 3 para 5

7.13 Housing Associations Act 1985 s1(1); Housing (Northern Ireland) Order 1992 art 3; HB 2(1) definition: 'housing association'; HB66+ 2(1); NIHB 2(1); NIHB66+ 2(1)

7.14-15 HB 2(1) definition: 'registered housing association', 13C(5)(a),(6), sch 2 para 3(1),(1A); HB66+ 2(1), 13C(5)(a),(6), sch 2 para 3(1),(1A); NIHB 2(1), 14C(5)(a), sch 3 para 3(b); NIHB66+ 2(1), 14C(5)(a), sch 3 para 3(a),(1A)

7.15   In Scotland and Wales, registered housing associations are known as 'registered social landlords'. In England, they are known as 'private registered providers of social housing' (often shortened to 'registered providers'). 'Private' here simply means non-council (because councils are also registered providers).

7.16   If your landlord is a registered housing association your eligible rent is normally worked out as a social renter. The only rare exceptions are when:

(a)   your landlord also provides you with care, support or supervision so that your home qualifies as 'exempt accommodation' (para 10.5) in which case your eligible rent is always worked out using the 'old scheme' rules (para 10.10);

(b)   (in England only) your landlord is profit-making and your home isn't social housing (para 7.17); or

(c)   the authority considers your rent to be unreasonably high, or (if you are pension age) your home unreasonably large, in which case your eligible rent is worked out using the rent referral rules (chapter 10).

But in the case of (b) and (c) your eligible rent is still worked out as a social renter if you have a secure tenancy or other pre-1989 agreement (para 7.39) (but see also paras 7.46-47).

7.17   In England only, if a registered housing association is profit-making, its lettings can be either social housing or private rented. A letting is 'social housing' if:

(a)   it is a shared ownership tenancy; or

(b)   it is made available for rent 'to people whose needs are not adequately served by the commercial [...] market', and 'the rent is below the market rate' (such as part of the Affordable Rent Programme).

In any other case (i.e. if it is let at a market rent) unless para 7.16(a) or (c) apply, eligible rent is worked out using the LHA rules (chapter 9).

Other not-for-profit landlords

7.18   If your landlord isn't the council/NIHE or a registered housing association, your eligible rent is usually worked out as a private renter (chapter 9) even if your landlord is a 'social landlord' in the broader sense (such as a charity). The only exceptions are if:

(a)   your home qualifies as exempt accommodation (para 7.19);

(b)   you live in a hostel (para 7.27) and exception (a) does not apply;

(c)   exception (a) does not apply and one of the other exclusions in table 9.1 does.

If (a) applies your eligible rent is always worked out using the 'old scheme' rules, or if (b) or (c) apply using the rent referral rules (chapter 10).

7.17   Housing and Regeneration Act 2008 s68-71 and 77; HB 13C(5)(a), sch 2 para 3(1A); HB66+ 13C(5)(a), sch 2 para 3(1A)

7.18   HB 13C(5)(a)-(d); HB66+ 13C(5)(a)-(d); NIHB 14C(5)(a)-(d); NIHB66+ 14C(5)(a)-(d)

7.19 Your home can only qualify as exempt accommodation if you meet the support condition (para 10.7) and your landlord is:

(a) a housing association (whether it is registered or not with the national regulator);

(b) a registered charity (para 7.20);

(c) a voluntary organisation (para 7.21); or

(d) an English county council that doesn't administer HB.

7.20 A 'registered charity' is a charity that is registered with the appropriate national regulator [www].

7.21 A 'voluntary organisation' is a 'body, other than a public authority or council, the activities of which are carried on otherwise than for profit'. Whether a landlord meets this description can involve looking at all the circumstances (not just the landlord's written constitution), and it is a 'commercial reality' that a voluntary organisation is likely to have contracts with profit-making third parties ([2013] UKUT 291 (AAC)).

Private landlords

7.22 If you pay rent to a private landlord your eligible rent is worked out using the LHA rules unless any of the exceptions in table 9.1 apply. For HB purposes, 'private landlord' means any landlord other than a council that administers HB or a registered housing association. It can include any kind of not-for-profit landlord in para 7.19. Apart from that a private landlord is usually an individual, a company or a firm (para 7.9).

Eligible rent: special kinds of accommodation

7.23 If you are a shared owner or live in non-permanent housing (e.g. lodger, hostel resident) the type of accommodation you live in can determine how your eligible rent is worked out. This section (paras 7.24-34) describes which eligible rent rules apply to you for each type of letting.

Shared ownership tenancies

7.24 If you are part renting and part buying your home you are a 'shared owner' (including if you have an equity sharing agreement). Your eligible rent is worked out as follows:

(a) if your landlord is the HB authority or a registered housing association (whether or not the authority considers your rent to be unreasonably high) your eligible rent is worked out as a social renter but without the social renter size criteria rules;

(b) in any other case your eligible rent is worked out using the LHA rules (or using the rent referral rules if any of the exceptions in table 9.1 apply).

7.19 CPR sch 3 para 4(10); NICPR sch 3 para 4(9)

7.20 England and Wales: www.gov.uk/government/organisations/charity-commission;
Scotland www.oscr.org.uk/; Northern Ireland: www.charitycommissionni.org.uk/

7.21 HB 2(1) 'voluntary organisation'; HB66+ 2(1); NIHB 2(1); NIHB66+ 2(1)

7.22 AA 134(1A),(1B); NIAA 126(1)(b),(c); HB 13C(2),(5)(a); HB66+ 13C(2),(5)(a); NIHB 14C(2),(5)(a); NIHB66+ 14C(2),(5)(a)

7.24 HB 12B(1),A13(2)(b),13C(5)(a)(iii), 14(2)(b), sch 2 para 12; HB66+ 13C(5)(a)(iii), 14(2)(b), sch 2 para 12;
NIHB 13A(1),A14(2)(b),14C(5)(a), 15(2)(b), sch 2 para 3; NIHB66+ 14C(5)(a)(iii), 15(2)(b), sch 2 para 3

Boarders

7.25   You are a boarder if your rent includes a charge for meals. If your landlord is the HB authority or a registered housing association then the eligible rent rules for that kind of accommodation apply. In any other case you are a private renter and your eligible rent is worked out using either the LHA or rent referral rules (and the rent officer decides which: paras 9.32-34). If you are a lodger see also para 7.9.

Supported accommodation

7.26   If you live in supported housing and your landlord is a not-for-profit landlord of the kind in para 7.19, your eligible rent is worked out using the 'old scheme' rules . In any other case your eligible rent is worked out using the LHA rules (chapter 9).

Hostels

7.27   If you live in a 'hostel' and your landlord is not the HB authority or a registered housing association your eligible rent is worked out using the rent referral rules (paras 10.35 and 10.39). Your dwelling only counts as a hostel if it meets the conditions in the next two paragraphs. (But if your landlord provides support see paras 7.18-19.)

7.28   A hostel is a building that:

  (a) provides accommodation for residents or a class of residents in units that are neither separate nor self-contained;

  (b) together with either meals or adequate facilities for preparing food; and

  (c) which is not a care home, independent hospital or Abbeyfield Home; and

  (d) meets at least one of the operating conditions in para 7.29.

7.29   The operating conditions referred to in para 7.28 are that the building is:

  (a) managed by a charity or voluntary organisation which provides care, support or supervision to help people be rehabilitated or resettled within the community; or

  (b) run on a non-commercial basis, and wholly or partly funded by a government department or agency or local authority; or

  (c) managed or owned by a registered housing association (para 7.14).

Condition (c) is only relevant if the housing association isn't your landlord (para 7.9), or is but the accommodation doesn't count as social housing (para 7.17) (because in any other case you would fall under the social renter rules).

Temporary accommodation

7.30   If your rent is due to the council (HB authority) or a registered housing association but you live in 'temporary accommodation' (para 7.32) that was provided because you were, or were at risk of being, homeless, your eligible rent is worked out as a social renter but the size criteria don't apply (paras 8.9-16).

7.25   HB 13C(5)(e), 14(2)(b), sch 2 para 12; HB66+ 13C(5)(e), 14(2)(b), sch 2 para 12;
        NIHB 14C(5)(a), 15(2)(b), sch 2 para 3; NIHB66+ 14C(5)(a)(iii), 15(2)(b), sch 2 para 3

7.27-29 HB 2(1) definition: 'hostel'; HB66+ 2(1); NIHB 2(1); NIHB66+ 2(1)

7.31 Temporary accommodation is often provided by the council/NIHE through an arrangement it has with a housing association or a private landlord (for example through properties it leases from them).

7.32 Your home only counts a 'temporary accommodation' if:

(a) it was made available to you by the authority or by a registered housing association (para 7.14) under an arrangement it has with the authority for the purpose of:

- satisfying a homelessness duty it owes you following your application for assistance (e.g. permanent housing wasn't available); or

- preventing you from becoming homeless (as defined in the homeless persons legislation); and

(b) the accommodation is:

- 'board and lodging' (as defined in para 21.35), or

- held by the authority or registered housing association on a short-term lease ('licensed accommodation' as defined in para 21.37), or

- provided by someone else but which the authority or registered housing association has a right to use under an agreement (other than a leasehold agreement: para 21.36).

But if you have been housed by the authority in one of its own properties (other than those in (b) above) then the social renter size criteria apply in the normal way.

Caravans, mobile homes and houseboats

7.33 If you live in a caravan, mobile home or houseboat and pay site fees or mooring charges your eligible rent is worked out using the rent referral rules (chapter 10) unless:

(a) you pay site fees or mooring charges to a local authority in Great Britain that administers HB (whether or not if you also pay rent for your dwelling and whether or not your rent is paid to the same or a different landlord); or

(b) you live on a gypsy or traveller site (para 7.34) and your landlord is an English county council,

in which case your eligible rent is worked out as a social renter (chapter 8) but without the social renter size criteria and paid as a rent allowance (para 18.6).

7.34 A gypsy or traveller site means a site provided for:

(a) people with a cultural tradition of nomadism or living in a caravan; or

(b) other people with a nomadic or cultural tradition of travelling regardless of their race or religion including travellers, show people, and those who no longer travel through reasons of health or age.

7.30-32 AA 134(1A); NIAA 126(1)(b); HB 12B(1),A13(2)(e),(3),(4); HB66+ 12D(1); NIHB 13A(1),A14(2)(e),(3),(4); NIHB66+ 13A(1)

7.33-34 HB 12B(1),A13(2)(c),13C(5)(d),14(2)(b),sch 2 para 3(1)(b),(c),(4); HB66+ 12B(1),13C(5)(d),14(2)(b), sch 2 para 3(1)(b),(c),(4)
NIHB 13A(1),A14(2)(c),14C(5)(d),15(4); NIHB66+ 13A(1),14C(5)(d),15(4)

Eligible rent: old claims and tenancies

7.35 In addition to your landlord and letting type, if you have an unbroken old HB claim or tenancy (usually 13 years or more in duration) it can also determine which eligible rent rules apply to you. If the exceptions in this section apply (para 7.36-43) then your eligible rent is worked out according to HB rules that applied at the start of your claim/tenancy but only until such time as you move home.

Private renters with pre-April 2008 HB claims

7.36 If you pay rent to a private landlord and none of the previous exceptions (paras 7.18-34) apply and you have been on HB continuously at the same address since 6th April 2008 (or earlier) then your eligible rent is worked out using the rent referral rules (chapter 10). But if there has been a break in your claim or you have moved the LHA rules apply (chapter 9).

'Old scheme' HB claims (pre-1996)

7.37 If you have an 'old HB claim' (para 7.38) your eligible rent is worked out in exactly the same way as if you live in exempt accommodation (para 10.10).

7.38 You have an 'old HB' claim only if all of the following apply:

(a) you have been getting HB continuously since 1st January 1996 (in Northern Ireland, 1st April 1996), ignoring breaks of four weeks or less;

(b) you have not moved home since then, or moved only because your home was made uninhabitable by fire, flood or natural disaster; and

(c) your landlord isn't the HB authority or a registered housing association.

Registered rent and similar tenancies

7.39 If you have a 'registered rent tenancy' (paras 7.41-43) your eligible rent is worked out in the same way as a social renter (chapter 8). The only exception is if you fall under the 'old scheme' rules (paras 7.19 and 7.38). For Great Britain see paras 7.41-42, for Northern Ireland see para 7.43.

7.40 In HB law these lettings are called 'excluded tenancies' because they cannot be referred to the rent officer for a rent determination (chapter 10). In landlord and tenant law they are private or housing association tenancies known as 'Rent Act' or 'regulated tenancies' but the HB definition is somewhat wider than this (para 7.41).

7.41 In Great Britain 'registered rent tenancy' means any kind of regulated tenancy where the rent officer has, or is entitled to, register the rent (i.e. set the legal maximum rent you can be charged). But for HB purposes it also includes any kind of letting agreement (for example a licence or housing association tenancy) that started before the relevant date (para 7.42) regardless of whether or not the rent officer is entitled to register the rent.

7.36   HB 13C(2)(a)-(c); HB66+ 13C(2)(b)-(c); NIHB 14C(2)(a)-(c); NIHB66+ 14C(2)(a)-(c);
        SI 2007/2868 reg 1(5),(6); SI 2007/2869 reg 1(5),(6); NISR 2008/103 reg 1(2),(3)

7.37   CPR sch 3 para 4(1)(a); NICPR sch 3 para 4(1)(a)

7.38   CPR sch 3 para 4(2)(aa),(3),(10); NICPR sch 3 para 4(1A)(aa),(2),(9)

7.39   HB 12B(1), 13C(5)(c), 14(2)(b); HB66+ 12B(1), 13C(5)(c), 14(2)(b); NIHB 13A(1), 14C(5)(c), 15(3)(b); NIHB66+ 13A(1), 14C(5)(c), 15(3)(b)

7.41   HB sch 2 paras 4-8; HB66+ sch 2 paras 4-8

7.42 The relevant date (para 7.41) is:

(a) in England and Wales 15th January 1989;

(b) in Scotland 2nd January 1989.

7.43 For HB purposes in Northern Ireland you have a 'registered rent tenancy' (para 7.39) if your rent is controlled (tied to a historic rateable value) or is fixed by a rent officer. In broad terms this applies to you if:

(a) in certain circumstances, your tenancy began before 1st October 1978; or

(b) your tenancy began on or after 14th June 2006; and

- your house or flat was built or converted before 6th November 1956; and

- it does not meet the fitness standard.

Rent restrictions and temporary protection

7.44 This section describes the general rules about how your eligible rent can be restricted (limited) depending on whether you are a social renter, private renter or if you fall within the 'old scheme' or rent referral rules (chapters 8-11). It also describes the common rules that give you time-limited protection from the restrictions described in those chapters.

High rents and over-sized accommodation

7.45 There are a number of rules about how your eligible rent can be reduced (or limited) if your rent is considered to be too high or your home to be too large. These are:

(a) the social renter size criteria (paras 8.9-16);

(b) the rules for exempt accommodation and old (pre-1996) HB claims (paras 10.9-20);

(c) the local housing allowance (LHA) rules (paras 9.4-9);

(d) the rent referral rules (paras 10.39-53);

(e) the rules for registered rent and similar tenancies (paras 7.39-43 and 8.8); and

(f) the default power to restrict rents (paras 7.46-47).

See also chapter 11 for general rules about the size criteria ('the bedroom tax'), and paras 7.48-58 to see if you qualify for time-limited protection from these.

The default power to restrict the rent

7.46 If your eligible rent 'appears [...] greater than it is reasonable to meet by way of HB', the authority has the power to reduce it to 'such lesser sum as seems [...] to be an appropriate rent'.

7.43   NIHB sch 3 para 4; NIHB66+ sch 3 para 4

7.46   HB 12B(6); HB66+ 12B(6); NIHB 13A(7); NIHB66+ 13A(7)

7.47   Although this default power to restrict can apply to council tenants (Burton v Camden LBC) the law is somewhat unclear and disputed as to when and how it can be used. It seems it can't be used if you fall under social renter size criteria or old scheme rules (para 7.45(a)-(b)); has disputed or limited use if you fall under the LHA or rent referral rules ([2011] UKUT 156 (AAC)); and therefore is only likely to affect you if none of these apply (e.g. you are a social renter unaffected by the size criteria: para 7.45(e) and table 8.1). If the power is used, the authority must take your personal circumstances into account as well as matters that relate to your rent (R v Westminster HBRB ex parte Laali).

Temporary protection from rent restrictions

7.48   If you are a protected renter (para 7.50) you are wholly or partly protected from your eligible rent being reduced (paras 7.45-47) for a period of up to 13 weeks or one year depending on which type of protection you qualify for (paras 7.49-56).

7.49   The protections apply whether your eligible rent is worked out under:

(a)   the rules if you are a social renter (chapter 8);

(b)   the LHA rules if you are a private renter (chapter 9);

(c)   the rules for exempt accommodation and old (pre-1996) HB claims (chapter 10); or

(d)   the rent referral rules if your claim is referred to the rent officer.

The footnotes give separate references for each of these.

Who is a protected renter

7.50   You are a protected renter if you:

(a)   could previously afford your rent; or

(b)   have had a death in your home; or

(c)   are considered vulnerable.

Protections (a) and (b) apply to all kinds of HB (para 7.49), and are described in paras 7.51-56. But protection (c) only applies if you live in exempt accommodation or have an old (pre-1996) HB claim, and is described in paras 10.22-25.

7.47   HB 12B(1); HB66+ 12B(1); NIHB 13A(1); NIHB66+ 13A(1)
         Burton v Camden LBC 17/12/97 CA 30 HLR 991;
         R (Laali) v Westminster CC HBRB 08/12/00 QBD

People who could previously afford their home

7.51   This protection applies if you meet the following conditions when you make a claim for HB:

(a) you or any combination of the occupiers of your home (para 7.57) could afford the financial commitments there when your liability for rent was entered into (no matter how long ago that was); and

(b) you have not received HB for any period during the 52 weeks before your award of HB starts, and nor has your partner (if you have one: table 1.1).

7.52   In this case, the protection lasts for the first 13 weeks of your award of HB. This may give you time to move or change your circumstances (e.g. by getting someone else to move in with you or improving your income) without the additional pressure of having insufficient HB. If you stop receiving HB (during or after the 13 weeks) the protection can only apply to a new HB claim if there are at least 52 weeks between the end of your old HB award and the start of the new one.

7.53   While the protection applies to you, your eligible rent is:

(a) the full actual rent payable on your home (para 7.3);

(b) minus an amount for service charges which are ineligible for HB (see paras 8.37-41) and in Northern Ireland an amount for rates unless you are billed separately.

People who have had a death in their home

7.54   This protection applies if you meet the following conditions when you make a claim for HB or during your award of HB:

(a) any of the occupiers of your home (para 7.57) has died within the past 12 months (including occupiers who were temporarily absent); and

(b) you were living there on the date of their death, or were temporarily absent in the UK or abroad (paras 3.5-12); and

(c) you have not moved since then.

But if you (the claimant) die, your HB ends. So this protection can only apply to someone who claims HB after your death if you counted as an occupier in their home (para 7.57).

7.51   Social renter: HB 12BA(6),(7); NIHB 13AA(6),(7)
         Private renter: HB 12D(5),(6); HB66+ 12D(5),(6); NIHB 13C(5),(6); NIHB66+ 13C(5),(6)
         Old scheme: HB Old 13(7),(8); HB66+ Old 13(7),(8); NIHB Old 14(7),(8); NIHB66+ Old 14(7),(8)
         Rent referral: HB 13(8), 13ZA(3),(4); HB66+ 13(8), 13ZA(3),(4); NIHB 14(8), 14A(3),(4); NIHB66+ 14(8), 14A(3),(4)

7.52   Social renter: HB 12BA(8); NIHB 13AA(8)
         Private renter: HB 12D(7)(b); HB66+ 12D(7)(b); NIHB 13C(7)(b); NIHB66+ 13C(7)(b)
         Old scheme: HB Old 13(7); HB66+ Old 13(7); NIHB Old 14(7); NIHB66+ Old 14(7)
         Rent referral: HB 13ZA(3); HB66+ 13ZA(3); NIHB 14A(3); NIHB66+ 14A(3)

7.53   Social renter: HB 12BA(6); NIHB 13AA(6)
         Private renter: HB 12D(5); HB66+ 12D(5); NIHB 13C(5); NIHB66+ 13C(5)
         Old scheme: HB Old 13(7); HB66+ Old 13(7); NIHB Old 14(7); NIHB66+ Old 14(7)
         Rent referral: HB 13ZA(3); HB66+ 13ZA(3); NIHB 14A(3); NIHB66+ 14A(3)

7.54-55 Social renter: HB 12BA(3),(4),(5); NIHB 13AA(3),(4),(5)
         Private renter: HB 12D(3),(4),(7)(a); HB66+ 12D(3),(4),(7)(a); NIHB 13C(3),(4),(7)(a); NIHB66+ 13C(3),(4),(7)(a)
         Old scheme: HB Old 13(5),(6); HB66+ Old 13(5),(6); NIHB Old 14(5),(6); NIHB66+ Old 14(5),(6)
         Rent referral: HB 13(8), 13ZA(1),(2); HB66+ 13(8), 13ZA(1),(2); NIHB 14(8), 14A(1),(2); NIHB66+ 14(8), 14A(1),(2)

7.55   In this case, the protection lasts for the 12 months following the date of the person's death. This may give you time to move or change your circumstances (e.g. by getting someone else to move in with you or improving your income) without the additional pressure of having insufficient HB. If you stop receiving HB and then make a new claim at the same address within the 12 months, the protection resumes until 12 months after the date of the person's death (in other words, it isn't extended). If you move, the protection ends.

7.56   While the protection applies to you:

(a) if you weren't on HB on the date of the person's death, your eligible rent is worked out in the same way as in para 7.53;

(b) if you were on HB on that date, your eligible rent must not be reduced below whatever it was immediately before that date (but it is increased if any rule requires this).

Occupiers related to a protected renter

7.57   In deciding if you qualify as a protected renter, the only 'occupiers' taken into account are:

(a) you (the claimant) (but only for the rule in paras 7.51-53);

(b) any members of your family (partner, children, young persons: para 4.2); and

(c) any 'relative' of you or your partner (including non-dependants and lodgers) who has no separate right to occupy the dwelling.

In the law, the term 'linked persons' is also used to refer to these occupiers.

Who is a 'relative'

7.58   A 'relative' is defined for all HB purposes as:

(a) a parent, daughter, son, sister or brother;

(b) a parent-in-law, daughter-in-law, son-in-law, step-daughter or step-son, including equivalent relations arising through civil partnership;

(c) a partner of any of the above (by marriage or civil partnership, or by living together as a married couple or as civil partners); or

(d) a grandparent, grandchild, aunt, uncle, niece or nephew.

7.56   Social renter: HB 12BA(3)(a),(b); NIHB 13AA(3)(a),(b)
            Private renter: HB 12D(3)(a),(b); HB66+ 12D(3)(a),(b); NIHB 13C(3)(a),(b); NIHB66+ 13C(3)(a),(b)
            Old scheme: HB Old 13(5); HB66+ Old 13(5); NIHB Old 14(5); NIHB66+ Old 14(5)
            Rent referral: HB 2(1) definition: 'reckonable rent', 13ZA(1); HB66+ 2(1), 13ZA(1); NIHB 2(1), 14A(1); NIHB66+ 2(1), 14A(1)

7.57   HB 2(1) definition: 'linked person', Old 13(10),(11); HB66+ 2(1), Old 13(10),(11); NIHB 2(1), Old 14(10),(11); NIHB66+ 2(1), Old 14(10),(11)

7.58   HB 2(1) definitions: 'close relative', 'couple', 'relative'; HB66+ 2(1); NIHB 2(1); NIHB66+ 2(1)

Examples: The protected groups

Redundancy

A claimant makes a claim for HB after he is made redundant. His actual rent is high. He moved to this address when he was in a well-paid job and could easily afford the rent and outgoings. He has not been on HB in the last 52 weeks.

Because of the protection for people who could formerly afford their accommodation, his eligible rent must not be restricted in any way for the first 13 weeks of his award of HB. During those weeks, his eligible rent is his actual rent minus amounts for any ineligible services.

Bereavement before claiming HB

A claimant makes a claim for HB after the death of her husband. She has not moved since her husband's death. Her actual rent is high.

Because of the protection for people who have had a bereavement, her eligible rent must not be restricted in any way until the first anniversary of her husband's death. Until then, her eligible rent is her actual rent minus amounts for any ineligible services.

Bereavement while on HB

A claimant is on HB and his mother lives with him as his non-dependant. His eligible rent takes account of the fact that he qualifies for two bedrooms (chapter 11) and is £125 per week. Following the death of his mother he only qualifies for one bedroom.

Because he has been bereaved while on HB he is a protected renter and his eligible rent must not be reduced below £125 per week until the first anniversary of his mother's death.

Chapter 8 **Social renters**

- Who is a social renter: see paras 8.2-3.
- Eligible rent for social renters: see paras 8.4-8.
- How your eligible rent is reduced if your home is too large: see paras 8.9-16.
- Service charges general rules: see paras 8.17-41.
- Eligible services: see paras 8.42-56.
- Ineligible services: see paras 8.57-74.
- Other items included in setting rents: see paras 8.75-82.

8.1 This chapter explains how your eligible rent is worked out if you rent your home from a social landlord (you are a 'social renter': para 8.2). It includes the general rules about service charges that also apply if you eligible rent is worked out using the rules in chapter 10.

Who is a social renter

8.2 You are a 'social renter' (or, for (e), you are treated as if you are) if:

(a) you live in Great Britain and your landlord is the council you claim HB from (para 7.11);

(b) your landlord is the Northern Ireland Housing Executive (para 7.11);

(c) you are a former council/NIHE ('stock transfer') tenant (para 7.12);

(d) in most cases, your landlord is a registered housing association (para 8.3); or

(e) you have an old style registered rent or similar tenancy (paras 7.39-43).

Where any of (a)-(e) apply 'landlord' (para 7.9) and 'tenant' includes a shared ownership/equity sharing agreement. For further details and exceptions see chapter 7.

Tenants of registered housing associations and other 'social' landlords

8.3 If your landlord is a registered housing association (paras 7.13-17) your eligible rent is worked out as a social renter unless:

(a) you live in exempt accommodation (paras 10.4-8); or

(b) you live in England and your home isn't social housing (para 7.17); or

(c) the council/NIHE considers your rent to be unreasonable (para 7.16).

If you rent your home from any other kind of 'social' landlord you are treated as a private renter unless any of the exceptions in table 9.1 apply.

8.2   AA134(1A), NIAA 126(1)(b); HB 12B(1), A13(1),(2); 13C(5)(a)-(c), 14(2)(b), sch 2; HB66+ 12B(1), 13C(5)(a)-(c), 14(2)(b), sch 2;
      NIHB 13A(1), A14(1),(2), 14C(5)(a)-(c), 15(3)(b), sch 3; NIHB66+ 13A(1), 14C(5)(a)-(c), 15(3)(b), sch 3

8.3   HB 12B(1), A13(1),(2); 13C(5)(1),(2),(a),(b), 14(2)(b), sch 2 para 3(1),(1A),(2)(b);
      HB66+ 12B(1), 13C(5)(1),(2),(a),(b), 14(2)(b), sch 2 para 3(1),(1A),(2);
      NIHB 13A(1), A14(1),(2), 14C(5)(1),(2),(a),(b), 15(3)(b), sch 3 para 3(b); NIHB66+ 13A(1), 14C(5)(1),(2),(a),(b), 15(3)(b), sch 3 para 3

Eligible rent

8.4   This section explains how your eligible rent is worked out if you are a social renter. Paras 8.5-7 are also the starting point for exempt accommodation and rent referral cases (chapter 10).

The general rule

8.5   Your eligible rent is:

(a) your actual weekly rent;

(b) minus an amount for service charges which are ineligible for HB (table 8.3) and in Northern Ireland an amount for rates unless you are billed separately.

Your actual weekly rent means the full weekly amount you are liable to pay on your home (para 7.3) before any rent discount for prompt payment, etc (paras 8.77-78). For items in your rent that are not services (e.g. overheads, management costs, garages, land, business premises and space for a carer) see paras 8.75-82.

Joint tenants

8.6   If you have at least one joint tenant who is not a member of your family (paras 4.42-46):

(a) first, the eligible rent for your dwelling is worked out as described in para 8.5;

(b) then it is apportioned (para 8.7) between you and the other joint tenant(s).

8.7   'Apportioning' means deciding how much is fairly attributable to each of you. To do this the authority takes account of:

(a) the number of joint tenants, including any who are ineligible for HB such as students (Nagshabandi v Camden LBC);

(b) the proportion of rent paid by each of you;

(c) the presence or absence of each of you (CH/3376/2002);

(d) the size and number of rooms each of you occupies;

(e) whether there is any written or other agreement between you; and

(f) any other relevant circumstances.

Eligible rent reductions

8.8   Your eligible rent may be reduced:

(a) under the social renter size criteria if your home is too large (paras 8.9-16);

(b) under the rent referral rules if you rent from a registered housing association, and

- the authority considers your rent to be unreasonably high (para 7.16); or

- you or your partner are state pension credit age and the authority considers your home to be too large (para 7.16);

(c) in any other case if your rent is unreasonable under the default power (para 7.46).

8.5   HB 12B(2), B13(2)(a); HB66+ 12B(2); NIHB 13A(2), B14(2)(a); NIHB66+ 13A(2)

8.6   HB 12B(4); HB66+ 12B(4); NIHB 13A(4); NIHB66+ 13A(4)

8.7   Nagshabandi v Camden LBC HBRB [2002] EWCA Civ 1038 www.bailii.org/ew/cases/EWCA/Civ/2002/1038.html

The social renter size criteria

8.9   This section explains how your eligible rent can be reduced if you have more bedrooms in your home than you qualify for. This is often called 'under-occupying' your home. In the law the reduced figure is known as the 'maximum rent social sector'.

8.10   The rules about this have applied in Great Britain since 1st April 2013 and in Northern Ireland from 20th February 2017. In Scotland and Northern Ireland if a reduction applies you are normally fully compensated through other payments (paras 23.9 and 23.29).

When a reduction applies

8.11   Your eligible rent is reduced if:

(a)   you are a social renter (para 8.2);

(b)   you – and also your partner(s) if you are in a couple or polygamous marriage – are under pension age (para 2.4);

(c)   you have more bedrooms than you qualify for (para 8.12); and

(d)   none of the exceptions in table 8.1 apply to you.

But if a member of your household has died or you could afford the rent before you claimed HB the reduction can be delayed for up to 13 weeks/one year (paras 7.48-58).

The amount of the reduction

8.12   The reduction is calculated as follows:

(a)   if your home has one bedroom more than you qualify for (table 11.1), your eligible rent is reduced by 14%;

(b)   if it has two or more bedrooms more than you qualify for, your eligible rent is reduced by 25%.

No reduction applies if your home has the same number of bedrooms as you qualify for, or fewer bedrooms.

The reduction for joint tenants

8.13   If you have at least one joint tenant who is not a member of your family (paras 4.42-46):

(a)   first, the reduction (of 14% or 25%) is made from the eligible rent for your dwelling;

(b)   then the resulting figure is apportioned (para 8.7) between you and the other joint tenant(s).

Eligible rent after a reduction

8.14   The reduced eligible rent is used in calculating your HB. Deductions for non-dependants (para 6.2) and/or because you have excess income (para 6.6) are made from the reduced eligible rent.

8.10   NISR 2016/326 reg 1(3); NISR 2016/452 reg 7

8.11   HB A13(1),(2)(d); NIHB A14(1),(2)(d)

8.12   HB B13(2)(b),(3); NIHB B14(2)(b),(3)

8.13   HB B13(2)(c); NIHB B14(2)(c)

Table 8.1 **Exceptions to the social renter size criteria**

The social renter size criteria don't apply to you if:

(a) you or your partner have reached pension age (para 2.4) (even if you don't have a pension age claim);

(b) you have a shared ownership tenancy (para 7.24); or

(c) your landlord is a registered housing association and the rent referral rules apply to you because the authority considers your rent is unreasonably high (table 10.3);

(d) you rent from a registered housing association and your home is exempt accommodation (paras 10.5-7);

(e) you live in temporary accommodation provided by the authority because you were homeless or to prevent you from becoming so (paras 7.30-32).

Note:

In Scotland and Northern Ireland if the social renter size criteria apply and your HB is reduced you are likely to be fully compensated through other payments (paras 23.9 and 23.29).

The number of bedrooms you qualify for

8.15   You qualify for the appropriate number of bedrooms for the occupiers of your home: see table 11.1.

Which occupiers are taken into account

8.16   The social sector size criteria take account of the occupiers of your dwelling. This means:

(a) you (the claimant) and members of your family (partner, children and young persons: para 4.2);

(b) non-dependants (para 4.26);

(c) lodgers (para 4.36);

(d) joint tenants (para 4.42); and

(e) any other person who occupies your dwelling as their home.

For further details, see paras 11.10-11.

T8.1   HB A13(2)(b)-(e),(3); CPR sch 3 para 4(1)(b); NIHB A14(2)(b)-(e),(3); NICPR sch 3 para 4(1)(b)

8.15   HB B13(5)-(7); NIHB B14(5)-(7)

Service charges: general rules

8.17   The remainder of this chapter (paras 8.18-82) deals with service charges (and related charges) and whether they are eligible for HB or not. It applies if:

(a) you are a social renter (para 8.2) (unless, in England, your home is not social housing: para 7.17); or

(b) your rent is assessed under the old scheme or rent referral rules described in chapter 10 (for example, if you live in 'exempt accommodation', or if you are a private tenant who has been on HB since before April 2008).

It does not apply if your eligible rent is assessed as a private renter under the LHA rules in chapter 9.

The importance of service charges

8.18   If you are a tenant you may pay for services either as part of your rent (whether or not it is mentioned in the letting agreement) or separately. As illustrated in the examples, there are two main methods of showing service charges in your letting agreement:

(a) your rent may be shown as so much per week (or month, etc) including certain services; or

(b) it may be shown as so much per week (or month, etc) with an amount for service charges being due on top of your rent.

8.19   If you are a tenant of a social landlord or your eligible rent is assessed under the old scheme or rent referral rules described in chapter 10, the council must consider whether the service charges you pay are eligible for HB (para 8.33).

(a) If a charge is 'eligible for HB', this means that it can be included in your eligible rent. It does not need to be valued; and no deduction is made for it at any stage in deciding the amount of your eligible rent unless the charge for it is excessive (para 8.39).

(b) If a charge is 'ineligible for HB', this means that it cannot be included in your eligible rent. With certain exceptions, it needs to be valued and deducted at some point in deciding your eligible rent (para 8.37).

8.20   The above points (para 8.19) can be particularly significant if you are not a social renter (para 8.2) but you live in supported housing that qualifies as 'exempt accommodation' (para 10.5). The council has a strong financial incentive to identify any ineligible services (such as support) to ensure your eligible rent does not exceed the rent officer's valuation (para 21.29). It is therefore essential for your landlord to provide a detailed breakdown of the charge for each service they provide.

8.16   HB B13(5); NIHB B14(5)

8.19   HB 83(5),(12),(12A); HB66+ 64(1),(1A),(5); NIHB 81(5),(12),(12A); NIHB66+ 62(1),(1A),(5)

Examples: Service charges

1. A council tenant's weekly rent is expressed as being £100 per week including £20 per week for fuel for their own flat and £10 per week for heating, lighting, cleaning and maintaining communal areas. In this case the eligible rent is £80 per week. The ineligible charge for fuel for the tenant's own flat is deducted.

2. A housing association tenant's weekly rent is expressed as being £70 per week plus £20 per week for fuel for the claimant's own room and £10 per week for heating, lighting, cleaning and maintaining communal areas. In this case the eligible rent is £80 per week. The eligible charge for the communal areas is added.

Notes:

- The facts in the two examples are the same but are expressed differently.

- Information about the service charges illustrated is given later in this chapter.

- The terms 'net rent' and 'gross rent' are sometimes used to distinguish between different methods of expressing a rent figure. But they are used in different ways nationally and are best avoided for HB purposes.

Who deals with your service charges for HB

8.21   If you live in Northern Ireland the NIHE deals with all matters for your HB claim to do with service charges. If you live in England, Scotland or Wales the council always identifies whether a charge is eligible/ineligible but either the authority or the rent officer is responsible for determining its value as follows:

(a) if your landlord is the authority, the authority values it;

(b) if your landlord is a registered housing association, you live in 'social housing' (paras 7.17) and the authority has not referred your rent to the rent officer (table 8.2, step 4), the council values it;

(c) if you live in 'exempt accommodation' (paras 10.5-8) or have a registered rent or other similar tenancy (paras 7.39-43), the council values it;

(d) in any other case, if your rent has been referred to the rent officer (for example, if your rent is unreasonably high, you have a pre-April 2008 award, or you live in a hostel or mobile home and so on: table 9.1), either the council or the rent officer values it depending on type of service (para 8.22). For ineligible services valued by the council see paras 8.37-38 for how this is done. For ineligible services valued by the rent officer see paras 8.22-23 and 10.51.

See table 8.2 for further details about how service charges are identified and assessed.

8.21   HB 12B(2),(5), B13(2)(a); HB66+ 12B(2),(5); CPR sch 3 para 5(1); NIHB 13A(2),(6), 14(2),(5),(7),(9), 15(1), sch 2 paras 6(2A),(3),7; NIHB66+ 13A(2),(6), 14(2),(5),(7), 15(1), sch 2 paras 6(2A),(3),7; NICPR sch 3 para 5(1)

Table 8.2 **How to assess service charges**

Step 1: Does the charge relate to a service performed or facility provided? (para 8.30)

- If yes, it is a service charge (and cannot be rent), go to step 2.
- If no, it is not a service charge but it may (or may not) be 'rent' (para 8.32).

Step 2: Does your right to occupy your home depend on payment? (para 8.33)

- If yes, go to step 3.
- If no, it is not eligible for HB.

Step 3: Does the charge relate to an ineligible service? (table 8.3 and paras 8.57-74)

- If no, go to step 4.
- If yes, it is not eligible for HB.

Step 4: Is your eligible rent worked out as a social renter? (paras 8.2-3)

- If yes, the council decides all issues including whether the service charge is excessive.
- If no, got to step 5.

Step 5: Do you live in 'exempt accommodation'? (paras 10.5-8)

- If yes, the council decides all issues including whether any eligible service charge is excessive. The authority must refer your rent and service charges to the rent officer but the council is not required to use the rent officer's valuation (but they should consider it with any other evidence) (paras 10.16 and 10.37).
- If no, your rent and service charges are assessed under rent referral rules. The council decides whether each service is eligible and either the council or the rent officer values it (para 8.22 and table 8.3). The council must use the rent officer's valuation.

Notes:

See para 8.21 for who is responsible for valuing a service charge once the council has identified it. For how a charge is valued, see paras 8.37-38.

8.22   When a claim is referred to the rent officer (para 8.21(d)) a service charge valuation is carried out as follows:

(a) the council   values any ineligible charges that are not valued by the rent officer (i.e. items with 'No' in both columns in table 8.3) and deducts them from the actual rent; except any charge for meals (see (e)) the result is the 'referred rent' (para 10.40) (and the rent officer is notified of these deductions when the referral is made);

T8.2   HB 12(1)(e),(8), 12B(2), 12C, B13(2), 13(2),(5),(7), sch 1; CPR sch 3 para 5(1); HB66+ 12(1)(e),(8), 12B(2), 12C, 13(2),(5), sch 1; NIHB 13(1)(e),(8), 13A(2), 13B, 14(2),(5),(7), sch 1; NIHB66+ 13(1)(e),(8), 13A(2), 13B, 14(2),(5), sch 1

8.22   HB 12C(2), 13(2)-(5),(7), 114A(3)(d)-(f),(4)(b),(6),(8)(a); HB66+ 12C(2), 13(2)-(5), 95A(3)(d)-(f),(4)(b),(6),(8)(a); ROO sch 1 paras 6(2A),(3), 7

(b) the rent officer takes the referred rent (which includes eligible services), and if he or she has made a significantly high, size-related or exceptionally high rent determination (paras 10.41-44) caps it at whichever of those determinations is the lowest (and in this case this is the 'claim-related rent');

(c) if none of the determinations in (b) apply, the rent officer values any ineligible service charges that he/she is responsible for (table 8.3) and deducts them from the referred rent (and in this case this is the 'claim-related rent'). See paras 10.51 for how the rent officer values ineligible services;

(d) if the rent officer has made a local reference rent or single room rent determination then that figure is passed back to the council and used instead of the claim-related rent (being the lower of the two); and

(e) where the rent includes meals the council deducts the appropriate amount (table 8.5) from the rent officer's lowest figure, but if it is a single room rent determination then that figure is the eligible rent unless the claim-related rent less the amount for meals results in a lower figure.

Ineligible charges in (a) above includes deductions from excessive eligible charges (para 8.39).

8.23   When the rent officer values a service (para 8.22(c)) he or she considers whether the service provided is value for money. The rent officer handbook [www] provides guidance about how this is done:

(a) evidence of service costs provided in the referral are used as a starting point but the value will only equate to the cost if the landlord is providing the service efficiently;

(b) if the landlord provides 'solid evidence' of service costs the rent officer does not normally deduct more; unless

(c) the service cost is very high or the service is not being provided in a cost efficient way.

Distinguishing 'rent' from service charges

8.24   Decision makers (the council/tribunals) pay more attention nowadays to the distinction between services (as described above) and other costs included when your landlord sets the rent. For example, your landlord's overheads such as vacant lettings cannot be a service because they do not provide any benefit to the tenant: CH/3528/2006 and para 8.30. For the same reason, rent collection costs including bad debt provision, and passing on costs like council tax, are usually regarded as rent rather than a service.

8.25   If you incur charges for: renting a garage or land, an additional room for a live-in carer, or additional rent to cover your arrears (all of which are 'rent' within its ordinary meaning) then special rules apply: see paragraphs 8.79-82 for details.

8.26   It is not always easy to distinguish between 'rent' and service charges and it is fairly common for landlords to classify charges incorrectly. Neither your landlord's classification nor the tenancy agreement determines whether an item is (or is not) rent or a service charge: it is the law which does so: [2009] UKUT 28 (AAC) (para 8.27). But the mere fact that your landlord classifies something incorrectly should not be held against them: CH/3528/2006.

8.23   https://www.gov.uk/guidance/rent-officer-handbook-housing-benefit-referral

8.24   HB 12(1)(e),(8); HB66+ 12(1)(e),(8); CPR sch 3 para 5(1); NIHB 13(1)(e),(8); NIHB66+ 13(1)(e),(8); NICPR sch 3 para 5(1)

8.27   If a charge relates to an item that falls within the definition of services (para 8.30) then it is a service charge (and it cannot be rent): CH/3528/2006. And if it is, the council must next decide if it is eligible: CH/3528/2006. So, for example, if your landlord provides you with support or counselling to help you sustain your tenancy (or to every tenant) as part of its housing management, it is a service and it is ineligible (table 8.3 and para 8.71). The fact that your landlord has classified it as 'housing management' or 'intensive housing management' does not mean that it is somehow eligible as 'rent' (para 8.26).

8.28   But just because an item is not a service it does not necessarily follow that the charge made for it must be rent (and therefore eligible for HB). It must still relate to a matter that is properly considered in setting the rent: CH/3528/2006.

8.29   A charge for a stair lift once installed, or presumably any other item that is physically attached to your property, is rent because it is an 'enhancement' of the premises: [2011] UKUT 513 (AAC).

Definition of 'services'

8.30   'Services' are defined as 'services performed or facilities… provided for, or rights made available to, the occupier…' and 'service charge' as any periodical charge for any such service. A helpful test is to ask: does the tenant derive any benefit or value from the function, or does the benefit or value wholly lie with the landlord?

8.31   A charge for the use of furniture and/or 'household equipment' (e.g. white goods, TV, etc) is treated as a service charge and is eligible for HB; unless those goods become part of your personal property (para 8.61), e.g. under a hire purchase agreement.

8.32   Any item that is not a service may (or may not) be part of the rent – provided it relates to a matter that is properly considered in setting the rent. In most cases provision for vacant tenancies (voids), bad debts and long-term maintenance are allowed as rent provided that the total charge (rent and eligible services) is not excessive: [2010] UKUT 222 (AAC).

Which service charges are eligible

8.33   A service charge is only eligible for HB if:

(a) you have to pay it as a condition for the right to occupy your home (whether the condition is part of the original tenancy agreement or a separate contract); and

(b) it is not listed in the regulations as ineligible (table 8.3, paras 8.57-74); and

(c) it is not excessive in relation to the service provided (para 8.39).

Details of which kinds of service charge are eligible for HB (subject to the above points) follow, and are summarised in table 8.3. For helpful advice see GM A4.700-950.

8.34   The first condition (para 8.33(a)) need not have applied from the start of your tenancy. It is eligible for HB (subject to the other conditions) from whenever you agreed to pay it, if the alternative would have been to lose your home.

8.30   HB 12(8); HB66+ 12(8); CPR sch 3 para 5(1); NIHB 13(8); NIHB66+ 13(8); NICPR sch 3 para 5(1)

8.31   HB 12(8), sch 1 para 1(b); HB66+ 12(8), sch 1 para 1(b); NIHB 13(8), sch 1 para 1(b), NIHB66+ 13(8), sch 1 para 1(b)

8.33   HB 12(1)(e),(8), sch 1 paras 1-5; HB66+ 12(1)(e),(8), sch 1 paras 1-5; CPR sch 3 para 5(1);
          NIHB 13(1)(e),(8), sch 1 paras 1-5; NIHB66+ 13(1)(e),(8), sch 1 paras 1-5; NICPR sch 3 para 5(1)

Table 8.3 **Service charges summary**

As described throughout this chapter, further details apply in many of the following cases.

Type of service charge	Eligible for HB	Valued by rent officer
Provision of a heating system	YES	NO
Fuel for communal areas	YES	NO
Other fuel	NO	YES
Meals	NO	NO
Water charges (personal use)	NO	YES*
Water charges communal areas	YES	NO
Laundry	NO	YES*
Leisure items	NO	YES*
Other day-to-day living expenses not included above	NO	YES*
Furniture/household equipment if the tenant becomes the owner (for example, under hire purchase)	NO	YES*
Any other furniture and household equipment (i.e. the landlord retains ownership)	YES	NO
Communal window cleaning	YES	NO
Other exterior window cleaning which the occupier(s) cannot do	YES	NO
Other window cleaning	NO	NO
Communal cleaning	YES	NO
Other cleaning	NO	NO
Emergency alarm systems	NO	NO
Counselling and support	NO	NO
Medical/nursing/personal care	NO	NO
Most communal services relating to the provision of 'adequate accommodation'	YES	NO
Any other service that is not related to the provision of adequate accommodation	NO	YES*

* The rent officer only makes a valuation when the council refers a claim to him/her (paras 8.22, 10.32 and table 10.3); in any other case the council values the charge.

T8.3   HB 114A(3)(d)-(f), sch 1 paras 1,2(1),5; HB66+ 95A(3)(d)-(f), sch 1 paras 1,2(1),5;
        NIHB 15(1), sch 1 paras 1,2(1),5; NIHB66+ 15(1), sch 1 paras 1,2(1),5

8.35 Some not-for-profit landlords sometimes provide services 'for free' but this is often because the charge is wholly funded from elsewhere. DWP guidance concerning hostel residents (though the point is relevant to all claims) states that 'HB should be based only on items included in the resident's charge. [The council] must confirm which services are included in the hostel charge' (GM A4.1950).

Management and administration costs of eligible services

8.36 If a service is eligible (table 8.3), the costs of any management and administrative support required (e.g. staff time) to provide it are also eligible, so long as the costs are reasonable and not excessive (para 8.40): [2010] UKUT 222 (AAC).

Valuing ineligible service charges

8.37 When the council is responsible for valuing ineligible charges this is done as follows:

(a) if the amount can be identified from your letting agreement or in some other way (e.g. a detailed breakdown provided by your landlord), the authority uses that value;

(b) but if the amount cannot be identified or is unrealistically low for the service provided, the council must decide what amount is fairly attributable to the value;

(c) however, different rules apply if the charge is for water, fuel or meals (paras 8.62-70).

In practice separating out charges is not always straightforward, particularly for not-for-profit landlords whose functions are often provided by staff whose duties include a mix of activities that are legitimately part of the rent (paras 8.24-32) and both eligible and ineligible services.

Valuing eligible service charges

8.38 When the council is responsible for valuing eligible service charges (para 8.21), it does so as follows:

(a) if the amount can be identified from the letting agreement or in some other way, it uses the amount so identified as the value;

(b) but if this identified amount is excessive, or if the amount cannot be identified, the council decides what amount is fairly attributable to the value.

Excessive eligible service charges

8.39 The authority must consider the cost of comparable services to decide whether the charge is excessive, and if it is the council must decide how much would be reasonable and disallow the excess. But even if a service charge is reasonable the council may still restrict the global rent if the total eligible charge (i.e. rent plus service charges) is unreasonable (paras 7.46, 10.15, 10.39).

8.37   HB 12B(2), B13(2)(a); HB66+ 12B(2); CPR sch 3 para 5(1); NIHB 13A(2); NIHB66+ 13A(2); NICPR sch 3 para 5(1)

8.38   HB 12B(2), B13(2)(a), sch 1 paras 3,4; HB66+ 12B(2), sch 1 paras 3,4; CPR sch 3 para 5(1);
          NIHB 13A(2), sch 1 paras 3,4; NIHB66+ 13A(2), sch 1 paras 3,4

8.39   HB sch 1 para 4; HB66+ sch 1 para 4; NIHB sch 1 para 4; NIHB66+ sch 1 para 4

8.40   The requirement to consider comparable costs does not prevent the authority from concluding that the charge is excessive for other reasons, and in particular it can take account of what is required to provide the service satisfactorily. For example, if the authority considered a concierge service could be adequately provided by using two workers but your landlord employed four, it could still restrict the charge even if your landlord's wage rates were shown to be comparable with others. In such cases the council is entitled to make a restriction even if it does not have sufficient evidence to put a precise figure on what a proper charge would be: [2010] UKUT 222 (AAC).

8.41   If you are already on HB and you are seeking to get your eligible rent increased (e.g. to reflect a service charge increase or to include a new service), the burden of proof (para 20.21) is on you to show that the increased charge is eligible by providing the necessary evidence. You cannot rely on the fact that the authority has no evidence with which to make a comparison to prevent it from restricting the charge: [2010] UKUT 222 (AAC).

Eligible services

8.42   This section relates to charges that are eligible for HB. Eligible charges often relate to communal areas. As a general rule, a service charge that would be ineligible if provided for your own exclusive use is eligible if it relates to communal areas. (For example, cleaning your own room is ineligible, but cleaning the communal areas is eligible.) In relation to all eligible services in this section see also paragraph 8.36 on the management and administrative costs of providing them.

'Communal areas'

8.43   Certain service charges relating to the cleaning, maintenance and fuel supplied to 'communal areas' are eligible for HB. For these limited purposes (and to determine who is a non-dependant: para 4.30) 'communal areas' means:

(a)   areas of common access in any type of accommodation (halls, corridors and stairways; also probably reception areas that do not count as a 'room'); and

(b)   in 'sheltered accommodation' only (para 8.44), common rooms (such as a lounge, dining room, or communal laundry facilities).

In all other situations communal areas are not defined and have their ordinary English meaning.

'Sheltered accommodation'

8.44   'Sheltered accommodation' is not defined in the regulations. The term is wide enough to include 'extra care', 'very sheltered' housing and 'supported housing' or indeed any accommodation that is 'more than ordinary accommodation [and is] for people who are in some way (and probably for some defined reason) more vulnerable than most people are, or are vulnerable in a particular kind of way'. If resident staff are at hand, there need not be a warden/manager or an alarm system: [2011] AACR 38, approving [2011] UKUT 136 (AAC) and [2016] AACR 19.

8.43   HB sch 1 para 8; HB66+ sch 1 para 8; NIHB sch 1 para 8; NIHB66+ sch 1 para 8;

Cleaning communal areas and other window cleaning

8.45   Except where the cost is separately met by the local authority under its powers to pay for housing-related support (para 8.71) the following charges are eligible for HB:

(a)   cleaning rooms and windows in 'communal areas' (para 8.43); and

(b)   cleaning the outside of windows which no-one in your household can do (for example, your windows if you live on one of the upper floors in a block of flats).

Any other cleaning charges (such as cleaning your own room) are not eligible (paras 8.60 and 8.71).

Fuel and water in communal areas

8.46   A charge for fuel used in communal areas (para 8.43) is eligible for HB, but only if it is separate from the fuel charge for your own accommodation.

8.47   Charges for water used by your landlord in communal areas (para 8.43), provided they can be separately identified, are eligible for HB because they relate to the provision of adequate accommodation (para 8.51): [2016] AACR 19. However, communal water charges that relate to an ineligible use such as community entertainment or personal laundry (para 8.59) must be deducted. So for example, water used by the landlord in sheltered housing for cleaning communal laundry facilities is eligible but any water used that relates to personal laundry would not: [2016] AACR 19.

Provision and maintenance of a heating system

8.48   A charge for providing a heating system (both in the common parts and in your own home) is eligible for HB, but only if it is separate from any charge for fuel.

Communal facilities

8.49   Charges for the following communal services are eligible for HB:

(a)   children's play areas;

(b)   equipment for receiving radio or 'Freeview' TV channels (e.g. an aerial for a block of flats) and their relay into your home through the communal areas, including any charges for the installation, upgrade and maintenance of that equipment (less any element included for subscription channels: paragraph 8.59). A similar argument seems likely to apply to charges for access to the internet (and see para 8.31);

(c)   communal laundry facilities (but not personal laundry service: paragraph 8.59);

(d)   any charge not otherwise specified as being eligible or ineligible by the HB rules, in respect of any part of the premises beyond those exclusive to you but which you have the right to use, for services related to the adequacy of those premises: CIS/1460/1995 and [2016] AACR 19. The council should not decide the question of 'adequacy' in terms of whether you have a personal need for the facilities but rather by having regard to the characteristics of residents in general for type of accommodation you occupy (for example, for residents with disabilities or vulnerable young people: [2016] AACR 19.

8.45   HB sch 1 para 1(a)(iv); HB66+ sch 1 para 1(a)(iv); NIHB sch 1 para 1(a)(iv), NIHB66+ sch 1 para 1(a)(iv)

8.46   HB sch 1 para 5; HB66+ sch 1 para 5; NIHB sch 1 para 5; NIHB66+ sch 1 para 5

8.48   HB sch 1 para 8; HB66+ sch 1 para 8; NIHB sch 1 para 8; NIHB66+ sch 1 para 8

8.50   Any other charge for leisure facilities (including sports facilities or television rental, licence and subscription fees) that is not covered above (para 8.49) is not eligible for HB.

All other eligible services (security, grounds maintenance, etc)

8.51   Except for any ineligible item (paras 8.59 and 8.71) any other charge for a service that is 'related to the provision of adequate accommodation' is eligible for HB. Items that fall under this heading are not restricted to services in respect of the common areas (although more often than not they will be).

8.52   The DWP advises (GM A4.730, A4 Annex D; DMG paras 78473-74) that this includes charges for:

(a)   portering and refuse removal;

(b)   the security of the dwelling (para 8.55);

(c)   lifts (including their repair), communal telephones and entry phones;

(d)   the upkeep and repair of communal pathways and gardens;

(e)   a car park attendant and the costs of a car park barrier; and

(f)   the time a scheme manager or similar person spends on eligible services (para 8.42).

8.53   What is meant by the 'provision of adequate accommodation' is fairly narrow and is restricted to only those services that are necessary for the enjoyment of your home (for example, a lift in a block of flats and costs associated with maintaining it): R v Swansea HBRB ex p. Littler/R v St Edmundsbury HBRB ex p Sandys.

8.54   In deciding what is necessary for the enjoyment of the dwelling, no account can be taken of your personal needs. It is only the adequacy of the accommodation that counts, not your ability to take advantage of it or any services you may need in order to do so (Littler/ Sandys and GM A4 Annex).

8.55   A charge for a concierge service (including any management and administrative support costs: para 8.36) is eligible so far as it relates to the safety and security of the dwelling: [2010] UKUT 222 (AAC). Note that while a charge for services that relate to the security of your home itself (such as a door entry system) is eligible, a service connected with you or your family's personal safety (such as a call out service for harassment) is not (para 8.74).

8.56   Charges for maintenance of communal areas are also eligible. This includes a charge for maintaining a communal garden provided that your landlord has an obligation to provide it and you merely have a right of access to it (rather than exclusive use): [2011] UKUT 22 (AAC). However, a charge for maintaining a garden (where you have exclusive use of it) is not eligible, even where your landlord has agreed to it: CH/755/2008 and [2011] UKUT 22 (AAC).

8.49-50   HB sch 1 para 1(a)(ii),(iii); HB66+ sch 1 para 1(a)(ii),(iii); NIHB sch 1 para 1(a)(ii),(iii); NIHB66+ sch 1 para 1(a)(ii),(iii)

8.51   HB sch 1 para 1(g); HB66+ sch 1 para 1(g); NIHB sch 1 para 1(g); NIHB66+ sch 1 para 1(g)

8.53   R v Swansea HBRB ex p Littler [1998] EWCA Civ 1214, 48 BMLR 24; R v St Edmundsbury HBRB ex p Sandys [1997] EWHC Admin 711, 30 HLR 800

8.56   HB sch 1 paras 1(g), 8; HB66+ sch 1 paras 1(g), 8; NIHB sch 1 paras 1(g), 8; NIHB66+ sch 1 paras 1(g), 8

Ineligible services

Day-to-day living expenses: the general rule

8.57   Charges for items that relate to you or your other household members' general living expenses are not eligible for HB, so any charges included in your rent must be deducted from it. Examples of items that count as daily living expenses under this rule are in para 8.59 (but this list is not exhaustive).

8.58   For certain items (e.g. fuel, meals) the law sets out how the ineligible charge should be calculated and these rules are described in the following paragraphs. In any other case the authority or the rent officer (as appropriate: paragraphs 8.21-22 and table 8.3) must decide the value.

8.59   All the following count as daily living expenses, and are ineligible for HB:

(a) fuel;

(b) water (other than that used in communal areas);

(c) meals;

(d) personal laundry (but see para 8.60);

(e) medical expenses or other expenses relating to personal hygiene;

(f) cleaning of rooms and window cleaning (but see para 8.45);

(g) transport;

(h) TV (and radio) rental, licence and subscription fees and any other charges for providing equipment to the individual home (e.g. a TV, individual satellite dish, set-top box) or any other leisure items.

8.60   Charges relating to fuel and water for heating and cleaning communal areas are eligible for HB (paras 8.46-47), as are charges for cleaning the outside of windows so long as no-one in your household can do them and the cost is not met by your council paying for it. Although personal laundry is not eligible, charges for equipment (such as a washing machine) and premises to enable you to do your own laundry are.

8.61   Note also that charges for renting household furniture and fittings are eligible for HB, but charges for acquiring them are not (para 8.31 and table 8.3).

Water charges

8.62   In Great Britain, water charges that relate to personal use (as opposed to water used in communal areas: para 8.47) are not eligible for HB so any charges included in the rent must be deducted. (But no deduction is made if you are billed by the water company and pay the bill yourself, since they are not then part of the rent.) The same applies in Northern Ireland, though for the time being, until a separate system for water charging is in place, water charges remain eligible for HB in respect of rates (although the rates element is deducted from your rent).

8.57   HB sch 1 paras 1(a),(e), 2(1), 5; HB66+ sch 1 para 1(a),(e), 2(1), 5; NIHB sch 1 para 1(a),(e), 2(1), 5; NIHB66+ sch 1 para 1(a),(e), 2(1), 5

8.58   HB sch 1 paras 2,5,6; HB66+ sch 1 paras 2,5,6; NIHB sch 1 paras 2,5,6; NIHB66+ sch 1 paras 2,5,6

8.59   HB sch 1 paras 1(a),(e),2(1),5; HB66+ sch 1 para 1(a),(e),2(1),5; NIHB sch 1 para 1(a),(e),2(1),5; NIHB66+ sch 1 para 1(a),(e),2(1),5

8.62   HB 2(1) – 'water charges', 12B(2),(5), B13(2)(a), 13(2); HB66+ 2(1),12B(2),(5), 13(2); ROO sch 1 paras 6A(2)(d),(3), 7; NIHB 2(1), 13A(2),(6),14(2), sch 2 paras 6(2A)(d),(3),7; NIHB66+ 2(1), 13A(2),(6),14(2), sch 2 paras 6(2A)(d),(3),7

8.63   The council decides the value of water charges, unless your claim is referred to the rent officer (para 8.21) in which case he or she does (para 8.22). If your dwelling is self-contained and the charge you pay relates solely to your personal use (as opposed to personal use and water used in other parts of the building) then the amount is calculated as follows:

(a) if you pay a flat rate charge, that amount;

(b) if the charge varies according to the amount of water used overall, typically where there is a water meter in use in a building which contains a number of self contained units or dwellings ([2016] AACR 19), the charge the authority considers can be fairly put down to your actual personal use or an estimate of it;

(c) otherwise, a proportion of the water charge for the self-contained unit you share equal to the floor area of your accommodation divided by the floor area of the self-contained unit as a whole (but in practice authorities sometimes use simpler methods).

8.64   In situations where your charge includes an amount for both personal and communal water use then the amount that relates to solely to personal use is deducted first (using the appropriate method above). Then any part of the remaining overall eligible rent (that includes an element for communal water) that relates to ineligible water charges is deducted from that figure: [2016] AACR 19. So for example, water used for cleaning the communal laundry facilities is eligible but any amount put down to personal laundry would not be.

Fuel

8.65   Charges for fuel used in your home (such as gas, electricity, etc, and also any standing charges or other supply costs) are not eligible for HB so any charges included in your rent must be deducted. (No deduction is made if you are billed by your energy company and pay the fuel bill yourself, since the fuel charges are not then part of your rent.) For charges for fuel used in the communal areas (e.g. heating and lighting) and providing a heating system, see paragraphs 8.46-48.

8.66   When the council is responsible for valuing any fuel charges (para 8.21), the rules depend on whether the amount of the charge is known (paras 8.67-68). If your claim is referred to the rent officer he or she is responsible for valuing fuel charges (para 8.22 and table 8.3).

8.67   If the charge is identifiable, the authority uses this figure as the fuel charge. However, if this is unrealistically low or includes an element for communal areas which cannot be separated out, the charge is treated as unidentifiable.

8.68   If the charge is not identified, the authority deducts the standard amounts, as shown in table 8.4 (a lower deduction applies if you only occupy one room). If the standard amounts are applied, the council must invite you to provide evidence from which the 'actual or approximate' charge can be estimated; and, if the evidence is reasonable, the authority must use the estimated amount instead.

8.63   HB 12B(2),(5), B13(2)(a); HB66+ 12B(2),(5); CPR sch 3 para 5(1); NIHB 13A(2),(6); NIHB66+ 13A(2),(6); NICPR sch 3 para 5(1)

8.65   HB sch 1 para 5; HB66+ sch 1 para 5; NIHB sch 1 para 5; NIHB66+ sch 1 para 5

8.66-67   HB sch 1 para 6(1); HB66+ sch 1 para 6(1); NIHB sch 1 para 6(1); NIHB66+ sch 1 para 6(1)

8.68   HB sch 1 para 6(2)-(4); HB66+ sch 1 para 6(2)-(4); NIHB sch 1 para 6(2)-(4); NIHB66+ sch 1 para 6(2)-(4)

Table 8.4 **Standard weekly fuel deductions 2021-22**

If the claimant and any family occupy more than one room

Fuel for heating	£34.30
Fuel for hot water	£4.00
Fuel for lighting	£2.75
Fuel for cooking	£4.00
Fuel for any other purpose	NIL
Fuel for all the above	£45.05

If the claimant and any family occupy one room only

Fuel for heating and any hot water and/or lighting	£20.53
Fuel for cooking	£4.00
Fuel for any other purpose	NIL
Fuel for all the above	£24.53

Meals

8.69 Charges for meals are not eligible for HB so if they are included in your rent a deduction must be made. For these purposes, 'a meal' includes preparation (e.g. where it is prepared somewhere else and then delivered) and also the provision of unprepared food (e.g. cereal, bread still in its wrappings).

Table 8.5 **Standard weekly meals deductions 2021-22**

A separate amount is assessed and deducted for each person whose meals are provided.

If at least three meals are provided every day

For the claimant, and each other person from the first Monday in September following his or her 16th birthday	£29.20
For each child	£14.80

If breakfast only is provided

For the claimant, and each other person of any age	£3.60

All other cases

For the claimant, and each other person from the first Monday in September following his or her 16th birthday	£19.45
For each child	£9.75

T8.4   HB sch 1 para 6(2)-(4); HB66+ sch 1 para 6(2)-(4); NIHB sch 1 para 6(2)-(4); NIHB66+ sch 1 para 6(2)-(4)

8.69   HB sch 1 para 2; HB66+ sch 1 para 2; NIHB sch 1 para 2; NIHB66+ sch 1 para 2

T8.5   HB sch 1 para 2; HB66+ sch 1 para 2; NIHB sch 1 para 2; NIHB66+ sch 1 para 2

8.70   The council (not the rent officer) makes the deduction for meals. The standard amounts for meals shown in table 8.5 are always deducted, never the actual amount your landlord charges. A deduction is made for each person in your household whose meals are included in your rent (whether this is for you, a member of your family or some other person in your household such as a non-dependant). No deduction is made for anyone whose meals are not included (for example, a baby). When appropriate, deductions are calculated separately (for example fewer meals may be provided for someone who goes out to work than for someone who does not).

Personal care and support charges

8.71   Support charges are never eligible for HB. This includes charges for:

(a)   cleaning and window cleaning over and above that mentioned in paras 8.45 and 8.60;

(b)   emergency alarm systems (to summon assistance in the event of a fall, an accident, etc, but see para 8.29 for other disability adaptations);

(c)   counselling and support; and

(d)   medical, nursing and personal care.

If you need any of these services you may be able to have the cost met by housing related support payments from your local council (formerly known as 'Supporting People') (in Northern Ireland from the NIHE) and independent of HB. For a detailed explanation of care, support and supervision in 'exempt accommodation' see table 10.1.

8.72   In theory the law is straightforward: support is not eligible for HB. In practice, separating any support charge from other eligible charges your landlord provides is more difficult because the member of staff who provides your support will also provide services that are eligible as part of the same job. The task of separating ineligible services from eligible is further complicated by the fact that some staff duties are rent (and so are not services at all) and some duties are services but contain both eligible and ineligible elements.

8.73   Whether a particular activity is a landlord function (and so eligible as part of the rent) or whether it constitutes a service is not determined by how the tenancy agreement describes it nor by the landlord's classification – it is the law that does so (para 8.26). The mere fact that the landlord classifies a charge as 'intensive housing management' does not mean a service that the law says is support is somehow eligible for HB (para 8.27).

8.70   HB 12B(2)(b), 12C(2), B13(2)(a), 13(5),(7), sch 1 para 2; HB66+ 12B(2), 12C(2), 13(5), sch 1 para 2;
        NIHB 13A(2)(b), 12B(2) 14(5),(7), sch 1 para 2; NIHB66+ 14(5),(7), sch 1 para 2

8.71   HB sch 1 para 1(a),(c)-(f); HB66+ sch 1 para 1(a),(c)-(f); sch 1 para 1(a),(c)-(f); NIHB sch 1 para 1(a),(c)-(f)

8.72   HB sch 1 para 1(f); HB66+ sch 1 para 1(f); sch 1 para 1(f); NIHB sch 1 para 1(f)

8.74   In separating rent, eligible and ineligible service charges the two key tests are:

(a) does the activity constitute a service (paras 8.27 and 8.30): in broad terms does it provide something that has value to you (as the tenant) rather than the landlord?; and

(b) if it is a service (and not an excluded item: paras 8.59 and 8.71), is it concerned with the 'provision of adequate accommodation' (paras 8.53-54), or is it provided to help you maintain your tenancy so that you can make use of the facilities (in which case it is support)?

So as a general rule any activity undertaken by your landlord that varies in intensity according to your personal needs is more likely to be considered support (and so not eligible for HB).

Other items included in setting rents

8.75   The distinction between services and other items that should be included as 'rent' are set out in paragraphs 8.24-32. Your landlord's overheads and management costs are usually rent (para 8.24) regardless of how your landlord has classified them (para 8.26).

8.76   If an item is 'rent' then it is eligible for HB without the further conditions that apply to services (para 8.33). In particular, if your landlord is liable for council tax (e.g. if you are a lodger or live in a house made up of bedsits) then the equivalent amount of your total charge is 'rent' (GM A4.160-161). Special rules apply to rent for garages, land and business premises (paras 8.80 and 8.82).

Rent discounts

8.77   Some social landlords have a rent discount scheme which reduces your rent as a payment incentive (e.g. for prompt payment, direct debit or online payments).

8.78   If you get such a discount, and your landlord's scheme is approved by the DWP, the discount is not deducted from your eligible rent. For example, if your eligible rent is normally £83.00 but your rent is reduced by £3.00 because you pay by direct debit, your eligible rent is still £83.00.

Increases to cover arrears of rent

8.79   If your rent has been increased to recover any arrears you owe, that part of the rent is not eligible for HB. This rule applies only to cover arrears you have personally incurred for rent on your current or former home. It does not apply if your landlord has increased the rent for all of his or her tenants as a result of arrears generally.

8.77-78 HB 12(2A),(2B); HB66+ 12(2A),(2B); Old 12(6A),(6B)

8.79   HB 11(3); HB66+ 11(2); NIHB 11(3); NIHB66+ 11(2)

Garages, land, etc

8.80   The rent on a garage, mobility scooter shed, or any other buildings, gardens or land included in your letting agreement, is eligible for HB if:

(a)   the facility provided is used for occupying the dwelling as your home; and

(b)   you acquired them at the same time as the dwelling; and

(c)   you had no option but to rent them at the same time.

Alternatively these facilities are also eligible for HB if you have made or are making reasonable efforts to end your liability for them.

Space for a carer

8.81   If you are a council/NIHE tenant, housing association tenant where referral to the rent officer is not required (para 7.16), or if you live in 'exempt accommodation' (para 10.5), a room for a live-in carer is included in your eligible rent in the normal way, even if your carer occupies a room down the corridor from you: [2009] UKUT 28 (AAC) and [2009] UKUT 116 (AAC). If the room is separated from your own (as in the second case) it is still counted as part of your accommodation because 'functionally and purposively, [you need two rooms to live – one for you and one for your] carer. Common sense dictates that it should not matter whether there is a connecting door between the two.' The situation is different if the carer does not live in your home (for example where you have a rota of carers); or if you want your parents to stay and care for you, but they live elsewhere: [2009] UKUT 79 (AAC). See also paragraphs 11.17-41.

Business premises

8.82   Rent on any part of your home which is used for business, commercial or other non-residential purposes is not eligible for HB. For example, if you rent both a shop and the flat above it, only the part of the rent relating to the flat is eligible for HB. If the rent on the business premises is not separately identified from the rent on the home, the council decides how much relates to each. If you are self-employed and work from home, see paras 14.43-44.

8.80   HB 2(4)(a); HB66+ 2(4)(a); NIHB 2(4)(a); NIHB66+ 2(4)(a)

8.82   HB 12B(3),12C(2), B13(2)(a); HB66+ 12B(3),12C(2); NIHB 13A(3),13B(2), B14(2)(a); NIHB66+ 13A(3),13B(2)

Chapter 9 **Private renters (LHAs)**

- Who the local housing allowance (LHA) rules apply to: see paras 9.2-3.
- Eligible rent: the LHA rules: see paras 9.4-9.
- The LHA figures and size of accommodation you qualify for: see paras 9.10-20.
- How LHAs are set: see paras 9.21-29.
- Boarders: see paras 9.30-34.

9.1   This chapter explains how your eligible rent is worked out if you are a private tenant and the local housing allowance (LHA) rules apply to you.

Who is a private renter

9.2   You are a 'private renter' if:

(a)   you rent from a private landlord (para 7.22); or

(b)   you rent from a registered housing association and your home isn't social housing (para 7.17); or

(c)   you rent from a not-for-profit landlord (para 7.19) and your home isn't exempt accommodation (para 10.5); or

(d)   you are a lodger (i.e. you pay rent to live in someone else's home, whether they are the owner or a tenant); or

(e)   you have a shared ownership enancy and your landlord is as described in (a)-(c).

For the meaning of 'rent' see paras 7.3-4.

Who falls within the LHA rules

9.3   The LHA rules apply to you if:

(a)   you are a private renter (para 9.2); and

(b)   you don't fall within any of the exclusions in table 9.1.

If your rent includes a charge for meals see paras 9.30-34.

9.2   HB 11(1), 13C(2),(5)(a); HB66+ 11(1), 13C(2),(5)(a); NIHB 11(1), 14C(2),(5)(a); NIHB66+ 11(1), 14C(2),(5)(a)

9.3   HB 13C(2),(5)(a)-(e); HB66+ 13C(2),(5)(a)-(e); NIHB 14C(2),(5)(a)(e); NIHB66+ 14C(2),(5)(a)-(e)

Table 9.1 **Private renters: exclusions from the LHA rules**

The LHA rules don't apply to you if:

(a) you rent from a not-for-profit landlord and your home is exempt accommodation (paras 7.19 and 10.5-8);

(b) you have an old (pre-1996) HB claim (paras 7.37-38); or

(c) you have an old 'registered rent' or similar tenancy (paras 7.39-43).

(d) you are a boarder and your rent includes substantial board and attendance (para 9.32);

(e) you live in a hostel (paras 7.27-29);

(f) you live in a caravan, mobile home or houseboat (paras 7.33-34);

(g) you have been receiving HB for your current home since before 7th April 2008 (para 7.36);

Note:

If (a) or (b) apply to you your eligible rent is always worked out using the 'old scheme' rules (paras 10.2-3). If (c) applies, your eligible rent is worked out the same way as for a social renter (chapter 8). In any other case, if (d)-(g) apply to you, your eligible rent is worked out using the rent referral rules (paras 10.39).

Eligible rent: LHA rules

9.4   This section explains how your eligible rent is worked out under the LHA rules. In HB law it is called the 'maximum rent (LHA)'.

The general rule

9.5   Your eligible rent is the lower of:

(a) the LHA figure that applies to you (para 9.10); and

(b) your actual weekly rent (para 7.3).

But if there has been a recent death in your home, or you could previously afford the rent (without HB) you are a 'protected renter', and the LHA rules can be delayed for up to 13 weeks/one year (paras 7.48-56). Otherwise the council may award you a discretionary housing payment (para 23.8).

9.6   Your actual weekly rent means the full weekly rent you are liable to pay on your home (para 7.3). This includes all service charges you are liable to pay, whether or not they would be eligible for HB in other types of HB case (table 8.3).

T9.1   HB 13C(2),(5)(a)-(e); HB66+ 13C(2),(5)(a)-(e); NIHB 14C(2),(5)(a)(e); NIHB66+ 14C(2),(5)(a)-(e)

9.5   HB 12D(3),(5), 13D(4),(5); HB66+ 12D(3),(5), 13D(4),(5); NIHB 13D(3),(5), 14D(4),(5); NIHB66+ 13D(3),(5), 14D(4),(5)

9.6   HB 13D(12); HB66+ 13D(12); NIHB 14D(10); NIHB66+ 14D(10)

Examples: Eligible rent and LHAs

1. Karen is aged 66 and moves home from rent-free accommodation to a privately rented flat where she pays rent of £160 per week. In her area, the LHA for a one-bedroom dwelling is £138 per week.

- ■ Karen's eligible rent is the lower of these two figures (para 9.5), which is £138.

2. Valentina is aged 66 and retires from a well-paid job that enabled her to afford an expensive privately rented flat. She pays rent there of £233 per week which doesn't include any services. In her area, the LHA for a one-bedroom dwelling is £167 per week.

- ■ Because Valentina could previously afford her home, her eligible rent is £233 per week for the first 13 weeks (para 7.51).
- ■ After that her eligible rent is £167 per week, but the council may agree to award a discretionary housing payment (para 23.8).

3. Julian is a private tenant aged 42 and has been getting HB for several years. He currently pays his landlord £116 per week. The LHA for one-bedroom accommodation in his area £121 per week.

- ■ Julian's eligible rent is the lower of these two figures (para 9.5), which is £116 per week.

4. Julian's rent goes up to £126 per week on 1st September and the LHA is still £121 per week.

- ■ His eligible rent is the lower of these two figures, which is now £121 per week.

Joint tenants

9.7 If there is at least one joint tenant who is part of your household but not your family (paras 4.42-46):

(a) first, the eligible rent for your dwelling is the lower of:
- ■ the actual rent for your dwelling, and
- ■ the LHA figure that applies to you (this takes account of you, your family and non-dependants, and also the joint tenant(s), their family members and non-dependants: para 9.17);

(b) then the resulting figure is apportioned (para 8.7) between you and the other joint tenant(s).

9.8 But if you have at least one joint tenant who maintains a separate household from you (paras 4.42-46):

(a) first, the actual weekly rent for your dwelling is apportioned (para 8.7) between you and the other joint tenant(s);

(b) then your eligible rent is the lower of:
- ■ your share of the actual rent, and
- ■ the LHA figure that applies to you (this takes account of you, your family and non-dependants, but not the joint tenant(s), their family members or non-dependants: para 9.17).

9.7-8   HB 12B(4), 13D(12); HB66+ 12B(4), 13D(12); NIHB 13A(4), 14D(10); NIHB66+ 13A(4), 14D(10)

Changes to your eligible rent

9.9   Your eligible rent is recalculated in the way described in paras 9.5-8 whenever there is a change in your actual rent or your LHA figure (para 9.15) or in the way the figures are apportioned between joint tenants.

Example: LHA rules for joint tenants

Sara and Janet are friends in their 70s. They jointly rent a flat from a private landlord, and Sara's daughter lives with them. Their actual rent is £252 per week. Sara pays two thirds and Janet pays one third which the council accepts is reasonable. In their area, LHAs are £229 per week for three bedrooms, £190 per week for two bedrooms and £150 per week for one-bedroom dwellings.

1. If Sara and Janet have a shared household (para 9.7):

- the eligible rent for their dwelling is the LHA figure of £229 per week;
- Sara's eligible rent is £152.67 per week (two thirds);
- Janet's eligible rent is £76.33 per week (one third).

2. If Sara and Janet have separate households (para 9.8);

- Sara's share of the actual rent is £168.00, which is higher than her LHA figure of £150, so her eligible rent is £150.00 per week;
- Janet's share of the actual rent is £84.00, which is lower than her LHA figure of £126, so her eligible rent is £84.00 per week.

The LHA figures and size criteria

9.10   This section (paras 9.11-20) explains which LHA figure applies to you and what size of accommodation you qualify for.

The LHA figures

9.11   LHA figures are set by the rent officer in Great Britain and the NIHE in Northern Ireland (para 9.21). Each year the rent officer/NIHE sets weekly figures for the sizes of accommodation in table 9.2, but in 2021-22 the figures remain unchanged from the previous year. All the figures are available online [www]; they vary from area to area but can never be greater than the maximum amounts in the table.

9.12   Each year's LHA figures apply from the first Monday in April (5th April 2021) if your rent is due weekly or in multiples of a week; or 1st April in other cases (e.g. if your rent is due monthly or daily).

9.9   HB 13C(2),(3); HB66+ 13C(2),(3); NIHB 14C(2),(3); NIHB66+ 14C(2),(3)

9.11   ROO 4B(2A),(2B),(3A),(3B), sch 3B para 2(3); NIED 3(2),(2A),(3),(3A)
Great Britain: https://lha-direct.voa.gov.uk/search.aspx
Northern Ireland: www.nihe.gov.uk/Housing-Help/Local-Housing-Allowance/Current-LHA-rent-levels

9.12   HB 12D(1),(2), 13C(2)(d),(3); HB66+ 12D(1),(2), 14C(2)(d),(3); NIHB 13D(1),(2), 14C(2)(d),(3); NIHB66+ 13D(1),(2), 14C(2)(d),(3)

Table 9.2 **LHA figures: sizes of accommodation and maximum amounts**

Sizes of accommodation	National weekly maximums
(a) One-bedroom shared accommodation	£295.49
(b) One-bedroom self-contained accommodation	£295.49
(c) Two-bedroom dwellings	£365.92
(d) Three-bedroom dwellings	£441.86
(e) Four-bedroom dwellings	£593.75

In practice, actual LHAs are usually lower (para 9.24), and these figures only affect a small number of areas in inner London. For which size of accommodation applies to you, see paras 9.16-20.

Which LHA figure applies to you

9.13 The LHA figure that applies to you is the one for:

(a) the size of accommodation you qualify for (para 9.16); and

(b) the area your home is in (para 9.27).

When you claim HB

9.14 When you make a claim for HB, your LHA figure is the one that applies on your date of claim (table 16.1).

When your LHA figure changes

9.15 Changes in your LHA figure affect your HB as follows:

(a) when you qualify for a different size of accommodation (e.g. if someone moves in or out), your HB changes from the date the change in circumstances takes effect (para 17.11) or up to 12 months later in the case of a death (para 7.54);

(b) when you move home, your HB changes from the same date as the move (para 17.18);

(c) when the new figures apply in April, your HB changes from the date in para 9.12;

(d) when the rent officer/NIHE corrects a wrongly calculated LHA figure (in practice this is rare), your HB changes from:

■ the date in para 9.12, if the new figure is higher, or

■ the Monday following the date of the correction, if the new figure is lower.

T9.2   ROO sch 3B para 2(2)(b); NIED sch para 2(2)(b); SI 2020/371; NISR 2020/53

9.13   HB 13D(1)(a),(b); HB66+ 13D(1)(a),(b); NIHB 14D(1)(a),(b); NIHB66+ 14D(1)(a),(b)

9.14   HB 13D(1); HB66+ 13D(1); NIHB 143D(1); NIHB66+ 14D(1)

9.15   HB 13C(2)(d); DAR 7A, 8(15); NIHB 14C(2)(d); NIDAR 7A

The size of the accommodation you qualify for

9.16   This is worked out as follows:

(a)   you qualify for accommodation with the appropriate number of bedrooms for the occupiers of your home: see table 11.1;

(b)   but the maximum number of bedrooms is always four;

(c)   and if you are the only occupier of your home, or you and your partner are, see para 9.18.

Which occupiers are taken into account

9.17   The LHA size criteria take account of the occupiers of your home. This means:

(a)   you (the claimant) and members of your family (partner, children and young persons: para 4.2);

(b)   non-dependants (para 4.26);

(c)   lodgers (para 4.36);

(d)   joint tenants who share your household (para 9.7): [2011] UKUT 156 (AAC); and

(e)   any other person who occupies your dwelling as their home (except joint tenants who maintain a separate household: para 9.8).

For further details see chapter 11.

One bedroom LHA figures

9.18   You qualify for one bedroom if:

(a)   you are a single claimant or couple without children;

(b)   there are no other occupiers in your home (para 9.17); and

(c)   you don't qualify for an additional bedroom for any of the reasons in paras 11.18-41.

But there are two LHA figures for one-bedroom accommodation, one for self-contained and one for shared accommodation. See table 9.3 for which of these applies to you.

When your home counts as self-contained

9.19   For the rules in table 9.3, your home counts as self-contained only if you have exclusive use of:

(a)   one room plus a bathroom and toilet (in the bathroom or separately) and a kitchen or cooking facilities; or

(b)   at least two rooms (counting only bedrooms and living rooms, but regardless of whether you share other facilities).

9.16   HB 13D(2); HB66+ 13D(2); NIHB 14D(2); NIHB66+ 14D(2)

9.17   HB 13D(3),(12); HB66+ 13D(3),(12); NIHB 14D(3),(10); NIHB66+ 14D(3),(10)

9.18   HB 13D(2)(a),(b); HB66+ 13D(2)(a),(b); NIHB 14D(2)(a),(b); NIHB66+ 14D(2)(a),(b)

9.19   HB 13D(2)(b); HB66+ 13D(2)(b); NIHB 14D(2)(b); NIHB66+ 14D(2)(b)

'Exclusive use' means the right to exclude others; and this must be a legal right, not just what happens in practice: [2011] UKUT 156 (AAC) and [2014] UKUT 36 (AAC). This has applied in the case of a couple who separated but remained in their home as joint tenants with a legal agreement that they each had exclusive use of part of it ([2018] UKUT 416 (AAC)). But it seems unlikely to apply to other joint tenants who maintain separate households (para 9.8).

Table 9.3 **The LHA one-bedroom categories**

Your circumstances	Your LHA category
Single claimants aged 35 or over	
▪ If your home counts as self-contained (para 9.19)	One-bedroom self-contained accommodation
▪ Otherwise	One-bedroom shared accommodation
Single claimants aged under 35	
▪ If you are in any of excepted groups (a) to (d) in para 9.20	One-bedroom self-contained accommodation
▪ Otherwise	One-bedroom shared accommodation
Couples of any age	
▪ If your home counts as self-contained (para 9.19)	One-bedroom self-contained accommodation
▪ If you or your partner are in excepted groups (a) or (b) in para 9.20	One-bedroom self-contained accommodation
▪ Otherwise	One-bedroom shared accommodation

Notes:

- ▪ This table applies when you qualify for only one bedroom (para 9.18).
- ▪ Single claimants under 35 who qualify for one-bedroom shared accommodation are called 'young individuals' in HB law.
- ▪ The shared accommodation rule doesn't amount to unlawful discrimination in the case of disabled people ([2020] UKUT 285 (AAC)).

T9.3   HB 13D(2)(a),(b); HB66+ 13D(2)(a),(b); NIHB 14D(2)(a),(b); NIHB66+ 14D(2)(a),(b)

Excepted groups for one-bedroom accommodation

9.20   You are in an excepted group for table 9.3 (and also for para 10.47) if:

(a) you or your partner meet the conditions for a severe disability premium (para 12.25);

(b) you or your partner are aged under 22, and were previously:

   ■   in social services care under a court order at any time after the age of 16, or

   ■   provided with accommodation by social services;

(c) you are aged 25 or over but under 35, and are an ex-offender managed under a level 2 or 3 multi-agency public protection agreement (MAPPA) (HB Circular A12/2011); or

(d) you are aged 25 or over but under 35, and:

   ■   you have occupied (or at any time formerly occupied) one or more hostels for homeless people for one or more periods totalling at least three months, and

   ■   while you were there, you were offered and you accepted support with rehabilitation or resettlement within the community.

A 'hostel for homeless people' means a hostel (paras 7.28-29) whose main purpose is to provide accommodation together with care, support or supervision, in order to assist homeless people to be rehabilitated or resettled in the community.

How LHAs are set

9.21   This section explains how the rent officer (in Great Britain) or the NIHE (in Northern Ireland) sets the LHA figures and areas.

9.22   Rent officers are independent of the council. They are government employees in the Valuation Office Agency (in England), the Rent Officers Wales or the Rent Service Scotland.

Setting the LHA figures

9.23   LHA figures apply from the beginning of April (para 9.12), and are set at the end of January using the data for the year ending on the preceding 30th September. But in 2021-22 the figures remain unchanged from the previous year after having been re-set at the 30th percentile (para 9.25) on 31st March 2020 due to the coronavirus.

9.24   LHA figures equal the rent at the 30th percentile (para 9.25). They are limited to the weekly maximum in table 9.2 if that is lower, but this affects only a small number of areas (table 9.2).

9.25   The 'rent at the 30th percentile' means the highest rent within the bottom 30% of rents in the rent officer's/NIHE's data. In broad terms this means that people on HB can afford rents in the lowest third of the rental market.

9.20   HB 2(1),(1A),(1B) definition: 'young individual', 13D(2)(a); NIHB 2(1),(1A),(1B), 14D(2)(a)

9.23-24   ROO 4B(2), sch 3B para 2(2); NIED 2(2); SI 2020/1519; NISR 2021/14

9.25   ROO sch 3B para 2(3)(b),(8); NIED sch para 2(3)(b),(8)

The data used to set the LHA figures

9.26 When setting LHA figures, the rent officer/NIHE:

(a) takes account of the range of rents payable (during the year ending on the preceding 30th September) on accommodation which:

- is the correct size and in the correct area or (if that area doesn't have enough accommodation of that size) in a comparable area or areas,

- is in a reasonable state of repair, and

- is let on an assured tenancy;

(b) excludes the value of all services that would be ineligible for HB in other types of HB case (para 8.5 and table 8.3);

(c) excludes rents which a landlord couldn't 'reasonably have been expected to obtain' (in practice this means very low or high rents); and

(d) assumes that 'no-one who would have been entitled to HB had sought or is seeking the tenancy' (in practice this means excluding rents paid by people on HB).

The LHA areas

9.27 LHA areas are called 'broad rental market areas' (BRMAs) and are defined by postcodes. They are drawn up by the rent officer/NIHE so that:

(a) a person 'could reasonably be expected to live [there] having regard to facilities and services for the purposes of health, education, recreation, personal banking and shopping, taking account of the distance of travel, by public and private transport, to and from those facilities and services';

(b) they contain 'residential premises of a variety of types' held as a 'variety of tenancies'; and

(c) they contain 'sufficient privately rented premises' to ensure that the LHA figures 'are representative of the rents that a landlord might reasonably be expected to obtain in that area'.

They can only be changed with the DWP's consent.

9.28 BRMAs in Great Britain are on average twice the size of council areas (following changes in the law since large areas were criticised in R (Heffernan) v the Rent Service). Their boundaries don't usually match council boundaries, so some councils are completely within one BRMA and others contain parts of more than one BRMA.

9.26   ROO sch 3B para 2(4),(5),(7); NIED sch para 2(4),(5),(7)

9.27   ROO 4B(1A), sch 3B paras 4,5; NIED sch paras 4,5
        R (Heffernan) v the Rent Service [2008] UKHL 58 www.bailii.org/uk/cases/UKHL/2008/58.html

Appeals about LHA figures and areas

9.29　　　You can appeal to a tribunal (para 20.41) about:

(a) whether the LHA rules apply to you (para 9.3); or

(b) whether the authority has correctly decided the size or category of accommodation you qualify for (paras 9.16-20) and therefore applies the correct LHA figure.

You can't appeal to a tribunal or a rent officer about the amount of your LHA figure or about how a BRMA was drawn up, but it may be possible to challenge these by judicial review (para 20.53).

Boarders

9.30　　　This section explains the eligible rent rules for boarders who rent from a private landlord – for example, you rent a room in someone's home and your rent includes meals. (See para 7.25 if you are a boarder and you pay rent to a social landlord.)

Who is a boarder

9.31　　　A 'boarder' means someone whose rent includes meals. But for private tenants the following additional rules apply.

Eligible rent

9.32　　　If you are a private renter (para 9.2) who is a boarder:

(a) you fall within the rent referral rules (paras 10.28-52) if your rent includes substantial board and attendance (para 9.33);

(b) otherwise you fall within the LHA rules (unless any of the exclusions in table 9.1(a)-(c) and (e)-(g) apply to you).

Substantial board and attendance

9.33　　　Your rent includes substantial board and attendance if:

(a) it includes 'board and attendance' – this means meals plus some further service such as serving the meals; and

(b) a 'substantial' amount of it is attributable to this – for example breakfast by itself isn't usually considered to be 'substantial'.

This is decided by making a board and attendance determination (para 9.34).

9.29　　　CPSA sch 7 para 6(2)(c); NICPSA sch 7 para 6(2)(c)

9.32-33　　HB 13C(5)(e), 13D(10); HB66+ 13C(5)(e), 13D(10); NIHB 14C(5)(e), 14D(8); NIHB66+ 14C(5)(e), 14D(8)

Board and attendance determinations

9.34   A 'board and attendance determination' is made by the rent officer in Great Britain or by the NIHE in Northern Ireland. It is only required if:

(a)   you are a private tenant who is a boarder; and

(b)   you are not excluded from the LHA rules for any of the reasons in table 9.1(a)-(c) and (e) to (g).

In Great Britain, the council applies to the rent officer for this determination. If the rent officer decides your rent includes substantial board and attendance, the council then makes a referral to the rent officer as described in para 10.31 and your eligible rent is worked out as in para 10.39 and table 10.5.

Example: Eligible rent for a boarder

Bobby is aged 68 and rent's a room in Philip's home. Bobby pays rent of £150 per week including all meals (which Philip cooks for him) but no other services. Bobby claims HB because a friend suggests he should.

The council gives the details to the rent officer (para 10.32), who first confirms that Bobby's rent includes substantial board and attendance (para 9.34) and then gives the council the following determinations:

- a claim-related rent of £120 per week (para 10.41);
- a local reference rent of £105 per week (para 10.45);
- no service charge determination (para 10.51).

The council calculates Bobby's weekly eligible rent as follows (para 10.5):

- local reference rent   £105.00
- minus all meals (table 8.5)   −£29.20
- equals eligible rent   £75.80

9.34   HB 13D(10), 114A(3),(4); HB66+ 13D(10), 95A(3),(4); NIHB 14D(10); NIHB66+ 14D(10)

Chapter 10 **Old scheme and rent referrals**

- Old scheme and exempt accommodation: see paras 10.1-8.
- Eligible rent in old scheme cases: see paras 10.9-27.
- Rent referral cases: see paras 10.28-37.
- Eligible rent and rent determinations: see paras 10.38-53.

10.1   This chapter only applies to rent allowance claims (para 18.6). It does not apply if your landlord is the authority (i.e. if your HB is paid as a rent rebate: para 18.4). It describes when and how your eligible rent is worked out if you fall under the old scheme (paras 10.2-27) or the rent referral rules (paras 10.28-53). Chapter 7 gives further details about when these rules apply.

What is the old scheme

10.2   This and the next section explain when and how your eligible rent is worked out under the old scheme rules. The old scheme rules only apply if:

(a) your landlord is not-for-profit (paras 7.13-21) and you live in 'exempt accommodation' (paras 10.4-8); or

(b) you rent from private rent landlord (para 7.22) and you have an 'old HB' claim (broadly, you have been on HB at the same address since 1996: para 7.37-38).

10.3   Local councils often refer to these claims as the 'old rules' or 'old scheme' because your eligible rent is based on the HB rules in force prior to 1996. These rules are now in 'old' HB regulations 12, 13 and 13ZA which are found in the HB Consequential Provisions Regulations.

Exempt accommodation

10.4   If you live in exempt accommodation your eligible rent is worked out using the old scheme rules regardless of how old your HB claim is. Exempt accommodation is so called because the authority is not bound by the LHA rates or rent officer determinations that apply to other rent allowance claims. (But your rent may be referred to the rent officer for subsidy purposes: para 10.37). For working age HB, all exempt accommodation is also 'supported accommodation' (para 2.13 and table 2.3) so you can get HB towards your housing costs if you claim UC and your HB doesn't count towards the benefit cap (para 6.28).

10.5   Your home is 'exempt accommodation' if:

(a) you meet both the 'landlord condition' and the 'support condition' (paras 10.6-7); or

(b) you live in resettlement accommodation (a hostel etc.) of the kind in para 10.8.

10.2-3   HB old 12,13,13ZA in CPR/NICPR sch 3 para 5

10.5-8   CPR sch 3 para 4(1)(b),(10); NICPR sch 3 para 4(1)(b),(9)

10.6   You meet the 'landlord condition' (para 10.5) if your landlord is:

(a) a registered housing association (paras 7.14-15); or

(b) not-for-profit – this means they are:

  ■   a housing association that is not registered (para 7.13),

  ■   a registered charity (para 7.20),

  ■   a voluntary organisation (para 7.21), or

  ■   an English county council that doesn't administer HB.

This means your immediate landlord (CH/3900/2005 and [2009] UKUT 12 (AAC)), and not, for example, the superior landlord or a managing agent (para 7.9).

10.7   The support condition (para 10.5) is that your landlord, or someone on their behalf, must be providing you with 'care, support or supervision'. There have been many appeals about this and the main cases are summarised in table 10.1.

10.8   Your dwelling counts as resettlement accommodation (para 10.5) if it is in Great Britain and your landlord has (in the past) received a resettlement grant paid under section 30 of the Jobseekers Act 1995. This mainly applies to hostels and similar kinds of temporary accommodation provided for people without a settled way of life.

Table 10.1 **Care, support and supervision: case law**

(a) Meaning of 'care, support or supervision' (CSS)

This part of the table applies to exempt accommodation (paras 10.5-8), and also to other kinds of supported accommodation (table 2.3(a)-(e)).

Meaning of CSS: the phrase 'care, support or supervision' has its ordinary English meaning (R(S) v Social Security Commissioner and Others, confirming R(H) 2/07).

Availability of CSS: The CSS must be available in reality to the tenant, and there must be a real prospect that they will find the service of use (R(H) 4/09; [2009] UKUT 109 (AAC)).

Meaning of 'support': 'Support' might well be characterised as 'the giving of advice and assistance to a claimant in coping with the practicalities of [their] life, and in particular [their] occupation of the property' ([2010] AACR 2). It is more than ordinary housing management ([2009] UKUT 107 (AAC)).

Continuity of support: The support provided must be on-going (R(H) 4/09). Help with gaining exemption from council tax because the tenant is severely mentally impaired is more like a setting up cost and is not enough ([2010] AACR 2).

Need for and provision of 'support': 'What matters is simply whether support is provided to more than a minimal extent, and it is… implicit that support is not "provided" unless there is in fact some need for it' ([2009] UKUT 150 (AAC)).

T10.1   R(S) v Social Security Commissioner and Ors [2008] EWHC 3097 Admin and [2009] EWHC 2221 Admin
          www.bailii.org/ew/cases/EWHC/Admin/2008/3097.html
          www.bailii.org/ew/cases/EWHC/Admin/2009/2221.html

Dwellings in a group: A dwelling in a group (e.g. sheltered accommodation) doesn't qualify as supported accommodation just because other dwellings in the group do: CSS must be provided to that particular dwelling (CH/1289/2007).

Amount of CSS: CSS must be more than minimal. An average of ten minutes per tenant per week was not enough (in R(H) 7/07), but three hours per tenant per week might be enough (in CH/1289/2007). Just helping with HB claims and reviews, and carrying out safety and security inspections, was not more than minimal; but 'proactively considering what physical improvements or alterations to the properties could usefully be made' in the case of adaptations for disability, could be enough ([2010] AACR 2).

When there is no relevant history: In a new development) it is necessary to look at what is contemplated ([2009] UKUT 109 (AAC)).

(b) Provision of CSS in exempt accommodation

This part of the table applies only to exempt accommodation (paras 10.5-7).

CSS provided by the landlord: A landlord can provide CSS by making arrangements for it, or by paying for someone to do it ([2009] UKUT 107 (AAC)).

CSS provided on behalf of the landlord: For CSS to be provided 'on behalf of' the landlord, there must be 'a sense of agency between the [CSS provider and the landlord], or… a contract, or something akin to it'. A joint venture is not enough; nor is a contract between the CSS provider and e.g. social services (R(S) v Social Security Commissioner, confirming R(H) 2/07).

CSS provided by landlord as well as care provider: The landlord may provide CSS without being the principal provider of it to that particular tenant ([2010] AACR 2).

Availability of CSS from elsewhere: 'The likely nature, extent and frequency of [the CSS], and the extent of support available to the claimant from elsewhere' are to be taken into account in considering whether the CSS provided by a landlord is more than minimal ([2009] UKUT 107 (AAC)).

Who pays for the CSS? It is irrelevant that the landlord is (or is not) paid to provide the CSS by someone else ([2009] UKUT 107 (AAC)).

Support vs housing management: 'Support' means that the landlord does more than an ordinary landlord would do (R(H) 4/09). It is more than ordinary housing management, e.g. repairs and maintenance. But if the tenancy agreement 'imposes unusually onerous repairing and maintenance obligations on the landlord', this can amount to support; as can the fact that a claimant's disabilities impose a 'materially greater burden on the landlord' ([2009] UKUT 107 (AAC)).

Live-in carers: While the presence of a live-in carer may or may not amount to CSS (depending on who provides the carer), the case law on carers can affect whether the size of the accommodation is reasonable (paras 10.13 and 11.10).

Eligible rent in old scheme cases

10.9   This section explains how your eligible rent is worked out if you live in exempt accommodation (paras 10.5-8). It also applies if you have an old (pre-1996) HB claim (para 7.37). If you have an old 'registered rent' or similar tenancy, see also para 7.39.

Eligible rent

10.10   Your eligible rent is worked out using the general rule for a social renter in paras 8.5-7 but the rules about how your eligible rent can be reduced are different (para 10.11). The social renter size criteria and LHA rules (paras 8.9-16 and chapter 9) don't apply to you. However, before the council decides to reduce the rent (paras 10.11-25) it must deduct any ineligible service charges, including charges for support (even if the landlord has classified it as housing management: para 8.27) and any charges it considers excessive (para 8.39).

Eligible rent reductions

10.11   Paras 10.12-20 explain when your eligible rent can be reduced. But if you are a 'protected renter', you are wholly or partly protected against these reductions (paras 10.21-27).

Unreasonably high rents

10.12   Your eligible rent may be reduced if your rent is 'unreasonably high'. This is decided by comparing the actual rent on your home with the rent payable on suitable alternative accommodation. See paras 10.15-16.

Unreasonably large dwellings

10.13   Your eligible rent may be reduced if your home is 'larger than reasonably required'. This is decided by comparing the size of your home with the size of suitable alternative accommodation for all the occupiers of your home. See paras 10.15-16.

Unreasonable rent increases

10.14   Your eligible rent may be reduced if you have a rent increase that:

(a)   is 'unreasonably high' compared with the level of increases for suitable alternative accommodation; or

(b)   is less than 12 months after the previous increase and is 'unreasonable having regard to the length of time since that previous increase'.

See paras 10.15-16.

10.10   HB 11(1)(d); HB66+ 11(1)(d); NIHB 11(1)(d); NIHB66+ 11(1)(d); old 12(3)-(5) in CPR/NICPR sch 3 para 5

10.11   HB old 13,13ZA; HB66+ old 13,13ZA; NIHB old 13,13ZA; NIHB66+ old 13,13ZA; (in CPR/NICPR sch 3 para 5

10.12   HB old 13(3)(a); HB66+ old 13(3)(a); NIHB old 13(3)(a); NIHB66+ old 13(3)(a) in CPR/NICPR sch 3 para 5

10.13   HB old 13(3)(b); HB66+ old 13(3)(b); NIHB old 13(3)(b); NIHB66+ old 13(3)(b) in CPR/NICPR sch 3 para 5

10.14   HB old 13ZA(1)(a); HB66+ old 13ZA(1)(a); NIHB old 13ZA(1)(a); NIHB66+ old 13ZA(1)(a) in CPR/NICPR sch 3 para 5

The amount of the reduction

10.15   When any of the rules in paras 10.12-14 apply to you the authority can:

(a)   reduce your eligible rent to the level of rent for suitable alternative accommodation (paras 10.17-18); or

(b)   make a smaller reduction.

Unless you are in a protected group (para 10.21); the authority must make some reduction, but it could be a small amount, or a small amount for the time being.

Decisions about reductions

10.16   When it makes a decision about whether to reduce your eligible rent or about the protected groups, the authority:

(a)   must take account of your individual circumstances and of suitable alternative accommodation (paras 10.17-18);

(b)   may take account of rent determinations made by the rent officer/NIHE (para 10.37), but must not automatically use these to reduce your eligible rent (para 10.27);

(c)   must not apply rigid rules that automatically treat every case the same way (GM A4.962);

(d)   must not allow subsidy considerations (paras 10.26-27) to override the HB rules and case law.

Table 10.2 summarises the case law about reductions and protections.

Suitable alternative accommodation

10.17   When deciding what is 'suitable alternative accommodation' (paras 10.12-16), the authority must take into account:

(a)   the nature of the alternative accommodation including any exclusive and shared facilities, having regard to the age and state of health of the occupiers of your home (paras 10.19-20). 'For example, if you are disabled or elderly you might have special needs and require expensive or larger accommodation' (GM para A4.1171);

(b)   only alternative accommodation with security of tenure which is reasonably equivalent to what you have.

The alternative accommodation can be either occupied or unoccupied (but at least some of it must be unoccupied if the protection in para 10.22 applies to you).

10.18   The authority normally only looks at alternative accommodation in its own area. If there is nothing comparable there it can look outside, but not at 'other parts of the country where accommodation costs differ widely from those which apply locally' (GM para A4.1172).

10.15   HB old 13(1),(9)(a) 13ZA(1),(9)(a); HB66+ old 13(1),(9)(a) 13ZA(1),(9)(a);
          NIHB old 13(1),(9)(a) 13ZA(1),(9)(a); NIHB66+ old 13(1),(9)(a) 13ZA(1),(9)(a) in CPR/NICPR sch 3 para 5

10.17   HB old 13(1),(9)(a); HB66+ old 13(1),(9)(a); NIHB old 13(1),(9)(a); NIHB66+ old 13(1),(9)(a); in CPR/NICPR sch 3 para 5

Table 10.2 **Old scheme eligible rent reductions: case law**

These cases apply equally to exempt accommodation (paras 10.5-8) and old (pre-1996) HB claims (para 7.37).

Decisions about unreasonably high rents: The authority must decide:

(a) the actual rent you pay (including all eligible and ineligible service charges);

(b) what would be suitable alternative accommodation (paras 10.17-18) including what services are needed to make it suitable and what other factors need to be taken into account;

(c) what the rent is for such accommodation; and

(d) whether (a) is 'unreasonably high' compared with (c).

    (R v Beverley BC ex parte Hare.)

'Unreasonably high': This means more than just 'higher' (Malcolm v Tweeddale DC HBRB).

Suitability of alternative accommodation: The authority must have 'sufficient information to ensure that like is being compared with like [...] Unless that can be done, no safe assessment can be made of the reasonableness of the rent in question or the proper level of value' (Malcolm v Tweeddale DC HBRB). Your home should be compared with 'more suitable' rather than 'less suitable' accommodation ([2009] UKUT 162 (AAC)).

Decisions about past periods: A decision about a past period should be made as if it was being made then. If evidence about that period is unavailable or unclear, findings of fact must be made about what was likely to have been the case ([2009] UKUT 162 (AAC)).

Decisions about the amount of a reduction: The authority should:

(a) consider whether any circumstances may make a small reduction appropriate;

(b) decide the appropriate level of a reduction; and

(c) be able to say how it arrived at (b).

    (Mehanne v Westminster CC HBRB and R v Beverley BC ex parte Hare).

Limits to reductions: Your eligible rent must not be reduced below the cost of suitable alternative accommodation (R v Brent LBC ex parte Connery).

People considered 'vulnerable': availability of suitable alternative accommodation: Although suitable alternative accommodation must be available if you are considered 'vulnerable' (para 10.24), this doesn't mean the authority is expected to find a home for you. It is 'quite sufficient if an active market is shown to exist in houses in an appropriate place at the appropriate level' (the level your eligible rent is reduced to). So long as the authority has evidence of this, it is sufficient 'to point to a range of properties, or a bloc of property,

---

T10.2   R v Beverley DC HBRB ex parte Hare 21/02/95 QBD HLR 637
          Malcolm v Tweeddale DC HBRB 06/08/91 CS 1994 SLT 1212
          R v Westminster HBRB ex parte Mehanne [2001] UKHL 11
          R v Brent LBC ex parte Connery 20/10/89 QBD 22 HLR 40
          R v East Devon DC HBRB ex parte Gibson 10/03/93 CA 25 HLR 487
          R v Sefton MBC ex parte Cunningham 22/05/91 QBD 23 HLR 534

which is available without specific identification of particular dwelling houses' (R v East Devon DC HBRB ex parte Gibson). If the authority doesn't have this evidence, it shouldn't reduce your eligible rent (CH/4306/2003).

People considered 'vulnerable': reasonableness of being expected to move: If you are considered 'vulnerable', the authority should have evidence that it has taken into account the effect a move would have (para 10.25) on employment and schooling (R v Sefton MBC ex parte Cunningham).

Which occupiers are taken into account

10.19   When the authority is deciding the nature and facilities of suitable alternative accommodation (para 10.17) or the rules about protected renters (para 10.21), only the following occupiers of your home are taken into account:

(a) you (the claimant) and members of your family (partner, children and young persons: paras 4.4 and 4.14); and

(b) any 'relative' (para 7.58) of you or your partner (including non-dependants, lodgers and joint tenants) who has no separate right to occupy your home.

10.20   But when the authority is deciding the size of suitable alternative accommodation (para 10.13), all the occupiers of your home are taken into account. This means everyone in para 10.19, and also anyone else (e.g. non-dependants, lodgers, joint tenants, foster children and carers) whether they are related to you or not. (Unlike all the other HB rules about accommodation size there are no exceptions.)

Protected renters

10.21   You may be protected against a reduction in your eligible rent if:

(a) you could previously afford the rent without help from HB: see paras 7.51-53; or

(b) an occupier of your home has died within the past year: see paras 7.54-56; or

(c) you or another occupier of your home is considered vulnerable: see paras 10.22-27.

All of these protections apply when your rent is too high or your home is too large (paras 10.12-13) but only (b) applies when you have an unreasonable rent increase (para 10.14).

Protection for people considered vulnerable

10.22   If you or another occupier of your home are considered to be 'vulnerable' (para 10.23), the authority must not reduce your eligible rent unless:

(a) there is cheaper suitable alternative accommodation available (para 10.24); and

(b) it is reasonable to expect you to move (para 10.25).

For this protection, only the occupiers in para 10.19 are taken into account. For case law see table 10.2.

10.19   HB old 13(10),(11); HB66+ old 13(10),(11); NIHB old 13(10),(11); NIHB66+ old 13(10),(11); in CPR/NICPR sch 3 para 5

10.21   HB old 13(5)-(8); HB66+ old 13(5)-(8); NIHB old 13(5)-(8); NIHB66+ old 13(5)-(8); in CPR/NICPR sch 3 para 5

10.22-23   HB old 13(4),(9)(b); HB66+ old 13(4),(9)(b); NIHB old 13(4),(9)(b); NIHB66+ old 13(4),(9)(b); in CPR/NICPR sch 3 para 5

10.23   Someone is considered to be 'vulnerable' only if they:

(a) have reached pension age (para 2.4); or

(b) are responsible for a child or young person in your household (paras 4.4-19); or

(c) have limited capability for work for ESA purposes (para 12.47).

The authority decides (a) and (b), but (c) is decided by the DWP (CH/4424/2004).

10.24   Suitable alternative accommodation is described in paras 10.17-20. The point here is that it must be available – and available more cheaply. For example, accommodation you have recently left, or an offer of accommodation you have refused, may be available – but only while it actually remains available to you, not after it has been let to someone else. The DWP advises that the authority 'should regard accommodation as not available if, in practice, there is a little or no possibility of [you] being able to obtain it, for example because it could only be obtained on payment of a large deposit which [you do] not have' (GM para A4.1222).

10.25   When deciding whether it is reasonable to expect you to move, the authority must take into account:

(a) your prospects of retaining employment; and

(b) the effect on the education of any children or young persons mentioned in para 10.23 who would have to change school.

The impact of subsidy

10.26   In exempt accommodation cases, a council in Great Britain can get less government subsidy (paras 21.29-32).

10.27   The authority must not take subsidy into account when it decides:

(a) whether your rent, accommodation size or rent increase is unreasonable; or

(b) any matter relating to the protected groups.

It may take subsidy into account when deciding the amount of a reduction (R v Brent LBC ex p Connery), but it must exercise its judgment and discretion (paras 20.23-24) and the DWP's advice is that it can't reduce your eligible rent 'on financial grounds alone' (GM para A4.1173).

Rent referral cases

10.28   This and the following section explain who falls within the 'rent referral' rules (also called the rent decision rules in Northern Ireland) and how your eligible rent is affected by the 'rent determinations' that are made in these cases.

Who falls within the rent referral rules

10.29   The rent referral rules only apply in the specific circumstances in table 10.3. If you are a private renter and you pay board, see also paras 9.30-34. The rent referral rules never apply if your landlord is the authority you claim HB from (para 7.11).

10.24   HB old 13(4); HB66+ old 13(4); NIHB old 13(4); NIHB66+ old 13(4); in CPR/NICPR sch 3 para 5

10.25   HB old 13(4),(9)(b); HB66+ old 13(4),(9)(b); NIHB old 13(4),(9)(b); NIHB66+ old 13(4),(9)(b); in CPR/NICPR sch 3 para 5

10.27   R v Brent LBC ex p Connery 20/10/89 QBD 22 HLR 40

Table 10.3 **Who the rent referral rules apply to**

(a) Private renters (paras 7.22 and 9.2)

You only fall with the rent referral rules if:

- you are a boarder and your rent includes substantial board and attendance (paras 9.33-34);
- you live in a hostel (paras 7.27-29);
- you live in a caravan, mobile home or houseboat (see paras 7.33-34 for further details and exceptions); or
- you have been receiving HB for your current home since before 7th April 2008.

If none of the above apply you fall under the LHA rules (chapter 9).

(b) Tenants of a registered housing association (paras 7.13-15)

You only fall within the rent referral rules if:

- the authority considers your rent is unreasonably high; or
- you have a pension age HB claim (table 2.2) and the authority considers your home is unreasonably large.

But if your home isn't social housing (para 7.17), the rules in (a) apply. See also (c) below if you are a former local authority ('stock transfer') tenant.

(c) Former local authority/NIHE ('stock transfer') tenants

If ownership of your home was transferred from the authority, new town or the NIHE to another landlord, you only fall within the rent referral rules if:

- the rent on your home has increased since the date of the transfer; and either
- the authority considers your rent is unreasonably high; or
- the transfer took place before 7th October 2002 and the authority considers your home unreasonably large.

But if your new landlord is a registered housing association, you only fall within the rent referral rules if (b) also applies to you.

(d) Exceptions

The rent referral rules do not apply to you in any of cases (a)-(c) if:

- you have an old (pre-1996) HB claim (para 7.37);
- you have a 'registered rent' or other similar old tenancy (para 7.39); or
- you have a shared ownership tenancy (para 7.24).

T10.3   HB 2(1) definitions: 'hostel', 'housing association', 'voluntary organisation', 12C(1), 13(1), 13C(5),(6), 14(1)(a)-(h), sch 2 paras 3, 11(2)(a);
HB66+ 12C(1), 13(1), 13C(5),(6), 14(1)(a)-(h), sch 2 paras 3, 11(2)(a);
NIHB 13B(1), 14(1), 14C(5),(6), 15(1),(4), sch 3 paras 3, 5(2)(a); NIHB66+ 13B(1), 14(1), 14C(5),(6), 15(1),(4), sch 3 paras 3, 5(2)(a)

Rent determinations

10.30   In rent referral cases, one or more rental valuations called 'rent determinations' are made, including a claim-related rent determination in all cases and a local reference and/or single room rent determination in some cases. A 'rent determination' means any of these individually, and also the overall decision about which of them apply to you. For the details, see paras 10.41-52.

Who makes rent determinations

10.31   In Great Britain, rent determinations are made by the rent officer as follows:

(a)   the authority refers details of your rent, accommodation and household composition to the rent officer – it should do this within three working days of a rent determination becoming required (para 10.32);

(b)   the rent officer then provides the authority with the rent determinations that apply to you – they should do this within five working days of receiving the referral or any further information they need (26 working days if they intend to visit your home).

In Northern Ireland, rent determinations are made by the NIHE itself – it should do this within three working days of a rent determination becoming required.

When rent determinations are required

10.32   A rent determination is required on each of the following occasions:

(a)   when you claim HB;

(b)   when you move home;

(c)   whenever there is a 'relevant change' in your circumstances: see table 10.4; and

(d)   whenever 52 weeks have passed since the most recent rent determination was made for your home.

But in cases (a) and (b), if there is already a valid rent determination for your home (para 10.33) this is used instead. For hostels, see also para 10.35.

10.33   For this purpose, a rent determination for your home is valid if:

(a)   it was made less than 52 weeks ago for you or another person (because you or they previously claimed or received HB there, or requested a pre-tenancy determination there: para 10.36); and

(b)   there is no difference that amounts to a 'relevant change' (table 10.4) between your current circumstances and your/their circumstances then.

10.30   HB 13(1),(5),(9); HB66+ 13(1),(5),(9); ROO sch 1; NIHB 14(1),(5),(9), sch 3; NIHB66+ 14(1),(5),(9), sch 3

10.31   AA 134(1); HB 14(1),(5),(9); HB66+ 14(1); ROO sch 1; NIAA 129(1); NIHB 15(1), sch 3; NIHB66+ 15(1), sch 3

10.32   HB 14(1)-(3),(6),(8), sch 2 para 2; HB66+ 14(1), sch 2 para 2; ROO sch 1; NIHB 15(1), sch 3 para 2; NIHB66+ 15(1), sch 3 para 2

10.33   DAR 7A(3), 8(6A),(6B); NIDAR 7A(3), 8(6A),(6B)

Table 10.4 'Relevant changes' in rent referral cases

Rent determinations are required in all these situations (paras 10.32 and 10.35):

Changes that could affect the size of accommodation you qualify for

(a) There is a change in the number of occupiers in your home – but this doesn't apply if you live in a hostel (para 10.35) or to the beginning or end of an armed forces absence (para 11.15).

(b) A child in your home reaches the age of 10 or 16 – but only if your most recent rent determination included a size-related rent determination (para 10.43).

(c) There is a change in the household composition of the occupiers of your home (e.g. two people start or stop being a couple) – but only if your most recent rent determination included a size-related rent determination (para 10.43).

(d) You start or stop qualifying for an additional bedroom for any of the reasons in para 11.19 (foster parents, overnight carers, and disabled people who need their own bedroom).

(e) You start to meet the conditions for a single room rent determination (which applies to certain single claimants under the age of 35: para 10.47) – e.g. because you are a care-leaver and have reached the age of 22 (para 9.20).

Other changes

(f) There is a substantial change in the terms of your letting agreement or the condition of your home (e.g. your landlord has made improvements) – this applies whether or not your rent changes (but not if the only change is in your rent).

(g) Your rent increases – but this only applies if:

  ■ the increase is under a term of your letting agreement (which needn't be in writing but must be a term of your letting, not just a provision of law: CH/3590/2007);

  ■ that term is the same (or substantially the same) as when your most recent rent determination was made; and

  ■ in your most recent rent determination, your referred rent was used as your claim related rent (para 10.41).

Note: Other increases in your rent don't count as a 'relevant change'. For reductions in your rent, see para 10.39. For moves, see paras 10.32-33.

T10.4   HB 14(1),(8), sch 2 para 2; HB66+ 14(1),(8), sch 2 para 2; NIHB 15(1), sch 3 para 2; NIHB66+ 15(1), sch 3 para 2

When rent determinations take effect

10.34   A rent determination relating to a claim takes effect when your HB starts (para 16.31). One relating to a move or relevant change takes effect when the move or change takes effect (para 17.18). One made because 52 weeks have passed takes effect as follows:

(a)   if it means you qualify for more HB (or the same amount), it takes effect on:

■   the day after the 52 weeks run out, but

■   if that isn't a Monday and your rent is due weekly or in multiples of weeks, on the preceding Monday;

(b)   if it means you qualify for less HB, it takes effect on the Monday following:

■   the day the authority receives the determination from the rent officer (Great Britain), or

■   the day the NIHE makes the determination (Northern Ireland).

Rent determinations for hostels

10.35   Once one rent determination has been made for a hostel (para 7.27), it applies for 12 months for all other lettings there that provide sleeping accommodation for the same number of people. If the hostel has lettings that provide sleeping accommodation for different numbers of people (e.g. single rooms and shared rooms) this applies separately for each kind. But rent determinations are required for 'relevant changes' (table 10.4) and when the 12 months run out.

Pre-tenancy determinations

10.36   If your landlord agrees, you can ask the authority to provide you with a 'pre-tenancy' rent determination (PTD) before you:

(a)   move into a new home; or

(b)   renew your letting agreement – so long as it is at least 11 months since your last agreement began.

This may help you decide whether you can afford the new home or new letting agreement. Advice to authorities on PTDs is in GM A4.2050-70.

Rent referrals for subsidy only

10.37   In old scheme cases (para 10.2) your rent is referred to the rent officer for subsidy purposes, but his/her determinations should not be used by the authority as the sole basis to set your eligible rent, for which they are advisory only (para 10.27). But a referral is not usually made if your landlord is a registered housing association (para 21.32), and never if you have a shared ownership, or a registered rent tenancy (paras 7.39-43).

10.34   DAR 7A, 8(6A),(6B); NIDAR 7A, 8(6A),(6B)

10.35   HB 14(2)(a),(7); HB66+ 14(2)(a),(7); NIHB 15; NIHB66+ 15

10.36   HB 14(4)(8); HB66+ 14(4),(8); ROO 3(1); NIHB 16, sch 1 para 3(1); NIHB66+ 16, sch 1 para 3(1)

Eligible rent and rent determinations

10.38   This section is about how your eligible rent is worked out in rent referral cases (para 10.29). It explains which rent determinations apply to you and how the rent officer/NIHE makes them. For appeals about rent determinations, see paras 20.54-61.

Eligible rent

10.39   In rent referral cases (other than a referral for subsidy only: para 10.37) your eligible rent is worked out as described in table 10.5 using the rent officer's determinations. These determinations are binding on the authority and set a maximum figure for your eligible rent as follows:

(a) if the rent officer has determined a single room rent your eligible rent can't exceed:

   ▪   the single room rent (para 10.47), or

   ▪   if your rent includes meals, the claim related rent minus the amount for meals (table 8.5) if this is a lower figure than the single room rent;

(b) if the rent officer has determined a local reference rent your eligible rent can't exceed:

   ▪   the local reference rent (para 10.45), or if meals are included, that figure minus the amount for meals;

(c) in any other case your eligible rent can't exceed:

   ▪   the claim related rent (para 10.41), minus

   ▪   a service charge determination if it applies (para 10.51), minus

   ▪   the amount for meals if they are included in your rent.

But if there has been a recent death in your home or you could previously afford the full rent you are a 'protected renter', and the rent determinations are not used to calculate your eligible rent for up to 13 weeks/one year (paras 7.48-58). If you are a joint tenant, adjustments are made as in table 10.5.

The referred rent and your actual rent

10.40   Rent determinations are made by reference to your 'referred rent' (i.e. the figure the authority passes to the rent officer). This means the full actual rent you are liable to pay your landlord including all eligible service charges together with most ineligible service charges except those, other than meals, which the authority values (see table 8.3). In Great Britain, the authority has to provide the rent officer with details of these and say which service charges are ineligible to be met by HB (table 8.3).

10.39   HB 13(1)-(3),(5),(7); HB66+ 13(1)-(3),(5),(7); NIHB 14(1)-(3),(5),(7); NIHB66+ 14(1)-(3),(5),(7)

10.40   HB 114A(3)(d),(4),(8)(a); HB66+ 95A(3)(d),(4),(8)(a); NIHB 16(a); NIHB66+ 16(a)

Table 10.5 **Eligible rent in rent referral cases**

Steps 1 and 2 apply to all rent referral cases. Steps 3 and 4 apply when rent determinations are binding (para 10.39).

Step 1: Rent determinations

The rent officer/NIHE may determine one or more (or none) of the following:

(a) a significantly high rent determination (para 10.42);

(b) a size-related rent determination (para 10.43);

(c) an exceptionally high rent determination (para 10.44);

(d) a local reference rent (paras 10.45-46);

(e) a single room rent (paras 10.47-48);

(f) a service charge determination (para 10.51).

Step 2: Your claim-related rent

The rent officer/NIHE always determines this. It is:

- the lowest of determinations (a) to (c); or

- if none of those apply to you, the referred rent (para 10.40).

Step 3: Adjustments to the figures

The authority then makes adjustments in the following order:

- if the referred rent is used as your claim-related rent, any service charge determination is deducted from it;

- if you have one or more joint tenants who are not a member of your family (para 4.43), the claim-related rent and any local reference rent are apportioned (para 8.7) between you;

- if necessary, convert all the figures to a weekly amount (para 6.34);

- if your actual rent includes meals, the standard amount (table 8.5) is deducted from the claim-related rent (in all cases) and any local reference rent (only if it includes board and attendance) – or from your share of these if you are a joint tenant.

Step 4: Your eligible rent

The authority decides this. It is the lowest of the following (after the above adjustments):

- your claim-related rent;

- the local reference rent (if any);

- the single room rent (if any).

But see para 10.39 for exceptions and protections.

T10.5   HB 2(1) – definition 'hostel', 12C, 13(1)-(3),(5),(7), 14(1),(2)(a),(3),(7),(8); HB66+ 2(1), 12C, 13(1)-(3),(5),(7), 14(1),(2)(a),(3),(7),(8);
          ROO 3(1), 6(2),(3),7, sch 1 paras 6,7,9, sch 4 paras 1,2;
          NIHB 2(1), 13B, 14(1)-(3),(5),(7), 15(1),(3),(4),sch 2 paras 6,7,12,13; NIHB66+ 2(1), 13B, 14(1)-(3),(5),(7), 15(1), (3),(4),sch 2 paras 6,7,12,13

Example: Eligible rent in a rent referral case

Suzie is aged 52 and has been getting HB on her home since 2007. She lives in a flat and currently pays her private landlord £110 per week which includes some ineligible services (table 8.3).

This is a rent referral case (table 10.3(a)) and the claim related rent is based on a two room dwelling (para 10.46, table 11.1). The council refers the rent because 52 weeks have passed since the last one was made (para 10.32). The rent officer gives the following determinations:

- a claim-related rent of £110 per week (para 10.41);
- no local reference rent (para 10.45);
- a service charge determination of £5 per week (para 10.51).

The council calculates Suzie's weekly eligible rent as follows (para 10.39) and table 10.5:

claim related rent	£110.00
minus service charge determination	-£5.00
equals eligible rent	£105.00

An example of a rent referral for a boarder follows para 9.34.

Claim-related rent determinations

10.41 The rent officer/NIHE always determines a 'claim-related rent'. This is the lowest of the following:

(a) a significantly high rent determination (para 10.42);

(b) a size-related rent determination (para 10.43);

(c) an exceptionally high rent determination (para 10.44);

or your referred rent (para 10.40) if none of (a) to (c) apply to you.

10.42 A 'significantly high rent determination' is a valuation of the reasonable market rent for your dwelling as it is (regardless of its size, etc). It only applies if your actual rent is 'significantly higher' than this.

10.43 A 'size-related rent determination' is a valuation of the highest reasonable market rent for a dwelling that is as similar as possible to yours but is of the size you qualify for (table 11.1). It only applies if your dwelling is larger than this. It doesn't apply if you live in a caravan, mobile home or houseboat (para 7.33).

10.41 HB 13(9); HB66+ 13(9); ROO sch 1 para 6; NIHB 14(9), sch 2 para 6; NIHB66+ 14(9), sch 2 para 6

10.42 ROO sch 1 para 1; NIHB sch 2 para 1; NIHB66+ sch 2 para 1

10.43 ROO 7, sch 1 para 2; NIHB 16(a), sch 2 para 2; NIHB66+ 16(a), sch 2 para 2

10.44   An 'exceptionally high rent determination' is a valuation of the highest reasonable market rent for a dwelling that is of the size you qualify for (table 11.1) that isn't 'exceptionally high' (in other words, the highest rent that isn't at the luxury end of the market: see also para 10.46). It only applies if your actual rent and/or the determination(s) in paras 10.42-43 are higher than this.

Local reference rent determinations

10.45   The rent officer/NIHE determines a 'local reference rent' (para 10.46) if this is lower than your claim-related rent (para 10.41). It doesn't apply if you live in a hostel (para 7.27).

10.46   The local reference rent is a valuation of the mid-point of market rents (ignoring exceptionally high or low ones: see Heffernan (No 2) v the Rent Service for how these are determined) for an appropriate dwelling. If you live in one room, this means a dwelling in the same category as yours. The categories are:

(a)   one-room dwellings where your rent includes 'board and attendance' (meals plus some further service such as serving the meals);

(b)   other one-room dwellings where you share a kitchen, living room, bathroom and toilet with someone who is not a member of your household; and

(c)   other one-room dwellings.

In any other case, it means a dwelling of the size you qualify for (table 11.1), or of the same size as yours if this is smaller.

Single room rent determinations

10.47   The rent officer/NIHE determines a 'single room rent' (para 10.48) if this is lower than your claim-related rent (para 10.41) and:

(a)   you are a single claimant aged under 35;

(b)   you aren't in any of the excepted groups in para 9.20 (ignoring references there to a partner) – in broad terms these are seriously disabled people, care-leavers, ex-offenders and former occupiers of hostels for homeless people;

(c)   there are no other occupiers in your home (para 10.53); and

(d)   you don't qualify for an additional bedroom for any of the reasons in para 11.19.

It doesn't apply if you live in a hostel (para 7.27) or rent from a registered housing association (paras 7.13-15).

10.44   ROO 6(2), sch 1 para 3; NIHB 16(a), sch 2 para 3; NIHB66+ 16(a), sch 2 para 3

10.45   ROO 6(2), sch 1 para 4; NIHB 16(a), sch 2 para 4; NIHB66+ 16(a), sch 2 para 4

10.46   Heffernan (No 2) v the Rent Service [2009] EWHC (Admin) 3539 www.bailii.org/ew/cases/EWHC/Admin/2009/3539.html

10.47   ROO 6(2), sch 1 para 5; NIHB 16(a), sch 2 para 5; NIHB66+ 16(a), sch 2 para 5

10.48 The single room rent is a valuation of the mid-point of market rents (ignoring exceptionally high or low ones) for a dwelling that:

(a) has exclusive use of (only) one bedroom;

(b) has shared use of a kitchen, living room, bathroom and toilet;

(c) has no exclusive use of facilities for cooking or preparing food; and

(d) does not provide 'board and attendance'.

General rules about rent determinations

10.49 When making rent determinations (paras 10.42-48) the rent officer/NIHE:

(a) takes account of the range of rents payable on accommodation which is in the correct area, is in a reasonable state of repair, and is let on an assured tenancy (in Northern Ireland, an uncontrolled tenancy);

(b) excludes rents payable to housing associations and charities; and

(c) excludes the value of all ineligible service charges apart from meals (which are deducted by the council: see para 10.39).

10.50 Rent determinations (paras 10.42-48) are set using rental data from the appropriate area in which your dwelling is located which is:

(a) the 'broad rental market area' for local reference and single room rent determinations (paras 9.27-28);

(b) the 'area immediately surrounding the dwelling' (the 'vicinity') for significantly high and size-related rent determinations;

(c) 'a distinct area of residential accommodation' (the 'neighbourhood') for exceptionally high rent determinations;

(d) in Northern Ireland only, the 'locality' is used in place of all the above.

Service charge determinations

10.51 The rent officer/NIHE determines the value of any ineligible service charges included in your rent apart from meals (paras 8.69-70). Because these are already excluded from all rent determinations (para 10.49) this valuation is only needed when the authority uses the referred rent as your claim-related rent (see table 10.5, which also explains the rules about meals). The rent officer manual provides useful guidance [www] on how rent officers value service charges.

The size of accommodation you qualify for

10.52 You qualify for the appropriate number of rooms (bedrooms/living rooms) for the occupiers of your home: see para 10.53 and table 11.1.

10.49-50 ROO sch 1 paras 1-5,7,8; NIHB sch 2 paras 1-5,7,8; NIHB66+ sch 2 paras 1-5,7,8

10.51   ROO sch 1 paras 6(3),7; NIHB sch 2 paras 6(3),7; NIHB66+ sch 2 paras 6(3),7
          https://tinyurl.com/RO-handbook see section on ineligible charges

10.52   ROO 2(1), sch 2 paras 1,1A,2,3; NIHB 2(1), sch 2 para 10; NIHB66+ 2(1) sch 2 para 10

Which occupiers are taken into account

10.53   The size criteria for rent referral cases take account of the occupiers of your dwelling. This means:

(a)   you (the claimant) and members of your family (partner, children and young persons: para 4.2);

(b)   non-dependants (para 4.26);

(c)   lodgers (para 4.36);

(d)   joint tenants (para 4.42); and

(e)   any other person who occupies your dwelling as their home.

The authority, not the rent officer, decides which occupiers are included: R v Swale BC HBRB ex parte Marchant. For further details see paras 11.11.

10.53   R v Swale BC HBRB ex p Marchant 09/11/99 CA, 32 HLR 856
           https://tinyurl.com//Swale-Marchant

Chapter 11 **The size criteria**

- The size criteria and eligible rent: see paras 11.1-9.
- Which occupiers are included: see paras 11.10-16.
- How many bedrooms you qualify for: see paras 11.17-20.
- Details of who qualifies for additional bedrooms: see paras 11.21-41.
- What counts as a bedroom: see paras 11.42-44.

The size criteria and eligible rent

11.1   This chapter explains the rules about the HB size criteria. Opponents of the rules claim they are a 'bedroom tax'; supporters claim they prevent a 'spare room subsidy'. The rules are not always the same as those used in UC (see volume 1 chapter 7).

11.2   The size criteria for social renters and private renters are summarised in paras 11.3-8. They depend on how your eligible rent is assessed: whether as an ordinary social renter, a private renter under the local housing allowance rules, or either kind of renter if your claim has been referred to the rent officer. Footnotes for each of these are given separately. See also para 23.8 for discretionary housing payments if you are affected by the size criteria.

The social renter size criteria

11.3   The social renter size criteria apply if you are a social renter (para 8.2) and you have a pension age claim (table 2.2). For exceptions see table 8.1.

11.4   If you are a social renter with a pension age claim:

(a) you qualify for the number of bedrooms in table 11.1 (with no upper limit);

(b) your eligible rent is normally reduced if you have more bedrooms than this in your home (paras 8.9-16).

The LHA size criteria

11.5   The LHA size criteria apply if you are a private renter of any age (para 9.2) and you fall within the LHA rules (para 9.3). For exceptions, see table 9.1 and para 9.5.

11.6   When the LHA size criteria apply:

(a) you qualify for the number of bedrooms in table 11.1, but only up to a maximum of four bedrooms;

(b) if this is one bedroom, there are further rules about what category of accommodation you qualify for (para 9.18);

(c) your eligible rent is normally limited to the LHA figure for the size (or category) of accommodation you qualify for (paras 9.4-20).

11.4   HB B13(2)(b),(3),(5); NIHB B14(2)(b),(3),(5)

11.6   HB 13D(2),(3); HB66+ 13D(2),(3); NIHB 14D(2),(3); NIHB66+ 14D(2),(3)

The rent referral size criteria

11.7　　The rent referral size criteria apply to certain social and private renters: see table 10.3.

11.8　　When the rent referral rules apply:

(a) you qualify for the number of bedrooms (with no upper limit) and living rooms in table 11.1;

(b) if you live in one room, or are single and under 35, there are further rules about the category of accommodation you qualify for (paras 10.45-48);

(c) your eligible rent is normally limited to the rent officer's or NIHE's rent determination for the size (or category) of accommodation you qualify for (para 10.39 and table 10.5).

But different rules apply if you live in exempt accommodation or have an old (pre-1996) HB claim (paras 10.1-27).

The size criteria and unlawful discrimination

11.9　　The European Court of Human Rights has decided that the size criteria unlawfully discriminate against women living in sanctuary schemes (A v UK). The size criteria don't unlawfully discriminate against:

(a) claimants who have a disabled adult child living with them (JD v UK);

(b) separated parents with shared care of a child (R (Cotton and Others) v SSWP);

(c) gypsy travellers ([2019] UKUT 43 (AAC)).

Another case resulted in changes to the law so that the rules in paras 11.25-41 no longer discriminate between adults and children (R (Daly and Others) v SSWP).

Which occupiers are included

11.10　　The size criteria take account of the occupiers of your dwelling. This means:

(a) you (the claimant) and the members of your family (partner, children and young persons: paras 4.4 and 4.14);

(b) non-dependants (para 4.26);

(c) lodgers (para 4.36);

(d) joint tenants (para 11.16); and

(e) any other person who occupies your dwelling as their home – for example family members of people in (b)-(d), resident carers (para 4.33) and employees (para 4.50).

See paras 11.11-41 for further details and exceptions.

11.8　　ROO sch 1 para 2(1), sch 2 paras 1, 2; NIHB sch 2 paras 2(1), 10, 11; NIHB66+ sch 2 paras 2(1), 10, 11

11.9　　JD and A v United Kingdom [2019] ECHR 753, www.bailii.org/eu/cases/ECHR/2019/753.html
　　　　R (Cotton and Others) v SSWP [2014] EWHC Admin 3437, www.bailii.org/ew/cases/EWHC/Admin/2014/3437.html
　　　　R (Daly and Others) v SSWP [2016] UKSC 58, www.bailii.org/uk/cases/UKSC/2016/58.html

11.10　Social renter: HB B13(5); NIHB B14(5)
　　　　LHA: HB 13D(3),(12); HB66+ 13D(3),(12); NIHB 14D(3),(10); NIHB66+ 14D(3),(10)
　　　　Rent referral: ROO sch 2 para 1; NIHB sch 2 para 10; NIHB66+ sch 2 para 10

11.11 The council decides who is an occupier (not, for example, the rent officer: R v Swale BC HBRB ex p Marchant). In doing so it should have regard to the general HB rules about this (chapter 3); and even though some of the law was written to apply to claimants and partners, it should be adapted to apply to non-dependants (for example): [2010] UKUT 129 (AAC). A decision about which occupiers are included is appealable to a tribunal: [2010] UKUT 79 (AAC).

Children and young persons

11.12 The size criteria take into account children and young persons for whom you, your partner or someone else in your household is responsible (para 4.18), including those who are temporarily absent (para 4.24).

11.13 The following are not included:

(a) children and young persons who are foster children or are placed for adoption (table 4.2(a) and (b)) – but in these cases see paras 11.21-24;

(b) children and young persons who don't live with you, or don't normally live with you (table 4.2(c) and (e)).

Students and others gradually leaving home

11.14 When a student starts at a university and lives in a hall of residence, coming home frequently, it is correct to include them as an occupier of the parent's home: [2009] UKUT 67 (AAC), [2010] UKUT 129 (AAC). By perhaps the second year, especially if the student has taken on the rent of a flat or house, this is less likely to be the case. There is no fixed rule, each case depending on its facts.

Armed forces absences

11.15 If your or your partner's son, daughter, step-son or step-daughter is in the armed forces (regular or reserve), he or she continues to count as an occupier of your home during an absence on operations, so long as he or she:

(a) was a non-dependant (paras 4.26-32) before that absence (regardless of whether a non-dependant deduction then applied); and

(b) intends to return to reside in your dwelling when that absence ends.

11.11 R v Swale BC HBRB ex p Marchant 09/11/99 CA 32 HLR 856
http://tinyurl.com/Swale-Marchant

11.12-13 All: HB 2(1) definitions: 'child' etc; HB66+ 2(1); NIHB 2(1); NIHB66+ 2(1)
Social renter: HB B13(5)(ba)-(e); NIHB B14(5)(b)-(f)
LHA: HB 13D(3)(ba)-(e); HB66+ 13D(3)(ba)-(e); NIHB 14D(3)(ba)-(e); NIHB66+ 14D(3)(ba)-(e)
Rent referral: ROO sch 2 para 1(ba)-(e); NIHB sch 2 para 10(ba)-(e); NIHB66+ sch 2 para 10(ba)-(e)

11.15 All: HB 2(1) definition: 'member of armed forces away on operations'; HB66+ 2(1); NIHB 2(1); NIHB66+ 2(1)
Social renter: HB B13(8); NIHB B14(8)
LHA: HB 13D(12); HB66+ 13D(12); NIHB 14D(10); NIHB66+ 14D(10)
Rent referral: ROO sch 2 para 2(4); NIHB sch 3 para 2(4); NIHB66+ sch 3 para 2(4)

Joint tenants

11.16   The size criteria take into account the following joint tenants (paras 4.42-46):

(a) if the social renter or rent referral size criteria apply to you (paras 11.3-4, 11.7-8), all joint tenants;

(b) if LHA size criteria apply to you (paras 11.5-6), joint tenants who share your household but not joint tenants who maintain a separate household.

Table 11.1 **The HB size criteria**

The social renter, LHA and rent referral size criteria (paras 11.3-8) are based on the occupiers of your dwelling (paras 11.10-16).

Bedrooms (all size criteria)

You qualify for one bedroom for each of the following occupiers:

- each couple (para 4.5);
- each other person aged 16 or over;
- two children under 16 of the same sex;
- two children under 10 of the same or opposite sex;
- each other child under 16.

Additional bedrooms (all size criteria)

You may qualify for one or more additional bedrooms for the following occupiers:

- a foster parent or pre-adopter (paras 11.21-24);
- a person who requires an overnight carer (paras 11.25-33);
- a disabled person who can't share a bedroom (paras 11.34-41).

Living rooms (rent referral size criteria only)

When the social renter or LHA rules apply, living rooms are ignored. But when the rent referral rules apply, you qualify for living rooms as follows:

- one if there are one to three occupiers;
- two if there are four to six occupiers;
- three if there are seven or more occupiers.

This applies regardless of the age of the occupiers.

Notes:

- When the LHA rules apply, the maximum number of bedrooms you can qualify for (including additional bedrooms) is four.
- When the LHA or rent referral rules apply, there are further rules about one-bedroom accommodation (paras 9.18 and 10.46-48).

11.16   See footnote to para 11.10

T11.1   Social renter: HB B13(5)-(9); NIHB B14(5)-(9)
         LHA: HB 13D(2)-(3B),(12); HB66+ 13D(2)-(3B),(12); NIHB 14D(2)-(3B),(10); NIHB66+ 14D(2)-(3B),(10)
         Rent referral: ROO sch 2 paras 1, 1A, 1B, 2, 3; NIHB sch 2 paras 10, 10A, 10B, 11, 15; NIHB66+ sch 2 para 10, 10A, 10B, 11, 15

How many bedrooms you qualify for

General rules

11.17 The general rules about how many bedrooms you qualify for are given in table 11.1. They take account of all the occupiers in your dwelling (paras 11.10-16).

Sharing a bedroom

11.18 The only occupiers who can be counted as sharing a bedroom (table 11.1) are:

(a) couples (para 4.5) – and for the size criteria this appears to include (only) two members of a polygamous marriage (table 1.1);

(b) children (para 4.15) – and if children could share bedrooms in different ways, you qualify for the smaller number of bedrooms (example 2 and para 11.36);

but not young persons (para 4.16) or anyone else aged 16 or over. If a couple or a child can't share a bedroom, see paras 11.34-41.

Examples: bedrooms – general rules

1. A lone parent has two children: a boy aged 7 and a girl aged 12.

Three bedrooms are allowed: one for the lone parent, and one each for the children (because they are not counted as sharing a bedroom: table 11.1).

2. A couple have four children: girls aged 8 and 12 and boys aged 5 and 14.

Three bedrooms are allowed: one for the couple, one for the two girls and one for the two boys (because this is fewer than if the two younger children shared a bedroom and the two older children had a bedroom each: para 11.18).

3. A lone parent has two young persons: daughters aged 17 and 19.

Three bedrooms are allowed: one for the claimant, and one each for the young persons (table 11.1).

4. A single claimant has two non-dependants: sons aged 21 and 25.

Three bedrooms are allowed: one for the claimant, and one each for the non-dependants (table 11.1).

5. A couple have a child of their own, a foster child, and two non-dependants who are themselves a couple.

Under the general rules, three bedrooms are allowed: one for the couple, one for their own child, and one for the non-dependent couple. But an additional bedroom is allowed because they are foster parents (para 11.21).

11.17-18   All: HB 2(1) definitions: 'child', 'couple'; HB66+ 2(1); NIHB 2(1); NIHB66+ 2(1)
          Social renter: HB B13(5); NIHB B14(5)
          LHA: HB 13D(3); HB66+ 13D(3); NIHB 14D(3); NIHB66+ 14D(3)
          Rent referral: ROO sch 2 para 1; NIHB sch 2 para 10; NIHB66+ sch 2 para 10

Additional bedrooms: carers and disabled people

11.19   You may qualify for an additional bedroom for someone in your home who:

(a) is a foster parent, or has a child placed with them for adoption (paras 11.21-24); or

(b) requires overnight care from a non-resident carer (paras 11.25-33); or

(c) can't share a bedroom due to their disability (paras 11.34-41).

11.20   You could qualify for one or more additional bedrooms under each of para 11.19(a), (b) and (c). But if you are a private renter and fall under the LHA rules, the maximum number of bedrooms (under the general rules and these rules) is always four.

Foster parents and pre-adopters

11.21   You may qualify for one or more additional bedrooms if an occupier of your home:

(a) is a foster parent (in Scotland a kinship carer) who has a child or young person placed with them; or

(b) has been approved as a foster parent (kinship carer) and is waiting for a placement or between placements – but only for up to 52 weeks in each period without a placement; or

(c) has a child or young person placed with them prior to adoption.

We use 'foster parent or pre-adopter' to mean any of these.

11.22   This rule can only apply to you, your partner, or (for social renters only) a joint tenant or the partner of a joint tenant.

Social renters

11.23   If you are a social renter (chapter 8), you are allowed:

(a) one additional bedroom if you or your partner are a foster parent or pre-adopter; and/or

(b) one additional bedroom if a joint tenant or their partner is a foster parent or pre-adopter.

So you could qualify for one additional bedroom under (a), or one under (b), or both of these. And in each case only one is allowed even when someone has more than one child or young person placed with them.

Private renters

11.24   If you are a private renter (chapter 9 or 10), only the rule in para 11.23(a) applies. So you could qualify for one additional bedroom under (a), but not more.

11.21-24   All: HB 2(1) definition: 'qualifying parent or carer'; HB66+ 2(1); NIHB 2(1); NIHB66+ 2(1)
             Social renter: HB B13(6)(b),(7),(9); NIHB B14(6)(b),(7),(9)
             LHA: HB 13D(3A)(b),(3B); HB66+ 13D(3A)(b),(3B); NIHB 14D(3A)(b),(3B); NIHB66+ 14D(3A)(b),(3B)
             Rent referral: ROO sch 2 paras 1A(b), 1B, 3; NIHB sch 2 paras 10, 10A(b), 10B, 15; NIHB66+ sch 2 paras 10, 10A(b), 10B, 15

People who need overnight care

11.25 You may qualify for one or more additional bedrooms if an occupier of your home:

(a) requires overnight care (para 11.29); and

(b) has arrangements in place for this (paras 11.30-31); and

(c) has an actual bedroom in your dwelling (para 11.32) that is in addition to those allowed for anyone else.

You may also qualify if the person is waiting to move in or is temporarily absent (para 11.33).

11.26 This rule can apply to any occupier of your dwelling (para 11.10). For example, you, your partner, a child or young person, a non-dependant, a joint tenant, and so on. Unlike the rest of this chapter, this rule can also apply to a child or young person who is placed with you or your partner as a foster child or prior to adoption.

Social renters

11.27 If you are a social renter (chapter 8), you are allowed:

(a) one additional bedroom if any occupier of your dwelling requires overnight care; or

(b) two additional bedrooms – but only if:

- you have one or more joint tenants (para 4.42), and

- at least one joint tenant or their partner requires overnight care, and

- at least one other occupier (not a joint tenant or their partner) requires overnight care.

So you could qualify for one additional bedroom under (a), or two under (b), but not more.

Private renters

11.28 If you are a private renter (chapter 9 or 10), only the rule in para 11.27(a) applies. So you could qualify for one additional bedroom under (a), but not more.

The need for overnight care

11.29 An occupier of your dwelling 'requires overnight care' (para 11.25) if they:

(a) are in receipt of:

- the daily living component of PIP,

- the highest or middle rate of the care component of DLA,

- attendance allowance, or constant attendance allowance paid with an industrial injury pension, or

- an armed forces independence payment; or

(b) don't receive any of the above, but have sufficient evidence to show that they require overnight care.

11.25-28   All: HB 2(1) definition: 'person who requires overnight care'; HB66+ 2(1); NIHB 2(1); NIHB66+ 2(1)
  Social renter: HB B13(6)(a),(ab),(7),(9); HB66+ B13(6)(a),(ab),(7),(9); NIHB B13(6)(a),(ab),(7),(9); NIHB66+ B13(6)(a),(ab),(7),(9)
  LHA: HB 13D(3A)(a),(3B); HB66+ 13D(3A)(a),(3B); NIHB 14D(3A)(a),(3B); NIHB66+ 14D(3A)(a),(3B)
  Rent referral: ROO sch 2 paras 1A(a), 1B, 3; NIHB sch 2 paras 10, 10A(a), 10B, 15; NIHB66+ sch 2 paras 10, 10A(a), 10B, 15

11.29-30   HB 2(1) definitions: 'attendance allowance', 'person who requires overnight care'; HB66+ 2(1); NIHB 2(1); NIHB66+ 2(1)

For example, someone who gets the lower rate of the care component of disability living allowance doesn't meet (a), but could meet (b), and the fact of getting the lower rate can be used as evidence of this ([2014] UKUT 325 (AAC)). Or someone who hasn't claimed any of the benefits in (a) could meet (b).

The arrangements for overnight care

11.30   For an additional bedroom to be allowed (para 11.25), the person requiring overnight care (or someone on their behalf) must reasonably require, and have in fact arranged, that one or more people who don't occupy your dwelling as their home:

(a) are engaged in providing the overnight care;

(b) regularly stay overnight in your dwelling for that purpose (para 11.31); and

(c) are provided with an additional bedroom for that purpose (para 11.32).

11.31   The carer could be the same person on each night a carer is required, or there could be a rota of carers. It is not enough to require a carer only by day. The carer(s) must stay overnight regularly. 'Regularly' does not mean normally, ordinarily or at reasonably even intervals, but is closer to habitually, customarily or commonly; so the question is whether the need for overnight care 'arises steadily and often enough to require a bedroom to be kept for the purpose', and a minority of nights can be enough: [2014] UKUT 325 (AAC).

11.32   There must be an actual bedroom provided for the carer(s), and it must be additional to those used by you, your family and the other occupiers of your dwelling. In this context, the Upper Tribunal has held that a bedroom means a room which has a bed in or is used for sleeping in: [2014] UKUT 48 (AAC). In that case, the claimant rented a two bedroom bungalow. He qualified for one bedroom for himself and his wife (table 11.1), but on medical advice they slept apart – one in each bedroom. Their daughter was an overnight carer, and she slept in a portable bed or sofa in the lounge. This met the condition for an additional bedroom. For further considerations about what is a bedroom, see paras 11.42-44 and table 11.2.

Examples: People who require overnight care

Both examples apply whether you are a social or a private renter.

1. A couple have a child who requires overnight care

The child meets all the conditions (paras 11.29-32) and their home has three bedrooms which include the one where the child's overnight carer stays. Three bedrooms are allowed: one for the couple, one for the child, and one for the carer to use.

2. A joint tenant who requires overnight care

A brother and sister are joint tenants of a social landlord. The brother meets all the conditions (paras 11.29-32) and their home has three bedrooms, which include the one where his overnight carers stay. Three bedrooms are allowed: one each for the brother and sister and one for the carers to use. (This applies in each claim if they both claim see para 8.6.)

Overnight care: waiting to move in and temporary absence

11.33   An additional bedroom is also allowed if:

(a) the person requiring overnight care (paras 11.26-28) is waiting to move in or temporarily absent; and

(b) there is an additional bedroom now, and the other arrangements in para 11.30 will be in place when they move in or return.

'Waiting to move in' and 'temporarily absent' have the same meanings as in paras 3.5-12 (adapting these as described in para 11.11).

Disabled people who can't share a bedroom

11.34   You may qualify for one or more additional bedrooms if an occupier of your home who would normally be expected to share a bedroom can't do so because of a disability (paras 11.39-41).

11.35   This rule:

(a) can only apply to couples, and to children (aged under 16) – apart from a foster child or a child placed for adoption;

(b) can't apply to single people, or to young persons (aged 16 or over) – because they qualify for their own bedroom under the general rules (table 11.1).

The couple or child can be any of the occupiers of your dwelling (para 11.10). For example, you and your partner, a child of yours, a couple who are non-dependants, a child of a joint tenant and so on.

11.36   If there are two or more children (para 11.25) in your dwelling, first a bedroom is allowed for each child who can't share a bedroom, then a bedroom or bedrooms are allowed under the general rules (table 11.1) for the other child(ren).

Social renters

11.37   If you are a social renter (chapter 8), you are allowed:

(a) one additional bedroom for each couple who can't share a bedroom; and/or

(b) one additional bedroom for each child who can't share a bedroom.

So you could qualify for one or more additional bedrooms under (a) or (b), or both of these.

Private renters

11.38   If you are a private renter (chapter 9 or 10), the rules are the same as in para 11.37. But for each additional bedroom you are allowed, there must be an actual bedroom in your dwelling (paras 11.42-44) that is in addition to those allowed for anyone else.

11.34-38   All: HB 2(1) definitions: 'child who cannot share a bedroom', 'member of a couple who cannot share a bedroom', (6); HB66+ 2(1),(6); NIHB 2(1),(6); NIHB66+ 2(1),(6)
Social sector: HB B13(5)(za),(zb),(ba); NIHB B14(5)(za),(zb),(c);
LHA: HB 13D(3)(za),(zb),(ba); HB66+ 13D(3)(za),(zb),(ba); NIHB 14D(3)(za),(zb),(ba); NIHB66+ 14D(3)(za),(zb),(ba)
Rent referral: ROO sch 2 paras 1(za),(zb),(ba),3

Examples: Disabled people who can't share a bedroom

Both examples apply whether you are a social or a private renter.

1. A couple can't share a bedroom

The couple meets all the conditions (para 11.39) and their home has two bedrooms. Two bedrooms are allowed: one for each of them.

2. A lone parent has three children, one is disabled

Two of the children are twin girls aged 12, one of whom is disabled and meets all the conditions (para 11.40). The other child is a boy aged 14, and their home has four bedrooms. Four bedrooms are allowed: one for the lone parent, one for the disabled child, and two for the other children because they aren't expected to share (para 11.36 and table 11.1).

Couples who can't share a bedroom

11.39   A couple meet the conditions for an additional bedroom if one partner is (or both partners are):

(a) due to their disability, not reasonably able to share a bedroom with their partner; and

(b) in receipt of:

- the daily living component of PIP,
- the highest or middle rate of the care component of DLA, or
- the higher rate of attendance allowance, or
- armed forces independence payment.

Children who can't share a bedroom

11.40   A child (under the age of 16) meets the conditions for an additional bedroom if he or she is:

(a) due to disability, not reasonably able to share a bedroom with another child; and

(b) entitled to (para 12.31) the highest or middle rate of the care component of DLA.

11.41   DWP advice in relation to children is in circular HB A21/2013. This focuses on whether the child requires overnight care and advises authorities to 'keep in mind the policy intention which is to safeguard the wellbeing of children and prevent them being put at risk of physical harm or having their sleep frequently and significantly disrupted by… sharing a bedroom when it is inappropriate to do so because of severe disability' (HB A21/2013 paras 10-11).

11.39-40   HB 2(1) definitions: 'attendance allowance', 'child who cannot share a bedroom', 'member of a couple who cannot share a bedroom'; HB66+ 2(1); NIHB 2(1); NIHB66+ 2(1)

What counts as a bedroom

11.42   Whether a particular room in your home is or isn't a bedroom can be important when the council is deciding the following matters, or when you are appealing about them:

(a) for social renters, whether you have more actual bedrooms than you qualify for in your HB (para 8.12);

(b) for social and private renters, whether you have enough actual bedrooms to qualify for an additional bedroom in your HB (paras 11.32 and 11.38).

11.43   There is no definition in the HB regulations of what counts as a bedroom, but there have been a number of court and Upper Tribunal decisions about this. These are summarised in table 11.2.

11.44   The council is entitled to use its judgment in deciding whether a room is or is not a bedroom (para 20.23). Initially it is likely to base this decision on how your landlord has categorised the rooms in your home (circular HB/CTB A4/2012), but it is not bound by this and should consider each case on its individual details in the light of the case law.

Table 11.2 **What counts as a bedroom: case law**

Assessing the room. The Court of Session has held that whether a room is a bedroom is determined by 'an objective assessment of the property as vacant which is not related to the residents or what their actual use or needs might be' ([2017] CSIH 35). In the same way, the Court of Appeal has held that the assessment should be 'carried out… in respect of a nominally vacant house' and that 'the characteristics of the particular individuals are irrelevant' ([2019] EWCA Civ 1080).

The term 'bedroom'. The term 'bedroom' has its ordinary or familiar English meaning ([2014] UKUT 525 (AAC)). The landlord's designation of the room or its description in the building's plans can be of use in borderline cases rather than being conclusive ([2014] UKUT 525 (AAC); [2018] UKUT 180 (AAC)). And a room can stop counting as a bedroom if exceptional circumstances relating to physical or mental disability mean it is now used as a living room ([2015] UKUT 282 (AAC)).

The description of the room by the landlord or in the building's plans. The council can take account of the description of the room by the original or current landlord (for example in the letting agreement or marketing materials) or in the plans or designs for the building. But this is 'a starting point' and is not conclusive ([2014] UKUT 525 (AAC)).

Practical factors. Factors to be considered include '(a) size, configuration and overall dimensions, (b) access, (c) natural and electronic lighting, (d) ventilation, and (e) privacy', taking account of the adults and children referred to in the regulations (paras 7.8-16), and the relationship of the room to the other rooms in the house ([2014] UKUT 525 (AAC), [2018] UKUT 180 (AAC)). So long as the room is accessible, it is not a requirement that the door opens all the way ([2020] UKUT 247 (AAC)). It should be possible to get into bed from within the room, and there should be somewhere to put clothes and a glass of water, for example a bedside cabinet with drawers ([2016] UKUT 164 (AAC); [2017] UKUT 443 (AAC)).

Overcrowding and unfitness. The overcrowding rules differ from the size criteria, taking into account living rooms as well as bedrooms, but they can sound 'warning bells' that a room with very small dimensions may not be a bedroom ([2014] UKUT 525 (AAC); [2016] UKUT 164 (AAC); [2017] UKUT 443 (AAC)). A room contaminated with asbestos cannot be counted as a bedroom ([2018] UKUT 287 (AAC)).

Chapter 12 **Applicable amounts**

- ■ What is an applicable amount: see paras 12.1-3.
- ■ Personal allowances for you and your family: see paras 12.4-18.
- ■ Additional amounts for disability and caring: see paras 12.19-50.
- ■ General rules: see paras 12.51-55.

What is an applicable amount

12.1　　Your 'applicable amount' represents your basic living expenses. It is compared to your income when your HB is calculated (paras 6.4-6). It is also used to decide other HB matters, such as the earnings disregards (tables 14.5 and 14.7).

How much is your applicable amount?

12.2　　Your applicable amount is the total of:

(a) a personal allowance for you, or for you and your partner (paras 12.5-8);

(b) up to two (or sometimes more) personal allowances for children and young persons in your family (paras 12.9-18); and

(c) additional amounts if someone in your family or someone you provide care for is disabled or long-term sick (paras 12.19-50).

12.3　　In this chapter a 'single person' means a single claimant or lone parent. For these and other family terms see table 1.1.

Personal allowances

12.4　　This section explains which personal allowances are included in your applicable amount. The figures are in table 12.1.

Personal allowances for you/your partner

12.5　　You qualify for a personal allowance for yourself, or for you and your partner:

(a) if you are a single person you get the single rate;

(b) if you are a couple you get the couple rate;

(c) if you are a polygamous marriage you get the couple rate plus the polygamous spouse rate for each spouse beyond two.

These are awarded at one of the rates in paras 12.6-8.

12.2　　CBA 135; NICBA 131; HB 22(1)(a),(b),(d)-(f), sch 3; HB66+ 22(a),(b),(e), sch 3; NIHB 20(1)(a),(b),(d)-(f), sch 4; NIHB66+ 20(a),(b),(e), sch 4

12.5　　HB 22(1)(a), sch 3 para 1; HB66+ 22(1)(a), sch 3 para 1; NIHB 20(1)(a), sch 4 para 1; NIHB66+ 20(1)(a), sch 4 para 1

Table 12.1 **Weekly HB applicable amounts: 2021-22**

Personal allowances

Single person	new pension age rate	£177.20
	old pension age rate	£191.15
	working age rate	£74.70
	lower rate	£59.20
Couple	new pension age rate	£270.30
	old pension age rate	£286.05
	working age rate	£117.40
	lower rate	£89.45
Polygamous spouse	new pension age rate	£93.20
	old pension age rate	£94.90
	working age/lower rate	£42.70
Child or young person	usually up to two amounts	£68.60

Additional amounts: any age

Disabled child premium	each child/young person	£65.94
Enhanced disability premium (child)	each child/young person	£26.67
Family premium	old HB cases	£17.65
Severe disability premium	single rate	£67.30
	double rate	£134.60
Carer premium	Claimant/partner/each	£37.70

Additional amounts: working age only

Disability premium	single person	£35.10
	couple	£50.05
Enhanced disability premium (adult)	single person	£17.20
	couple	£24.60
Support component	single person/couple	£39.40
WRA component	single person/couple	£29.70

Note: Examples are later in this chapter.

T12.1　　HB sch 3 paras 1, 2, 20; HB66+ sch 3 paras 1, 2, 12; SI 2018/281; NIHB sch 4 paras 1, 2, 20; NIHB66+ sch 4 paras 1, 2, 12; NISR 2018/58

Pension age rate

12.6   There are two pension age rates depending on when you reached age 66:

(a) the new pension age rate applies if you are:

- a single person and reached 66 on or after 1st April 2021, or
- a couple (or polygamous marriage) and at least one of you reached 66 on or after that date;

(b) the old pension age rate applies if you are:

- a single person and reached 66 before 1st April 2021, or
- a couple (or polygamous marriage) and both (or all) of you reached 66 on or before that date.

Working age rate

12.7   The working age rate applies if you are:

(a) a single person and are aged under 66; or

(b) a couple (or polygamous marriage) and both (or all) of you are aged under 66.

Lower rate

12.8   The lower age rate only applies if you are:

(a) a single claimant under 25 or a lone parent under 18, and aren't on the main phase of ESA (para 12.48); or

(b) a couple (or polygamous marriage) and are both (or all) under 18, and you (the claimant) aren't on the main phase of ESA.

Personal allowances: children and young persons

12.9   You qualify for personal allowances for the children and young persons in your family, but in many cases there is a 'two child limit' (paras 12.10-18).

The two child limit

12.10   The two child limit applies to personal allowances for children/young persons, but not to premiums (paras 12.22-23). The Court of Appeal has ruled that it isn't unlawful discrimination (R(SC and Others) v SSWP [2019] EWCA Civ 615) [www].

How the two child limit works

12.11   If you have one child/young person in your family, you get a personal allowance for him or her. Or if you have two, you get personal allowances for each of them.

12.6   HB66+ sch 3 para 1(1)(b),(2)(b),(4); NIHB66+ sch 4 para 1(1)(b),(2)(b),(4)

12.7   HB sch 3 para 1(1)(a),(b),(2)(a),(b),(3)(a),(b); NIHB sch 4 para 1(1)(a),(b),(2)(a),(b),(3)(a),(b)

12.8   HB sch 3 para 1(1)(c),(2)(c),(3)(c); NIHB sch 4 para 1(1)(c),(2)(c),(3)(c)

12.9   HB 22(1)(b), sch 3 para 2(1); HB66+ 22(1)(b), sch 3 para 2(1); NIHB 20(1)(b), sch 4 para 2(1); NIHB66+ 20(1)(b), sch 4 para 2(1)

12.10-11   HB 22(1)(b); HB66+ 22(1)(b); NIHB 20(1)(b); NIHB66+ 20(1)(b) www.bailii.org/ew/cases/EWCA/Civ/2019/615.html

12.12   But if you have three or more, you only get two personal allowances for them unless you qualify for more because:

(a) you have claimed CTC (paras 12.13-16); or

(b) you get transitional protection (paras 12.17-18).

Exception if you have claimed child tax credit

12.13   This exception to the two child limit applies if:

(a) you have claimed CTC; and

(b) your CTC assessment included more than two children/young persons (para 12.15).

You don't have to be getting CTC. It is enough if you were assessed for it but weren't awarded it (e.g. because of the level of your income). The council can ask to see your CTC decision notice as evidence of this.

12.14   When this exception applies to you, you qualify for an HB personal allowance for each child/young person who is included in your CTC assessment.

12.15   Your CTC can include more than two children/young persons if one or more of them:

(a) is adopted or placed with you for adoption;

(b) receives non-parental care from you and:

- lives with you under formal arrangements made by social services or a court, or confirmed by you getting guardian's allowance for them, or

- lives with you under informal arrangements made by you and would otherwise be likely to enter local authority care, or

- was born to a child under 16 who is in your family; or

(c) is one of twins, triplets or a larger multiple birth; or

(d) was conceived because of rape or controlling or coercive behaviour; or

(e) was born before 6th April 2017 in Great Britain or 11th May 2017 in Northern Ireland.

12.16   HMRC decides – when it assesses your CTC – whether a child/young person meets the conditions in para 12.15. So, it can be necessary to claim CTC (even if you won't qualify for it because of your income) to get HB for more than two of them.

Exception if you haven't claimed CTC

12.17   This exception to the two child limit applies if:

(a) you were entitled to HB on 5th April 2017 in Great Britain or 10th May 2017 in Northern Ireland; and:

(b) you have one or more 'protected' children/young persons – this means anyone who:

- was included in your family then, and

- is included in your family now (regardless of absences in between); and

---

12.12   HB 22(2)-(4); HB66+ 22(5A)-(5C); SI 2017/376 reg 9; NIHB 20(2)-(4); NIHB66+ 20(3)-(5); NISR 2017/79 reg 8

12.13   HB 22(2),(3); HB66+ 22(5A),(5B); NIHB 20(2),(3); NIHB66+ 20(3),(4)

12.14   HB 22(3),(4); HB66+ 22(5B),(5C); SI 2017/376 reg 9; NIHB 20(2),(3); NIHB66+ 20(3),(4); NISR 2017/79 reg 8

12.15   The Child Tax Credit (Amendment) Regulations 2017 No. 387, reg 5 (includes Northern Ireland)

(c) you haven't made a new claim for HB since then (e.g. following a break in your entitlement or a move to a new local authority area); and

(d) you haven't claimed CTC (para 12.13).

12.18 When this exception applies to you, you qualify for a personal allowance for:

(a) each protected child/young person (para 12.17(b)) no matter how many this is; and

(b) either:

- one other child/young person (if you have just one protected one), or

- no other children/young persons (if you have two or more protected ones).

In some cases, you could be better off if you claim CTC (paras 12.13-16).

Additional amounts: any age

12.19 The additional amounts in this section (called premiums) are for disabled children and young persons, severely disabled adults and their carers, and certain old HB cases. If you meet their conditions they are included in your applicable amount.

12.20 You can get these additions whatever age you are (working age or pension age). If you are a couple (or polygamous marriage) you can get these whatever age you and your partner(s) are.

12.21 The figures are in table 12.1 and the details are in paras 12.22-33. Paras 12.51-55 give general rules about going into hospital, etc. If you are working age you may also qualify for the premiums and components in paras 12.37-50.

Disabled child premium

12.22 You qualify for this premium for each child or young person in your family who:

(a) receives PIP (either component at any rate); or

(b) receives DLA (either component at any rate); or

(c) receives armed forces independence payment (young persons only); or

(d) is severely sight impaired (para 12.54).

Enhanced disability premium (child)

12.23 You qualify for this premium for each child or young person who receives:

(a) the enhanced rate of the daily living component of PIP; or

(b) the highest rate of the care component of DLA; or

(c) armed forces independence payment (young persons only).

12.17   SI 2017/376, reg 9; NISR 2017/79, reg 8

12.18   SI 2017/376, reg 9(4)-(9); NISR 2017/79, reg 8(4)-(9)

12.19   HB 22(1)(d)-(f); HB66+ 22(1)(e); NIHB 20(1)(d)-(f); NIHB66+ 20(1)(e)

12.22   HB sch 3 paras 16, 20(9)(b); HB66+ sch 3 paras 8, 12(3); NIHB sch 4 paras 16, 20(9)(b); NIHB66+ sch 4 paras 8, 12(3)

12.23   HB sch 3 paras 15(1)(b)-(d) 20(9)(a); HB66+ sch 3 paras 7(1)(a)-(c), 12(2);
         NIHB sch 4 paras 15(1)(aa),(b),(c), 20(9)(a); NIHB66+ sch 4 paras 7(1)(a),(b), 12(2)

Examples: Applicable amounts

1. Pension age couple, no children

A couple in their 70s claim HB. They do not have any disabilities.

Personal allowance

- Couple, old pension age rate   £286.05

Total weekly applicable amount   £286.05

2. Working age single person, one child

A single person aged 30 claims HB on supported accommodation. She has one child aged three. Neither of them has any disabilities. The claimant gets carer's allowance for caring for her mother.

Personal allowances

- Single person, working age rate   £74.70
- One child   £68.60

Additional amount

- Carer premium   £37.70

Total weekly applicable amount   £181.00

3. Pension age single person, one disabled child

A single person who has just reached 66 claims HB. Her grandson aged eight lives with her, and he gets the mobility component of PIP.

Personal allowances

- Single person, new pension age rate   £177.10
- One child   £68.60

Additional amount

- Disabled child premium   £65.94

Total weekly applicable amount   £311.64

4. Working age couple, two children, one disabled

A couple in their 40s have been on HB for some time (para 2.8). They have two children aged 11 and 13. One child gets the enhanced rate of the daily living component of PIP.

Personal allowances

- Couple, working age rate   £117.40
- Two children   £137.20

Additional amounts

- Disabled child premium   £65.94
- Enhanced disability premium (child)   £26.67

Total weekly applicable amount   £347.21

Family premium

12.24   This premium has been abolished for new HB claims. You only qualify for it if:

(a) you were entitled to HB on 30th April 2016 in Great Britain or 4th September 2016 in Northern Ireland; and

(b) at least one child or young person has been included in your family since then (not necessarily the same one throughout); and

(c) you haven't made a new claim for HB since then (e.g. following a break in your entitlement or a move to a new local authority area).

Severe disability premium

12.25   You qualify for this premium if:

(a) you receive:

- the daily living component of PIP, or

- the middle or highest rate of the care component of DLA, or

- attendance allowance, or

- constant attendance allowance paid with an industrial injury or war disablement pension, or

- armed forces independence payment; and

(b) you have no non-dependants living with you (para 4.26) apart from non-dependants who receive any of the benefits in (a) or are severely sight impaired (para 12.54); and

(c) no-one receives carer's allowance or the carer element of UC for caring for you (para 12.28).

12.26   If you are a single person, you qualify for the single rate of this premium if you meet all three conditions (para 12.25).

12.27   If you are a couple you qualify for:

(a) the double rate if you both meet all three conditions (para 12.25);

(b) the single rate if:

- you (the claimant) meet all three conditions, and

- your partner is severely sight impaired (para 12.54); or

(b) the single rate if:

- one of you meets all three conditions, and

- the other meets only the first two conditions (para 12.25(a)-(b)).

12.24   HB 22(1)(c), sch 3 para 3; HB66+ 22(1)(c), sch 3 para 3;
NIHB 20(1)(c), sch 4 para 3; NIHB66+ 20(1)(c), sch 4 para 3; regs 2,4 of SI 2015/1857, regs 2, 4; NISR 2016/310, regs 3, 5

12.25   HB 2(1) definition: 'attendance allowance', sch 3 para 14(2); HB66+ 2(1), sch 3 para 6(2);
NIHB 2(1), sch 4 para 14(2); NIHB66+ 2(1), sch 4 para 6(2)

12.26   HB sch 3 paras 14(2)(a), 20(6)(a); HB66+ sch 3 paras 6(2)(a), 12(1)(a);
NIHB sch 4 paras 14(2)(a), 20(6)(a); NIHB66+ sch 4 paras 6(2)(a), 12(1)(a)

12.27   HB sch 3 paras 14(2)(b),(3),(4), 20(6)(b); HB66+ sch 3 paras 6(2)(b),(3),(6), 12(1)(b);
NIHB sch 4 paras 14(2)(b),(3),(4), 20(6)(b); NIHB66+ sch 4 paras 6(2)(b),(3),(6), 12(1)(b)

If you are in a polygamous marriage, you qualify for the double rate if you all meet all three conditions; or the single rate if you meet all three conditions and all your partners are severely sight impaired; or the single rate if all but one of you meet all three conditions and the other one meets only the first two conditions.

12.28   For the third condition of this premium (para 12.25(c)), your carer:

(a)   counts as getting carer's allowance or the UC carer element even if it stops when you have been in hospital for four weeks;

(b)   counts as getting carer's allowance even if it stops as a penalty for a benefit fraud conviction;

(c)   doesn't count as getting carer's allowance if it isn't paid because it is overlapped by another benefit;

(d)   doesn't count as getting carer's allowance or UC carer element in periods for which it is backdated. This means that your carer's arrears don't cause your HB to be overpaid.

Carer premium

12.29   You qualify for this premium if:

(a)   you receive carer's allowance; or

(b)   you are 'entitled to' (para 12.31) carer's allowance but it isn't paid because it is overlapped by another benefit or you are taking part in a government training scheme; or

(c)   you stopped being 'entitled to' carer's allowance (for any reason) within the past eight weeks.

12.30   If you are a single person, you get one carer premium if you qualify (para 12.29). If you are a couple (or polygamous marriage) you get a carer premium for each one of you who qualifies.

12.31   You are 'entitled to' a benefit (even if it isn't in payment) if you meet all the qualifying conditions (Insurance Officer v McCaffrey [1985]) and have made a claim for it (SSWP v Nelligan [2003]). The qualifying conditions for carer's allowance are:

(a)   you regularly and substantially care for someone for at least 35 hours per week; and

(b)   that person receives one of the benefits in para 12.25(a); and

(c)   you are not in full time employment or full-time education (both are defined differently to HB).

Once you have claimed a benefit you remain 'entitled to' it for as long as you continue to meet all the qualifying conditions. You don't have to make a further claim for carer's allowance to get the carer premium even if you claim HB later (CIS/367/2003).

12.28   HB sch 3 para 14(6),(7); HB66+ sch 3 para 6(8); NIHB sch 4 para 14(6),(7); NIHB66+ sch 4 para 6(8)

12.29   HB sch 3 paras 7(1),(2), 17(1),(2),(4); HB66+ sch 3 paras 5(1),(2), 9(1),(2),(4);
         NIHB sch 4 paras 7(1),(2), 17(1),(2),(4); NIHB66+ sch 4 paras 5(1),(2), 9(1),(2),(4)

12.30   HB sch 3 para 20(8); HB66+ sch 3 para 12(4); NIHB sch 4 para 20(8); NIHB66+ sch 4 para 12(4)

12.31   AA 1(1); NIAA 1(1); Insurance Officer v McCaffrey [1985]) 1 All ER (HL) 5
         www.bailii.org/ew/cases/EWCA/Civ/2003/555.html (paras 13-15)

Carer premium and severe disability premium

12.32   These premiums both include conditions relating to carer's allowance (paras 12.25 and 12.29). This means that usually either the carer gets the carer premium or the person cared for gets severe disability premium, but not both at the same time.

12.33   However, when carer's allowance is overlapped by another DWP benefit, the carer gets carer premium (para 12.29(b)) and the person cared for can get the severe disability premium at the same time (para 12.28(c)). And if a couple provide care for each other, it is possible for them to qualify for two carer premiums and a severe disability premium (at the single or double rate) at the same time.

Additional amounts: working age only

12.34   The additional amounts in this section are for adults who are disabled or long-term sick. If you meet their conditions they are included in your applicable amount.

12.35   You can only get these additions if you are working age (which means under 66). If you are a couple (or polygamous marriage) you can only get these if you (the claimant) are working age, but your partner(s) can be working age or pension age.

12.36   The figures are in table 12.1 and the details are in paras 12.37-50. Paras 12.51-55 give general rules about going into hospital, etc. You may also qualify for the additions in paras 12.22-33.

Disability premium

12.37   You qualify for the single rate of this premium if you are a single person and:

(a)   you are under 66 (para 2.4); and

(b)   you aren't on ESA or ESA credits (paras 12.45-46); and

(c)   you meet the disability condition (para 12.39).

12.38   You qualify for the couple rate if you are a couple (or polygamous marriage) and:

(a)   you (the claimant) are under 66; and

(b)   you (the claimant) aren't on ESA or ESA credits; and

(c)   either:

   ■   you meet the disability condition, or

   ■   your partner is also under 66 and they meet the disability condition.

12.33   HB sch 3 para 19; HB66+ sch 3 para 11; NIHB sch 4 para 19; NIHB66+ sch 4 para 11

12.37   HB sch 3 paras 12, 13(9); NIHB sch 4 paras 12, 13(9)

12.38   HB sch 3 para 20(5); NIHB sch 4 para 20(5)

12.39   You meet the disability condition (see paras 12.37-38) if:

(a) you receive:

■   PIP (either component at any rate),

■   DLA (either component at any rate),

■   the disability element or severe disability element of WTC,

■   attendance allowance,

■   constant attendance allowance paid with an industrial injury pension or war disablement pension,

■   armed forces independence payment, or

■   war pensioner's mobility supplement; or

(b) you are severely sight impaired (para 12.54); or

(c) you get DWP payments for car running costs or have an invalid vehicle supplied by the NHS.

The same applies to your partner if they are under 66.

Enhanced disability premium (adult)

12.40   You qualify for the single rate of this premium if you are a single person and:

(a) you are under 66 (para 2.4); and

(b) you receive:

■   the enhanced rate of the daily living component of PIP, or

■   the highest rate of the care component of DLA, or

■   armed forces independence payment, or

■   the support component of ESA or equivalent ESA credits (paras 12.45-49).

12.41   You qualify for the couple rate if you are a couple (or polygamous marriage) and:

(a) you (the claimant) are under 66; and

(b) either:

■   you receive one of the benefits in para 12.40(b), or

■   your partner is also under 66 and they receive one of the first three benefits in para 12.40(b) (it is not enough if your partner gets the support component of ESA or equivalent ESA credits).

12.39   HB 2(1) definition: 'attendance allowance', sch 3 para 13(1)(a)(i),(iv),(v); NIHB 2(1), sch 4 para 13(1)(a)(i),(iv),(v)

12.40   HB sch 3 paras 15(1)(a)-(d), 20(9)(b); NIHB sch 4 paras 15(1)(a),(aa),(b),(c), 20(9)(b)

12.41   HB sch 3 paras 15(1)(b)-(d), 20(9)(c); NIHB sch 4 paras 15(1)(aa),(b),(c), 20(9)(c)

Support component and WRA component

12.42   These components occur in both HB and ESA, and the general rule is that people who get a component in their ESA get the same component in their HB. For most older claims you can get either component (but not both), but for new claims you can only get the support component. Paras 12.43-44 explain the HB rules and paras 12.45-49 give the ESA background.

12.43   If you are a single person you qualify for a component in your HB if:

(a) you are under 66 (para 2.4); and

(b) you are entitled to a component in your ESA or ESA credits (paras 12.45-49).

You get the same component in your HB as you get in your ESA.

12.44   If you are a couple (or polygamous marriage) you qualify for a component in your HB if:

(a) you (the claimant) are under 66; and

(b) at least one of you is entitled to a component in your ESA or ESA credits.

If only one of you gets an ESA component, you get the same component in your HB. If each of you gets an ESA component, you get the same component in your HB as you (the claimant) get in your ESA (even if this is the lower of them).

ESA and ESA credits

12.45   There two types of ESA: ESA(IR) has been replaced for new claims by UC, but ESA(C) continues alongside UC (and is also known as new-style ESA). Paras 12.46-49 apply to both of these.

12.46   ESA credits are national insurance credits that you get instead of ESA when you don't meet the contribution conditions or when your ESA(C) has been ended because you have been getting it for a year. For HB applicable amounts, ESA credits are treated as though they were ESA.

ESA phases and components

12.47   The ESA 'assessment phase' runs for the first 13 weeks of your ESA claim. You get your ESA personal allowance(s), and the DWP assesses whether you are in:

(a) the 'support group' which is for people who have both limited capability for work and limited capability for work-related activity; or

(b) the 'work-related activity group' (WRA group) which is for people who have limited capability for work but can carry out work-related activity.

12.42   HB sch 3 paras 21, 24, 26; SI 2017/204, sch 1 para 6(7), sch 2 paras 1-7; NIHB sch 4 paras 21, 24, 26;
         NISR 2017/51, sch 1 para 6(7), sch 2 paras 1-7

12.43   HB sch 3 paras 21, 21A, 24, 26; NIHB sch 4 paras 21, 21A, 24, 26

12.44   HB sch 3 paras 21, 21A, 22(2), 24, 26; NIHB sch 4 paras 21, 21A, 22(2), 24, 26

12.46   HB sch 3 paras 1A, 21(2), 21A; NIHB sch 4 paras 1A, 21(2), 21A

12.48   The ESA 'main phase' runs from week 14 of your ESA claim onwards. You continue to get your ESA personal allowance(s), and:

  (a) if you are in the support group, you get an ESA support component; but

  (b) if you are in the WRA group, you can usually only get an ESA WRA component if your ESA claim began before 3rd April 2017 or is linked to an ESA award which began before that date (para 12.49).

ESA linking rules

12.49   Your ESA is 'linked' to a previous ESA award if the gap between them is no more than 12 weeks. In this case your ESA assessment period starts on the first day of your previous award, so some or all of the 13 weeks of the ESA assessment phase (para 12.47) have already been completed in your current ESA claim.

Transitional addition if you transferred onto ESA

12.50   You qualify for a transitional addition if your disability premium stopped because you started getting a component (paras 12.42-44) when you transferred from long-term IB, SDA or incapacity credits (under the old fitness for work test) onto ESA/ESA credits. Your transitional addition is the difference between your old and new applicable amount at the time you transferred. After that any increase in your HB applicable amount (due to the annual uprating or a change in your circumstances) is deducted from your transitional addition until:

  (a) it reduces to nil; or

  (b) if earlier, when your ESA(C) or HB ends – unless you start back on HB within 12 weeks in which case it is restored.

General rules

Going into hospital

12.51   If you or a member of your family goes into hospital, you continue to qualify for your personal allowances. In most cases you also continue to qualify for your premiums (table 12.2), and your components continue as long as they do in your ESA.

12.52   But your HB ends if you (the claimant) are likely to be in hospital for more than 52 weeks (paras 3.6-12 and table 3.1). Or if a member of your family is likely to be in hospital for more than 52 weeks, that person stops being included in your applicable amount so your HB reduces (para 4.25).

12.48(b) SI 2017/204, sch 1 para 6(7), sch 2 paras 1-7; NISR 2017/51, sch 1 para 6(7), sch 2 paras 1-7

12.49   SI 2008/794, reg 145; NISR 2008/280, reg 145

12.50   HB sch 3 paras 27, 28, 30; NIHB sch 4 paras 27, 28, 30

12.52   HB 21(1),(2); HB66+ 21(1),(2); HB 19(1),(2); HB66+ 19(1),(2)

Table 12.2 **Premiums after a period in hospital**

How PIP and DLA affect HB

(a) If you or your partner go into hospital, PIP/DLA stop after four weeks. If this is the only reason they stop:

- disability premium continues;
- enhanced disability premium (adult) continues;
- severe disability premium ends if you are a single person, but continues at the single rate if you are a couple (or polygamous marriage) and were previously getting the couple rate.

(b) If a young person aged 18 or over goes into hospital, PIP/DLA stop after four weeks. If this is the only reason they stop:

- disabled child premium continues;
- enhanced disability premium (child) continues.

They also continue if a child or young person under 18 goes into hospital, because in their case PIP/DLA don't stop.

How carer's allowance affects HB

(c) If you or your partner go into hospital, carer's allowance stops after 12 weeks. If this is the only reason it stops:

- carer premium continues for a further eight weeks (making 20 weeks in total).

(d) If the person you or your partner care for goes into hospital, PIP/DLA stop after four weeks. If this is the only reason they stop:

- carer premium continues for a further eight weeks (making 12 weeks in total).

Note:

The four weeks in (a) and (d) don't have to be continuous but can be made up of two or more periods which are less than 29 days apart.

T12.2(a) HB sch 3 paras 13(1)(a)(iii),(iiia), 14(5), 15(1)(b),(c),(2), 20(6)(b); HB66+ sch 3 para 6(7);
NIHB sch 4 paras 13(1)(a)(iii),(iiia), 14(5), 15(1)(b),(c),(2), 20(6)(b); NIHB66+ sch 4 para 6(7)

T12.2(b) HB sch 3 paras 15(1)(b),(c), 16(a),(d); HB66+ sch 3 paras 7(1)(a),(b), 8(a),(d);
NIHB sch 4 paras 15(1)(b),(c), 16(a),(d); NIHB66+ sch 4 paras 7(1)(a),(b), 8(a),(d)

T12.2(c) HB sch 3 para 17(2)(b),(4)(b); HB66+ sch 3 para 9(2)(b); NIHB sch 4 para 17(2)(b),(4)(b); NIHB66+ sch 4 para 9(2)(b)

A death in your family

12.53   If a child or young person dies who met the conditions for a disabled child premium or enhanced disability premium (child), these continue for eight weeks after their death. Apart from that, if any member of your family dies your applicable amount changes to take account of your new circumstances; or if you (the claimant) die your HB stops (para 17.35).

Severely sight impaired

12.54   For all HB purposes you count as 'severely sight impaired' if:

(a) a consultant ophthalmologist has certified you as 'severely sight impaired' or 'blind'; or

(b) you have regained your sight and (a) stopped applying to you within the past 28 weeks following the date on which you stopped being certified.

DWP concessionary payments

12.55   For the premiums in this chapter, a DWP concessionary payment compensating for non-payment of a DWP benefit counts as if it was that benefit.

12.53   HB sch 3 paras 15(1A), 16(c); HB66+ sch 3 paras 7(2), 8(c); NIHB sch 4 paras 15(1A), 16(c); NIHB66+ sch 4 paras 7(2), 8(c)

12.54   HB sch 3 para 13(1)(a)(v),(2); HB66+ sch 3 para 6(4),(5); NIHB sch 4 para 13(1)(a)(v),(2); NIHB66+ sch 4 para 6(4),(5)

12.55   HB sch 3 para 18; HB66+ sch 3 para 10; NIHB sch 4 para 18; NIHB66+ sch 4 para 10

Chapter 13 **Income**

- General rules about assessing income: see paras 13.1-8.
- State benefits, pensions and payments: see paras 13.9-22.
- Council benefits and payments: see paras 13.23-25.
- Private pensions, maintenance, rent, student income, etc: see paras 13.26-44.
- Additional rules about income disregards: see paras 13.45-49.
- Notional income: see paras 13.50-61.

Assessing income

13.1 This chapter and chapter 14 explain how your income is assessed for HB purposes, including:

(a) unearned income (paras 13.9-44);

(b) earned income (chapter 14);

(c) notional income (paras 13.50-61); and

(d) assumed income from your capital (para 15.5).

This section gives rules relating to all types of income.

'Your' income

13.2 If you are single, your own income is taken into account. If you are in a couple, the income of your partner is taken into account as well as yours. If you are in a polygamous marriage, the income of all your partners is included. In this chapter and chapter 14, 'your' income always includes the income of your partner (or partners). But if a child or young person in your family has income of their own, this is never included and nor is the income of a non-dependant (but see para 13.61).

How your income affects your HB

13.3 If you are on a passport benefit (see para 13.5), all your income is disregarded (ignored) and you qualify for maximum HB: para 6.2-3.

13.4 If you are not on a passport benefit, some kinds of income are counted and some are wholly or partly disregarded. The details are in this chapter and chapter 14. The more income you have (apart from disregarded income) above your applicable amount, the less HB you qualify for: para 6.4-6.

13.1   HB 27(1)(a),(b),(4); HB66+ 25, 29(1),(2); NIHB 24(1)(a),(b),(4); NIHB66+ 23, 27(1),(2)

13.2   CBA 136(1); HB 25; HB66+ 23; NICBA 132(1); NIHB 22; NIHB66+ 21

13.3   CBA 130(1)(c)(i),(3)(a); HB sch 4 para 12, sch 5 paras 4,5; HB66+ 26; NICBA 129(1)(c)(i),(3)(a); NIHB sch 5 para 12, sch 6 paras 4,5; NIHB66+ 24

13.4   CBA 130(1)(c),(3); HB 36(2), 38(2), 40(2), sch 4, sch 5; HB66+ 33(8),(9), sch 4, sch 5; NICBA 129(1)(c),(3); NIHB 33(2), 35(2), 37(2), sch 5, sch 6; NIHB66+ 31(8),(9), sch 5, sch 6

The passport benefits

13.5   The passport benefits are:

(a) the guarantee credit of SPC;

(b) universal credit in supported or temporary accommodation (table 2.3);

(c) income-based JSA;

(d) income-related ESA; and

(e) income support.

Current income

13.6   Your current income is taken into account for the period it covers (apart from the amounts which are disregarded). In the case of a state benefit this means the period for which it is payable.

Arrears of income

13.7   The rules in para 13.6 also apply to arrears of income. So income paid for a past period counts as income in that past period (apart from the amounts which are disregarded). Para 15.13 explains when arrears of income turn into capital.

Weekly income

13.8   HB is a weekly benefit, so your income is assessed as a weekly figure. The law says this is done by accurately calculating or estimating the likely amount of your average weekly income. In practice this means:

(a) the actual weekly amount if your income is paid weekly; or

(b) the weekly equivalent if your income is paid on a non-weekly basis (see para 6.37).

In working age HB, unearned income must not be averaged over a period longer than 52 weeks. In pension age HB claims, it is not in practice averaged over a period longer than one year. For earned income see paras 14.8-10 and 14.29-31.

Examples: Assessing income

1. A working age HB claim

Geoff and Julia are on HB and have two children at school. Geoff works full time and his net earnings (after disregards) are £286 pw. Julia receives child maintenance from the children's father, child benefit, and child tax credit of £110 pw. They have £3,000 in a savings account.

13.5   HB sch 4 para 12, sch 5 paras 4,5, sch 6 paras 5,6; HB66+ 26; NIHB sch 5 para 12, sch 6 paras 4,5, sch 7 paras 5,6; NIHB66+ 24

13.6   HB 27(1), 31(1),(2); HB66+ 30(1), 33(1),(6); NIHB 24(1), 28(1),(2); NIHB66+ 28(1), 31(1),(6)

13.7   HB 27(1), 31(1),(2); HB66+ 30(1), 33(1),(6); NIHB 24(1), 28(1),(2); NIHB66+ 28(1), 31(1),(6)

13.8   CBA 136(4); HB 27(1), 29-31; HB66+ 30(1), 33(1); NICBA 132(3); NIHB 24(1), 26-28; NIHB66+ 28(1), 31(1)

Their income is assessed as follows:

- the child benefit and the child maintenance are disregarded (tables 13.1 and 13.6)
- the child tax credit is counted as income (para 13.12)   £110 pw
- the earnings are counted (chapter 14)   £286 pw
- they do not have assumed income from their capital (para 15.5)

So their total income for HB purposes is   £396 pw

2. A pension age HB claim

Jacqui is on HB and receives a state pension, a private pension, and a war widow's pension. She has £12,000 in a savings account.

Her income is assessed as follows:

- her council runs a local scheme which disregards the whole of the war widow's pension (paras 13.16-18)
- the state pension and the private pension are counted as her income (paras 13.13 and 13.27): they work out as   £170.95 pw
- she has assumed income from her capital (para 15.5) of   £4.00 pw

So her total income for HB purposes is   £174.95 pw

State benefits, pensions and payments

13.9 Table 13.1 lists which state benefits, pensions and other payments are disregarded. Table 13.2 lists the ones which are taken into account, and summarises the other rules which apply.

Table 13.1 **Disregarded state benefits, pension, etc**

Income from all the following is wholly disregarded. For the 'passport benefits' (a)-(c) see also para 13.3.

- (a) the guarantee credit of SPC
- (b) universal credit
- (c) JSA(IB), ESA(IR) and IS
- (d) disability living allowance (DLA)
- (e) personal independence payment (PIP)
- (f) attendance allowance and equivalent benefits (para 13.10)

T13.1   HB 40(2), sch 5; HB66+ 29(1), 33(9), sch 5; NIHB 37(2), sch 6; NIHB66+ 27(1), 31(9), sch 6

T13.1(a)-(c) HB sch 5 para 4; HB66+ 26, 29(1)(j)(zi); NIHB sch 6 para 4; NIHB66+ 24, 27(1)(h)(zi)

T13.1(d)-(e) HB sch 5 para 6; HB66+ 29(1)(j)(i),(ia); NIHB sch 6 para 7; NIHB66+ 27(1)(h)(i)

T13.1(f)   HB 2(1) definition: 'attendance allowance', sch 5 para 9; HB66+ 2(1), 29(1)(j) (ii)-(v); NIHB 2(1), sch 6 para 10; NIHB66+ 2(1), 27(1)(h) (ii)-(iv)

(g) bereavement support payments other than the initial lump sum (para 15.51)

(h) child tax credit (CTC) in pension age HB (para 13.12)

(i) child benefit

(j) guardian's allowance

(k) Christmas bonus

(l) social fund payments and local welfare assistance

(m) in Northern Ireland, welfare supplementary payments (23.20)

(n) carer's allowance supplement, Scottish child payment, early years assistance, short-term assistance and funeral expense assistance (all paid by Social Security Scotland)

(o) government and related payments to disabled people to help with obtaining or retaining work (for example by buying special equipment)

(p) payments from government work programme training schemes. There are rare exceptions in working age claims (see GM paras BW 2.597-611), but even in these cases expenses for travel etc are always disregarded

(q) payments compensating for non-payment of:

- ▪ (a) to (f) in working age HB
- ▪ all the above in pension age HB.

Note: Payments (l) to (p) and in most cases (q) are also disregarded as capital. See paras 15.50-52 for details about this and about arrears of benefits.

Table 13.2 **Counted state benefits, pensions etc**

Income from the following is counted in full.

(a) contribution-based JSA (JSA(C)) (para 13.11)

(b) contributory ESA (ESA(C)) (para 13.11)

(c) working tax credit (WTC) (para 13.12)

(d) child tax credit (CTC) in working age HB (para 13.12)

T13.1(g)   HB sch 5 para 67; HB66+ 29(1)(j)(xiii); NIHB sch 6 para 65; NIHB66+ 27(1)(h)(xi)

T13.1(h)   HB66+ 29(1); NIHB66+ 27(1)

T13.1(i),(j) HB sch 5 paras 50, 65; HB66+ 29(1)(j)(vi),(viii); NIHB sch 6 paras 52, 64; NIHB66+ 27(1)(h)(v),(vi)

T13.1(k)   HB sch 5 para 32; HB66+ 29(1)(j)(x); NIHB sch 6 para 33; NIHB66+ 27(1)(h)(ix)

T13.1(l)   HB sch 5 paras 31,31A; sch 6 paras 20,20A; HB66+ 29(1)(j)(ix); NIHB sch 6 para 32, sch 7 para 21; NIHB66+ 27(1)(h)(viii)

T13.1(m)   NISR 2016/178 reg 12; NISR 2017/35 reg 14

T13.1(n)   HB sch 5 paras 68-72; HB66+ 29(1)(b)(xviib)-(viih); NIHB sch 6 paras 66-68; NIHB66+ 27(1)(h)(xva)-(xvd)

T13.1(o)   HB sch 5 para 49, sch 6 paras 43,44; HB66+ 29(1); NIHB sch 6 para 51, sch 7 para 44; NIHB66+ 27(1)

T13.1(p)   HB 2(1) definitions, sch 5 paras A2-A5,13,58,60,61; HB66+ 29(1); NIHB 2(1), sch 6 paras 13,15,60; NIHB66+ 27(1)

T13.1(q)   HB 2(1) definition: 'concessionary payment', sch 5 para 7; HB66+ 2(1), 29(1)(u); NIHB 2(1), sch 6 para 8; NIHB66+ 2(1), 27(1)(s)

(e) state retirement pension (para 13.13)

(f) the savings credit of SPC (para 13.14)

(g) carer's allowance (but in Scotland see T13.1(g))

(h) maternity allowance

(i) severe disablement allowance (SDA)

(j) widow's pension

(k) industrial death benefit

The following have individual rules.

(l) widowed mother's allowance and widowed parent's allowance: disregard £15 per week and count the rest as income (for deaths occurring before 6th April 2017)

(m) industrial injuries disablement benefit: disregard any increase for attendance and count the rest as income

(n) war pensions: see paras 13.16-18

(o) increases in benefits for dependants: see para 13.20

(p) reductions in benefits: see para 13.21

(q) statutory sick, maternity, paternity and adoption pay: count as earned income (see table 14.1(c) and paras 14.15-16)

Note: See table 15.2 for arrears of payments (c), (d) and (f).

Benefits equivalent to attendance allowance

13.10 The following benefits are equivalent to attendance allowance:

(a) increases in industrial injuries benefit for constant attendance or exceptionally severe disablement;

(b) increases in a war disablement pension for attendance, constant attendance or exceptionally severe disablement;

(c) an armed forces independence payment;

(d) payments for attendance under the Personal Injuries (Civilians) scheme; or

(e) adult disability payment and child disability payment in Scotland.

JSA(C) and ESA(C)

13.11 Contribution-based JSA and contributory ESA are counted in full as your income: see para 13.22 if payments are reduced due to sanctions. They are also called 'new style' JSA/ESA or just JSA and ESA.

T13.2(a)-(k) HB 31(1),(3), 40(1); HB66+ 29(1)(b),(c),(j); NIHB 28(1),(3), 37(1); NIHB66+ 27(1)(b),(c),(h)

T13.2(l) HB sch 5 para 16; HB66+ sch 5 paras 7,8; NIHB sch 6 para 17; NIHB66+ sch 6 paras 8,9

T13.2(m) HB 2(1) definition: 'attendance allowance', sch 5 para 9; HB66+ 2(1), 29(1)(j)(iii),(n); sch 5 para 2; NIHB 2(1), sch 6 para 10; NIHB66+ 2(1), 27(1)(h)(iii),(l), sch 6 para 3

13.11 HB 31(1),(2), 40(1); HB66+ 29(1)(j), 33(6); NIHB 28(1),(2), 37(1); NIHB66+ 27(1)(h), 31(6)

WTC and CTC

13.12   Working tax credit is counted in full as your income (in working age and pension age HB). Child tax credit is counted in full as your income in working age HB, but is wholly disregarded in pension age HB. In some uncommon cases, part of the earned income disregards can be deducted from your WTC or CTC: see para 14.61(c) and (d). For the £500 lump sum paid by HMRC in 2021-22 due to coronavirus see para 15.51.

State retirement pension

13.13   State retirement pension is counted in full as your income. If you defer your state pension:

(a) it is not included as your income until you begin receiving it. Any increase you receive (because you deferred it) is then included;

(b) any lump sum you receive (because you deferred your state pension) is disregarded as your capital until your state pension begins.

Savings credit

13.14   The savings credit of state pension credit (SPC) is counted in full as your income. But if you are also on the guarantee credit of SPC, see para 13.3.

Table 13.3 **People on savings credit: adjusting the DWP's figures**

If you are on savings credit, the following adjustments are made whenever the DWP tells the council your income and capital (para 13.15).

Your income

The DWP tells the council:

- the amount of your savings credit; and

- your 'assessed income figure' (AIF). This is the DWP's assessment of your income (apart from savings credit).

The council adds these together, and then deducts the following amounts:

If you receive:	The amount is:
(a) maintenance from a current or former husband, wife or civil partner	the full HB disregard (table 13.6)
(b) a war disablement or bereavement pension	any amount disregarded under a local scheme (in other words, any amount over £10: para 13.18)

13.12   HB 31(1), 32, 40(1),(6),46(9),49(2)(f),(g); HB66+ 29(1)(b),(5), 32; NIHB 28(1), 29, 37(1),(4),43(8),46(2)(f),(g); NIHB66+ 27(1)(b),(5), 30

13.13   HB66+ sch 6 para 26A as implied by CPR 2; SI 2005/2677 regs 11,12; NIHB66+ sch 7 para 28

13.14   HB 31(1),(2), 40(1); HB66+ 27(4)(a), 33(6); NIHB 28(1),(2), 37(1); NIHB66+ 25(4)(a), 31(6)

T13.3   HB66+ 27(3)-(8); NIHB66+ 25(3)-(8)

(c)	earned income and you are a lone parent	£5
(d)	earned income from 'permitted work'	£143 or £20 (as shown in table 14.5)
(e)	earned income and you qualify for the HB child care disregard	the full HB disregard (para 14.63)
(f)	earned income and you qualify for the HB additional earnings disregard	£17.10 (para 14.68)

If you have a partner who was excluded from your savings credit claim but is included in your HB claim, the council assesses their income and adds it.

Your capital

The DWP tells the council the amount of your capital. The council changes this only if your capital increases to more than £16,000, in which case your HB stops.

Other rules if you are on savings credit

13.15	The following rules apply if you are on savings credit (but not guarantee credit):

(a)	the DWP assesses your income and capital as part of your savings credit claim;

(b)	the DWP tells the council these income and capital figures (when you first claim HB or savings credit, and then whenever your circumstances change);

(c)	the council adjusts these figures as shown in table 13.3;

(d)	the council uses the adjusted figures to calculate your HB.

War disablement and bereavement pensions

13.16	Table 13.4 gives the rules for assessing income from:

(a)	pensions under the Armed Forces Pensions and Compensation schemes (and similar payments) for:

- war disablement;
- war widows;
- war widowers; and
- war bereaved civil partners;

(b)	payments compensating for non-payment of the above;

(c)	equivalent payments from governments outside the UK; and

(d)	pensions paid by any (non-UK) government to the victims of Nazi persecution.

The payments in (a) include both 'service attributable pensions' for service before 5th April 2005 and 'guaranteed income payments' for service on or after that date.

13.17	War pensions not included in para 13.16 are assessed in the same way as private pensions: see para 13.27.

13.15	HB66+ 27(1)-(3); NIHB66+ 25(1)-(3)

13.16	HB sch 5 para 15; HB66+ 29(1)(e)-(h),(l)-(m), sch 5 para 1; NIHB sch 6 para 15; NIHB66+ 27(1)(e)-(f),(j)-(k), sch 6 para 1

Local schemes for war disablement and bereavement pensions

13.18   Councils in Great Britain can run a 'local scheme' to disregard more than £10 per week of the war disablement and bereavement pensions in para 13.16 (apart from those which are always wholly disregarded: see table 13.4).

13.19   Most councils do this, and some disregard the whole amount. The government pays councils up to 75% of the cost of running a local scheme (see para 21.4), but decisions about local schemes are not appealable to a tribunal (see table 20.4).

Table 13.4 **War disablement and bereavement pensions**

This table applies to the pensions etc in para 13.16.

Assessment in Great Britain

   (a)   Disregard the whole amount of:

   ■   'pre-1973' special payments to war widows, war widowers and war bereaved civil partners (currently £98.44 per week: HB circular A2/2021);

   ■   a mobility supplement paid with any war disablement or bereavement pension; and

   ■   an increase for constant attendance paid with any war disablement pension (including war injured civilians) or an Armed Forces independence payment.

   (b)   Disregard £10 per week from the total of any other war disablement or bereavement pension. But see paras 13.18-19 (local schemes).

Assessment in Northern Ireland

   (c)   Disregard the whole amount of all war disablement and bereavement pensions.

Increases in benefits for dependants

13.20   The following applies if you receive an increase for a dependant in any of the state benefits which count as income (table 13.2):

   (a)   if the increase is for your partner, it is included as your income;

   (b)   if the increase is for a child or young person in your family, it is included as your income in working age HB, but disregarded in pension age HB;

   (c)   if the increase is for someone not in your family, it is disregarded.

13.18   AA 134(8)-(10); SI 2007 No. 1619

T13.4   HB 2(1) definitions: 'attendance allowance', 'guaranteed income payment', 'war pension' etc, 27(1)(a), 31(1), 40(1), sch 5 paras 8,9,15,53-55; HB66+ 2(1), 29(1)(e)-(h),(l),(m), 30(1)(a), sch 5 paras 1-6; NIHB 2(1), 24(1)(a), 28(1), 37(1), sch 6 paras 9,10,15,55-57; NIHB66+ 2(1), 27(1)(f),(j),(k), 28(1)(a), sch 6 paras 1-7

13.20   HB 27(1)(a), 40(1), sch 5 para 52; HB66+ 29(1)(j)(viii), 30(1)(a), sch 5 para 13; NIHB 24(1)(a), 37(1), sch 6 para 54; NIHB66+ 27(1)(h)(vii), 28(1)(a), sch 6 para 14

Reductions in benefits

13.21   If you receive a reduced amount of any of the state benefits which count as income (see table 13.2) only the reduced amount is counted as your income if the reduction is:

(a)   because of the rules about overlapping state benefits;

(b)   because your WTC or CTC is reduced to recover an earlier year's overpayment;

(c)   because your incapacity benefit is reduced when you have an occupational pension (CH/51/2008); or

(d)   in pension age HB, because a state benefit is reduced when you are in hospital.

13.22   But the gross amount (the amount before the reduction is made) is counted as your income in any other circumstances, for example if a state benefit (but not WTC or CTC) is reduced:

(a)   to recover an overpayment; or

(b)   to pay your rent, fuel, water or other priority debts; or

(c)   as a result of a work-related sanction in JSA(C) or ESA(C) (and in the case of ESA(C) the law expressly says so).

Council benefits and payments

13.23   This section gives the rules for benefits, allowances and other payments from local councils.

13.24   Table 13.5 lists which council allowances and payments are disregarded.

Social services and similar payments for care and support

13.25   The payments in table 13.5 (a)-(h) are disregarded if they are paid by:

(a)   a social services department in Great Britain;

(b)   the Health and Social Services Board, a Health and Social Services Trust or a Juvenile Justice Centre in Northern Ireland;

(c)   a voluntary organisation on behalf of the above; or

(d)   in the case of respite care payments, a Primary Care Trust.

13.21   HB 27(1)(a), 40(1),(6); HB66+ 29(3)-(5), 30(1)(a); NIHB 24(1)(a), 37(1),(4); NIHB66+ 27(3)-(5), 28(1)(a)

13.22   HB 40(1),(5),(5A); HB66+ 29(3),(5); NIHB 37(1),(3),(3A); NIHB66+ 27(3),(5)

13.25   HB 2(1), sch 5 paras 25-28A,57; HB66+ 29(1); NIHB 2(1), sch 6 paras 26-29A,59; NIHB66+ 27(1)

Table 13.5 **Disregarded council payments**

Income from the following is wholly disregarded. For payments (a) to (h) see also para 13.25.

  (a) foster care payments, also called kinship care payments in Scotland;

  (b) adoption allowances;

  (c) special guardianship payments;

  (d) payments to avoid taking children into care;

  (e) payments to care leavers, including payments passed on to you by a care leaver aged 18 or more who lives with you;

  (f) boarding out and respite care payments, including contributions you receive from the person you are caring for;

  (g) community care payments;

  (h) direct care payments;

  (i) supporting people payments, for housing-related support to help you maintain your tenancy;

  (j) 'local welfare assistance' or equivalent payments in Scotland, Wales and Northern Ireland (para 23.35);

  (k) discretionary housing payments (para 23.1) and in Northern Ireland welfare supplementary payments (para 23.20);

  (l) council tax rebates, other council tax reductions, and HB itself.

Note: In some cases these are also disregarded as capital. See para 15.50 for details about this.

T13.5(a)-(f) HB 2(1) definition: 'voluntary organisation', sch 5 paras 25-28A; HB66+ 29(1); NIHB 2(1), sch 6 paras 26-29A; NIHB66+ 27(1)

T13.5(g)-(h) HB sch 5 para 57; HB66+ 29(1); NIHB sch 6 para 59; NIHB66+ 27(1)

T13.5(i)   HB sch 5 para 63; HB66+ 29(1); NIHB sch 6 para 63; NIHB66+ 27(1)

T13.5(j)   HB 2(1) definition – 'local welfare provision', sch 5 para 31A; HB66+ 29(1)

T13.5(k)   HB sch 5 para 62; HB66+ 29(1); NIHB sch 6 para 62; NIHB66+ 27(1)

T13.5(l)   HB sch 5 para 41; HB66+ 29(1); NIHB sch 6 para 43; NIHB66+ 27(1)

Other unearned income

13.26 This section gives the rules for private pensions, maintenance, charitable and voluntary payments, rent, student income and other unearned income. For assumed income from capital see para 15.5.

Private pensions

13.27 Income from a private pension is counted in full, after any deductions have been made for tax paid on it. This applies to any kind of:

(a) occupational pension;

(b) personal pension; or

(c) pension from the Pension Protection Fund.

But if a court has ordered part of your pension to be paid to someone else (for example your former partner), that part is disregarded (CH/1672/2007). See also paras 13.54-55 and 13.60.

Maintenance

13.28 Table 13.6 gives the rules for assessing maintenance you receive from a former partner or anyone else (other than your current partner).

13.29 If you pay maintenance for a child or anyone else, the amount you pay cannot be deducted when your income is assessed. But if it is for a student son or daughter, see para 13.47.

Charitable and voluntary payments

13.30 Payments of income you receive which are charitable and/or voluntary are wholly disregarded. For example, these could be from a charity, family, friends, etc (but for maintenance see table 13.6). For payments of capital see para 15.53. If the only money you have is charitable or voluntary income, you qualify for maximum HB (see paras 6.5 and 16.30).

Rent

13.31 Table 13.7 gives the rules for assessing rent you receive from people living in your home. Table 13.8 gives the rules for rent you receive on other property. But if you are self-employed and you receive rent as part of your business, see para 15.33.

Annuities

13.32 If you have an annuity, you get payments from an insurance or similar company in return for investing an initial capital sum with them. Payments from an annuity are counted in full as unearned income (not capital), after any deductions have been made for tax paid on them.

13.27   HB 2(1), definition – 'occupational pension' 31(1), 35(2), sch 5 para 1; HB66+ 2(1), 29(1)(c),(d),(t),(x), 30(1)(a), 33(12), 35(2); NIHB 2(1), 28(1), 32(2), sch 6 para 1; NIHB66+ 2(1), 27(1)(c),(d),(r),(v), 28(1)(a), 31(12), 33(2)

13.29   HB 31(1); HB66+ 30(1); NIHB 28(1); NIHB66+ 28(1)

13.30   HB sch 5 para 14(1)(a),(b),(2); HB66+ 29(1); NIHB sch 6 para 14(1)(a),(b),(2); NIHB66+ 27(1)

13.32   HB 41(2), sch 5 para 1; HB66+ 29(1)(d), 33(12); NIHB 38(2), sch 6 para 1; NIHB66+ 27(1)(d), 31(11)

Table 13.6 **Income from maintenance**

	Assessment
Maintenance for a child or young person	

Working age HB:

  (a) if it is paid by:

      ▪ a husband, wife or civil partner you or your partner are separated from, or

      ▪ a parent or step-parent of the child/young person, or

      ▪ someone whose payments of maintenance mean they can reasonably be treated as the father of the child or young person — *Disregard in full*

  (b) if it is paid by someone else — *Count in full*

Pension age HB:

  (c) whoever it is paid by — *Disregard in full*

Maintenance for you or your partner, if you have a child or young person

Working age HB:

  (d) if it is paid by your or your partner's former partner — *Disregard £15 pw*

  (e) if it is paid by someone else — *Count in full*

Pension age HB:

  (f) if it is paid by your or your partner's current or former husband, wife or civil partner — *Disregard £15 pw*

  (g) if it is paid by someone else — *Disregard in full*

Maintenance for you or your partner, if you do not have a child or young person

Working age HB:

  (h) whoever it is paid by — *Count in full*

Pension age HB:

  (i) if it is paid by your or your partner's current or former husband, wife or civil partner — *Count in full*

  (j) if it is paid by someone else — *Disregard in full*

Maintenance for a non-dependant

  (k) working age HB: — *Same as (d), (e) or (h)*

  (l) pension age HB: — *Disregard in full*

Note: 'Partner', 'child', 'young person', and 'non-dependant' have the same meanings as in chapter 4. But 'husband', 'wife' and 'civil partner' have their ordinary English meanings.

T13.6   HB 31(1), sch 5 paras 47,47A; HB66+ 29(1)(o), sch 5 para 20; NIHB 28(1), sch 6 para 49,49A; NIHB66+ 27(1)(m), sch 6 para 21

Table 13.7 **Rent from people in your home**

(a) Household members

Rent (or 'keep') you receive from a child, young person or non-dependant in your home is wholly disregarded.

(b) Lodgers whose rent includes meals (boarders)

If you receive rent from one or more lodgers in your home and their rent includes meals (see para 4.38):

- start with the total amount your lodger(s) pay you each week (for rent, meals and any other services);
- deduct £20 for each lodger you charge for (counting adults and children);
- divide the result by two;
- this gives your weekly income.

(c) Lodgers whose rent does not include meals

If you receive rent from one or more lodgers in your home and their rent does not include meals:

- start with the total amount your lodger(s) pay you each week (for rent and any other services);
- deduct £20 for each separate letting;
- this gives your weekly income.

Examples: Letting out a room

1. A lodger whose rent does not include meals

A couple on HB have a spare room. They let it out to a lodger for £80 per week inclusive of fuel and water, but not meals.

Their income from this lodger (table 13.7(c)) is £80 minus £20, which is £60 per week.

2. A lodger whose rent includes meals

The couple increase the lodger's rent to £90 per week because they now provide meals.

Their income from the lodger (table 13.7(b)) is now £90 minus £20, which is £70, the result being divided by two, which is £35 per week.

T13.7(a) HB sch 5 para 21; HB66+ 29(1); NIHB sch 6 para 22; NIHB66+ 27(1)

T13.7(b) HB sch 5 para 42; HB66+ 2(1) definition: 'board and lodging accommodation', 2(1), 29(1)(p), sch 5 para 9;
          NIHB sch 6 para 44; NIHB66+ 27(1)(n), sch 6 para 10

T13.7(c) HB sch 5 para 22; HB66+ 29(1)(v), sch 5 para 10; NIHB sch 6 para 23; NIHB66+ 27(1)(t), sch 6 para 11

Table 13.8 **Rent from property other than your home**

(a) When the rent counts as income

The rent you receive counts as unearned income:

- only in working age HB; and
- only if the property's capital value is disregarded for any of the reasons in table 15.1(b) to (g).

In these cases your unearned income equals the rent you receive on the property, minus outgoings you pay on the property (during the period the rent covers) for:

- mortgage payments (both interest and capital);
- council tax (rates in Northern Ireland);
- water charges; and
- tax paid on the resulting income.

No other outgoings can be deducted.

(b) When the rent counts as capital

The rent you receive counts as capital (not income):

- in working age HB other than as described in (a); and
- in all pension age HB.

In these cases, your capital:

- increases when you receive the rent;
- but decreases when you pay for outgoings on the property, for example agent's fees, repairs, cleaning, etc, as well as those listed in (a).

Home income plans

13.33   A home income plan is an annuity in which the invested capital sum is a loan secured against your home. The payments you receive are assessed as unearned income (para 13.32). But if you were over pension age when you began the home income plan (or began it before 6th December 2018 and were over 65), the following amounts are disregarded from the payments:

(a) tax paid on them;

(b) mortgage repayments made using them; and

(c) repayments on the loan.

T13.8(a) HB sch 5 paras 1, 17(2),(3); NIHB sch 6 paras 1, 18(2),(3)

T13.8(b) HB 46(4), sch 5 paras 1, 17(1); HB66+ 29(1), sch 5 para 22; NIHB 43(4), sch 6 paras 1, 18(1); NIHB66+ 27(1), sch 6 para 23

13.33   HB 41(2), sch 5 para 1; HB66+ 29(1)(d), 33(12), sch 5 para 11; NIHB 38(2), sch 6 para 1; NIHB66+ 27(1)(d), 31(11), sch 6 para 12

Equity release schemes

13.34   If you are in an equity release scheme, the payments you receive are a form of loan secured against your home. In pension age HB, payments from an equity release scheme count in full as unearned income. This also seems likely to be the case in working age HB (because of the way loans are treated in HB: see para 15.54).

Mortgage and loan protection policies

13.35   If you have insurance against being unable to pay your mortgage or another loan (because of unemployment, sickness, etc), payments you receive from that policy are assessed as follows:

(a)   in pension age HB, the payments are wholly disregarded;

(b)   in working age HB, payments for the following are disregarded:

- the mortgage or loan repayments;

- the payments due on the policy;

- in the case of a mortgage protection policy, the payments due on another policy you were required to have to insure against loss or damage to your home,

and the rest (if any) counts as your income.

Income from trusts

13.36   Income you receive from a trust is counted as your unearned income, with the following exceptions:

(a)   income from some government supported trust funds is wholly disregarded (para 15.42);

(b)   income from personal injury trusts is wholly disregarded (paras 15.43-45);

(c)   in pension age HB, if you receive discretionary income from a trust:

- £20 per week is disregarded if it is for your rent (other than any part of the rent which is not met by HB because of a non-dependant deduction), mortgage interest or other housing costs that could be met by the guarantee credit of SPC, council tax (in Northern Ireland rates), water charges, household fuel, food, or ordinary clothing or footwear;

- the whole amount is disregarded if it is for anything else.

For further details about trusts see paras 15.37-41.

13.34   HB66+ 29(1)(w),(8); NIHB66+ 27(1)(u),(8)

13.35   HB sch 5 para 29; HB66+ 29(1); NIHB sch 6 para 30; NIHB66+ 27(1)

13.36(c) HB 31(1), sch 5 para 14(1)(c); HB66+ 29(1)(i), sch 5 para 12; NIHB 28(1), sch 6 para 14(1)(c); NIHB66+ 27(1)(g), sch 6 para 13

Student income

13.37   In pension age HB, student income is wholly disregarded. If you are eligible for working age HB (paras 2.26-27) the rules are in paras 13.38-43, but we have not given all the special cases for loans and grants (see GM chapter C2). If you are a student couple, the rules and disregards apply to each of you separately.

Student loans

13.38   Student maintenance loans (loans towards living costs) are counted as your income as described in table 13.9. But the following are wholly disregarded:

(a)   special support loans (for students on means tested benefits); and

(b)   student fee loans.

Table 13.9   **Student maintenance loans**

(a)   Start with the annual amount of your loan, including contributions due from your parents or others even if they don't pay them.

(b)   Disregard 70% in the case of a postgraduate master's degree loan.

(c)   Subtract £693 (an annual allowance towards books, travel and equipment).

(d)   Average the result over the period:

■   from the first Monday in September, or the first Monday in your academic year if it falls in August;

■   to the last Sunday in June (or the last Sunday in your course in your final year).

(e)   Disregard £10 (a standard weekly amount) (see also para 13.49).

(f)   In your first year, disregard the whole amount in the weeks falling before your course begins (CIS/3735/2004).

Note: Most full-time UK students on courses at level 4 or above (HNCs, HNDs, degrees, etc) qualify for a student loan. If you choose not to apply for one, or to take only part of the loan, you are counted at step (a) as having the full amount you qualify for. Religious beliefs aren't likely to be accepted as preventing you from applying (CH/4422/2006).

13.37   HB 54; HB66+ 29(1); NIHB 51; NIHB66+ 27(1)
         England: www.gov.uk/student-finance
         www.practitioners.slc.co.uk/policy/
         Scotland: www.saas.gov.uk/
         Wales: www.studentfinancewales.co.uk
         Northern Ireland: www.studentfinanceni.co.uk
         NHS and social work: www.nhsbsa.nhs.uk/student-services

13.38   HB 53(1) definitions: 'contribution', 'student loan', 64(1), 64A; NIHB 50(1), 61(1), 62

T13.9   HB 40(7)-(9), 53(1) definitions: 'academic year', 'last day of course', 64, 64B; NIHB 37(3)-(7), 50(1), 61

Student grants

13.39   Student maintenance grants (loans towards living costs) are counted as your income as described in table 13.10. But the following are wholly disregarded:

(a) special support grants (for students on means-tested benefits);

(b) education maintenance allowances (EMAs);

(c) 16-19 bursary fund payments (the English replacement for EMAs);

(d) parent's learning allowances (awarded for dependants); and

(e) higher education bursaries (awards to care leavers in England and Wales).

Table 13.10 **Student grants**

(a) Start with the annual amount of your grant, including contributions due from your parents or others even if they don't pay them.

(b) Disregard all amounts for:

- any disability you have,
- childcare costs,
- travel,
- books and equipment,
- tuition or examination fees,
- maintenance of two homes,
- term-time residential study away from your educational establishment,
- anyone outside the UK who is not included in your application amount.

(c) If you don't qualify for a student loan (table 13.9), subtract £693, even if amounts are deducted for travel and books and equipment at step (b).

(d) Average the result over the period it is payable for. In many (but not all) cases this means that:

- amounts for an adult or child dependant are averaged over the same period as the student loan if you qualify for one (table 13.9), or over the full calendar year if you don't,
- care leaver's grants are averaged over the summer vacation,
- other amounts are averaged over the academic year, but the long summer vacation is excluded (if you get one), and so are periods of work experience in a sandwich course.

13.39   HB 53(1) definitions: 'contribution', 'grant', 'grant income', 64(1),(4)(a)(ii),(b)(ii), 66, 67; NIHB 50(1), 61(1),(4)(a)(ii),(b)(ii), 64, 65

T13.10   HB 40(7)-(9), 53(1) definition: 'grant income', 59; NIHB 37(3)-(7), 50(1), 56

Using other income to supplement a student loan or grant

13.40   If you have income from a student loan or grant, you may qualify for an extra disregard towards your expenditure. This is calculated as follows:

(a) work out your expenditure for the year on the items in table 13.10(b), but only include expenditure which is necessary for you to attend your course;

(b) add together the following figures:

  ■ £693,

  ■ your higher education bursary (if you get one),

  ■ any amounts you get in your grant for the items in table 13.10(b);

(c) if the total of (a) is greater than the total of (b), you qualify for a disregard equal to the difference. In practice this is averaged over the year (or a more appropriate period) to give the weekly amount of the disregard.

But this disregard can only be made from income 'intended' for this purpose (CIS/3107/2003), for example if you have to take a part-time job to pay for your travel. It cannot be made from the student loan or grant, or from income you would have anyway.

Access funds, learner support funds and financial contingency funds

13.41   Educational establishments can make payments to students from 'access funds' or 'learner support funds', and Welsh Ministers can make payments to students from 'financial contingency funds'. These are sometimes called hardship payments. They are assessed as follows:

(a) payments towards your living costs (see para 13.42) are counted as your income or capital as appropriate. But if they are income (in other words regular payments):

  ■ the whole amount is disregarded if they are paid before your course begins, or to tide you over until you receive your student loan,

  ■ £20 per week is disregarded in other situations (see also para 13.49);

(b) payments for anything else (for example course-related expenses) are disregarded as income and as capital for 52 weeks.

13.42   Your living costs mean rent (other than any part of the rent which is not eligible for HB, or not met by HB because of a non-dependant deduction), council tax (in Northern Ireland rates), water charges, household fuel, food or ordinary clothing or footwear.

Sports Council awards

13.43   Sports Council awards are assessed as follows:

(a) payments towards your living costs (see para 13.42) are counted in full as your income or capital as appropriate;

(b) payments for anything else (including vitamins, minerals or performance-enhancing dietary supplements) are disregarded as income, and as capital for 26 weeks.

13.40   HB 63; NIHB 60

13.41   HB 53(1) definition: 'access funds', 65,68(2),(4); NIHB 50(1), 63,66(2),(4)

13.43   HB 2(1) definition: 'sports award', sch 5 para 59, sch 6 para 50; NIHB 2(1), sch 6 para 61, sch 7 para 49

Other sources of unearned income

13.44   Any other kind of unearned income is:

(a)   disregarded in pension age HB;

(b)   counted as unearned income in working age HB, except as in table 13.11 and para 13.46.

Additional rules about income disregards

13.45   The rules about disregards for each kind of unearned income are given earlier in this chapter. Those for earned income are in chapter 14. This section gives further rules about disregards which can apply to more than one kind of unearned or earned income.

Income tax

13.46   Income tax paid on any kind of unearned income is always deducted in the assessment of that income. For earned income see paras 14.19-21 and 14.53-55.

Parental contributions to a student

13.47   If you make a parental contribution to a son or daughter who is a UK student, the following amount is disregarded from the total of your unearned and earned income:

(a)   if you were assessed as having to make a contribution towards their student loan or grant, the whole of that contribution;

(b)   if (a) does not apply, and they are under 25, any amount you contribute up to:

- the lower rate of the single person's personal allowance (table 12.1);

- minus the weekly amount of any discretionary grant they receive.

Income outside the UK

13.48   Unearned or earned income you receive outside the UK is assessed in the normal way (as described in this chapter and chapter 14), and any commission for converting it to sterling is then disregarded. But if you are prohibited (by the country you receive the income in) from bringing it to the UK, the whole amount is disregarded.

Table 13.11 **Other unearned income disregards**

The following kinds of income are wholly disregarded (except as shown in (k) to (n)):

(a)   expenses you receive as a volunteer or for charitable or voluntary work;

(b) · expenses you receive as a member of a service user group (for example when these are run by local councils, social landlords or health authorities);

13.44   HB 31(1), sch 5 para 1; HB66+ 29(1); NIHB 28(1), sch 5 para 1; NIHB66+ 27(1)

13.46   HB sch 5 para 1; HB66+ 33(12); NIHB sch 6 para 1; NIHB66+ 31(11)

13.47   HB sch 4 para 11, sch 5 paras 19,20; HB66+ sch 4 para 6, sch 5 paras 18,19; NIHB sch 6 paras 20,21; NIHB66+ sch 5 para 6, sch 6 paras 19,20

13.48   HB sch 4 paras 13,14, sch 5 paras 24,33; HB66+ 29(1)(k), 33(7), sch 4 para 10, sch 5 paras 16,17; NIHB sch 5 paras 13,14, sch 6 paras 25,34; NIHB66+ 27(1)(i), 31(7), sch 5 para 10, sch 6 paras 17,18

(c)   expenses you receive from your employer (for exceptions see table 14.1(n));

(d)   payments you receive as a teacher under the Student Loans Repayment Scheme (but student loan repayments can't be deducted from any other income);

(e)   payments for travel for hospital visits;

(f)   payments for health service supplies;

(g)   payments replacing free milk and vitamins and/or healthy start vouchers;

(h)   payments for travel for prison visits;

(i)   payments from the National Emergency Trust, the We Love Manchester Emergency Fund, and in relation to the Grenfell Tower fire;

(j)   payments you receive as a holder of the Victoria Cross or George Cross, and similar payments (para 15.48);

(k)   payments in kind (in other words, in goods rather than money or vouchers)

   ▪ but in working age HB, goods bought for you by someone who receives income on your behalf can count as notional income: see para 13.54;

(l)   concessionary coal

   ▪ but in working age HB, cash in lieu of it is counted as unearned income (R v Doncaster MBC and another ex parte Bolton);

(m) juror's allowance

   ▪ but in working age HB, compensation for loss of earnings or state benefits is counted as unearned income;

(n)   career development loans paid by banks in Great Britain under arrangements in s2 of the Employment and Training Act 1973;

   ▪ but in working age HB, loans for living expenses are counted as unearned income until the course you are on ends.

Note: In working age HB, payments (e) to (h) are also disregarded as capital for 52 weeks.

T13.11(a)   HB sch 5 para 2; HB66+ 29(1); NIHB sch 6 para 2; NIHB66+ 27(1)

T13.11(b)   HB 2(1) definition: 'service user group', 35(2)(d), sch 5 para 2A; HB66+ 29(1), 35(2)(f);
               NIHB 2(1), 32(2)(d), sch 6 para 2A; NIHB66+ 27(1), 33(2)(e)

T13.11(c)   HB 35(2)(b), sch 5 para 3; HB66+ 29(1), 35(2)(b); NIHB 32(2)(b), sch 6 para 3; NIHB66+ 27(1), 33(2)(b)

T13.11(d)   HB sch 5 para 12; HB66+ 29(1); NIHB66+ 27(1)

T13.11(e),(f) HB sch 5 para 44; HB66+ 29(1); NIHB sch 6 para 46; NIHB66+ 27(1)

T13.11(g)   HB sch 5 para 45; HB66+ 29(1); NIHB sch 6 para 47; NIHB66+ 27(1)

T13.11(h)   HB sch 5 para 46; HB66+ 29(1); NIHB sch 6 para 48; NIHB66+ 27(1)

T13.11(i)   HB 2(1), sch 5 para 35; HB66+ 29(1); NIHB 2(1), sch 6 para 37; NIHB66+ 27(1)

T13.11(j)   HB sch 5 para 10; HB66+ 29(1); NIHB sch 6 para 11; NIHB66+ 27(1)

T13.11(k)   HB 35(2)(a), sch 5 para 23; HB66+ 29(1); NIHB 32(2)(a), sch 6 para 24; NIHB66+ 27(1)

T13.11(l)   HB66+ 29(1); NIHB66+ 27(1); R v Doncaster MBC & Another ex p Boulton 11/12/92 QBD 25 HLR 195

T13.11(m)   HB sch 5 para 39; HB66+ 29(1); NIHB sch 6 para 41; NIHB66+ 27(1)

T13.11(n)   HB 41(4), sch 5 para 13(1)(c); HB66+ 29(1)

The over-riding limit on certain disregards

13.49 If you qualify for more than one of the following unearned income disregards, the disregard from all of them is limited to £20 per week:

(a) the £15 disregard from widowed mother's/parent's allowance (table 13.2(l));

(b) in Great Britain, the £10 disregard from war pensions for disablement or bereavement (table 13.4(b)), but your council may also run a local scheme (para 13.18);

(c) in pension age HB, the £20 disregard from discretionary trust income (para 13.36(c));

(d) in working age HB, the £10 disregard from income from student loans (table 13.9(e));

(e) in working age HB, the £20 disregard from income from student access funds (para 13.41).

Apart from that, you get the full amount of any disregard you qualify for.

Notional income

13.50 This section explains when you are counted as having unearned or earned income you do not in fact have. This is called 'notional' income.

13.51 For working age HB, this section also includes rules about notional capital when these are similar. The main rules about notional capital are in paras 15.56-59.

Types of notional income

13.52 You can be counted as having notional income when:

(a) there is income available to you (paras 13.54-56);

(b) in working age HB, you are paid income on behalf of someone else (paras 13.57 and 13.59);

(c) someone else is paid income on your behalf (paras 13.58-59);

(d) you have deprived yourself of income (para 13.60);

(e) a non-dependant has more income and capital than you (para 13.61); or

(f) in working age HB, you are paid less than the going rate for a job (para 14.24).

Assessing notional income

13.53 If you are counted as having notional income, it is assessed in the same way as actual income and all the disregards given earlier in this chapter and in chapter 14 apply. This means this section does not apply if you are on a passport benefit.

13.49   HB sch 5 para 34; HB66+ sch 5 para 12(3)(b),(c); NIHB sch 6 para 35; NIHB66+ sch 6 para 13(3)(b),(c)

13.53   HB 42(11),(12); HB66+ 25; NIHB 39(11),(12); NIHB66+ 23

Money which is available to you

13.54   If income is available to you and you could get it by applying for it, it is counted as your notional income (but only from when you would get it if you did apply). In working age HB, this rule also applies to capital. For further details see paras 13.55-56.

13.55   In pension age HB, the rule in para 13.54 applies only to income from:

(a)   a private pension (para 13.27); or

(b)   a state pension unless you have deferred it (para 13.13).

For DWP guidance, see GM paras BP2.680-750.

13.56   In working age HB, the rule in para 13.54 applies to any kind of income or capital except for:

(a)   income/capital from a private pension (para 13.27) if you (the claimant) are under 66;

(b)   income/capital from a personal injury payment (paras 15.43-44);

(c)   income/capital from a discretionary trust;

(d)   income/capital from WTC or CTC;

(e)   income from expenses or earnings as a service user group member;

(f)   income from a DWP rehabilitation allowance; or

(g)   capital from a loan you could raise against disregarded property or against other disregarded capital.

The DWP says this rule should not be used in the case of any state benefit if there is a doubt about whether you would qualify or how much you would get (see GM para BW2.682). See also paras 13.53 and 15.60.

Payments received by one person on behalf of another

13.57   In working age HB, if you receive payments of income on behalf of someone else, they are counted as your notional income if you keep or use them for yourself or your family. This rule also applies to payments of capital. For exceptions see para 13.59.

13.54   HB 42(2), 49(2); HB66+ 41(1),(4); NIHB 39(2), 46(2); NIHB66+ 39(1),(4)

13.55   HB66+ 41(1)-(7); NIHB66+ 39(1)-(7)

13.56   HB 42(2),(12A), 49(2); NIHB 39(2),(12A), 46(2)

13.57   HB 42(6)(c), 49(3)(c); NIHB 39(6)(c), 46(3)(c)

13.58   If someone else receives payments of income on your behalf, they are counted as your notional income if they are from:

(a)   a private pension (paras 13.27 and 13.59(a)); or

(b)   some other source, but in this case only if the payment is used for your or your family's:

■   rent (other than any part of the rent which is not eligible for HB, or not met by HB because of a non-dependant deduction);

■   council tax (rates in Northern Ireland); or

■   water charges, household fuel, food or ordinary clothing or footwear (apart from school uniform/sportswear).

In working age HB, this rule also applies to payments of capital. For exceptions see para 13.59.

13.59   The rules in paras 13.57-58 do not apply to

(a)   income/capital from a private pension (para 13.27) if:

■   the person whose pension it is, is bankrupt (or sequestered in Scotland) and has no other income; and

■   the person it is paid to is their trustee in bankruptcy or someone else acting on behalf of their creditors;

(b)   income/capital from the government-sponsored trusts and funds in paras 15.42(a) to (d);

(c)   income/capital from government work programme training schemes;

(d)   income from expenses or earnings as a service user group member; or

(e)   income from cash in lieu of concessionary coal.

See also paras 13.53 and 15.59.

Income you have deprived yourself of

13.60   If you have deprived yourself of income, it is counted as your notional income. To 'deprive' yourself of income means:

(a)   you have disposed of it (for example by stopping it being paid); and

(b)   your purpose in doing so was to make yourself entitled to HB or to more HB.

This rule is likely to be interpreted in a similar way to the rule about deprivation of capital (see table 15.3(a) to (e)). In practice it is rare, but could in some cases apply if you sell your right to receive income from a private pension by 'assigning' your pension annuity (HB G8/2016). It does not apply to income from expenses or earnings as a service user group member, or to income from a state pension you have deferred (para 13.13). See also para 13.53.

13.58   HB 2(1) definition: 'ordinary clothing and footwear', 42(6)(a),(b),(13), 49(3)(a),(b),(8), sch 5 para 23(2); HB66+ 42(1); NIHB 2(1), 39(6)(a),(b),(14), 46(3)(a),(b),(8), sch 6 para 24(2); NIHB66+ 40(1)

13.59   HB 42(7),(12A), 49(4); HB66+ 29(1), 42(2),(3); NIHB 39(7),(12A), 46(4); NIHB66+ 27(1), 40(2),(3)

13.60   HB 42(1),(12A); HB66+ 41(8)-(8C),(11),(12); NIHB 39(1),(12A); NIHB66+ 39(8)-(10A),(13),(14)

If your non-dependant has more income and capital than you

13.61   You are counted as having your non-dependant's income and capital (instead of yours) if:

(a) they have more income and capital than you; and

(b) you and they arranged to 'take advantage of' (abuse) the HB scheme, for example by deliberately making them your non-dependant rather than making you their non-dependant.

This rule is in practice rare. It does not apply if you are on a passport benefit.

13.61   HB 26; HB66+ 24, 27(4)(f); NIHB 23; NIHB66+ 22, 25(4)(f)

Chapter 14 **Earned income**

- General rules: see paras 14.1-4.
- Employed earnings and how they are assessed: see paras 14.5-16.
- Calculating net earnings: see paras 14.17-25.
- Self-employed earnings and how they are assessed: see paras 14.26-35.
- Calculating net profit: see paras 14.36-59.
- Earnings disregards: see paras 14.60-73.

Assessing earned income

14.1   This chapter explains how your earned income is assessed for HB purposes.

14.2   In this chapter, 'your' earned income always includes the earned income of your partner. See paras 13.1-8 for details about this and for other general rules.

14.3   The rules in this chapter apply to income from employment or self-employment in the UK (England, Wales, Scotland and Northern Ireland). If you are claiming HB in Northern Ireland they also apply to income from employment or self-employment in the Republic of Ireland. For other countries see para 13.48.

The amount of your earned income

14.4   For HB purposes, the amount of your earned income is:

(a) the weekly amount of your (and your partner's):

- net earnings from employment (para 14.17), and/or
- net profit from self-employment (para 14.36);

(b) minus the earned income disregards which apply to you (para 14.60).

It can also include notional earnings (see 14.24).

Example: Earned income

One partner in a couple is employed and has net earnings of £230 per week. The other is self-employed and has a net profit of £150 per week. They qualify for a standard earned income disregard of £10 per week.

Their combined earned income after the disregard has been made is £370 per week. This figure is used in calculating their HB.

14.4   HB 2(1) definition: 'earnings', 36(1),(2), 38(1),(2); HB66+ 2(1), 33(8)(a), 36(1), 39(1);
        NIHB 2(1), 33(1),(2), 35(1),(2); NIHB66+ 2(1), 31(8)(a), 34(1), 37(1)

Employed earnings

14.5   This section explains what employed earnings are and the information used to assess them. This information is needed to calculate your 'net earnings', which is the figure used in HB. (The calculation is in paras 14.17-32.)

What are employed earnings

14.6   Your employed earnings are your earnings from employment 'under a contract of service' (an employment contract) or 'in an office', and includes amounts paid to employees who are furloughed due to coronavirus. An 'office' means the kind of job that may not have an employment contract. People employed in an office include directors of limited companies, local authority councillors and clergy.

14.7   Table 14.1 explains which payments count as employed earnings and which do not. Payments which count as employed earnings are usually shown on your pay slip. For arrears of earnings see para 13.7.

Table 14.1 **Employed earnings**

The following count as employed earnings:

(a) Employed earnings generally (see para 14.6).

(b) Employed earnings paid in a lump sum (see also paras 14.58-59).

(c) Sick, maternity, paternity, shared parental and adoption pay from your employer.

(d) Statutory sick, maternity, paternity, shared parental and adoption pay.

(e) Holiday pay.

(f) Retainers.

(g) Bonuses and commission.

(h) Tips.

(i) Payments in lieu of notice.

(j) Payments in lieu of earnings (but for redundancy payments see (q) below).

14.6   CBA 2(1)(a); NICBA 2(1)(a); HB 2(1) definition: employed earner; HB66+ 2(1), 29(1)(a); NIHB 2(1); NIHB66+ 2(1), 27(1)(a)

14.7   HB 35; HB66+ 35; NIHB 32; NIHB66+ 33

T14.1(a)   HB 35(1); HB66+ 35(1); NIHB 32(1); NIHB66+ 33(1)

T14.1(b)   HB 41(3); HB66+ 33(4); NIHB 38(3); NIHB66+ 24

T14.1(c)   HB 35(1)(j); HB66+ 35(1)(k); NIHB 32(1)(k); NIHB66+ 33(1)(k)

T14.1(d)   HB 35(1)(i); HB66+ 35(1)(h)-(j); NIHB 32(1)(i); NIHB66+ 33(1)(h)-(j)

T14.1(e)   HB 35(1)(d); HB66+ 35(1)(d); NIHB 32(1)(d); NIHB66+ 33(1)(d)

T14.1(f)   HB 35(1)(e); HB66+ 35(1)(e); NIHB 32(1)(e); NIHB66+ 33(1)(e)

T14.1(g)   HB 35(1)(a); HB66+ 35(1)(a); NIHB 32(1)(a); NIHB66+ 33(1)(a)

T14.1(h)   HB 35(1); HB66+ 35(1); NIHB 32(1); NIHB66+ 33(1)

T14.1(i)   HB 35(1)(c); HB66+ 35(1)(c); NIHB 32(1)(c); NIHB66+ 33(1)(c)

T14.1(j)   HB 35(1)(b); HB66+ 35(1)(b); NIHB 32(1)(b); NIHB66+ 33(1)(b)

(k) Non-cash vouchers which are earnings for national insurance purposes.

(l) Councillor's allowances, but for expenses see (n) below (R(IS) 6/92). For detailed guidance see GM paras BW2.83-95.

(m) Company director's income (para 14.6).

The following have individual rules:

(n) Expenses paid by your employer:

- these are disregarded if they are 'wholly, exclusively and necessarily incurred' in carrying out your employment. For example, for travel between workplaces (R(IS) 16/93, CIS 507/94), or all travel if you don't have a fixed workplace and can be asked to work anywhere in your area (CH/1330/2008, in which the claimant was a care worker);

- apart from that, they count as your employed earnings. For example, for travel between your home and workplace, or for caring for a member of your family.

(o) Expenses you receive as a participant service user are disregarded (for example where you are being consulted by councils, social landlords or health authorities).

(p) Compensation payments for unfair dismissal or under laws about equal pay etc, whether made by an employment tribunal or in an out of court settlement:

- count as your employed earnings in working age HB claims;

- do not count as your employed earnings in pension age HB (but are likely to be included as your capital).

(q) Redundancy payments count as your capital, not earnings (but for payments in lieu of notice see (j) above).

(r) Payments in kind (in other words, in goods rather than money or vouchers) are disregarded (see also table 13.11(k)). But payments in private currencies count as your employed earnings, for example in local exchange trading schemes (GM paras BW2.99-101) or in internet currencies.

(s) Bounty payments you receive as a part-time firefighter, a part-time lifeboat worker, an auxiliary coastguard or a member of the Territorial Army or similar reserve forces – all these count as your capital, not earnings, if they are paid to you annually or at longer intervals (see also table 14.5(f)).

T14.1(k)   HB 35(1)(k); HB66+ 35(1)(g); NIHB 32(1)(l); NIHB66+ 33(1)(g)

T14.1(l)   HB 35(1); HB66+ 35(1); NIHB 32(1); NIHB66+ 33(1)

T14.1(m)   HB 35(1); HB66+ 35(1); NIHB 32(1); NIHB66+ 33(1)

T14.1(n)   HB 35(1)(f),(2)(b); HB66+ 35(1)(f),(2)(b); NIHB 32(1)(f),(2)(b); NIHB66+ 33(1)(f),(2)(b)

T14.1(o)   HB 2(5) definition: 'participating as a service user' 35(2)(d); HB66+ 2(6), 35(2)(f); NIHB 2(4A), 32(2)(d); NIHB66+ 2(5A), 33(2)(e)

T14.1(p)   HB 35(1)(g),(gg),(h), 41(3); HB66+ 35(2)(e); NIHB 32(1)(g),(gg),(h), 38(3); NIHB66+ 33(2)(d)

T14.1(q)   HB 35(1)(b), 44(1); HB66+ 35(1)(b), 44(1); NIHB 32(1)(b), 41(1); NIHB66+ 33(1)(b), 44(1)

T14.1(r)   HB 35(2)(a),(3); HB66+ 35(2)(a),(3); NIHB 32(2)(a),(3); NIHB66+ 33(2)(a),(3)

T14.1(s)   HB 46(1); NIHB 43(1)

(t) Advances of earnings and loans from your employer count as your capital, not earnings.

(u) Tax refunds on your earnings count as your capital, not earnings.

(v) Occupational pensions count as your unearned income (para 13.27).

(w) Strike pay counts as your unearned income in working age HB claims, but is disregarded in pension age HB.

(x) Self-employed earnings are assessed separately (paras 14.26-35, and for royalties and similar payments paras 14.58-59).

Notes

■ The rules in (b), (s), (t) and (u) are given in the law for working age HB. They are also likely to apply for pension age HB.

■ See also paras 14.13-16 if you are absent from work or your job ends.

Assessing employed earnings

14.8   When your employed earnings are assessed, the purpose is to estimate 'the amount which is likely to be' your average weekly net earnings (for net earnings see para 14.17). This is done using information from an assessment period or employer's estimate (paras 14.9-11), but other relevant information should also be taken into account in order to obtain a fair and accurate result. For these purposes, your earnings count as belonging to the period they cover, whether they are paid at the beginning or end of that period or part way through it.

Assessment periods

14.9   In working age HB claims, when you make your claim your assessment period is usually:

(a) the two months before you claimed if you are paid monthly; or

(b) the five weeks before you claimed if you are paid weekly; or

(c) if you have not been working long enough for the above to apply:

■   the period you have been working if what you have been paid is representative;

■   if what you have been paid is not representative, or you haven't yet been paid, an employer's estimate is used (para 14.11);

(d) but if your earnings vary, whatever period gives a more accurate result.

If your earnings change while you are on HB, your assessment period is whatever period gives an accurate result. But it must not be longer than 52 weeks, and must not include periods before the change occurred ([2015] UKUT 237 (AAC)).

T14.1(t)   HB 46(5); NIHB 43(5)

T14.1(u)   HB 46(2); NIHB 43(2)

T14.1(v)   HB 35(2)(c); HB66+ 35(2)(c); NIHB 32(2)(c); NIHB66+ 33(2)(c)

T14.1(w)   HB 35(1); HB66+ 29(1); NIHB 32(1); NIHB66+ 27(1)

14.8   HB 27(1)(a), 29(1)-(3), 29A; HB66+ 30(1)(a), 33(2),(2A),(3),(3A); NIHB 24(1)(a), 26(1)-(3), 26A; NIHB66+ 28(1)(a), 31(2),(2A),(3),(3A)

14.9   HB 2(1) definition: 'assessment period', 29(1)-(3); NIHB 2(1), 26(1)-(3);

14.10 In pension age HB, when you make your claim your assessment period usually uses the following information:

(a) your most recent two payments if they are one month or more apart; or

(b) your most recent four payments in other cases; or

(c) whatever payments give a more accurate result;

(d) but if your hours vary over a recognisable cycle (for example you work a regular pattern of shifts, or you work in term-times but not school holidays), information about the whole of that cycle.

If your earnings change while you are on HB, the rules in (c) or (d) usually apply.

Employer's estimates

14.11 Your council can ask your employer to provide information about your earnings (see also para 16.22), or can ask you to obtain this information from your employer. Many councils have a 'certificate of earnings' form which can be used for this.

Examples: Assessing employed earnings

1. A claimant's weekly earnings have been the same over the five weeks before she claimed HB.

   ▪ Her weekly net earnings are calculated from this weekly amount.

2. A claimant's monthly earnings have varied over the two months before he claimed HB. Evidence about his earlier earnings shows that an average can fairly be taken over the past six months.

   ▪ His weekly net earnings are calculated from the past six months' figures.

3. A claimant has moved to the area for a new job. She claims HB a few days after starting work.

   ▪ She is asked to provide an employer's estimate, and her weekly net earnings are calculated from that.

Starting a job

14.12 When you start a job, your earnings can be estimated to begin with (paras 14.9(c) and 14.11). They are taken into account from the Monday following the first day you are paid for, even if your first pay day is later on. But if you have been out of work for 26 weeks or more, you may qualify for an 'extended payment' of HB (para 17.32).

Leaving a job

14.13 When you leave a job, your earnings are taken into account until the Sunday following the last day you are paid for. But in working age HB, holiday pay counts as your capital, not earnings, if it is payable more than four weeks after you left.

14.10   HB66+ 2(1) definition: 'assessment period', 33(2),(3); NIHB66+ 2(1),31(2),(3)

14.12   HB 29A(b); HB66+ 33 (2A)(b),(3A)(b); NIHB 26A(b); NIHB66+ 31(2A)(b),(3A)(b)

14.13   HB 35(1)(d), 46(3); NIHB 32(1)(d), 43(3)

14.14   And if your job ended before your first day of entitlement to HB:

(a) in working age HB, all your earnings from that job are disregarded except for compensation (see table 14.1(p)) and retainers;

(b) in pension age HB, all your earnings from that job are disregarded.

Absences from work

14.15   When you are absent from work, your earnings are reassessed if they change. This applies to all absences, whether they are:

(a) due to sickness (with or without leave);

(b) due to maternity, paternity, shared parental or adoption leave;

(c) 'with good cause' (for example you are furloughed or laid off);

(d) on holiday;

(e) on strike; or

(f) for any other reason (including absences 'without good cause').

But in working age HB, holiday pay counts as your capital, not earnings, if it is payable more than four weeks after your absence began.

14.16   And in working age HB, if your absence:

(a) began before your first day of entitlement to HB; and

(b) is for one of the reasons in para 14.15(a), (b) or (c),

all your earnings from that job are disregarded except for employer's and statutory sick, maternity, paternity, shared parental or adoption pay, compensation (table 14.1(p)) and retainers.

Calculating net earnings

14.17   It is your 'net earnings' which are used in assessing your HB. They are calculated as follows, using the information described in paras 14.8-16:

(a) start with your gross earnings: para 14.18;

(b) deduct amounts for tax and national insurance: paras 14.19-21;

(c) deduct half of your pension contributions: para 14.22;

(d) convert the result to a weekly figure: para 6.37;

(e) this gives your weekly net earnings: para 14.23.

See also paras 14.60-73 for the earned income disregards.

14.14   HB sch 4 paras 1(a),(b), 2(a),(b),(i), 16; HB66+ sch 4 para 8; NIHB sch 5 paras 1(a),(b), 2(a),(b),(i), 16; NIHB66+ sch 4 para 8

14.15   HB 35(1)(d), 46(3); NIHB 32(1)(d), 43(3)

14.16   HB sch 4 paras 1(c), 2(a),(b),(ii), 16; NIHB sch 5 paras 1(c), 2(a),(b),(ii), 16;

14.17   HB 2(1) definition: 'net earnings', 29(4), 36; HB66+ 2(1), 28, 36; NIHB 2(1), 26(4), 33; NIHB66+ 2(1), 26, 34

Example: Calculation of net earnings

Rosa has gross earnings are £1,450 per month. From this, her employer deducts £92.51 each month for tax, £89.74 each month for class 1 national insurance contributions (NICs), and £58 each month towards a pension scheme. Rosa's net earnings are calculated as follows.

From her gross earnings	£1,450 pcm
deduct:	
■ tax	£92.51 pcm
■ NICs	£89.74 pcm
■ half her pension contributions	£29.00 pcm
This gives her net earnings	£1,238.75 pcm
They are converted to a weekly figure:	
■ £1,238.75 x 12 ÷ 52	£285.86 pw

The earned income disregards which apply to her are then deducted (para 14.60).

Gross earnings

14.18   Your 'gross earnings' are the total of your employed earnings: see paras 14.5-16 and table 14.1.

Deductions for tax and national insurance

14.19   Deductions are made from your gross earnings for:

(a)   income tax; and

(b)   class 1 national insurance contributions (NICs).

The deductions equal the amounts deducted by your employer for these. The amounts should be shown on your pay slip. The exceptions to this are in paras 14.20-21.

14.20   If your gross earnings were assessed using an employer's estimate (para 14.11) or you have notional earnings (para 14.24), the deductions are calculated by the council. They equal what would be deducted (if they were actual earnings) for:

(a)   income tax, using only the specific personal reliefs that you are entitled to (i.e. the personal allowance, the blind person's allowance, the tax deduction for married couples and civil partners where one was born before 6th April 1935 and the transferable tax allowance for married couples and civil partners) [www]; and using the basic rate of tax, or for a Scottish taxpayer, the Scottish basic rate; and

(b)   class 1 NICs.

14.18   HB 35; HB66+ 35; NIHB 32; NIHB66+ 33

14.19   HB 36(3),(a),(d); HB66+ 36(2),(a),(d); NIHB 33(3),(a),(d); NIHB66+ 34(2),(a),(d)

14.20   HB 2(1) definitions: 'basic rate', 'Scottish basic rate', 'Scottish taxpayer', 36(6),(a),(b), 42(12)(a),(b);
          HB66+ 2(1),36(5),(a),(b); NIHB 2(1),33(6),(a),(b),39(12)(a),(b); NIHB66+ 2(1),34(5),(a),(b)
          www.gov.uk/income-tax-rates

14.21   If you are claiming HB in Northern Ireland and work in the Republic of Ireland, the deductions are calculated by the NIHE. They equal what would be deducted for tax and class 1 NICs if you worked in Northern Ireland.

Deductions for pension contributions

14.22   If you make contributions towards an occupational or personal pension, one half of the amount you contribute is deducted from your gross earnings. If your gross earnings were assessed using an employer's estimate (para 14.11) or you have notional earnings (para 14.24), the deduction is calculated by the council. It equals one half of what you would contribute (if they were actual earnings).

Net earnings

14.23   The above calculation (paras 14.18-22) gives your net earnings. They are converted to a weekly figure (para 6.37). No other amounts can be deducted from them, even if you have to pay work expenses which are not met by your employer. Your weekly net earnings are used in calculating your HB (but only after the earned income disregards have been made: paras 14.60-73).

Notional earnings

14.24   In working age HB, you are counted as having 'notional' earnings (para 13.52(f)) if:

(a)   you work or provide a service for someone;

(b)   they pay you less than the rate for comparable employment in the area, or do not pay you; and

(c)   none of the exceptions in para 14.25 apply.

Your notional earnings equal the amount (if any) which would be reasonable for the comparable employment. Apart from that, notional earnings are assessed in the same way as actual earnings (but see paras 14.20 and 14.22).

14.25   The rule in para 14.24 does not apply to work you do or a service you provide:

(a)   for someone whose means are insufficient to pay you, or to pay you more; or

(b)   for a charitable or voluntary organisation or as a volunteer, if it is reasonable for you to work without being paid; or

(c)   in a government work programme training scheme or work placement.

14.21   NIHB 33(7); NIHB66+ 34(6)

14.22   HB 36(3)(b),(c),(4),(5),(6)(c), 42(12)(c); HB66+ 36(2)(b),(c),(3),(4),(5)(c);
         NIHB 33(3)(b),(c),(4),(5),(6)(c), 39(12)(c); NIHB66+ 34(2)(b),(c),(3),(4),(5)(c)

14.23   HB 2(1) definition: 'net earnings', 29(4), 36; HB66+ 2(1), 28, 36; NIHB 2(1), 26(4), 33; NIHB66+ 2(1), 26, 34

14.24   HB 27(4), 42(9),(12); NIHB 24(4), 39(9),(12)

14.25   HB 42(9),(10),(10A),(12A); NIHB 39(9),(10),(10A),(12A)

Self-employed earnings

14.26   This section explains what self-employed earnings are, and the information used to assess them. This information is needed to calculate your 'net profit', which is the figure used in HB. (The calculation is in paras 14.36-57.)

What are self-employed earnings

14.27   Your self-employed earnings are your earnings which:

(a) are from 'gainful employment'; but

(b) are not employed earner's earnings (para 14.6).

This applies whether you are a sole trader or in a partnership, and includes payments you receive under the self-employed income support scheme due to coronavirus. Royalties and similar payments also usually count as self-employed earnings (paras 14.58-59).

14.28   Your self-employed earnings only include payments which:

(a) are income (not capital); and

(b) are 'derived from' your self-employment.

Table 14.2 lists payments which (for those reasons) do not count as self-employed earnings. Apart from that, self-employed earnings include payments in money, in kind (in other words, in goods) and in any other form (for example barter).

Table 14.2 **Self-employed earnings: exclusions**

The following do not count as self-employed earnings:

(a) Your business assets. These are capital (not income) and are disregarded (para 15.33).

(b) Grants and loans to your business. These are usually capital and (if so) are disregarded as part of your business assets.

(c) New enterprise allowance. This can help you start up in business if you are on UC, JSA, ESA or IS [www]. It is unearned income and can include a low cost loan. These are disregarded.

(d) Access to work. This can help you start up in business if you have a disability [www]. It is unearned income and is disregarded (table 13.1(o)).

(e) Other government work programme training schemes. Payments from these are usually disregarded (table 13.1(p)).

(f) Sports Council awards. These are usually disregarded (para 13.43).

(g) Foster care and kinship care payments. These are disregarded (table 13.5(a)).

(h) Boarding out and respite care payments. These are disregarded (table 13.5(f)).

14.27   CBA 2(1)(b); NICBA 2(1)(b); HB 2(1) definition: 'self-employed earner', 37(1); HB66+ 2(1), 38(1); NIHB 2(1), 34(1); NIHB66+ 2(1), 36(1)

14.28   HB 37(1); HB66+ 38(1); NIHB 34(1); NIHB66+ 36(1)

T14.2   HB 37(2); HB66+ 38(2); NIHB 34(2); NIHB66+ 36(2); www.gov.uk/new-enterprise-allowance; www.gov.uk/access-to-work

(i)   Rent you receive on your home (table 13.7).

(j)   Rent you receive on other property: R(FC) 2/92 (table 13.8). But if you rent out property as a business this counts as self-employed earnings (para 15.33).

(k)   Employed earnings are assessed separately (paras 14.5-16).

(l)   Income you receive as a director of a limited company counts as employed earnings (not self-employed earnings).

Assessing self-employed earnings

14.29   When your self-employed earnings are assessed, the purpose is to estimate 'the amount which is likely to be' your average weekly net profit (for net profit see para 14.36). This is done using information from an assessment period, but other information should be taken into account to obtain a fair and accurate result.

Assessment periods

14.30   Your assessment period is whatever period is appropriate to enable the most accurate estimation of your weekly net profit (CH/329/2003, [2003] UKUT 104 (AAC)). In working age HB it must not be longer than one year, and in pension age HB it is a year unless this would not be appropriate.

14.31   When you make your claim for HB your assessment period is usually:

(a)   the most recent full year for which you have accounts or other records; or

(b)   the period you have been self-employed if this is less than a year; or

(c)   in either case, a shorter or different period if this would be more representative;

(d)   but if you are just starting self-employment, an estimated future period (see para 14.33).

If your self-employed earnings change while you are on HB (para 14.35), your assessment period should usually be from the date the change occurred to the most recent date you have figures for (CH/329/2003, [2003] UKUT 104 (AAC)). For DWP guidance on assessment periods see GM paras BW2.330, BW2.333.

Providing accounts or other records

14.32   You are expected to provide information about your income and expenses in your assessment period. You can draw up accounts or other records yourself, or get someone else to do this for you. They can be drawn up on:

(a)   a cash basis, counting income when it comes in, and expenses when you pay them; or

(b)   an accrual basis, counting income when you issue a bill and expenses when you get a bill,

so long as you are reasonable, consistent, and fairly reflect your income and expenses.

14.29   HB 27(1)(a), 30(1); HB66+ 30(1)(a), 37; NIHB 24(1)(a), 27(1); NIHB66+ 28(1)(a), 35

14.30   HB 2(1) definition: 'assessment period', 30(1); HB66+ 2(1), 37; NIHB 2(1), 27(1); NIHB66+ 2(1), 35

Example: Self-employed earnings and net profit

Dennie is a self-employed window-cleaner. The records of his most recent year's trading show he had gross income of £10,268, and spent £354 on telephone, postage and stationery, £3,534 on petrol and other costs for his van, £187 on overalls and disposable equipment, £507 on advertising, and £613 to pay someone to cover his round while he was on holiday. His mileage records show that two-thirds of his use of the van is for his business (para 14.41).

The council decides that year is appropriate as his assessment period (see para 14.31), as the figures are likely to represent his current income and expenses. His pre-tax profit (para 14.46) is calculated as follows.

From his gross income	£10,268 pa
Deduct his allowable expenses (see table 14.3):	
telephone, postage and stationery	£354 pa
business use of van (⅔ of £3,534)	£2,356 pa
overalls and disposable equipment	£187 pa
advertising	£507 pa
holiday cover payments	£613 pa
This gives his pre-tax profit	£6,251 pa

This is used to calculate his weekly net profit (para 14.36). The earned income disregards which apply to him are then deducted (para 14.60).

Starting self-employment

14.33   When you start self-employment, your self-employed earnings can be estimated to begin with (para 14.31(d)). The estimate usually covers the first 13 weeks you will be self-employed. Most councils have a form you can use to give your estimated income and expenses for this period, and expect you to provide records of your actual income and expenses after that. If you have been out of work for 26 weeks or more, you may qualify for an 'extended payment' of HB (para 17.32).

Stopping self-employment

14.34   When you stop self-employment, any self-employed earnings are disregarded from the date you stopped, except for royalties etc (para 14.58-59).

14.34   HB sch 4 para 2A; NIHB sch 5 para 2A

Changes in your self-employed earnings

14.35   Your self-employed earnings can change in different ways. Generally speaking:

(a) short-term variations in your cash flow (for example from month to month) are a normal part of being self-employed, and do not mean your HB should be reassessed; but

(b) significant changes in your trading pattern mean your HB should be reassessed. For example, this could be because you change from full-time to part-time or from part-time to full-time, or gain or lose a major customer, or have a break from trading because you are sick or caring for someone or due to coronavirus.

Calculating net profit

14.36   It is your 'net profit' which the council uses to calculate your HB. It is calculated as follows using the information described in paras 14.29-35:

(a) start with your gross income: para 14.37;

(b) deduct your allowable expenses: paras 14.38-45 or 14.52;

(c) this gives your pre-tax profit (or if you are in a partnership your share is your pre-tax profit): paras 14.46-52;

(d) deduct amounts for tax and national insurance: paras 14.53-55;

(e) deduct half your pension contributions: para 14.56;

(f) convert the result to a weekly figure: para 6.37;

(g) this gives your weekly net profit: para 14.57.

See also paras 14.60-73 for the earned income disregards.

Gross income

14.37   Your gross income is the total of your self-employed earnings before any deductions have been made from them: see paras 14.26-35.

Allowable expenses

14.38   Your allowable expenses are deducted from your gross income. There are two main conditions about this:

(a) expenses are only allowable if they are 'wholly and exclusively incurred' for the purposes of the business: paras 14.40-44;

(b) but expenses are not allowable if they are not 'reasonably incurred': para 14.45.

Some types of expenses also have special rules, and these are all included in table 14.3.

14.39   Table 14.3 summarises which expenses are allowable and which are not, and further details are in paras 14.40-45. Different rules apply if you are a childminder: see para 14.52.

14.36   HB 2(1) definition: 'net profit', 30(2), 38; HB66+ 2(1), 28,39; NIHB 2(1), 27(2), 32; NIHB66+ 2(1), 26,37

14.37   HB 37(1); HB66+ 38(1); NIHB 34(1); NIHB66+ 36(1)

14.38   HB 38(3)(a),(4),(7); HB66+ 39(2)(a),(3),(6); NIHB 35(3)(a),(4),(7); NIHB66+ 37(2)(a),(3),(6)

Table 14.3 **Self-employed expenses**

Allowable expenses

(a) Expenditure (from your income) on repairing an existing business asset, apart from costs covered by an insurance policy.

(b) Capital repayments on a loan used for repairing an existing business asset, apart from costs covered by an insurance policy.

(c) Capital repayments on a loan used for replacing business equipment or machinery (this includes a loan for replacing a car: R(H) 5/07).

(d) Interest payments on any business loan.

(e) Any VAT you pay (minus any VAT you receive).

(f) Any other expenditure which meets the conditions in para 14.38. For example:
- computer, telephone, postage, stationery and delivery costs,
- transport and vehicle costs and hire and leasing charges,
- materials, supplies, stock and protective clothing,
- advertising and subscriptions to trade and professional bodies,
- bank charges, insurance costs, and accountancy and legal fees,
- staff costs and payments to subcontractors,
- premises costs such as rent, rates, cleaning and fuel.

Non-allowable expenses

(g) Capital expenditure, such as buying a vehicle, equipment of a lasting nature, or business premises.

(h) Capital repayments on a loan, unless (b) or (c) above applies.

(i) Depreciation of capital assets.

(j) Expenditure on setting up or expanding your business (but interest on loans for this is allowable: see (d) above).

(k) Losses you have incurred before your assessment period (paras 14.30-31).

(l) Expenditure on business entertainment.

(m) Unpaid bills you have sent out, unless they are proven bad debts.

(n) Expenditure for domestic or private purposes (see also paras 14.41-44).

(o) Any other expenditure which does not meet the conditions in para 14.38.

T14.3(a)-(e)   HB 38(6),(8)(b); HB66+ 39(5),(7)(b); NIHB 35(6),(8)(b); NIHB66+ 37(5),(7)(b)

T14.3(f)   HB 38(3)(a),(4),(7); HB66+ 39(2)(a),(3),(6); NIHB 35(3)(a),(4),(7); NIHB66+ 37(2)(a),(3),(6)

T14.3(g)-(n)   HB 38(5),(8)(a); HB66+ 39(4),(7)(a); NIHB 35(5),(8)(a); NIHB66+ 37(4),(7)(a)

'Wholly and exclusively incurred' expenses

14.40   An expense is wholly and exclusively incurred for your business if all of it is for your business and no part of it is for anything else. For example, if you use a van only for your business (and do not use it for domestic, private or other purposes), your vehicle costs for the van are allowable expenses. See also paras 14.41-44.

Expenses for mixed purposes

14.41   If an expense is partly for your business and partly for another purpose, you can separate it out to find the business part. This is also called 'apportioning' expenses. For example, if you use a car for both business and personal purposes, you can keep records of your mileage and then separate the costs on that basis. The business part is then allowable. But the calculation does not have to be that detailed, so long as the method you use is fair and reasonable.

14.42   Even expenses you would incur anyway can be apportioned. For example you would have to pay for insurance and a vehicle licence on a car (and perhaps repay a car loan) even if you did not use it for your business, but you can apportion these expenses in the same way as the petrol you use (R(H) 5/07, which followed R(FC) 1/91).

Expenses if you work from home

14.43   If you work from home, part of your accommodation costs are an allowable expense. For example, this can include part of your fuel for heating and lighting, standing charges, and rent (see also para 14.44). The business part of these should be calculated in a fair and reasonable way, taking into account the size of your working area compared with the size of the rest of your home, and the amount of time you use it for business rather than domestic purposes. In one case a self-employed claimant used the second bedroom in their home only for business purposes. The difference between the total rent on their home and the rent officer's valuation of the rent for a one-bedroom flat was accepted as an appropriate allowable expense (para 12 of R(H) 5/07).

14.44   But when part of your rent is allowed as a business expense, that part cannot be included in your eligible rent: para 8.82. This affects you if your eligible rent is based on your actual rent (see chapters 8 and 10), but not if it is based on a local housing allowance (chapter 9).

14.40   HB 38(3)(a),(4); HB66+ 39(2)(a),(3); NIHB 35(3)(a),(4); NIHB66+ 37(2)(a),(3)

'Reasonably incurred' expenses

14.45   Whether an expense is reasonably incurred depends on the circumstances of the individual case (R(P) 2/54), including how much you earn from your business (R(G) 1/56). If an expense is appropriate and necessary, it should always be considered reasonably incurred unless it is excessive (R(G) 7/62). If an expense is excessive only the part which is reasonable is allowable.

Pre-tax profit (chargeable income)

14.46   Deducting your allowable expenses from your gross income gives your pre-tax profit. In the law it is called your 'chargeable income'. Further rules about pre-tax profit are in paras 14.47-52. See also paras 14.53-56 for deductions for tax etc.

Pre-tax profit for business partnerships

14.47   If you are self-employed in a partnership, your pre-tax profit is worked out for your business and then divided between you. The same applies if you are a share fisherman. The division is made in the same way as you actually share the net profit derived from the business. For example if you are one of two business partners and you get one-third of the net profit (perhaps reflecting the different hours you work in the business or the terms of a partnership agreement), then this is the proportion of the pre-tax profit of the business that the council should use in the calculation of your HB.

Pre-tax profit and couples

14.48   If you are a couple and are also business partners, your pre-tax profit is divided between you (see para 14.47). If you are self-employed and employ your partner, the pre-tax profit isn't shared between you. But the wages or salary you pay them are your allowable expenses, and are your partner's employed earnings.

If you make a loss

14.49   If your allowable expenses are greater than (or equal to) your gross income, your pre-tax profit is nil, so your self-employed earnings are nil (R(H) 5/08).

14.50   Your losses cannot be deducted from any other employed or self-employed earnings you have, or your partner or any other family member has (R(H) 5/08).

Pre-tax profit and drawings

14.51   If you take drawings from your business (for example as a kind of wage or salary you pay yourself), this has no effect on the calculation of your pre-tax profit. Drawings are not part of your gross income (R(H) 6/09) and are not an allowable business expense (GM paras BW2.390-396).

14.45   HB 38(7); HB66+ 39(6); NIHB 35(7); NIHB66+ 37(6)

14.46   HB 38(3)(a); HB66+ 39(3)(a); NIHB 35(3)(a); NIHB66+ 37(3)(a)

14.47   HB 38(1)(b); HB66+ 39(1)(b); NIHB 35(1)(b); NIHB66+ 37(1)(b)

14.50   HB 38(10); HB66+ 39(9); NIHB 35(10); NIHB66+ 37(9)

Pre-tax profit if you are a childminder

14.52   If you are a self-employed childminder:

(a)   your expenses are not deducted from your gross income;

(b)   instead, your pre-tax profit always equals one-third of your gross income.

This is intended to make the calculation easier.

Example: A self-employed childminder

Hendl is a self-employed childminder. She gets gross income from her childminding which averages £240 per week. She works from her home and it would be difficult to assess her expenses, but she does not have to do this because her pre-tax profit is calculated as follows.

Her gross income is	£240
Of this only one-third is counted as her pre-tax profit	£80
This is too low for deductions for tax and national insurance.	
So her net profit is also	£80

The earned income disregards which apply to her are then deducted (para 14.60).

Deductions for tax and national insurance

14.53   Deductions are made from your pre-tax profit for:

(a)   income tax; and

(b)   classes 2 and 4 national insurance contributions (NICs).

The deductions are calculated by the council and are called 'notional tax' and 'notional NICs'. They are unlikely to be the same as the amounts you actually pay HMRC, for a number of reasons, e.g. different assessment periods and differences in what expenses are treated as allowable for income tax and for HB.

14.54   Table 14.4 shows how the deductions are calculated. It gives the figures for the tax year from 6th April 2021 to 5th April 2022 (this tax year contains 365 days). The calculation:

(a)   uses annual figures. So if your pre-tax profit is not an annual amount it is converted to an annual figure;

(b)   uses the tax and NICs figures for the tax year which is 'applicable to' your assessment period (paras 14.30-31). If your assessment period spanned two tax years, councils interpret this in different ways. Many use the most straightforward method of using the figures for the tax year containing your date of claim for HB (or the date your HB is reassessed).

When making the calculation, councils can ignore national changes in the tax and NICs rates and allowances for up to 30 weeks.

14.52   HB 39(3)(b); HB66+ 40(3)(b); NIHB 36(3)(b); NIHB66+ 38(3)(b)

14.53   HB 38(1)(b)(i),(3)(b),(9)(a), 39; HB66+ 39(1)(b)(i),(2)(b),(8)(a), 40; NIHB 35(1)(b)(i),(3)(b),(9)(a), 36; NIHB66+ 37(1)(b)(i),(2)(b),(8)(a), 38

14.54   HB 2(1) definitions: 'basic rate', 'tax year', 'Scottish basic rate', 'Scottish taxpayer', 34, 39(1),(2);
         HB66+ 2(1), 34, 40(1),(2); NIHB 2(1), 31, 36(1),(2); NIHB66+ 2(1), 32, 38(1),(2)

14.55 The calculations in table 14.4 apply in Northern Ireland even if your self-employment is based in the Republic of Ireland.

Table 14.4 **Notional tax and NICs: 2021-22 tax year**

This table shows how your notional tax and national insurance contributions (NICs) are calculated if you are self-employed. All three calculations are made (though one or more of them may give a figure of nil).

(a) Income tax

- start with your annual pre-tax profit
- subtract the personal relief(s) which apply to you, e.g. the £12,750 personal allowance
- if there is a remainder, multiply it by the basic rate of tax (20%) or in the case of a Scottish taxpayer, the Scottish basic rate (20%)
- the result is the annual amount of your notional tax.

(b) Class 2 NICs

- if your annual pre-tax profit is £6,515 or more, the annual amount of your notional class 2 NICs is £158.60.

(c) Class 4 NICs

- start with your annual pre-tax profit;
- multiply the first £9,568 by 0%, the rest up to £50,270 by 9%, and any remainder by 2%;
- the result is the annual amount of your notional class 4 NICs.

Notes:

(a) The personal reliefs that may be applicable dependent upon your circumstances are: the personal allowance, the blind person's allowance, the tax deduction for married couples and civil partners where one was born before 6th April 1935 and the transferable tax allowance for married couples and civil partners [www];

(b) £158.60 is 52 times the weekly class 2 NICs of £3.05, there being 52 Sundays in the 2021-22 tax year. If your pre-tax profit is below £6,515, your notional class 2 NICs are nil (even if you have not applied to HMRC for exemption).

14.55   NIHB 35(12); NIHB66+ 37(11)

T14.4   HB 2(1) definitions: 'basic rate', 'tax year', 'Scottish basic rate', 'Scottish taxpayer', 39; HB66+ 2(1), 40;
NIHB 2(1), 36; NIHB66+ 2(1), 38; SI 2020/299
www.gov.uk/income-tax-rates

Example: Notional tax and NICs

Florence is a self-employed book-keeper who lives in England. She provides her most recent accounts for a full year. The council decides that year is appropriate as her assessment period (para 14.31). In that year she had gross income of £15,150 and allowable expenses of £1,400, so her pre-tax profit is £13,750. She doesn't contribute to a pension scheme. Her notional tax and national insurance contributions (NICs) are calculated as follows (table 14.4).

(a) Notional tax

▪ from her pre-tax profit	£13,750.00 pa
▪ subtract the personal allowance	£12,570.00 pa
	= £1,180.00 pa
▪ and multiply this by the basic rate (20%) to give her notional tax	£236.00 pa

(b) Notional class 2 NICs

▪ her pre-tax profit is greater than £6,475 so her notional class 2 NICs are	£158.60 pa

(c) Notional class 4 NICs

▪ from her pre-tax profit	£13,750.00 pa
▪ subtract the lower earnings threshold	£9,568.00 pa
	= £4,182.00 pa
▪ and multiply this by 9% to give her notional class 4 NICs	£376.38 pa

(d) Net profit

▪ from her pre-tax profit deduct:	£13,750.00 pa
▪ her notional tax	£236.00 pa
▪ her notional class 2 NICs	£158.60 pa
▪ her notional class 4 NICs	£376.82 pa
▪ this gives her annual net profit	£13,137.62 pa
▪ it is converted to a weekly figure:	
▪ £13,137.62 ÷ 365 x 7	£251.95 pw

The earned income disregards which apply to her are then deducted (para 14.60).

Deductions for pension contributions

14.56   If you make regular contributions towards a qualifying personal pension scheme (i.e. a scheme that qualifies for tax relief) half of the amount you contribute is deducted from your pre-tax profit. If your contributions change (or you start or stop making contributions) your HB is reassessed.

14.56   HB 2(1) definition: 'personal pension scheme', 38(1)(b)(ii),(3)(c),(9)(b),(11),(12); HB66+ 2(1),39(1)(b)(ii),(2)(c),(8)(b),(10),(11);
         NIHB 2(1),35(1)(b)(ii),(3)(c),(9)(b),(11),(13); NIHB66+ 2(1),37(1)(b)(ii),(2)(c),(8)(b),(10),(12)

Example: Pension contributions

A couple of months after Florence (in the previous example) claimed HB, she begins making pension contributions of £40 per month. Her HB is reassessed to take account of this as follows. (Her trading pattern has not changed so her income and expenses do not need to be reassessed: para 14.35.)

Her weekly net profit was	£251.95 pw
From this, deduct the weekly equivalent of half of her qualifying pension contributions (para 14.56):	
■ £20 x 12 ÷ 365 x 7	£4.60 pw
This gives her new weekly net profit	£247.35 pw

The earned income disregards which apply to her are then deducted (para 14.60).

Net profit

14.57 The above calculation (paras 14.37-56) gives your net profit. This is converted to a weekly figure (para 6.37). The council uses your weekly net profit to calculate your HB (but only after the earned income disregards have been made: paras 14.60-73).

Royalties and similar payments

14.58 The following payments count as earned income. In working age HB they are assessed as self-employed earnings (para 14.36), and in practice this is also done in pension age HB:

(a) royalties or other payments you receive for the use of, or right to use, a copyright, design, patent or trademark;

(b) payments you receive as an author under the Public Lending Right scheme or a similar international scheme; and

(c) in pension age HB, any other 'occasional' payment you earn.

The rules in (a) and (b) only apply if you are the first owner of the copyright etc or an original contributor to the book etc. If you have inherited the right to receive royalties etc, this is unearned income (para 13.44).

14.59 Because these payments are often annual, six monthly or irregular, there are special rules saying what period they cover:

(a) in pension age HB, they are averaged over the year beginning with the date of payment. For example, a payment of £364 is gross income of £7 per week over that year (see para 6.37);

14.57   HB 2(1) definition: 'net profit', 30(2), 38; HB66+ 2(1), 28,39; NIHB 2(1), 27(2), 35; NIHB66+ 2(1), 26,37

14.58   HB 37(3); HB66+ 29(1)(q),(r), 33(5),(8)(b),(8A); NIHB 34(3); NIHB66+ 27(1)(o),(p), 31(5),(8)(b),(8A)

14.59   HB 37(4); HB66+ 33(4); NIHB 34(4); NIHB66+ 31(4)

(b) in working age HB, work through the following steps:

   ■   start with the weekly amount of your HB (calculated as though you did not receive the royalties etc);

   ■   add to that all the earned income disregards which apply to you (para 14.60);

   ■   the result is your gross income for each week until payment is used up. For example, if your HB is £90 per week and you qualify for only the £10 per week earned income disregard, a payment of £364 is gross income of £100 per week for three weeks, then £64 in the fourth week.

Earned income disregards

14.60   This section describes the amounts which are disregarded from your earned income. You may qualify for one, two, or all three of the following:

   (a) a standard earned income disregard (para 14.62);

   (b) a child care disregard (paras 14.63-67);

   (c) an additional earned income disregard (para 14.68).

They can be described as the amounts you are allowed to 'keep' before your earned income affects the amount of your HB.

How the disregards work

14.61   The earned income disregards work as follows:

   (a) first add together all your (and your partner's):

   ■   weekly net earnings from employment (para 14.17), and

   ■   weekly net profit from self-employment (para 14.36);

   (b) then (from that total) deduct the standard earned income disregard;

   (c) then deduct the child care disregard if you qualify for it. But if:

   ■   the result of (b) is not enough to deduct the whole of the child care disregard, and

   ■   you are on working tax credit or child tax credit,

   the balance of the child care disregard is deducted from your WTC and/or CTC;

   (d) then deduct the additional earned income disregard if you qualify for it. But if:

   ■   the result of (c) is not enough to deduct the whole of the additional earned income disregard (£17.10 as shown in para 14.68), and

   ■   you are on working tax credit,

   the whole of the additional earned income disregard (not just the balance) is instead deducted from your WTC.

Except as described in (c) and (d), no part of the earned income disregards can be deducted from your unearned income. (See para 13.47 if you make parental contributions to a student.)

14.61   HB 2(1) definition: 'earnings' 27(1)(c),(2), 36(2), 38(2), sch 4 paras 3-10A, sch 5 para 56; SI 2020/371 reg 5;
          HB66+ 2(1), 30(1)(c),(2), 33(8), sch 4 paras 1-5A, 7, 9(1),(3), sch 5 para 21;
          NIHB 2(1), 24(1)(c),(2), 33(2), 35(2), sch 5 paras 3-10A, sch 6 para 58; NISR 2020/53 reg 5;
          NIHB66+ 2(1), 28(1)(c),(2), 31(8), sch 5 paras 1-5A, 7, 9(1),(3), sch 6 para 22

Examples: Earned income disregards

1. A couple without children

A couple in their 40s are both employed for 35 hours a week. Their combined net earnings are £500 per week. They do not have children.

From their weekly net earnings:	£500.00
Deduct:	
▪ the standard earned income disregard for a couple (table 14.5 (g))	£10.00
▪ the additional earned income disregard (para 14.68 and table 14.7(b))	£17.10
This gives the figure used in calculating their HB	£472.90

2. A lone parent with child care costs

A lone parent aged 30 is self-employed for 20 hours a week, and his net earnings are £250 per week. He pays child care charges of £70 per week for his daughter aged 9.

From his weekly earnings:	£250.00
Deduct:	
▪ the standard earned income disregard for a lone parent (table 14.5(b))	£25.00
▪ the child care disregard (paras 14.63-64)	£70.00
▪ the additional earned income disregard (para 14.68 and table 14.7(c))	£17.10
This gives the figure used in calculating his HB	£137.90

The standard earned income disregard

14.62   Everyone who has earned income qualifies for a standard earned income disregard. The disregard has different amounts, but whether you are a single claimant, a lone parent, or a couple, you qualify for only one amount. Table 14.5 explains the conditions for each amount, and which one you qualify for.

14.62   HB sch 4 paras 3-10A; HB66+ sch 4 paras 1-5A, 7; NIHB sch 5 paras 3-10A; NIHB66+ sch 5 paras 1-5A, 7

Table 14.5 **The standard earned income disregard**

The standard earned income disregard has different amounts (para 14.62), all given in this table. You qualify for the first amount you meet the conditions for.

(a) 'Permitted work' approved by the DWP: £143 per week

The disregard is £143 per week if you are in 'permitted work'. This means work the DWP has agreed you can do while you are receiving:

- ESA(C);
- incapacity benefit;
- severe disablement allowance; or
- national insurance credits instead of those benefits.

If you are a couple and only one of you is in permitted work, it is disregarded from that one's earned income. But if that is less than £143 per week, the balance up to £20 per week is disregarded from the other one's earned income. The disregard is set at 16 times the national living wage, rounded up to the next 50 pence.

(b) Lone parents: £25 per week

Unless (a) applies to you, the disregard is £25 per week if you are a lone parent.

(c) Sickness or disability: £20 per week: working age HB

In working age HB, unless (a) or (b) apply to you, the disregard is £20 per week if you or your partner:

- get main phase ESA (para 12.48);
- qualify for a disability premium (para 12.37); or
- qualify for a severe disability premium (para 12.25).

(d) Sickness or disability: £20 per week: pension age HB

In pension age HB claims, unless (a) or (b) apply to you, the disregard is £20 per week if you or your partner:

- receive attendance allowance or constant attendance allowance paid with an industrial injury or war disablement pension;
- receive personal independence payment or disability living allowance.
- receive the disability element or severe disability element of working tax credit;
- receive an armed forces independence payment;

T14.5(a)   HB sch 4 para 10A; HB66+ sch 4 para 5A; NIHB sch 5 para 10A; NIHB66+ sch 5 para 5A
           SI 2008/794 reg 45(3),(9A); SI 2013/379 reg 39(1),(4); NISR 2008/280 reg 45(3),(9A); NISR 2016/219 reg 39(1),(4)

T14.5(b)   HB sch 4 para 4; HB66+ sch 4 paras 1(a),2; NIHB sch 5 para 4; NIHB66+ sch 5 paras 1(a),2

T14.5(c)   HB sch 4 para 3; ; NIHB sch 5 para 3;

T14.5(d)   HB66+ 2(1) definition: 'attendance allowance', sch 4 para 5; NIHB66+ 2(1), sch 5 para 5

- receive war pensioner's mobility supplement;

- receive main phase ESA, or national insurance contributions instead of it (para 12.46);

- meet the old work fitness test (incapacity benefit). But in the case of national insurance credits the qualifying period is 28 weeks (not one year). And unlike the rules for the disability premium it can be you or your partner who meets this condition; or

- qualified for the £20 per week disregard (as described in (c) above) at any time in the eight weeks before you reached pension age (para 2.4), and there have been no breaks in either your entitlement to HB or your employment since you reached that age.

(e) Carers: £20 per week

Unless (a) to (d) apply to you, the disregard is £20 per week if your applicable amount includes a carer premium (para 12.29).

If you are a couple and only one of you is a carer, it is disregarded from the carer's earned income. But if that is less than £20 per week, the balance up to £10 per week is disregarded from the other one's earned income.

(f) Special occupations: £20 per week

Unless (a) to (e) apply to you, the disregard is £20 per week if you or your partner are:

- a part-time fire-fighter;

- a part-time lifeboat worker;

- an auxiliary coastguard; or

- a member of the Territorial Army or similar reserve forces.

(See also table 14.1(s).)

(g) Couples: £10 per week

For all other couples, the disregard is £10 per week.

(h) Single claimants: £5 per week

For all other single claimants, the disregard is £5 per week.

T14.5(e) HB sch 4 paras 5,6; HB66+ sch 4 paras 1(b),4; NIHB sch 5 paras 5,6; NIHB66+ sch 5 paras 1(b),4

T14.5(f) HB sch 4 paras 8,9; HB66+ sch 4 paras 1(b),3; NIHB sch 5 paras 8,9; NIHB66+ sch 5 paras 1(b),3

T14.5(g) HB sch 4 para 7; HB66+ sch 4 para 7(b); NIHB sch 5 para 7; NIHB66+ sch 5 para 7(b)

T14.5(h) HB sch 4 para 10; HB66+ sch 4 para 7(a); NIHB sch 5 para 10; NIHB66+ sch 5 para 7(a)

The child care disregard

14.63   You qualify for the child care disregard if:

  (a) you pay child care charges to one or more of the providers in table 14.6;

  (b) you pay them for one or more children who meet the age condition (para 14.66); and

  (c) you are:

  ▪   a lone parent and you work at least 16 hours per week, or

  ▪   a couple and you both work at least 16 hours per week, or

  ▪   a couple and one of you works at least 16 hours per week and the other one meets one or more of the conditions in para 14.67.

Paragraphs 14.69-72 explain when you count as working at least 16 hours per week.

14.64   The disregard equals the weekly amount of child care charges you pay (para 14.65), up to:

  (a) £175 per week if the charges are for one child;

  (b) £300 per week if the charges are for two or more children.

See para 14.61(c) for further information about how the disregard works.

14.65   Table 14.6 explains which child care charges are taken into account. The weekly amount is found by averaging them over whatever period, up to one year, gives an accurate figure. The council can ask the person providing the care for the information about this.

Table 14.6 **Child care providers**

Charges you have paid or will pay to the following are taken into account for the child care disregard (paras 14.63-66):

  (a) A registered child minder, nursery or play scheme.

  (b) A child minding scheme that does not have to be registered, for example, one run by a school or local authority or in Northern Ireland on Crown property.

  (c) Any child care provider if the child care has been approved for working tax credit purposes.

  (d) An out-of-school-hours scheme provided by a school on school premises, by a local authority, or in Northern Ireland by an education and library board or HSS trust. But in this case only, the child must be aged 8 or more.

  (e) A foster parent or kinship carer (apart from the child's own foster parent or kinship carer) under the Fostering Services Regulations 2002, or equivalent provisions in Wales, or the Looked After Children (Scotland) Regulations 2009.

14.63   HB 28(1) ; HB66+ 31(1); NIHB 25(1) ; NIHB66+ 29(1)

14.64   HB 27(3); HB66+ 30(3); NIHB 24(3); NIHB66+ 28(3)

14.65   HB 28(5),(10); HB66+ 31(5),(10); NIHB 25(5),(10); NIHB66+ 29(5),(10)

(f) A domiciliary care worker under the Domiciliary Care Agencies Regulations 2002, or equivalent provisions in Wales.

(g) Anyone else who provides care wholly or mainly in the child's home, for example, a friend who comes in to provide care for the child. But this does not apply if they are your partner or a relative of the child. See para 7.58 for who counts as a 'relative'.

But payments you make in respect of compulsory education do not count towards the child care disregard.

14.66 A child meets the age condition for the child care disregard from birth until:

(a) the first Monday in September following their 15th birthday; or

(b) if they meet the conditions for a disabled child premium (para 12.22), the first Monday in September following their 16th birthday.

14.67 The conditions listed in this paragraph are about the child care disregard for couples (para 14.63(c)). If you are a couple and one of you works at least 16 hours per week, the other one does not have to do so if they:

(a) meet the conditions for:

- a work-related activity component (para 12.44),

- a support component (para 12.44), or

- a disability premium (para 12.37); or

(b) are receiving:

- disability living allowance (DLA),

- personal independence payment (PIP),

- attendance allowance, or constant attendance allowance paid with an industrial injury or war disablement pension,

or would do so except that they are in hospital (para 12.51 and table 12.2); or

(c) are receiving:

- main phase ESA (para 12.48), or

- severe disablement allowance; or

(d) have been accepted by the DWP as having limited capability for work (para 12.47(a) or (b)) for a continuous period of 28 weeks, ignoring breaks of up to 12 weeks; or

---

T14.6   HB 28(5),(7)-(9); HB66+ 31(5),(7)-(9); NIHB 25(5),(7)-(9); NIHB66+ 29(5),(7)-(9)

14.66   HB 28(6),(9),(13); HB66+ 31(6),(9),(13); NIHB 25(6),(9),(13); NIHB66+ 29(6),(9),(13)

14.67   HB 28(1)(c),(11); HB66+ 31(1)(c),(11) ; NIHB 25(1)(c),(11); NIHB66+ 29(1)(c),(11)

14.67(a)   HB 28(11)(a),(b),(ba); HB66+ 31(11),(b),(ba); NIHB 25(11)(a),(b),(ba); NIHB66+ 29(11),(b),(ba)

14.67(b),(c) HB 28(11)(d)-(f); HB66+ 31(11),(d)-(f); NIHB 25(11)(d)-(f); NIHB66+ 29(11),(d)-(f)

14.67(d)   HB 28(11)(c),(ca),(12),(12A); HB66+ 31(11)(c),(ca),(12),(12A); NIHB 25(11)(c),(ca),(12),(12A); NIHB66+ 29(11)(c),(ca),(12),(12A)

(e)   have an invalid carriage or similar vehicle; or

(f)   are aged 80 or more; or

(g)   are in hospital; or

(h)   are in prison (serving a sentence or on remand).

Condition (d) only applies to the HB claimant but if you want to swap roles with your partner this usually ends your HB (paras 2.6.9, 16.2).

The additional earned income disregard

14.68   You qualify for the additional earned income disregard if you meet one or more of the conditions in table 14.7. The amount of the disregard is £17.10 per week. See para 14.61(d) for further information about how the disregard works. For the treatment of the one-off coronavirus payment of £500 paid by HMRC in 2021 if you are entitled to WTC, see para 15.51.

Working at least 16 hours per week

14.69   You count as working at least 16 hours per week if:

(a)   you are employed or self-employed in work for which payment is made or expected; and

(b)   you work at least 16 hours per week every week, or on average (para 14.70).

The law calls this 'remunerative work'.

14.70   If your hours vary, they are averaged as follows:

(a)   if there is no recognisable cycle to your work, over five weeks or whatever period would give a more accurate figure;

(b)   if your work has a recognisable cycle (for example you work a regular pattern of shifts), over the whole of that cycle. In this case, the averaging includes periods you don't work;

(c)   but if your work has a recognisable cycle of a year (for example you work in term-times but not school holidays) over the whole year. In this case, the averaging excludes periods you don't work but the result applies throughout the year. (So if you work at least 16 hours every week in term-times, you count as working at least 16 hours per

---

14.67(e)   HB 2(1) definition: 'invalid carriage', 28(11)(g); HB66+ 2(1), 31(11)(g) ; NIHB 2(1), 25(11)(g); NIHB66+ 2(1), 29(11)(g)

14.67(f)   HB66+ 31(11)(a); ; NIHB66+ 29(11)(a)

14.67(g),(h) HB 28(1)(c); HB66+ 31(1)(c); NIHB 25(1)(c); NIHB66+ 29(1)(c)

14.68   HB sch 4 para 17; HB66+ sch 4 para 9; SI 2020/371 reg 5; NIHB sch 5 para 17; NIHB66+ sch 5 para 9; NISR 2020/53 reg 5

14.69   HB 2(1) definition: 'remunerative work'; HB66+ 2(1), 6(1); NIHB 2(1), 6(1); NIHB66+ 2(1), 6(1)

14.70   HB 6(2)-(4); HB66+ 6(2)-(4); NIHB 6(2)-(4); NIHB66+ 6(2)-(4)

Table 14.7 **The additional earned income disregard**

You qualify for the additional earned income disregard (see para 14.68) if you meet one or more of the conditions (a) to (e). Paras 14.69-73 explain when you count as working at least 16 or 30 hours per week. The examples illustrate how the conditions work for couples.

(a) You receive working tax credit and it includes the WTC '30 hour element'.

If you are a couple, at least one of you has to qualify for the WTC 30 hour element. See example 1.

(b) You:

- are aged 25 or more; and

- work at least 30 hours per week.

If you are a couple, at least one of you has to meet both halves of this condition. See example 2.

(c) You:

- are responsible for one or more children or young persons; and

- work at least 16 hours per week.

If you are a couple, only one of you has to work at least 16 hours per week. See example 3.

(d) In working age HB, you:

- qualify for a work-related activity component, a support component, or a disability premium, or are on main phase ESA but can't get a component (see paras 12.37-39 and 12.42-49); and

- work at least 16 hours per week.

If you are a couple, at least one of you has to meet both halves of this condition. See example 4.

(e) In pension age HB, you:

- qualify for the £20 disregard for sickness or disability (see table 14.5(d)); and

- work at least 16 hours per week

If you are a couple, at least one of you has to meet both halves of this condition. See example 5.

Note:

For condition (a) you have to be on WTC (and getting the WTC 30 hour element). For conditions (b) to (e) you don't have to be on WTC (but they are the same as the conditions used in WTC for getting the 30 hour element).

T14.7   HB sch 4 para 17(2); HB66+ sch 4 para 9(2); NIHB sch 5 para 17(2); NIHB66+ sch 5 para 9(2)

Examples: The additional earned income disregard for couples

1. A couple on working tax credit

A couple are on WTC. One of them has been awarded the WTC '30 hour element'.

- ■ They qualify for the additional earned income disregard: see table 14.7(a).

2. A couple without children

A couple are aged 22 and 27. The 22-year-old works for 35 hours a week. The 27-year-old does not work.

- ■ They do not qualify for the additional earned income disregard: see table 14.7(b). (They would qualify if the 27-year-old worked at least 30 hours a week.)

3. A couple with a child

A couple with a baby. One of them works for 20 hours a week. The other one does not work.

- ■ They qualify for the additional earned income disregard: see table 14.7(c).

4. A working age couple, one with a disability

A couple are in their 50s. One of them receives personal independence payment (PIP) and works for 20 hours a week.

- ■ They qualify for the additional earned income disregard: see table 14.7(d).

5. A pension age couple, one with a disability

A couple are in their 70s. One of them receives attendance allowance and does not work. The other one works for 20 hours a week.

- ■ They do not qualify for the additional earned income disregard: see table 14.7(e). (They would qualify if the one on attendance allowance worked at least 16 hours a week, or they both did.)

week throughout the year.)

14.71 Once you count as working at least 16 hours per week (paras 14.69-70):

(a) you continue to do so during the following absences from work:
- ■ while you are on holiday, or
- ■ while you are absent from work 'without good cause';

(b) for the purposes of the child care disregard (only), you also continue to do so:
- ■ while you are on maternity, paternity, shared parental or adoption leave. This only applies while you are getting statutory maternity, paternity, shared parental or adoption pay, or maternity allowance, or income support because of paternity leave (these can be paid for up to 39 weeks; and if you are getting the child element of WTC when they stop, it continues to apply until the WTC child element stops), or
- ■ while you are on sick leave. This is limited to 28 weeks. And it only applies while you are getting statutory sick pay, incapacity benefit at the short-term lower rate, ESA, income support because of incapacity for work, or national insurance credits

---

14.71-72   HB 2(1) definitions: 'adoption leave', 'maternity leave', 'paternity leave', 'shared parental', 'sports award', 6(1),(5)-(8), 28(2)-(4),(14),(15); HB66+ 2(1), 6(1),(5)-(8), 31(2)-(4),(14)-(16); NIHB 2(1), 6(1),(5)-(8), 25(2)-(4),(14),(15); NIHB66+ 2(1), 6(1),(5)-(8), 29(2)-(4),(14)-(16)

instead of these.

14.72   You do not count as working at least 16 hours per week:

(a) while you are absent from work 'with good cause' (for example you are laid off);

(b) while you are doing unpaid work;

(c) while your only income is from a Sports Council award (para 13.43);

(d) in any benefit week in which you are on JSA(IB), ESA(IR) or income support for more than three days;

(e) while you are on maternity, paternity, shared parental or adoption leave, with the right to return to work under your contract or under employment law; or

(f) while you are absent from work due to illness, whether or not you are being paid.

There are exceptions to (e) and (f) in relation to the child care disregard: see para 14.71(b).

Working at least 30 hours per week

14.73   The rules about whether you count as working at least 30 hours per week are the same as in paras 14.69-72, apart from the different number of hours.

14.73   HB sch 4 para 17(4); HB66+ sch 4 para 9(4); NIHB sch 5 para 17(4); NIHB66+ sch 5 para 9(4)

Chapter 15 **Capital**

- General rules about assessing capital: see paras 15.1-13.
- How capital is valued: see paras 15.14-20.
- Savings and investments: see paras 15.21-27.
- Property and possessions: see paras 15.28-35.
- Trust funds, compensation payments and other capital: see paras 15.36-55.
- Notional capital: see paras 15.56-70.

Assessing capital

15.1　This chapter explains how your capital is assessed for HB purposes, including actual capital (paras 15.21-55) and notional capital (paras 15.56-70). This section gives rules relating to all types of capital.

'Your' capital

15.2　If you are single, your own capital is taken into account. If you are in a couple, the capital of your partner is taken into account as well as yours. If you are in a polygamous marriage, the capital of all your partners is included. In this chapter, 'your' capital always includes the capital of your partner (or partners). But if a child or young person has capital of their own, this is never included.

How your capital affects your HB

15.3　If you are on a passport benefit (para 13.5), all your capital is disregarded (ignored) and you qualify for maximum HB: see paras 6.2-3.

15.4　If you are not on a passport benefit, some kinds of capital are counted and some are disregarded. The details are in this chapter. Once the amount of your capital is valued (paras 15.14-20), it is taken into account as follows:

(a) if it is more than £16,000 you are not entitled to HB; otherwise

(b) the first £6,000 is ignored in working age HB claims;

(c) the first £10,000 is ignored in pension age HB claims;

(d) the remainder up to £16,000 is counted as providing you with an assumed amount of income (para 15.5).

(See also para 13.15 if you are on the savings credit of SPC.)

15.1　HB 44(1); HB66+ 44(1); NIHB 41(1); NIHB66+ 42(1)

15.2　CBA 136(1); HB 25, 45; HB66+ 23; NICBA 132(1); NIHB 22, 42; NIHB66+ 21

15.3　HB sch 6 paras 5,6; HB66+ 26; NIHB sch 7 paras 5, 6; NIHB66+ 24

15.4　CBA 134(1); HB 43, 44(2), 52(1), sch 6; HB66+ 28, 29(2), 43, 44(2); NICBA 130(1), NIHB 40, 41(2), 49(1), sch 7; NIHB66+ 26, 27(2), 41, 42(2)

Assumed income from capital (tariff income)

15.5   The assumed income from your capital (apart from disregarded capital) is calculated as follows (in the law it is also called 'tariff income'):

(a)   in working age HB, deduct £6,000 from your capital and divide the remainder by 250;

(b)   in pension age HB , deduct £10,000 from your capital and divide the remainder by 500;

(c)   if the result of (a) or (b) is not an exact multiple of £1, round the result up to the next £1.

This gives the weekly amount of your assumed income from capital. It is added to your other income: see para 13.1. (For interest and other kinds of actual income from capital see para 15.26.)

Examples: Assessing capital and assumed income from capital

1. A working age HB claim

Leroy is in his 40s and has £14,085 in his bank account. Of this, £2,000 is an insurance payment he received three weeks ago to replace his motorbike after an accident. He has no other capital.

Assessment:

- The £2,000 is disregarded (table 15.1(j))
- So his capital for HB purposes is   £12,085

Assumed income from capital (tariff income):

- From the £12,085, £6,000 is deducted leaving   £6,085
- Dividing this by 250 gives   £24.34
- Rounding up to the next whole pound gives   £25
- So he has £25 per week of assumed income from capital

2. A pension age HB claim

Nadia and Idris are in their 80s and have £15,085 in their bank account. Of this, £3,000 is arrears of attendance allowance they received three months ago after winning an appeal. They have no other capital.

Assessment:

- The £3,000 is disregarded (table 15.2)
- So their capital for HB purposes is   £12,085

Assumed income from capital (tariff income):

- From the £12,085, £10,000 is deducted leaving   £2,085
- Dividing this by 500 gives   £4.17
- Rounding up to the next whole pound gives   £5
- So they have £5 per week of assumed income from capital

15.5   CBA 136(2); HB 27(1)(b), 52; HB66+ 30(1)(b), 29(2); NICBA 132(2); NIHB 24(1)(b), 49; NIHB66+ 28(1)(b), 27(2)

Distinguishing capital from income

15.6 HB law does not give a definition of capital or income. Instead the rules 'operate at a stage after the money has been classified' (CH/1561/2005). But the distinction is usually straightforward: see paras 15.7-13.

Capital you hold

15.7 DWP guidance says 'As a general rule, capital includes all categories of holdings which have a clear monetary value' (GM para BW1.70). The rules for savings, investments, property and other items are given later in this chapter, including when they count as your capital and when they are disregarded.

Capital someone else holds for you

15.8 If someone else holds your capital for you, it counts as yours. For example, this includes money held for you by the Court of Protection ([2011] UKUT 157 (AAC)) or by someone who has power of attorney for you.

Capital you hold for someone else

15.9 If you hold someone else's capital for them, it does not count as yours. For example, you might be looking after your child's savings for them, or someone you are caring for may have put your name on a joint bank account with them so you can deal with their money for them. It is up to you to provide evidence that the money is not yours, but you do not need to be a formally documented trustee for them ([2010] UKUT 437 (AAC)). (If you are a trustee, see para 15.41.)

Payments of income and capital

15.10 A payment you receive can be income (for example earnings or benefits) or capital (for example an inheritance). This is decided by looking at 'the true characteristics of the payment in the hands of the recipient' (in other words, what it is to you), rather than whether the person pays it you periodically or in a lump sum or whether they (or you) call it 'income' or 'capital' (Minter v Hull City Council). DWP guidance says it is more likely to be capital if it is '(i) made without being tied to a period, (ii) made without being tied to any past payment, and (iii) not intended to form part of a series of payments' (GM para BW1.71).

Payments of arrears of income

15.11 A payment of arrears of income is assessed in both the following ways:

(a) it is income for a past period, except when that kind of income is disregarded. This may mean you have been overpaid HB (chapter 19);

(b) it is capital from when you receive it until when you spend it. But arrears of some benefits are disregarded as capital for 52 weeks or longer (para 15.52).

The fact that arrears of income can affect your capital does not stop them being income for a past period. For example a large lump sum settlement of an equal pay claim can be income for a past period if it is 'properly characterised as wages' (Minter vs Hull City Council).

15.10-11   Minter v Hull CC 13/10/11 CA [2011] EWCA Civ 1155 www.bailii.org/ew/cases/EWCA/Civ/2011/1155.html

15.11   HB 27(1), 31(1),(2), 44(1); HB66+ 30, 33(1),(6), 44(1); NIHB 24(1), 28(1),(2), 41(1); NIHB66+ 28, 31(1),(6), 42(1)

Payments of capital in instalments

15.12   If capital is payable to you in instalments, outstanding instalments are assessed as follows:

(a)   in pension age HB, they do not count as your capital until you receive them;

(b)   in working age HB, they count as your capital straight away (in other words even before you receive them). But if they would take your capital over £16,000, they count instead as your income.

When payments of income become capital

15.13   Income you do not spend becomes capital. 'A payment of income… remains income for the period in which it is paid. Any surplus at the end of that period metamorphoses into capital' (CH/1561/2005). This applies to counted income (for example earnings) and also to disregarded income (for example fostering allowances: CIS/3101/2007). So if your income is paid monthly, only what is left at the end of the month is capital. Different rules apply to arrears of income (para 15.11).

Valuing capital

15.14   The value of each item of capital you have (apart from disregarded capital) is assessed by working through the following steps:

(a)   start with its current market or surrender value (para 15.15);

(b)   then deduct 10% if selling it would involve costs (para 15.16);

(c)   then deduct any debt or charge secured against it (para 15.17).

Further rules are in paras 15.18-20. See para 13.15 if you are on the savings credit of state pension credit.

Market or surrender value

15.15   Dwellings, non-residential property, and many other items have a market value. It is what they would fetch if you sold them on the open market. Your council can ask the Valuation Office Agency to assist them in valuing these (forms for this are in GM BW1 annexes D and E, and further DWP guidance is in circular A25/2009). Insurance policies and some other investments have a surrender value. It is what you would be paid if you cashed them in now. For cash in a bank account see para 15.22.

Sales costs

15.16   If selling a capital item would mean you had to pay a fee or other costs, 10% is deducted from its value. For example this applies to property and shares. You do not have to work out what the actual sales costs would be. Instead, the 10% deduction always applies.

15.12   HB 41(1), 44(1), sch 6 para 18; HB66+ 44(1); NIHB 38(1), 41(1), sch 7 para 19; NIHB66+ 42(1)

15.14   HB 47; HB66+ 45; NIHB 44; NIHB66+ 43

15.15   HB 47; HB66+ 45; NIHB 44; NIHB66+ 43

15.16   HB 47(a); HB66+ 45(a); NIHB 44(a); NIHB66+ 43(a)

Secured debts or charges

15.17   Any debt or charge secured against a capital item is deducted from its value. For example this includes the outstanding mortgage on a property. Only secured debts and charges can be deducted (the law calls them 'encumbrances'). Other debts (such as rent arrears) cannot be deducted from your capital (CH/3729/2007).

Jointly owned capital

15.18   If you own a capital item jointly with one or more other people (other than just your partner), only your share of its capital value is taken into account. This means:

(a) your actual share if you own it in known shares (e.g. if you own a one-third share and another person owns a two-thirds share): R(IS) 4/03 – and in appropriate cases this could be your beneficial share (the share that is intended to be of benefit to you): [2018] UKUT 25 (AAC)

(b) an equal share in other cases (for example one-half if there are two of you).

Your share is valued as described in paras 15.14-16. The reason your share is valued rather than the whole item, is that the value of a half-share (for example) can be less than half the value of the whole item. In some cases the value of a share of capital can be minimal (CH/1953/2003).

Examples: Valuing capital

1. Shares in a company

Wilma owns 1,000 shares. Their sell price is currently £0.78 each.

- Their market value is 1,000 x £0.78   £780
- Deduct 10% for sales costs   £78
- Their value for HB purposes is   £702

2. Jointly owned land

Fred and his two brothers jointly own some land in equal shares. It is worth £35,000, but the value of a one-third share is £10,500. Fred is on HB. He took out a loan using his share of the land as security and £5,400 of the loan remains to be paid.

- The market value of his share is   £10,500
- Deduct 10% for sales costs   £1,050
- Deduct the loan   £5,400
- The value of his share for HB purposes is   £4,050

15.17   HB 47(b); HB66+ 45(b); NIHB 44(b); NIHB66+ 43(b)

15.18   HB 51; HB66+ 49; NIHB 48; NIHB66+ 47

Capital outside the UK

15.19   If you own capital in a country outside the UK:

(a)   its market or surrender value in that country is taken into account (see also para 15.20);

(b)   but if you are prohibited (by that country) from bringing the money to the UK, it is valued at what a willing buyer in the UK would give for it.

In each case steps (b) and (c) in para 15.14 then apply.

Capital not in sterling

15.20   If you have capital in a currency other than sterling, any banking charge or commission for converting it to sterling is deducted.

Savings and investments

15.21   This section gives the rules for savings and various kinds of investment. (For property and possessions, see paras 15.28-35.)

Savings and cash

15.22   Your savings are counted in full as your capital whether you keep them as cash or in a bank, and interest is included as capital from when it is due. But if you have more than one bank account, and the bank has the power to use money in one to pay an overdraft on another, it is the net amount (across those accounts) which is counted: [2011] UKUT 63 (AAC). See also para 15.13 if your income is paid into an account.

Savings certificates

15.23   National Savings and Ulster Savings certificates count in full as your capital. You can find out their current value using an online calculator, and the DWP says your council should use this to value them (GM BW1.440-451).

Shares and similar investments

15.24   Shares, unit trusts, income bonds and similar investments count in full as your capital. Shares and unit trusts are valued at their current 'sell' price. Then 10% is deducted for sales costs in the case of shares (see para 15.16), but not normally for unit trusts because their sell price already allows for this.

Pension schemes, annuities, life insurance and funeral plans

15.25   Capital held in the following is wholly disregarded:

(a)   an occupational or personal pension scheme (para 13.27);

(b)   an annuity (paras 13.32-33);

15.19   HB 48; HB66+ 46; NIHB 45; NIHB66+ 44

15.20   HB sch 6 para 23; HB66+ sch 6 para 23; NIHB sch 7 para 24; NIHB66+ sch 7 para 23

15.22   HB 44(1); HB66+ 44(1); NIHB 41(1); NIHB66+ 42(1)

15.23   HB 44(1); HB66+ 44(1); NIHB 41(1); NIHB66+ 42(1)

15.24   HB 44(1), 47(a); HB66+ 44(1), 45(a); NIHB 41(1), 44(a); NIHB66+ 42(1), 43(a)

(c) a life insurance policy, including a bond or similar investment which has a life insurance element (R(IS) 7/98) and including compensation paid by the UK government (£5,000) to holders of Equitable Life pre-1992 policies (HB G10/2013);

(d) in pension age HB claims, a funeral plan contract if its sole purpose is to provide a funeral in the UK for you and/or your partner.

Their surrender value is also disregarded (this means what you would get if you cashed them in), but capital you actually receive from them (if you do cash in part or all) is counted in full.

Interest and other actual income from capital

15.26   Interest you receive on a bank account, and other kinds of actual income you receive on capital, are counted as increasing your capital from when they are due. (They are not counted as income, because instead there are rules about assumed income from capital: see para 15.5.) But see tables 13.7 and 13.8 if you receive rent on property you have let out, and para 15.33 for income you receive on business assets.

The value of your right to receive an asset in the future or future income

15.27   Your right to receive an asset in the future can be sold. And the income from some investments can be sold (the purchaser would receive the income in the future instead of you). So each of these has a capital value. But this capital value is disregarded in the case of reversionary interest (table 15.1(g)), occupational and personal pensions, annuities, rent, a life interest/life rent (para 15.31) and any kind of income you cannot bring to the UK (para 13.48).

Property and possessions

15.28   This section gives the rules for property, money relating to property, personal possessions, and business assets. (For property held in a trust see paras 15.37-40.)

Property

15.29   The rules about property apply to dwellings and non-residential premises. Your home and some other property is disregarded: see the first part of table 15.1. Property which is not disregarded is counted as your capital. Its value is assessed as described in paras 15.14-20. If you have rented it out, this is taken into account in valuing it. For example the presence of a sitting tenant can reduce the value of a dwelling (CH/1953/2003). If ownership of a property is in dispute, it may have no value until the dispute is settled.

15.25   SI 2013/2980 reg 5; HB 2(1) definition: 'policy of life insurance', sch 6 paras 13,17,32; HB66+ 2(1), sch 6 paras 11,12,24,29; NIHB 2(1), sch 7 paras 13,18,31A,33; NIHB66+ 2(1), sch 7 paras 11,12,24,31,31A

15.26   HB 46(4); HB66+ 29(1)(i), sch 5 paras 22,24; NIHB 43(4); NIHB66+ 27(1)(g), sch 6 paras 23,25

15.27   HB sch 6 paras 7,13,15,16,31,33; HB66+ sch 6 paras 5,24,27-29; NIHB sch 7 paras 7,13,16,17,32,34; NIHB66+ sch 7 paras 5,24,29-31

15.29   HB 44, sch 6; HB66+ 44(1),(2), sch 6; NIHB 41, sch 7; NIHB66+ 42(1),(2), sch 7

Table 15.1 **Capital disregards relating to property**

Your home and other property

Working age and pension age HB: disregards (a) to (g)

In (a) to (e) only one dwelling can be a person's home at any one time. In (a) to (c) there is no time limit. (if you rent out property as a self-employed business see para 15.33.)

(a) Your home, and any land or buildings (including croft land in Scotland) which are part of it or are impracticable to sell separately. For example, your home is disregarded if you are a shared owner, or an owner claiming HB for rates in Northern Ireland, or are claiming HB temporarily on other accommodation (see paras 3.13, 3.14).

(b) The home of a partner or 'relative' (para 7.58) of yours or of anyone in your family, if that partner/relative:

   ▪ has reached state pension age (para 2.4); or

   ▪ is 'incapacitated'. This word has its ordinary English meaning. For example it is not limited to people on ESA or similar benefits.

(c) The home of your partner if:

   ▪ you have not divorced, dissolved your civil partnership or become estranged (in other words your relationship has not ended: CH/3777/2007); but

   ▪ you no longer count as a couple (or polygamous marriage) for HB purposes (para 4.6).

(d) A home you intend to occupy if:

   ▪ you acquired it within the past 26 weeks*; or

   ▪ you are taking steps to obtain possession of it, and first sought legal advice about this or began legal proceedings within the past 26 weeks*; or

   ▪ you are carrying out essential repairs or alterations to make it fit for occupation or re-occupation, and began doing so within the past 26 weeks*.

(e) Your former home, and any land or buildings (including croft land in Scotland) which are part of it or are impracticable to sell separately, if:

   ▪ you ceased to occupy it because you have divorced, dissolved your civil partnership or become estranged from your partner (in other words your relationship has ended: [2019] UKUT 360 (AAC)); and either

---

T15.1   HB 44(2), sch 6; HB66+ 44(2), sch 6; NIHB 41(2), sch 7; NIHB66+ 42(2), sch 7

T15.1(a)   HB sch 6 para 1; HB66+ sch 6 para 26; NIHB sch 7 para 1; NIHB66+ sch 7 para 26

T15.1(b)   HB sch 6 para 4(a); HB66+ sch 6 para 4(a); NIHB sch 7 para 4(a); NIHB66+ sch 7 para 4(a)

T15.1(c)   HB sch 6 para 4(b); HB66+ sch 6 para 4(b); NIHB sch 7 para 4(b); NIHB66+ sch 7 para 4(b)

T15.1(d)   HB sch 6 paras 2, 27, 28; HB66+ sch 6 paras 1-3; NIHB sch 7 paras 2, 28,29; NIHB66+ sch 7 paras 1-3

T15.1(e)   HB sch 6 para 25; HB66+ sch 6 para 6; NIHB sch 7 para 26; NIHB66+ sch 7 para 6

- they are now a lone parent and live in it as their home (in this case there is no time limit); or

- you ceased to occupy it within the past 26 weeks (this time limit cannot be extended).

(f) A home and any other premises you are taking reasonable steps to dispose of, and began doing so within the past 26 weeks*.

(g) Any property you will not own until a future event occurs (for example you reach a particular age). This is called a 'reversionary interest'. (But for a life interest/life rent see para 15.31.)

Money relating to property

Working age HB: disregards (h) to (m)

(h) Money which:

- is from the sale of your former home (including compensation for compulsory purchase but not a home loss payment) and which you intend to use to buy a home within 26 weeks* of the date of sale; or

- was deposited with a housing association as a condition of occupying your home and which you intend to use to buy a home within 26 weeks* of the date the deposit was returned (DMG chapter 28 para 295330).

This disregard does not apply if you haven't yet decided what to do with the money (CH/2255/2006).

(i) A local authority grant you received as a council tenant within the past 26 weeks*, for:

- buying a home; or

- carrying out repairs or alterations to make a future home fit for occupation.

(j) Insurance or compensation payments you received within the past 26 weeks* for repairs or replacements following loss or damage to your home or personal possessions.

(k) Any other payments received within the past 26 weeks* solely for essential repairs or improvements to your home.

(l) Money deposited with a housing association as a condition of occupying your home.

(m) Tax refunds for interest on a mortgage, or on a loan for home repairs or improvements.

T15.1(f) HB sch 6 para 26; HB66+ sch 6 para 7; NIHB sch 7 para 27; NIHB66+ sch 7 para 7

T15.1(g) HB sch 6 para 7; HB66+ sch 6 para 5; NIHB sch 7 para 7; NIHB66+ sch 7 para 5

T15.1(h) HB 2(1) definition: 'housing association', sch 6 paras 3, 11(b); NIHB 2(1) definition: 'housing association', sch 7 paras 3, 11(a)

T15.1(i) HB sch 6 para 38; NIHB sch 7 para 39

T15.1(j) HB sch 6 para 10(a); NIHB sch 7 para 10(a)

T15.1(k) HB sch 6 para 10(b);;NIHB sch 7 para 10(b);

T15.1(l) HB 2(1) definition: 'housing association', sch 6 para 11(a); NIHB 2(1) definition: 'housing association', sch 7 para 11(a)

Pension age HB: disregards (n) to (p)

(n) Any money paid to you (or deposited in your name) within the past year for the sole purpose of buying a home. For example this can include money from the sale of your former home, compensation for compulsory purchase, local authority grants, and gifts or loans from relatives or friends.

(o) Insurance or compensation payments you received within the past year for repairs or replacements following loss or damage to your home or personal possessions.

(p) Any other payments you received within the past year solely for essential repairs or improvements to your home or a future home.

Extending the 26-week time limits

*   The time limits marked with an asterisk can be extended if it is reasonable to do so in the circumstances. But the time limit in (h) is not extended if your only reason for needing longer is that you are taking a hard line in negotiations about your share of the money from the sale of your home (CH/2255/2006).

Examples: Property

1. The home of a relative

A man owns a house where his mother lives. She is aged 87. He claims HB on the flat he is renting.

■   The value of the house is disregarded: table 15.1(b).

2. A couple end their relationship

A couple jointly own a house where they live with their school-age children. They decide to end their relationship. The man moves out and rents a flat. He claims HB there. The woman remains in the home with the children.

■   His share of the value of the house is disregarded: table 15.1(e).

3. A new partner moves in

Nine months after the man moved out (see example 2) the woman's new partner moves in with her and the children.

■   The man's share of the value of the house is no longer disregarded, because the woman is no longer a lone parent and because more than 26 weeks have passed since he moved out: table 15.1(e).

T15.1(m)   HB sch 6 para 21; NIHB sch 7 para 22

T15.1(n)   HB66+ sch 6 paras 18,20(a); NIHB66+ sch 7 paras 18,20(a)

T15.1(o)   HB66+ sch 6 paras 18,19; NIHB66+ sch 7 paras 18,19

T15.1(p)   HB66+ sch 6 paras 18,20(b); NIHB66+ sch 7 paras 18,20(b)

4. The house is put up for sale

The former partners (see examples 2 and 3) decide to sell the house. They put it on the market.

- The man's share of the value of the house is disregarded for 26 weeks, or longer if this is reasonable to allow a sale to take place: see table 15.1(f).

5. Money for buying a home

A woman sells her home and moves to a rented flat in a new area while she looks for a new property to buy. She claims HB on the flat. She has £240,000 from the sale, and a further £50,000 which her brother gave her towards a new home.

- If she is over state pension credit age, both these amounts are disregarded for one year, but no longer: table 15.1(n).
- If she is under state pension credit age, only the money from the sale is disregarded, and only for 26 weeks or longer if reasonable: see table 15.1(h).

6. A property which is rented out

A couple own a house which is rented out to a tenant through an agency. The house has a market value of £200,000 and there is an outstanding mortgage on it of £175,000. They claim HB on a flat they are renting.

- The market value of the house is £200,000.
- Deduct 10% for sales costs, leaving £180,000.
- Deduct the outstanding mortgage, leaving £5,000.
- This £5,000 is their capital for HB purposes.
- The rent they receive on the house also counts as their capital (not income), after allowing for the mortgage interest, agency fees, and other outgoings they pay on it: table 13.8(b).

Money relating to property

15.30   Money for buying, repairing or improving a home (e.g. including adaptations for people who are elderly or disabled) can be disregarded: see the second part of table 15.1. If you receive rent on a property you have let out, see table 13.8.

Life interest and life rent

15.31   If you have a life interest (or in Scotland a life rent) in property or any other asset, this means you have the right to use it until you die, or someone else dies. Unless the property or other asset is disregarded (see for example table 15.1), the value of the life interest or life rent (if it has a value) is counted as your capital.

15.30   HB sch 6; HB66+ sch 6; NIHB sch 7; NIHB66+ sch 7

15.31   HB 44(1); HB66+ 44(1); NIHB 42(1); NIHB66+ 42(1)

Personal possessions

15.32   The value of your personal possessions is disregarded. This means any physical assets apart from land, property and business assets (R(H)7/08). Payments for loss or damage to your personal possessions are also disregarded (table 15.1(j) and (o)). But in working age claims, personal possessions you bought with the purpose of gaining HB are counted as your capital (para 15.63).

Self-employed business assets

15.33   If you are self-employed (para 14.27) your business assets are disregarded:

(a)   while you are self-employed;

(b)   if you are not self-employed because of sickness or disability but intend to return to the self-employment, for 26 weeks, or longer if you reasonably need longer to return;

(c)   if you have ceased to be self-employed, for as long as you reasonably need to dispose of the assets.

'Business assets' means assets held in the course of your self-employment (CH/4258/2004). In some circumstances they can include property you rent out, though this is unlikely if you just rent out one property as a single letting ([2016] UKUT 357 (AAC)). Business capital is disregarded (as a business asset) if it is 'part of the fund employed and risked in the business' (R (SB) 4/85), which is unlikely to be the case unless you keep it separate from your personal savings. But rent and other income you receive on your business assets counts as part of your self-employed earnings (para 14.28).

Company ownership

15.34   Companies can take several different forms: public limited company (PLC), private limited company (Ltd) and so on. A company is separate legal entity from its shareholders (who are its members). Normally its assets cannot be attributed to its members (R(SB) 57/83) – it is your shares that are valued. However, particularly in the case of a small private limited company, the council may consider that your relationship to the business is more like that of a sole owner or partner. In these circumstances the council may, and for pension age claims must, adopt a different approach.

15.35   If the council decides that your relationship in the business is like that of a sole owner or partner it should:

(a)   disregard the value of your shares in the company; and

(b)   decide whether you are engaged in activities in the course of the company's business (R(IS) 13/93).

If the council decides that you aren't so engaged it must treat you as having notional capital (para 15.56-58) equal to the value (or your share of the value) of the capital of the company, i.e. its net worth (R(IS) 13/93). But if the council decides that you are engaged any notional capital it treats you as having is disregarded.

15.32   HB sch 6 para 12; HB66+ sch 6 para 8; NIHB sch 7 para 12; NIHB66+ sch 7 para 8

15.33   HB sch 6 para 8(1),(2); HB66+ sch 6 paras 9,10; NIHB sch 7 para 8(1),(2); NIHB66+ sch 7 paras 9,10

15.34-35   HB 49(5),(6);HB66+ 47(3),(4);NIHB 46(5),(6);NIHB66+ 45(3),(4)

Trusts and compensation

15.36   This section gives the rules for trusts, personal injury payments, and other compensation and gallantry payments. (For compensation relating to property and possessions see table 15.1.)

Trusts

15.37   Assets held in a trust, such as cash, investments or property are legally owned by the trustees (or trustee) of the trust, and beneficially owned by the beneficiary (or beneficiaries) of the trust. The trustees have a duty to use the assets under the terms of the trust for the benefit of the beneficiary, for example by making payments to them. Paras 15.38-41 explain how this is assessed.

If you are a beneficiary of a trust

15.38   Capital held in a trust for you counts in full as your capital, but see para 15.39 for exceptions. If you are not the only beneficiary of the trust, it is your share of the capital which is taken into account (para 15.18).

15.39   Capital held in a trust for you is disregarded:

(a) if you cannot obtain it until a particular event occurs, for example when you reach a certain age (this is called a 'reversionary' trust); or

(b) if it relates to a personal injury (para 15.43); or

(c) in pension age HB if:

   ■   it is property, and

   ■   the trustees make payments to you, or could do so.

15.40   If you receive a payment of capital from a trust (whether the capital in the trust itself is counted or disregarded):

(a) it is disregarded if any of the disregards in this chapter apply to it (see for example table 15.1(k), (n) and (p));

(b) otherwise it counts in full as your capital.

For payments of income from a trust see para 13.36.

If you are a trustee of a trust

15.41   Capital you hold as a trustee is wholly disregarded. But to count as a trustee it is not enough just to say that you are holding money (or other assets) for someone else, or plan to give it to them. You must have received it on clearly stated terms requiring you to hold it for them, or you must have clearly and consistently expressed that you hold it for them and have given up all intentions of using it for yourself (R(IS)1/90). If you meet these conditions it is not necessary for the trust to be legally documented ([2012] UKUT 115 (AAC); [2018] UKUT 63(AAC)).

15.38   HB 44(1); HB66+ 44(1); NIHB 41(1); NIHB66+ 42(1)

15.39   HB sch 6 paras 7,14; HB66+ sch 6 para 30; NIHB sch 7 paras 7,14; NIHB66+ sch 7 para 32

15.40   HB 44; HB66+ 44(1),(2); NIHB 41; NIHB66+ 42(1),(2)

Government sponsored trust funds

15.42   Any payment of capital or income you receive from the following is disregarded:

(a) the Independent Living Funds (which help severely disabled people live independently);

(b) government schemes for people infected with HIV or hepatitis C from NHS blood and other products and government Thalidomide trusts;

(c) the Variant Creutzfeldt-Jacob Disease (vCJD) Trust; and

(d) the London Bombings Relief Charitable Fund, the London Emergency Trust and the Manchester Emergency Fund (for victims of the attacks and bombings in 2005 and 2017).

The disregards in (a), (b) and (d) have no time limit. The disregard in (c) has no time limit if the payment is to the person with vCJD or their partner or surviving partner, but is limited to two years if it is to a parent or guardian of a child with vCJD. The disregards in (b) to (d) can continue if the payment is passed on to a relative as a gift or inheritance (but the usual HB definition of 'relative' does not always apply here). For further details see GM para BW2.620.

Personal injury payments

15.43   The following payments of capital are disregarded if they relate to a personal injury you or your partner have had:

(a) damages for personal injury which are:

  ▪ held by a court and administered by it, or

  ▪ held by someone else and can only be used under a court order or direction;

(b) any payment for personal injury which is held in a trust; and

(c) any other payment for personal injury except for capital paid to you by a trust (but see para 15.40(a)).

The disregards in (a) and (b) have no time limit. The disregard in (c) has no time limit in pension age HB, but in working age HB it is limited to 52 weeks from the day you receive the first or only payment. (It does not start again if you receive a further payment for that injury.) The 52 weeks is called a 'grace period' because it should give you time to form a trust to hold the money (see (b) above) or invest it in an annuity (para 15.25(b)).

15.44   Payments of income you receive for a personal injury to you or your partner are wholly disregarded. For example this includes income paid to you by a trust or from an annuity in which a personal injury payment was invested. In pension age HB, payments of income are also disregarded if they are paid to you by order of a court for a personal injury to your child.

15.42   HB 2(1) definitions: 'Independent Living Fund' etc, sch 5 para 35, sch 6 paras 24, 34, 55,63; HB66+ 2(1), 29(1), sch 6 paras 14,16,30,26l; NIHB 2(1), sch 6 para 37, sch 7 paras 25,35,52; NIHB66+ 2(1), 27(1), sch 7 paras 14,16,32

15.43   HB sch 6 paras 14, 14A, 45, 46; HB66+ sch 6 para 17; NIHB sch 7 paras 14,15,45; NIHB66+ sch 7 para 17

15.44   HB sch 5 para 14(1)(c)-(e); HB66+ sch 5 paras 14,15; NIHB sch 6 para 14(1)(c)-(e); NIHB66+ sch 6 paras 15,16

Examples: Personal injury payments

1. Working age HB

A woman in her 20s is awarded £500,000 for a personal injury. It is paid into her bank account.

- This is disregarded for 52 weeks (para 15.43(c)).

Five months later a trust is formed, with her parents and solicitor as the trustees and her as the beneficiary. The whole of the personal injury payment is paid into the trust.

- This is now disregarded without time limit (para 15.43(b)).

The trust pays her an income of £70 per week.

- This is disregarded in the assessment of her income (para 15.44).

The trust later pays her a lump sum of £75,000 for the cost of adapting her home to improve wheelchair access.

- This is disregarded for 26 weeks, or longer if this is reasonable, to allow the work to take place (para 15.40(a) and table 15.1(k)).

2. Pension age HB

A man in his 70s is awarded £500,000 for a personal injury. It is paid into his bank account.

- This is disregarded without time limit (para 15.43(c)).

Payments compensating for death of a parent

15.45   If you are under 18, compensation you receive for the death of a parent is wholly disregarded if it is held by a court and administered by it, or held by someone else and can only be used under a court order or direction.

Second World War payments

15.46   Payments of compensation are wholly disregarded if they were paid because – during the Second World War – you, your partner, or your or your partner's deceased husband, wife or civil partner:

(a)   were a slave labourer or forced labourer; or

(b)   suffered property loss or personal injury; or

(c)   were a parent of a child who died; or

(d)   were imprisoned or interned by the Japanese.

There is no time limit. The disregard in (d) is always £10,000 (which is the standard amount paid in these cases), and £10,000 is disregarded from the total of your capital without any time limit (so you do not need to keep track of the money).

The families of the disappeared

15.47   In Northern Ireland, compensation paid to the families of the disappeared is disregarded for 52 weeks from the date of payment.

15.45   HB sch 6 para 45, 46; NIHB sch 7 para 45

15.46   HB sch 6 paras 54, 56; HB66+ sch 6 paras 13,15; NIHB sch 7 paras 51,53; NIHB66+ sch 7 paras 13,15

15.47   NIHB sch 7 para 58; NIHB66+ sch 7 para 27

Gallantry payments

15.48   Payments you receive as a holder of the Victoria Cross or George Cross, and similar payments, are wholly disregarded:

(a) in working age HB in the assessment of both your income and your capital;

(b) in pension age HB in the assessment of your income.

Other capital

15.49   This section gives the rules for benefits which are paid as a lump sum, arrears of benefits, charitable and voluntary payments, loans, and other kinds of capital.

Employment programmes and local authority support

15.50   Lump sum payments of the following are wholly disregarded:

(a) government and related payments to disabled people to help with obtaining or retaining employment;

(b) payments from government work programme training schemes;

(c) in working age HB claims:

  ▪ adoption payments,

  ▪ special guardianship payments,

  ▪ payments to avoid taking children into care, and

  ▪ payments to care leavers;

(d) community care payments;

(e) direct care payments;

(f) payment for a housing-related support service to help you live independently in your accommodation (formerly known as 'Supporting People' payments); and

(g) 'local welfare assistance' or equivalent payments in Scotland, Wales and Northern Ireland (para 23.35).

All are also disregarded as income (table 13.1).

15.48   HB sch 5 para 10, sch 6 para 47; HB66+ 29(1); NIHB sch 6 para 11, sch 7 para 46; NIHB66+ 27(1)

15.50(a)   HB sch 6 paras 43, 44; NIHB sch 7 para 44

15.50(b)   HB 46(7),(8), sch 6 paras A2,A3, 8(3),(4), 35,49,52,55; NIHB 43(7),(8), sch 7 paras 8(3),(4), 36,48,52

15.50(c)   HB sch 6 paras 19,19A,59-61; NIHB sch 7 paras 20,20A,56,57

15.50(d),(e) HB sch 6 para 58; HB66+ sch 6 paras 26D,26F; NIHB sch 7 para 55; NIHB66+ sch 7 para 28C

15.50(f)   HB sch 6 para 57; HB66+ sch 6 paras 18,21(1)(e); NIHB sch 7 para 63; NIHB66+ sch 7 paras 18,21(1)(e)

15.50(g)   HB sch 6 para 20A; HB66+ sch 6 paras 18,21(1)(f)

Table 15.2 **Capital disregards: arrears of benefits**

(a) Disregarded arrears

Arrears of all the following are disregarded when your capital is assessed:

- state pension credit (both guarantee credit and savings credit)
- universal credit
- JSA(IB), ESA(IR), IS and HB
- WTC and CTC
- disability living allowance
- personal independence payment
- attendance allowance, or equivalent benefits (para 13.10)
- bereavement support payments (other than the initial lump sum: para 15.51)
- maternity allowance
- any Scottish child payment or short-term assistance and, in pension age claims, the benefits in para 15.51(d)-(g)
- discretionary housing payments (para 23.1) and in Northern Ireland welfare supplementary payments (para 23.20).

(b) Standard time limit

The disregard lasts for 52 weeks in working age HB, and one year in pension age HB, in each case beginning with the day you received the arrears.

(c) Extended time limit

If the arrears:

- are £5,000 or more;
- are paid while you are on HB; and
- are because you were underpaid due to official error (paras 20.38-39),

the disregard continues for as long as you or your partner remain continuously on HB (including periods one of you remains continuously on HB after the other one's death).

(d) Arrears of war disablement and bereavement pensions

Arrears of the war disablement and bereavement pensions in table 13.4(a) are disregarded:

- for 52 weeks in working age HB claims (the extended time limit does not apply);
- without time limit in pension age HB claims.

Note:

The rules in (a) to (c) above also apply to payments compensating for non-payment of the benefits.

T15.2   CBA 123 definition: 'income related benefit'; HB 46(9), sch 6 para 9; HB66+ 44(3), sch 6 paras 18, 21(1)(a)-(d),(2), 22;
NICBA 122; NIHB 43(8), sch 7 para 9; NIHB66+ 42(3), sch 7 paras 18, 21(1)(a)-(d),(2), 22

DWP and other benefits paid as a lump sum

15.51   Lump sum payments of the following are disregarded:

   (a)   social fund payments (winter fuel payments, cold weather payments, Sure Start
         maternity grant and funeral expenses payment);

   (b)   in Northern Ireland, welfare supplementary payments;

   (c)   for 52 weeks, the initial lump sum of bereavement support payment;

   (d)   winter heating assistance;

   (e)   carers assistance (young carers grant);

   (f)   early years assistance;

   (g)   funeral expense assistance; and

   (h)   the £500 paid by HMRC in 2021 due to coronavirus if you are entitled to WTC
         (see Welfare Direct Bulletin 3/2021 paras 15-19).

The benefits (d)-(g) are paid by Social Security Scotland.

Arrears of benefits and compensation relating to benefits

15.52   Table 15.2 explains when the capital value of arrears of benefits is disregarded. The
same rules apply to payments compensating for non-payment of the benefits. Arrears of
benefits not included in the table are taken into account as described in para 15.11.

Charitable and voluntary payments

15.53   Payments of capital you receive which are charitable and/or voluntary are counted
as your capital. But in working age HB claims, payments in kind (in other words in goods not
money) are disregarded. For payments of income see para 13.30.

Loans

15.54   Money which was loaned to you (and which you still have) is counted as your capital.
But in pension age HB claims, loans for buying a home are disregarded (table 15.1(n)). And
the following count as income, not capital:

   (a)   in working age HB, student loans (para 13.38);

   (b)   in working age HB, career development loans (table 13.11(n));

   (c)   in pension age HB, payments from an equity release scheme (para 13.34).

Other loans can be counted as income if the council has clear evidence that they should be
(R(IS) 6/03, R(H) 8/08). This is likely to mean that (c) above also applies in working age HB.

Other kinds of capital

15.55   If you have any other kind of capital, it is counted in full. But for payments you receive
as an earner see chapter 14.

15.51   HB sch 6 paras 20, 62, 65-68; HB66+ sch 6 paras 18, 21(1),(2)(n),(q),(r),(u),(w) 26H, 26J, 26K
         NIHB sch 7 paras 21, 59, 61, 62; NIHB66+ sch 7 paras 18, 21(1),(2)(m),(o),(p), 28D; NISR 2016/178 reg 12; NISR 2017/35, reg 14

15.53   HB 44(1), 46(6), sch 6 para 34; HB66+ 44(1); NIHB 41(1), 43(6), sch 7 para 35; NIHB66+ 42(1)

15.55   HB 44(1); HB66+ 44(1); NIHB 41(1); NIHB66+ 42(1)

Notional capital

15.56   This section explains when you are counted as having capital you do not in fact have. This is called 'notional capital'.

Types of notional capital

15.57   In working age HB, you can be counted as having notional capital when:

(a) you have deprived yourself of capital (paras 15.60-62);

(b) there is capital available to you (paras 13.54 and 13.56);

(c) you are paid capital on behalf of someone (paras 13.57 and 13.59);

(d) someone else is paid capital on your behalf (paras 13.58-59);

(e) a non-dependant has more income and capital than you (para 13.61); or

(f) you are counted as an owner or partner in relation to a company (para 15.35).

15.58   In pension age HB, you can be counted as having notional capital when:

(a) you have deprived yourself of capital (paras 15.60-62);

(b) a non-dependant has more income and capital than you (para 13.61); or

(c) you are counted as an owner or partner in relation to a company (para 15.35).

Assessing notional capital

15.59   If you are counted as having notional capital, it is assessed in the same way as actual capital. All the rules and disregards given earlier in this chapter apply. This means this section does not apply if you are on a passport benefit (except as described in table 15.3(e)).

Capital you have deprived yourself of

15.60   If you have deprived yourself of capital, it is counted as your notional capital. To 'deprive' yourself of capital means:

(a) you have disposed of it (for example by spending it or giving or lending it to someone); and

(b) your purpose in doing so was to make yourself entitled to HB, or to more HB (we use 'gain HB' to cover both these).

This is called the 'deprivation of capital rule'.

15.61   Table 15.3 explains how the rule works. See paras 15.62-64 for exceptions and further details. See paras 15.59 and 15.65-70 for how notional capital is assessed and how it reduces.

15.59   HB 49(7); HB66+ 47(5); NIHB 46(7); NIHB66+ 45(5)

15.60   HB 49(1); HB66+ 47(1); NIHB 46(1); NIHB66+ 45(1)

Table 15.3 **Deprivation of capital: case law**

This table is about the deprivation of capital rule (see paras 15.60-62).

(a) *The test of purpose:* To count as depriving yourself of capital, 'the test is one of purpose'. Gaining HB must have formed 'a positive part of [your] planning'. [2011] UKUT 500 (AAC).

(b) *Thinking about the consequences:* You can only count as depriving yourself if you knew what you were doing. If you did not think about the consequences, you cannot have acted with the purpose of gaining HB. [2011] UKUT 500 (AAC). And if you had no legitimate choice but to spend capital, this cannot count as deprivation: [2015] UKUT 15 (AAC).

(c) *Your personal circumstances:* Your mental state and capabilities are taken into account. A schizophrenic man without an appointee, who lived in 'an intolerable level of chaos', spent almost all of a big windfall on 'alcohol and high living'. He did not count as depriving himself, because it was not shown that he appreciated what he was doing or what the consequences would be. R(H)1/06.

(d) *Mixed motives:* If you had some other reason for disposing of capital (which is 'almost always' the case), you count as depriving yourself of it if gaining HB was 'a significant operative purpose' of doing so. This includes looking at 'whether, given [your] knowledge, it was reasonable in all the circumstances' to act as you did, bearing in mind your obligations (for example, to support yourself, and to other people). [2009] UKUT 145 (AAC), which cited CJSA/1425/2005.

(e) *Passport benefits and HB:* If you deprived yourself of capital to gain a passport benefit, you also count as depriving yourself to gain HB if you plainly expected that getting the passport benefit would lead to getting HB. [2009] UKUT 145 (AAC).

(f) *Buying an asset whose capital value is disregarded:* Even if what you bought is disregarded, you count as depriving yourself if your purpose was gaining HB (see para 15.63). [2009] UKUT 145 (AAC), which cited R(SB) 40/85 and R(IS) 8/04.

(g) *Buying personal possessions:* In working age HB claims, if you bought a personal possession with the purpose of gaining HB (in this case, a caravan) its value counts as actual (not notional) capital (see para 15.63). [2009] UKUT 145 (AAC).

(h) *Providing receipts:* If you are asked to provide receipts for capital you have spent, this 'is primarily to enable [the council] to be satisfied the money has not been retained' (see para 15.63). But it 'can also form the basis as to the reasonableness of the expenditure'. [2009] UKUT 145 (AAC).

(i) *Seeking to recover the money:* It is irrelevant whether you seek to recover money you deprived yourself of. [2009] UKUT 96 (AAC).

Exceptions

15.62   In pension age HB, the deprivation of capital rule does not apply to capital you have used to:

(a)   buy goods or services which are reasonable in your circumstances; or

(b)   repay or reduce a debt you owe.

In working age and pension age HB, the rule does not apply if you are on a passport benefit, except as described in table 15.3(e).

Distinguishing notional capital from actual capital

15.63   In general terms, capital you have is your actual capital, and capital you disposed of to gain HB is your notional capital. The Upper Tribunal has summarised the following possibilities ([2009] UKUT 145 (AAC)):

(a)   if you have spent capital on an item which counts as capital (for example shares), the item is your actual capital;

(b)   if you have spent capital with the purpose of gaining HB (and (a) does not apply), this is your notional capital;

(c)   the exception to (b) is that in working age HB claims, if you bought personal possessions with the purpose of gaining HB, they are counted as your actual capital;

(d)   if you spent capital without the purpose of gaining HB (and (a) does not apply), this is neither actual nor notional capital;

(e)   if you say you have spent capital but in fact you still have it (for example in an undisclosed bank account), this is your actual capital.

For pension age HB, see also para 15.62.

15.64   There are also differences in other situations. For example:

(a)   if one person holds capital on behalf of another, there are rules about whether it is your actual capital (paras 15.8-9);

(b)   the exception is that in working age HB claims, if one person is paid capital on behalf of another, there are rules about whether it is your notional capital (paras 13.57-59).

How notional capital reduces

15.65   If you have notional capital because of the deprivation of capital rule (paras 15.60-62), your notional capital reduces each week: paras 15.66-70. This is called the 'diminishing notional capital rule'. It is illustrated in the example.

15.62   HB66+ 47(2); NIHB66+ 45(2)

15.63   HB 44, 49(1), sch 6 para 12; HB66+ 44(1),(2), 47(1),(2); NIHB 41, 46(1), sch 7 para 12; NIHB66+ 42(1),(2), 45(1),(2)

15.65   HB 49(1), 50; HB66+ 47(1), 48; NIHB 46(1), 47; NIHB66+ 45(1), 46

The amount of the reduction

15.66   The reduction equals the amount of HB and other benefits you have lost as a result of having notional capital: see paras 15.67-70. But the only benefits taken into account are HB, JSA(IB), ESA(IR), IS and SPC. If the figures for these (apart from HB) relate to a part-week, they are converted to a weekly equivalent.

People who still qualify for HB

15.67   In weeks in which you qualify for HB, the reduction equals the amount you have lost in that particular week.

People who don't qualify for HB

15.68   In weeks in which you don't qualify for HB, the reduction is made at a fixed rate (paras 15.69-70), but only in pension age HB, or in working age HB if you live in supported or temporary accommodation (because otherwise you can't reclaim HB: chapter 2).

15.69   The fixed rate of the reduction equals the amount you lost in the most recent of the following weeks:

(a)   the week your notional capital was first taken into account; or

(b)   the first week you did not qualify for HB; or

(c)   any week in which the fixed rate is recalculated (para 15.70).

15.70   The fixed rate is recalculated only if you make a new unsuccessful claim for HB (in other words you claim but do not qualify for HB) at least 26 weeks after the fixed rate was:

(a)   first calculated (para 15.69(a) or (b)); or

(b)   most recently recalculated (as described in this paragraph).

The new fixed rate is then used if it is higher than (or equal to) the old fixed rate. If it is lower, the old fixed rate continues (but this still counts as a recalculation for (b) above). The fixed rate is not recalculated if you make an unsuccessful claim for HB within the 26 weeks (but the old fixed rate continues). If you make a successful claim for HB (at any time) see para 15.67.

15.66   HB 50(1)-(4),(8); HB66+ 48(1)-(4),(8); NIHB 47(1)-(4),(8); NIHB66+ 46(1)-(4),(8)

15.67   HB 50(1)(a),(2),(3),(8); HB66+ 48(1)(a),(2),(3),(8); NIHB 47(1)(a),(2),(3),(8); NIHB66+ 46(1)(a),(2),(3),(8)

15.69   HB 50(1)(b),(4),(8); HB66+ 48(1)(b),(4),(8); NIHB 47(1)(b),(4),(8); NIHB66+ 46(1)(b),(4),(8)

15.70   HB 50(1)(b),(5)-(8); HB66+ 48(1)(b),(5)-(8); NIHB 47(1)(b),(5)-(8); NIHB66+ 46(1)(b),(5)-(8)

Example: Diminishing notional capital

Catalina claims HB

Catalina is aged 68. She has actual capital of £15,000, and with just this she would qualify for HB of £50 per week. But she is found to have deprived herself of £5,000 and this counts as her notional capital (paras 15.60-70).

- Notional capital   £5,000
- Actual capital   £15,000
- Total capital   £20,000

She does not qualify for HB. The notional capital means she has lost £50 per week. This is the fixed rate reduction.

Catalina claims HB 20 weeks later

- Notional capital (reduced by 20 x £50 = £1,000)   £4,000
- Actual capital (has reduced for other reasons to)   £13,000
- Total capital   £17,000

She does not qualify for HB. The fixed rate of reduction is not recalculated (less than 26 weeks have passed).

Catalina claims HB 10 further weeks later

- Notional capital (further reduced by 10 x £50 = £500)   £3,500
- Actual capital (has not changed)   £13,000
- Total capital   £16,500

She does not qualify for HB. The fixed rate of reduction is recalculated (at least 26 weeks have passed). But the new figure turns out to be £40 per week, so the existing £50 per week fixed rate continues.

Catalina claims HB 20 further weeks later

- Notional capital (further reduced by 20 x £50 = £1,000)   £2,500
- Actual capital (has reduced to)   £12,000
- Total capital   £14,500

She qualifies for and is awarded HB. Actual rates of reduction are used while she is on HB.

Chapter 16 **Claims**

- Making a claim: see paras 16.1-21.
- Information and evidence: see paras 16.22-30.
- HB start dates and backdating: see paras 16.31-50.

Making a claim

16.1   You have to make a claim to get HB. This chapter explains how to do this. It applies whether you are making your first ever claim or are claiming again following a period when you weren't on HB.

Pension age and working age HB

16.2   Anyone can make a claim for pension age HB, but you can only make a claim for working age HB if you live in supported or temporary accommodation (para 2.6).

16.3   If you are already on HB and you move home or have another kind of change in your circumstances, see chapter 17.

Who makes the claim

16.4   You make your HB claim yourself, and can ask a friend, relative, advice worker or someone else to help you. If you are a couple (or in a polygamous marriage) you have to choose one of you to be the claimant. Or if you can't agree the council chooses for you.

Attorneys and appointees if you are unable to act

16.5   Someone can make a claim on your behalf if you are unable, for the time being, to act. They take over all rights and responsibilities in relation to your HB claim. However, no-one can make a claim for you after your death (R (IS) 3/04).

16.6   If someone has power of attorney for you, the council must accept a written claim from them. The council must also accept a claim from a deputy appointed by the Court of Protection; in Scotland, a judicial factor or other guardian; or in Northern Ireland, a controller appointed by the High Court.

16.7   In any other case the council may accept a written request from an individual over 18, or from a firm or organisation, to be your 'appointee' – for example, a friend or relative, a social worker or solicitor, or someone appointed by the DWP to act for you in relation to one of your benefits. Either the council or appointee can terminate the appointment by giving four weeks' written notice.

16.1   AA 1, 5; NIAA 1, 5

16.2   UCTP 4A, 5(2)(a), 6(1),(8); NIUCTP 2B, 3(2)(a), 4(1),(8)

16.4   CBA 134(2); HB 82(1); HB66+ 63(1); NICBA 130(2); NIHB 80(1); NIHB66+ 61(1)

16.5-7   HB 82(2)-(6); HB66+ 63(2)-(6); NIHB 80(2)-(6); NIHB66+ 61(2)-(6)

Where to claim

16.8   You claim HB from your council. Or if you are claiming SPC, JSA, ESA or IS, you can claim HB from the DWP.

Claiming HB from the council

16.9   Each council has at least one office where you can make your HB claim (called a 'designated office' in the law). This is normally the council's benefit office. Some councils in England also allow claims at a county council office or via a social landlord's address.

16.10   You can make a claim to the council in writing (typically on the council's claim form but it could be in a letter). The council must provide claim forms free of charge. Alternatively, you may make a claim online via a web form or app if the council allows this. But the council can only accept electronic claims if its Chief Executive has made a direction permitting it (HB A18/2006). You can also claim by telephone if the council has published a number for this purpose. Sometimes the council may require a signed confirmation from you of the details given in the call.

Claiming HB via the DWP

16.11   When you claim SPC, JSA, ESA or IS from the DWP, you can usually claim HB at the same time and in the same way (e.g. at an interview, by telephone, etc). You have made a claim for HB if you answered the question (or ticked the box, etc) about whether you pay rent (CP/3444/2003). You can do this at any time before your SPC/JSA/ESA/IS claim is decided. But when you claim other benefits from the DWP, including UC in temporary or supported accommodation, you have to make a separate HB claim to the council.

16.12   If you claim HB via the DWP, the DWP sends details of your claim to the council. Before that, it may ask you to provide information and evidence for the council. If it does, the rules in paras 16.16-17 also apply to the DWP.

Telling the council or DWP you want to claim

16.13   If you tell the council or DWP that you intend to claim, this can count as your date of claim (table 16.1(b)). You could notify your intention in any way, such as requesting a claim form or asking how to claim.

Completing your claim

16.14   The council doesn't have to decide your claim or award you HB until your claim is complete.

16.8   HB 83(4)(a),(b); HB66+ 64(5)(a),(b); NIHB 81(4)(a),(b); NIHB66+ 62(5)(a),(b)

16.9-10   HB 2(1) definition: 'designated office', 83(1),(4A), 83A, sch 11; HB66+ 64(2),(5A), 64A, sch 10;
           NIHB 2(1), 81(1),(4A), 81A, sch 11; NIHB66+ 2(1), 62(2),(5A), 62A, sch 10

16.11-12   HB 83(5)(d); HB66+ 64(6)(d); NIHB 81(5)(d); NIHB66+ 62(6)(d)

16.13   HB 83(4D),(4DA),(4E),(6),(7),(8); HB66+ 64(5E),(EA),(5F),(7),(8),(9)
           NIHB 81(4D),(4DA),(4E),(6),(7),(8); NIHB66+ 62(5E),(5EA),(5F),(7),(8),(9)

16.14   HB 83(1),(6); HB66+ 64(2),(7); NIHB 81(1),(6); NIHB66+ 62(2),(7)

16.15 A 'complete' (or 'valid') HB claim means one that:

(a) meets the council's instructions – for example you need to answer all the questions that apply to you; and

(b) provides the information and evidence the council requires (para 16.22).

Completing an incomplete claim

16.16 If your claim is incomplete ('defective') the council must give you the opportunity to do whatever is needed to complete it. For example, it should:

(a) send you an application form if you asked for one or tell you how to claim;

(b) ask questions that arise from the information you have provided;

(c) ask questions you haven't yet answered;

(d) ask for information and evidence you haven't yet provided.

16.17 The council must allow you a month to respond, and if you claimed by telephone this period starts from when the council/DWP last drew attention to what it required of you. So long as you respond within the month, or longer if reasonable, your date of claim isn't delayed. This is the case even if the council took a long time to ask you in the first place, for example, if it initially failed to recognise your letter as being a claim (para 16.10) (CP/3444/2003).

Deciding your claim

16.18 Once you complete your claim, the council must decide whether you qualify for HB and, if so, from what date (para 16.31).

16.19 The council must also decide your claim if you don't complete it, and in this case it could:

(a) decide it has enough information to award you HB; or

(b) decide that your failure to provide information or evidence, or to answer questions, means that you don't meet the conditions of entitlement to HB (para 16.14); or

(c) make a reasonable assumption that you don't qualify (draw an 'adverse inference'), for example, assume that you still have capital if you refuse to say where it went.

16.20 Even if the council can't get all the information it needs, it must make a decision (para 16.19), send you a notice (para 20.6) and allow you the appeal rights in chapter 20 (R(H) 3/05).

Amending or withdrawing a claim

16.21 You can amend your HB claim at any time before the council makes a decision on it. Or you can withdraw your claim and the council need take no further action on it – in this case you should be sure you don't want HB.

16.15　AA 1(1), 5(1)(a),(1A); HB 83(1),(4C),(9), 86(1); HB66+ 64(2),(5D),(10), 67(1)
　　　　NIAA 1(1), 5(1)(a),(1A); NIHB 81(1),(4C),(9), 82(1); NIHB66+ 62(2),(5D),(10), 63(1)

16.16-17　HB 83(4D),(4DA),(4E),(7),(7A),(8),(8A), 86(1); HB66+ 64(5E),(5EA),(5F),(8),(8A),(9),(9A), 67(1)
　　　　　 NIHB 81(4D),(4DA),(4E),(7),(8), 82(1); NIHB66+ 62(5E),(5EA),(5F),(8),(9), 63(1)

16.18-20　HB 83(4E),(4F),(8), 89, 90; HB66+ 64(5F),(5G),(9), 70, 71; NIHB 81(4E),(4F),(8), 85, 86; NIHB66+ 62(5F),(5G),(9), 66, 67

16.21　HB 87; HB66+ 68; NIHB 83; NIHB66+ 64

Information and evidence

16.22   The council can ask you for 'certificates, documents, information and evidence' that it reasonably needs to decide your entitlement to HB. This applies when you make your claim, and also while you are getting HB (para 17.8).

Information and evidence normally requested

16.23   The council should tell you what information and evidence it requires to support your claim. You will always be asked for evidence of your and your partner's identity (i.e. name, address) and (in most cases) national insurance number (paras 16.26-27). But apart from that, any other information and evidence requested depends on the council's approach to verifying claims. Many follow the guidance (HB S11/2011) and adopt a risk-based approach whereby the level of checking depends on the probability of fraud or error associated with your category of claim (e.g. pensioner, hostel-dweller). Your risk category may also determine the form of evidence the council accepts (e.g. electronic submission, photocopies or original documents). Changes in the number and type of HB claims due to the roll-out of UC may lead councils to review their approach to information and evidence gathering.

16.24   When you claim on a paper application form you should sign it. If you are a couple (or in a polygamous marriage) your partner(s) should also sign if the form requires this.

Information and evidence that can't be requested

16.25   The council shouldn't ask you for information and evidence about payments from certain government trust funds (para 15.42) or payments in kind (goods not money) from a charity or most other sources.

National insurance numbers

16.26   You must give the council your national insurance number (NINO), and your partner's if you are a couple, along with supporting evidence. Or if you don't have one you must apply for one.

16.27   But a NINO isn't required:

(a) for you (or your partner) if you live in a hostel (para 7.27); or

(b) for your partner if s/he requires 'leave' to be in the UK but does not have it (table 2.4) – typically if s/he has an outstanding application with the Home Office. In these cases, where your partner's NINO has been refused due to 'immigration status invalid' the council should allocate a dummy NINO so the claim can be processed (GM D1.284-86). The council may inform the Home Office, because getting a personal allowance as a couple rather than as a single person counts as 'public funds', and this may affect your partner's leave (GM C4.218-19).

16.22   AA 5(1A); HB 83(1), 86(1); HB66+ 64(2), 67(1); NIAA 5(1A); NIHB 81(1), 82(1); NIHB66+ 62(2), 63(1)

16.25   HB 86(2),(4); HB66+ 67(2),(4); NIHB 82(2),(4); NIHB66+ 63(2),(4)

16.26-27   AA 1(1A)-(1C); HB 4; HB66+ 4; NIAA 1(1A)-(1C); NIHB 4; NIHB66+ 4

Using information supplied by the DWP

16.28   Where the DWP has supplied the council with information about any benefits used in connection with your claim (but not UC) the council must normally use that information without verifying its accuracy. Exceptions to this rule include where the information was given to the council more than 12 months after the DWP used it or the council has reasons for thinking it has changed.

16.29   If you have been awarded a passport benefit (table 6.1), you automatically meet the income and capital conditions for getting maximum HB (R v Penwith DC ex parte Menear; R v South Ribble HBRB ex parte Hamilton). If you have been refused a passport benefit, the council must make its own assessment of your income and capital ([2017] UKUT 362 (AAC)).

Nil income claims

16.30   If you have no income, the council mustn't refuse you HB on the grounds that you 'ought' to claim SPC or UC. If you claim HB while waiting for SPC or UC, the council shouldn't delay your HB if you can show that you are living off voluntary support or your savings.

HB start dates and backdating

Your HB start date

16.31   The general rule is that your HB starts on the Monday following:

(a)   your date of claim (table 16.1); or

(b)   your backdated date of claim (paras 16.36-42).

If your date of claim or backdated date of claim is a Monday, this means the following Monday. Exceptions to the general rule are in paras 16.32-35.

When you move home

16.32   Paras 16.33-34 apply to claims for HB when you move home or become liable for rent for any other reason. But if you were already on HB at your old address, moves within your council's area are taken into account without you having to make a claim (para 16.50 and table 17.3).

16.28   AA 7B; SI 2007/2911; NIAA 5B; NISR 2007/467

16.29   R v Penwith DC ex p Menear 11/10/91 QBD 24 HLR 115
               R v South Ribble HBRB ex p Hamilton [2000] EWCA Civ 518 www.bailii.org/ew/cases/EWCA/Civ/2000/518.html

16.31   HB 76(1); HB66+ 57(1); NIHB 74(1); NIHB66+ 55(1)

Table 16.1 **Your date of claim**

Date of claim	Conditions you have to meet
(a) The day the council or DWP received your HB claim (paras 16.8-12).	All cases unless (b)-(e) give an earlier date.
(b) The day you first told the council or DWP you want to claim HB (para 16.13).	You made your HB claim within one month of telling them or of being sent a claim form (even if the form was issued later).
(c) The day your partner died or you separated, if they were getting HB at the time.	The council or DWP received your HB claim within one month of the death or separation.
(d) The day your SPC guarantee credit or UC began.	The council or DWP received your HB claim within one month of the DWP receiving your SPC/UC claim.
(e) The day your liability for rent began, if you were on SPC guarantee credit or UC at the time.	The council or DWP received your HB claim within one month of the liability beginning.

Note: See paras 16.35-42 for advance and backdated claims.

The new liability rule

16.33 This rule applies when all the following occur in the same benefit week (para 16.49):

(a) your date of claim (table 16.1) or backdated date of claim (paras 16.36-42) is in that benefit week; and

(b) your or your partner's liability for rent begins in that benefit week; and

(c) you move in during or before that benefit week.

In this case, your HB starts on the day your liability begins, or the day you move in if that is later in the week ([2014] UKUT 411 (AAC)). If you don't meet conditions (a) to (c), the general rule applies.

The rule for daily rents

16.34 This rule only applies if you are liable to pay your rent daily to:

(a) a hostel (para 7.27); or

(b) temporary accommodation (para 7.32).

In this case, your HB starts on the day you move in. This applies regardless of when you make your claim (HB A8/2006, A2/2007), but it is a good idea to make your claim as soon as you can so that you still have the information and evidence you need.

T16.1   HB 83(5),(12),(12A); HB66+ 64(1),(1A),(5); NIHB 81(5),(12),(12A); NIHB66+ 62(1),(1A),(5)

16.33   HB 76(2); HB66+ 57(2); NIHB 74(2); NIHB66+ 55(2)

16.34   HB 76(3)-(5); HB66+ 57(2)-(4); NIHB 74(3)-(5); NIHB66+ 55(2)-(4)

Examples: When HB starts

1. Pension age HB: general rule

Sian is aged 70 and is on a low income. Her online claim for HB is received by the council on Friday 2nd April 2021.

- Her date of claim is automatically backdated for three months to Saturday 2nd January 2021 (para 16.36).
- Her HB starts on Monday 4th January (para 16.31).

2. Working age HB: a new home

Murdo is aged 30 and moves into supported accommodation on Monday 15th March 2021. His weekly rent starts on the same day, and his HB application form reaches the council on Friday 19th March 2021.

- His date of claim is Friday 19th March 2021 (table 16.1(a)).
- His HB starts on Monday 15th March 2021 (para 16.31).

Advance claims

16.35 Making an advance claim can mean you get HB when you need it, rather than having to wait for HB and possibly building up rent arrears. You can make an advance claim for HB:

(a) up to 17 weeks before you will become entitled to pension age HB (e.g. because you are approaching pension age or planning to retire from work);

(b) up to 13 weeks before you will become entitled to working age HB (e.g. you are planning to move to your first rented home).

In these cases your date of claim is treated as being in the benefit week (para 16.49) before your entitlement begins and your HB starts on the day you become entitled to it. But this rule only applies if you are habitually resident in the UK or the rest of the CTA (table 2.4).

Backdating pension age HB

16.36 When you claim pension age HB your date of claim is automatically backdated for three months (or back to the date you or your partner reached pension age if this is later). You don't have to request this: it applies in all cases. See paras 16.31-34 for the date your HB starts.

If you also claim SPC

16.37 SPC is also automatically backdated for three months (or back to the date you qualify from if this is later: para 22.42).

16.38 If you claim HB within one month of claiming SPC guarantee credit, your HB date of claim is the day your SPC was backdated to (table 16.1(d)).

16.35   HB 83(10),(11); NIHB 81(10),(11)

16.36   HB66+ 64(1),(1A); NIHB66+ 62(1),(1A)

16.38   HB66+ 64(1A),(6)(a); NIHB66+ 62(1A),(6)(a)

Backdating working age HB

16.39   When you claim working age HB, your date of claim is backdated if you:

(a)   request this – either when you claim or separately later; and

(b)   had continuous 'good cause' (para 16.44) for not making your claim/request earlier.

16.40   If you meet these conditions, your date of claim is backdated for one month before the council received your request or (if shorter) for whatever period you had good cause. See table 16.1 for the date your HB starts.

If you also claim UC

16.41   UC is also backdated for up to one month, but normally only if you are disabled, or were ill, or the UC online system wasn't working (volume 1 chapter 3).

16.42   If you claim HB within one month of claiming UC, your date of claim is the day your UC was backdated to (table 16.1(d)). If your UC was backdated for less than a month, you can request backdated HB for the remainder of the month (paras 16.39-40).

HB during a backdated period

16.43   During a backdated period, your HB is:

(a)   calculated using your circumstances and HB rules that applied then; and

(b)   only awarded for the parts of the period in which you qualify.

'Good cause' for backdating working age HB

16.44   You are likely to have good cause for backdating working age HB if:

(a)   you were so ill (physically or mentally) or otherwise unable to act that you could not claim and could not ask someone to claim for you;

(b)   someone you have been able to rely on (such as the council, the DWP, an advice agency and possibly others) advised you that you could not get HB when in fact you could;

(c)   there were good reasons for you not believing you could claim, amounting to more than just not thinking or caring;

(d)   some external factor prevented you from making a claim (e.g. failure of the postal services, imprisonment); or

(e)   there is some other good reason for your failure to claim or request backdating earlier.

Table 16.2 summarises case law about this.

16.45   When you request backdated HB, you don't have to use legal terminology, so long as you ask for HB for a past period and give your reasons (CH/3402/2005). The council can ask you for information and evidence to support your request and must base its decision on your individual circumstances. You can ask the council to reconsider its decision and appeal to a First-tier Tribunal (para 20.41) and then an Upper Tribunal (para 20.52) because 'good cause' is a question of law as well as fact (R(SB) 39/91).

16.39-40 HB 83(12),(12A); NIHB 81(12),(12A)

16.42   HB 83(5)(aa),(12),(12A); NIHB 81(5)(aa),(12),(12A)

Table 16.2 **Good cause: case law**

- *Reasonableness:* Good cause includes 'any fact that would probably have caused a reasonable person to act as the claimant did' (CH/4501/2004 approving C.S. 371/49). What is 'reasonable' is objective rather than subjective ([2010] UKUT 64 (AAC)).

- *Ignorance of rights and attempts to ascertain them:* Claimants are expected to take reasonable steps to ascertain what their rights may be, but 'cannot always be assumed to have an understanding of public administration' (C.S. 371/49). Though ignorance of itself is not good cause, it may be a factor to take into account since the law does not 'require a person to be acquainted with the "rules and regulations"' ([2010] UKUT 64 (AAC)).

- *A mistaken belief reasonably held:* Good cause can include a firmly held misunderstanding which amounts to a mistaken belief reasonably held, particularly when the claimant has not been careless or attempted to obtain benefit they are not entitled to (CH/4501/2004 approving earlier cases). This could include believing that you don't have to pay housing costs (and so don't have to claim HB) if you are on a passport benefit (CH/4501/2004), or that you can't get HB if you haven't paid national insurance contributions (CH/2198/2008).

- *Illness:* Good cause is related not to the severity or seriousness of an illness but to the resulting incapability of the claimant to claim (CH/5135/2001).

- *Mental incapacity:* In deciding good cause, a mentally disabled person is treated as having their mental age, not their chronological age (CH/393/2003).

- *Inability to speak English:* By itself, an inability to speak English is not normally good cause (CH/3579/2003).

- *Not receiving a document from the council:* Good cause can include non-receipt of a document from the council (e.g. requesting information and evidence) if this meant your HB stopped and you have reapplied (CH/3402/2005).

- *Misleading or incorrect advice and other factors:* Case law about other benefits is binding on HB (CH/5221/2001). Misinformation on an official website such as gov.uk can be misadvice and amount to good cause ([2015] UKUT 616(AAC)).

- *Who has to have good cause:* Only you (the claimant) have to show good cause not, for example, your partner (CH/3817/2004).

- *Good cause and qualifying for HB:* If you have good cause your claim is backdated even if you only qualify for HB for part of the backdated period (CH/1237/2004). But the council doesn't have to consider whether you have good cause if you don't qualify for any of the backdated period (CH/996/2004).

Lost, mislaid or delayed claim forms

16.46   If you sent the council a claim form or enquiry about claiming (para 16.13) but the council has no record of this, the question of whether and when it reached the council is decided by looking at the evidence and surrounding circumstances (paras 20.19-21). If the council received your form or enquiry but didn't act on it (for the above or other reasons) your HB is awarded based on the date the council received it, without this counting as 'backdating' your HB (CP/3477/2003). If you claimed SPC/JSA/ESA/IS at the DWP and you indicated on the claim form that you pay rent (usually by ticking a box) this is a HB claim even if the council wasn't made aware of it (CP/3477/2003).

Definition of 'month'

16.47   Many of the rules in this guide refer to allowing you a 'month' to complete your claim or appeal, etc. This means a calendar month, counted as follows (RI(IB) 4/02):

(a)   if the council requests something on 26th June, you have provided it within one month if you get it to the council by the end of 26th July;

(b)   if the council requests something on 31st January, you have provided it within a month if you get it to the council by the end of 28th (or 29th) February.

16.48   Things sent out by the council (such as requests for information or evidence, decision letters) are counted in the law as being sent out on the date of posting. Things received by the council (such as claims, information and evidence) are counted in the law as being received on the date of receipt. In the case of online communications, this means the date recorded by the computer as the date of sending or receipt unless the council reasonably directs otherwise.

Definition of 'benefit week'

16.49   Many of the rules in this guide refer to 'benefit week'. A benefit week always begins on a Monday and ends on the following Sunday.

Duration of your HB award

16.50   There is no fixed limit to an award of HB. Your award may change if your circumstances change (para 17.1) but this does not end your HB (even if the council asks you to complete a new form). Your HB award continues until you:

(a)   transfer onto UC (para 1.26);

(b)   move home to an area where a different council administers HB (para 17.18);

(c)   are no longer entitled – i.e. don't meet all the basic and financial conditions (table 2.1);

(d)   voluntarily relinquish your award by telling the council you want to end it (HB circular G10/2008 and CJSA/3979/1999). But once you do your decision can't be reversed if you later change your mind, and you might not be able to claim HB again (para 16.2); or

(e)   fail to respond to a request for information or evidence and this causes your HB to be terminated (para 17.44).

16.48   DAR 2; HB sch 11 para 4; HB66+ sch 10 para 4; NIDAR 2; NIHB sch 11 para 4; NIHB66+ sch 10 para 4

16.49   HB 2(1) definition: 'benefit week'; HB66+ 2(1); NIHB 2(1); NIHB66+ 2(1)

16.50   HB 79(1),(8); HB66+ 59(1),(8); NIHB 77(1),(10); NIHB66+ 57(1),(10)

Chapter 17 **Changes**

- ■ Changes of circumstances: see paras 17.1-10.
- ■ When changes take effect: see paras 17.11-15.
- ■ Rent increases, moving home, transferring to UC, changes in state benefits, starting work etc: see paras 17.16-39.
- ■ Suspending, restoring and terminating HB: see paras 17.40-45.

Changes of circumstances

17.1　This chapter explains how your HB changes when there is a change in your or someone else's circumstances. It applies when:

(a) you or someone else report a change; or

(b) the council becomes aware of a change without it being reported.

The duty to report changes

17.2　You have a duty to tell the council about any 'relevant' change of circumstances. The same duty applies to anyone acting for you (paras 16.5-7), and your landlord/agent if HB is paid to them (para 18.22). This means any change which you (or they) could reasonably be expected to know might affect:

(a) your entitlement to HB; or

(b) the amount of your HB; or

(c) how your HB is paid or who it is paid to.

17.3　This duty begins on the date your claim is made, and continues for as long as you are receiving HB. Table 17.1 summarises the main changes you should tell the council about.

How to notify changes

17.4　You must notify changes to the council. Some councils accept notification by telephone or online, though they can require written rather than telephone notifications, or require written or electronic records to be kept by those making online notifications.

17.5　In all other cases, you must notify changes to the council's 'designated office' (para 16.9). However, the council may accept notification by any other method it agrees to in a particular case.

17.6　If you or your partner are on JSA or IS and are starting work, and this will mean that your JSA/IS will stop (or JSA(C) will change), you may notify this by telephone to the DWP. This is part of the DWP's 'in and out of work' process.

17.2-3　HB 88(1); HB66+ 69(1); NIHB 84(1); NIHB66+ 65(1)

17.4　HB 88(1),(6), 88A, sch 11; HB66+ 69(1),(9), 69A, sch 10; NIHB 84(1),(3), 84A, sch 11; NIHB66+ 65(1),(2), 65A, sch 10

Table 17.1 **Changes you should notify**

(a) Changes in your personal details – e.g. becoming a couple or a single person.

(b) Changes in your family details – e.g. a child or young person moving out or stopping being your responsibility.

(c) Changes relating to non-dependants – e.g. moving in or a change in their income.

(d) Changes in your rent (unless you are a council or NIHE tenant) or letting details.

(e) Stopping qualifying for UC, JSA(IB), ESA(IR) or IS (but it is the DWP's duty to notify changes to SPC).

(f) Changes in other DWP benefits.

(g) Changes in your earned or unearned income or capital.

(h) Changes affecting your entitlement to HB – e.g. becoming a student, or absences likely to be over 13 weeks.

(i) If you are a couple, changes (as above) relating to your partner as well as yourself.

(j) Any other changes affecting your entitlement to HB, the amount of your HB, how it is paid or who it is paid to.

Reporting changes promptly

17.7   You should tell the council promptly about changes. If you delay reporting a change that increases your HB, you may end up getting less HB than you could have (table 17.2).

Information and evidence

17.8   The council can ask you for information and evidence it reasonably requires in order to make a decision about a change (para 16.22), and must take this into account if you provide it within one month, or longer if reasonable.

Decisions and notices

17.9   The council makes a decision about the change, and must send you a decision notice telling you:

(a) how the change affects your HB;

(b) if it does, when the change takes effect;

(c) your rights (para 20.1).

17.10   The change to your HB is also called a 'supersession' or (in a few cases) a 'revision' – these terms are explained in para 20.32.

T17.1   HB 88; HB66+ 69; NIHB; NIHB66+ 65

17.8   AA 5(1A); NIAA 5(1A); HB 86(1); HB66+ 67(1); NIHB 82(1); NIHB66+ 63(1); DAR 4(5), 7(5); NIDAR 4(4), 7(5)

17.9   HB 89(1), 90(1)(b), sch 9; HB66+ 70(1), 71(1)(b), sch 8; NIHB 85(1), 86(1)(b), sch 10; NIHB66+ 66(1), 67(1)(b), sch 9

When changes take effect

17.11   When there is a change in your personal, financial or other circumstances, the change takes effect (alters or ends your HB) as in table 17.2.

17.12   But there are different rules for rent increases, moving home, entitlement to UC, SPC and other benefits, reaching pension age, and starting work (paras 17.16-39).

Table 17.2 **When changes of circumstances take effect**

Type of change	When it takes effect
Changes increasing your HB	
(a) Reported to the council, or made by the council, within the time limit (one month or in some cases up to 13 months: para 17.15)	The Monday following the date the change occurred
(b) Reported outside the time limit	The Monday following the date the change was reported, or the council makes the change (if this is earlier)
Changes reducing or ending your HB	
(c) Changes reducing your HB	The Monday following the date the change occurred
(d) Changes ending your HB	The last day of your HB is the Sunday at the end of the benefit week that contains the change, or the exact day of the change if your rent is due on a daily basis

Notes:
- In the law, (a) to (d) are all supersessions.
- For exceptions see paras 17.16-39.

Example: Late notified change increasing HB

Anjali is on HB. Her wages went down four months ago, but she did not inform the council until today. The council asks why she delayed, but she has no special circumstances.

The change is implemented from the Monday following the day her notification of the change was received by the council. She does not get arrears of HB because she has no special circumstances for notifying late.

T17.2   HB 79(1),(8); HB66+ 59(1),(8); DAR 7(2)(a)(i), 8(2)-(5); NIHB 77(1),(8); HB66+ 57(1),(8); NIDAR 7(2)(a)(i), 8(2)-(5)

Time limit for getting your arrears

17.13   When a change increases your HB, you only get all your arrears if you report it within the time limit. Table 17.2 shows how the time limit affects you. It doesn't apply to changes in most state benefits (para 17.26)

17.14   A change is reported within the time limit if:

(a) you report the change to the council within one month of when it occurred; or

(b) you report the change within 13 months and the council agrees to extend the time limit (para 17.15); or

(c) the council (without being notified by you) makes the change within one month of when it occurred.

Extending the time limit

17.15   The time limit for reporting a change is extended if:

(a) you report the change within 13 months of when it occurred;

(b) you say you are reporting it late and give the reasons for your delay;

(c) there are special circumstances why it wasn't practicable for you to report the change earlier; and

(d) it is reasonable to accept your delay – the longer you delay the more compelling your special circumstances have to be.

Special cases

Rent increases

17.16   If you are a council or NIHE tenant, an increase (or decrease) in your rent or service charges usually affects your eligible rent (para 8.5). When it does, your HB changes on the exact day, and the rule about late reported changes (para 17.13) doesn't apply.

17.17   For all other tenants, an increase (or decrease) in your rent or service charges may or may not affect your eligible rent (paras 8.5 9.5, 10.10 or 10.39). When it does, your HB changes on the exact day, but if you are late reporting the change, you don't get all your arrears (table 17.2(b)).

Moving home

17.18   Table 17.3 shows how and when your HB changes if you move home. See also paras 3.29-38 if you qualify for HB before moving in or after moving out.

17.13   DAR 8(2); NIDAR 8(2)

17.14   DAR 7(2)(a),(3), 8(3),(5); NIDAR 7(2)(a), 8(3),(5)

17.15   DAR 9; NIDAR 9

17.16-17   HB 79(2),(8), 80(3)(b),(c),(8); HB66+ 59(2),(8), 61(3)(b),(c),(8)
           NIHB 77(2),(8), 78(3)(b),(c),(8); HB66+ 57(2),(8), 59(3)(b),(c),(8)

Table 17.3 **When HB changes if you move home**

Details of move	HB on old home	HB on new home
General rules (all pension age moves – and working age moves unless the exceptions apply)		
(a) Moves within the same council's area	Last day of HB = day before move	First day of HB = day of move (if you report the move promptly: para 17.13)
(b) Moves to a different council's area	Last day of HB = day before move	First day of HB = day of move (if you claim HB on time: table 16.1)
(c) Moves to somewhere HB can't be paid (paras 5.15-35 or table 7.2)	Last day of HB = end of benefit week that contains day of move (or exact day if daily rent)	You can't get HB
Exception for working age HB if you aren't on UC		
(d) Moves to general accommodation in a different council's area	Last day of HB = end of transitional HB (this runs for two weeks from date of UC claim: para 17.19)	You can't get HB, but you can claim UC towards your housing costs
Exception for working age HB if you are on UC (in supported or temporary accommodation)		
(e) Moves to general accommodation in the same or a different council's area	Last day of HB = end of benefit week that contains day of move (or exact day if daily rent)	You can't get HB, but you can claim UC towards your housing costs

Notes:

- 'Supported or temporary accommodation' means any accommodation in table 2.3.
- 'General accommodation' means any other accommodation.
- In situation (d), your UC can be backdated for up to one month (volume 1 chapter 3) if you claim UC promptly when you are told by your new council that you can no longer claim HB ([2020] UKUT 309 (AAC)).

T17.3   HB 79(2A)(a),(8), 80(3)(c),(8); HB66+ 59(2A)(a),(8),61(3)(e), (8); UCTP 5(2)(a), 6(8), 8(1),(2A),(3),(5),(8A);
         NIHB 77(2A)(a),(8), 78(3)(c),(8); NIHB66+ 57(2A)(a),(8),59(3)(c)(9); NIUCTP 3(2)(a), 4(8), 6(1),(2A),(6A)

Examples: Moving home

1. Moving within a council's area

Ginger moves within a council's area on Friday 28th May 2021. She is liable for rent at her old address up to and including Thursday 27th May and at her new address from Friday 28th May.

- ■ Her HB changes on and from Friday 28th May to reflect her new eligible rent.

2. Moving out of rented accommodation

Fred moves out of rented accommodation (to go and live with his parents) on Saturday 15th May 2021. He is liable for rent at his old address (but not on a daily basis) up to and including Friday 14th May.

- ■ His HB ends at the end of the benefit week containing the day of the move, in other words his last day of HB is Sunday 16th May.

Claiming UC – the two-week run on

17.19   If you are on working age HB and you claim UC:

(a)   while you are living in general accommodation (para 2.3); or

(b)   when you move to general accommodation in a different council's area (table 17.3(d));

you get a two-week run on of HB and (if you are on them) JSA(IB), ESA(IR) or IS (para 1.29).

Transitional HB

17.20   The HB run on is awarded from the first day of your UC and lasts exactly two weeks. It is designed to help you avoid rent arrears while waiting for your UC decision, and isn't repayable even if you turn out not to qualify for UC.

17.21   If you claimed UC as part of 'natural migration' (para 1.27):

(a)   you qualify for maximum HB throughout the two-week HB run on; and

(b)   this is calculated in the same way as if you were on any passport benefit (paras 6.2-3), using your current rent and non-dependant details.

17.22   If you claimed UC as part of 'managed migration' (para 1.28):

(a)   your two-week HB run on continues at whatever amount your HB was on the first day of the two weeks; and

(b)   no changes of circumstances are taken into account after that first day.

17.19   UCTP 8(1),(2A),(3),(5); NIUCTP 6(1),(2A),(3),(5)

17.20   reg 5 of SI 2019/1152; reg 4 of NISR 2019/152

17.21   UCTP 8A(a); NIUCTP 6A(a)

17.22   UCTP 8A(c); NIUCTP 6A(c)

17.23 Your two-week HB run on is paid to you if your HB was being paid to you, or to your landlord/agent if it was being paid to them. But if you claimed UC following a move, it is paid by the council whose area you've left, and must be paid to you, not your landlord/agent.

Examples: Transitional HB

1. Managed migration to UC

Rosemary gets HB of £70 per week. She gets a migration notice from the DWP and claims UC on Friday 12th November 2021.

- The first day of her UC is Friday 12th November.
- She gets two weeks transitional HB from Friday 12th November to Thursday 25th November of £70 per week

2. Natural migration to UC

Arthur gets HB and moves to a rented home in a new area. He claims UC on the day he moves, which is Thursday 7th October 2021.

- The first day of his UC is Thursday 7th October.
- He gets two weeks of transitional HB from Thursday 7th October to Wednesday 20th October, which equals maximum HB (his new weekly eligible rent minus deductions for any non-dependants at his new home).

Becoming a couple with someone on UC

17.24 When you become a couple with someone who is already on UC:

(a) if you move out of your home (e.g. because you are moving in with your partner), the last day of your HB is the Sunday at the end of the HB benefit week (para 16.49) containing the day of your move;

(b) if you remain in your home (e.g. because your partner is moving in with you), the last day of your HB is the day before the first day of the UC assessment period in which you become a couple.

In these circumstances you don't qualify for the two-week HB run on.

Example: Becoming a couple with someone on UC

Jack's new partner, Jill, moves in with him on 19th September. She is on UC and her assessment periods begin on the 7th of each month. Jack is added to Jill's UC claim from 7th September (the first day of the assessment period).

- Their UC starts to include housing costs on Jack's home (now their home) on 7th September.
- The last day of Jack's HB is 6th September.

17.23   UCTP 8A(b); NIUCTP 6A(b)

17.24   UCTP 5(2)(b), 7(1)-(3),(5),(6); NIUCTP 4(2)(b), 5(1)-(3),(5),(6)

Changes in state benefits – the 'relevant benefit rule'

17.25   When SPC, UC or any other state benefit starts, changes or ends, this takes effect as in table 17.4. This is often called the 'relevant benefit rule'. It applies to benefits received by (or for) you, your partner or a child or a young person in your family.

17.26   It is the DWP's duty to tell the council when your SPC starts, changes or ends, so the rule about late reported changes (para 17.13) doesn't apply. It is your duty to tell the council when any other benefit starts, changes or ends, but the rule about late reported changes also doesn't apply to any of these except WTC and CTC.

Examples: Changes in state benefits

1. Award of PIP following a claim

Bruno is aged 45 and is getting HB. He claims PIP and is awarded it from 18th May. This increases his HB (chapter 12).

- ■ His HB is increased from 18th May (table 17.4(m)).

2. Award of attendance allowance following an appeal

Lilian is aged 75 and is getting HB. Following an appeal she is awarded attendance allowance for the past 18 months. This increases her HB (chapter 12).

- ■ Her HB is increased back to the date her attendance allowance is awarded from (table 17.4(m)) so she gets 18 months of arrears of this increase.

Table 17.4 **When changes in state benefits take effect**

What the change is	When it takes effect
Changes in SPC	
(a) Guarantee credit starts	HB increases on the following Monday
(b) Guarantee credit ends (except as in (c) or (d))	HB reduces on the following Monday
(c) Guarantee credit is replaced by savings credit (except as in (d))	HB reduces on the following Monday or, if later, the Monday following the day the DWP tells the council
(d) Guarantee credit is replaced by savings credit and you delayed telling the DWP about the change that led to that	HB reduces on the Monday following the day savings credit begins
(e) Savings credit starts	HB reduces on the following Monday or, if later, the Monday following the day the DWP tells the council
(f) Savings credit ends (except as in (g))	HB increases on the following Monday

---

17.25-26   DAR 4(7B),(7C), 7(2)(i), 8(14); NIDAR 4(6B),(6C),7(2)(h), 8(12)

(g) Savings credit is replaced by guarantee credit	HB increases on the Monday of the benefit week in which guarantee credit begins
(h) Savings credit increases	HB reduces on the following Monday or, if later, the Monday following the day the DWP tells the council
(i) Savings credit reduces	HB increases on the Monday of the benefit week in which it reduces
Changes in other state benefits	
(j) UC starts in temporary or supported accommodation	HB increases on the exact day
(k) UC ends in temporary or supported accommodation	HB reduces on the following Monday
(l) WTC or CTC starts, changes or ends	HB changes as described in table 17.2
(m) Any other state benefit starts or increases	The exact day if HB starts or increases, or the following Monday if HB reduces
(n) Any other state benefit reduces or ends	The following Monday (whether HB increases or reduces)

Note: In all the above cases, if the change means your HB ends, it ends as described in table 17.2(d). For changes due to the benefit cap see paras 6.32-33.

Reaching pension age

17.27   The pension age HB rules start to apply to you on the day that:

(a) you reach 66, if you are single; or

(b) the younger of you reaches 66, if you are a couple.

When differences between working age and pension age rules affect your HB, the change takes place on the exact day of that birthday.

Start of SPC at pension age

17.28   You can get SPC (para 22.9) from the day you reach 66 (or the younger partner in a couple does) if you claim it no more than four months earlier or three months later (paras 22.42-43). The rules in paras 17.29-30 are designed to help you avoid rent arrears when you claim SPC while you wait for your decision, but in the case of a UC run-on (para 17-29) it applies even if you don't claim or don't qualify for SPC.

T17.4   HB 41(9), 60, 79(1); HB66+ 39(11), 58, 59(1), 60; DAR 4(7B),(7C), 7(2)(i), 8(14);
          NIHB 39(9), 58, 77(1); NIHB66+ 37(11), 56, 57(1), 58; NIDAR 4(6B),(6C), 7(2)(h), 8(12)

17.27   HB 5; HB66+ 5); NIHB 5; NIHB66+ 5

End of UC at pension age

17.29   If you are getting UC, it continues until the end of the UC assessment period containing the date you reach 66 (or the younger partner in a couple does). Your HB is worked out in the normal way (paras 6.5-6) but your UC is disregarded. After that your new circumstances are taken into account in your HB.

End of JSA(IB)/ESA(IR)/IS at pension age

17.30   If you are getting JSA(IB)/ESA(IR)/IS, it ends on the day before you reach 66 (or the younger partner in a couple does). In this case, you get continuing payment of the maximum HB for four weeks plus any odd days to make it end on a Sunday. After that your new circumstances are taken into account in your HB.

Example: End of UC at pension age

Raj is on UC and HB (in supported accommodation) when he reaches 66 on 26th May. His UC assessment periods begin on the 3rd of each month.

- His UC continues until 2nd June but is disregarded so he gets maximum HB (para 17.29).
- By then the DWP has decided he qualifies for guarantee credit of SPC, so he continues to get maximum HB.

Starting work

17.31   When you or your partner start work, your HB changes on the Monday following your first day of employment or self-employment (paras 14.12, 14.33).

Extended payments of HB

17.32   You qualify for an extended payment of four weeks of HB if:

(a) you or your partner start employment or self-employment, or increase your hours or earnings; and

(b) this is expected to last at least five weeks; and.

(c) either:

- you are on JSA(IB), ESA(IR) or IS which stops due to (a), and
- you have been on those benefits or JSA(C) in any combination for 26 weeks;

(d) or:

- you are on ESA(C), IB or SDA which stops due to (a), and
- you have been on those benefits (in any combination) for 26 weeks.

17.29   HB66+ 27(1)(zi); SI 2013/381, sch 1 para 26; UCTP 5(8A); NIHB66+ 21(1)(zi); NISR 2016/221, sch 1 para 26; NIUCTP 4(8A)

17.30   HB66+ 54; NIHB66+ 52

17.31   HB 79(1); HB66+59(1); NIHB 77(1); NIHB66+ 57(1)

17.32-33   HB 72-73E, 115, 116; HB66+ 52-53E, 96, 97
           NIHB 70-71D, 110, 111; NIHB66+51-51C, 94, 95

17.33 In each of the four weeks your extended payment equals:

(a) the weekly amount of HB you were getting before the extended payment began, but ignoring the benefit cap (para 6.21); or

(b) if higher, the amount you qualify for in that particular week under the ordinary HB rules.

But you don't get an extended payment in a rent-free week (para 6.35). And after the four weeks of your extended payment, your HB is calculated under the ordinary HB rules.

Example: Extended payments of HB

Aaron meets all the conditions for an extended payment when he starts work on Monday 2nd August 2021.

His award of HB continues up to and including Sunday 8th August. His extended payment covers the period from Monday 9th August to Sunday 6th September. If he then continues to qualify for HB after that, the new amount of HB is awarded from Monday 6th September.

Stopping work

17.34 When you or your partner stop work, your HB changes on the Monday following the first day you aren't employed or aren't self-employed (paras 14.13, 14.34).

Death

17.35 Your HB ends at the end of the benefit week that contains your date of death (because you are no longer in occupation: table 2.1(a)). Your executors can't continue your HB claim, but a bereaved partner can make their own HB claim (table 16.1(c)).

Other changes

17.36 When any other change in circumstances affects your HB, your HB alters or ends as in table 17.2.

Amendments to regulations and up-ratings

17.37 When the HB regulations are amended, your HB:

(a) changes from the date of the amendment, if you continue to qualify for HB; or

(b) ends at the end of the benefit week (para 16.49) containing the date of the amendment, if you no longer qualify for HB.

But if the April up-rating for social security benefits or tax credits is different from that for HB (para 1.16), they are treated as up-rated on the same day as HB.

17.34   HB 79(1); HB66+59(1); NIHB 77(1); NIHB66+ 57(1)

17.35-36   AA 130(1)(a); HB 79(1); HB66+59(1); NIAA 129(i)(a); NIHB 77(1); NIHB66+ 57(1)

17.37   HB 79(3); HB66+ 60(3); DAR 7(2)(q),(s), 8(10),(14E),(14G)
NIHB 77(3); NIHB66+ 58(3); NIDAR 8(12)

New case law

17.38   When new case law (in another person's appeal) affects your HB, it takes effect from the date the Upper Tribunal, Northern Ireland Commissioners or court gives its judgment in that case. The main exception is that your HB can be altered from an earlier date if a First-tier Tribunal 'stayed' your own appeal to await that judgment.

More than one change

17.39   If you have more than one change, each is dealt with in turn. But the following rules apply when changes which actually occur in the same benefit week (para 16.49) would have an effect (under the earlier rules in this chapter) in different benefit weeks:

(a)   If one of the changes is in the annual up-rating in cases when this takes effect on the first Monday in April, the other changes take effect when that applies.

(b)   Otherwise, if one of the changes is in your rent (or your address if you move within the council's area), the other changes take effect when that applies.

(c)   In all other cases, all the changes take effect from the Monday of the benefit week in which the changes actually occur.

Suspending, restoring and terminating HB

17.40   This section describes how the council can suspend, restore and terminate HB. To suspend means stopping making payments for the time being, usually in order to avoid an overpayment or to seek information or evidence. To restore means starting payments again – either at the same amount as before or at a different amount, depending on the circumstances. To terminate means ending an award of HB altogether.

Suspending HB

17.41   The council may suspend HB if any of the following circumstances apply:

(a)   the council doubts whether the conditions of entitlement to HB are fulfilled;

(b)   the council is considering whether to change a decision about HB;

(c)   the council considers there may be a recoverable overpayment of HB;

(d)   a First-tier or Upper Tribunal has made a decision (in this or another case) and the council is awaiting the decision or a statement of reasons, or is considering making a further appeal;

(e)   an appeal has been made, or leave to appeal has been sought, against a decision of a First-tier or Upper Tribunal or court in the case to be suspended;

(f)   an appeal has been made, or leave to appeal has been sought, against a decision of an Upper Tribunal (in Northern Ireland, appeal tribunal/Commissioner) or court in a different HB case, and this may affect the case to be suspended;

17.38   CPSA sch 7 paras 4(5),(6),18; DAR 7(2)(b); NICPSA sch 7 paras 4(4),(5); NIDAR 7(2)(b)

17.39   HB 42(8), 79(4),(5); HB66+ 41(9),(10), 59(4),(5); DAR 7(2)(q), 8(14E);
             NIHB 39(8), 77(6),(7); NIHB66+ 39(11),(12), 57(6),(7); NIDAR 7(2)(h), 8(11)

17.41   DAR 11,13(1),(2); NIDAR 11,13(1),(2)

(g) you (or another person affected) have failed to provide information or evidence needed by the council to consider changing a decision about HB.

In such cases, HB is usually suspended in full (though the law permits the council to suspend only part).

Restoring HB

17.42   When payments of HB have been suspended, the council must restore them (to the extent that you are still entitled) within 14 days or as soon as reasonably practicable after that, as follows:

- in cases (a) to (c) (para 17.41), the council is satisfied that HB is properly payable and no outstanding matters remain to be resolved;
- in case (d), the council decides not to make the further appeal (if it decides to make the further appeal case (e) or (f) then applies);
- in cases (e) and (f), the appeal or request for leave has been determined;
- in case (g), the claimant has responded as required (para 17.43).

Information and evidence

17.43   When payments of HB have been suspended for failure to provide information or evidence (para 17.41(g)), the council must notify you of the suspension and of what information and evidence is required. You must then, within one month or such longer period as the council considers necessary:

(a) provide the information or evidence required; or

(b) satisfy the council that the information or evidence does not exist, or is impossible for you to obtain.

Terminating HB

17.44   When payments of HB have been suspended for failure to provide information or evidence (para 17.41(g)) and you have failed to respond as required (para 17.43) your HB entitlement is terminated from the date on which the payments were suspended (i.e. no further payments are made). The rule cannot be used to end HB from an earlier date ([2020] UKUT 71 (AAC)) so if entitlement did end earlier, this is done as an (ordinary) supersession from that earlier date.

17.42   DAR 12,13(5); NIDAR 12,13(5)

17.43   DAR 13(3),(4); NIDAR 13(3),(4)

17.44   DAR 14; NIDAR 14

Decisions and appeals

17.45   The council must notify you if it suspends, restores or terminates your HB, and you can ask it to reconsider any of these matters. You then have a right of appeal to a tribunal about a decision to terminate HB (CH/402/2007), or to restore HB at a different amount or for a different reason; but not about a determination to suspend HB, or to restore HB at the same amount for the same reasons. A decision to suspend HB may, however, be challenged by judicial review if it is irrational: R (Sanneh) v SSWP.

Example: Suspending and restoring HB

Karel is on HB. The council obtains information that he has changed jobs. It suspends his award immediately and writes to him allowing him one month to respond.

After two weeks, he sends in the necessary information and evidence, and he remains entitled to HB.

The council restores his HB from the date payments were suspended, making any change in his entitlement from the Monday after the day he got the new job.

17.45   R (Sanneh) v SSWP [2012] EWHC 1840 (Admin)
         www.bailii.org/ew/cases/EWHC/Admin/2012/1840.html

Chapter 18 **Payments**

- HB payments: rebates, allowances and payments on account: see paras 18.1-16.
- Paying HB to someone on your behalf: see paras 18.17-21.
- Paying HB to your landlord or agent: see paras 18.22-54.

How HB is paid

18.1　　This section explains how and when your HB is paid, how soon the first payment should be made, and who your HB is paid to. You can ask the council to reconsider a decision it makes about any of these things (para 20.25), but only some of them can be appealed to a tribunal (para 20.42 and table 20.4).

Rebate or allowance

18.2　　Your HB is paid:

(a) as a rent rebate if you are a council or NIHE tenant: see paras 18.4-5;

(b) as a rent allowance in all other cases: see paras 18.6-54.

18.3　　In England, Scotland and Wales there are two exceptions:

(a) if you are renting a houseboat, mobile home or caravan (para 7.33) and you pay:

- your mooring charges or site charges to the council, but
- your rent to someone else (for example a private landlord)

your HB for each of these is paid as a rent allowance;

(b) if you pay your rent to the council because your home is subject to a management order or empty dwelling management order (EDMO), your HB is paid as a rent allowance.

Rent rebates

18.4　　If your HB is paid as rent rebate (paras 18.2-3), this means it is paid straight into your rent account. You do not get a payment yourself, but you have less rent to pay (and in some cases no rent to pay).

When rent rebates are paid

18.5　　The council should make the first payment into your rent account within 14 days of the date it receives your HB claim or as soon as reasonably practicable after that. It should then usually make payments into your rent account on the days your rent is due.

18.2　　AA 134(1A),(1B),(2); NIAA 126(1),(2); NIHB 88,93(5); NIHB66+ 69, 74(5)

18.3　　AA 134(1A); HB 91A; HB66+ 72A

18.4　　AA 134(1A); NIAA 126(1)(b),(c)

18.5　　HB 91(3); HB66+ 72(3); NIHB 87(3); NIHB66+ 68(3)

Rent allowances

18.6   If your HB is paid as a rent allowance (paras 18.2-3), this means it is paid:

(a) to you (the HB claimant);

(b) to someone on your behalf (paras 18.17-21); or

(c) to your landlord or agent (paras 18.22-54).

The council decides how to make payments, and should take into account your (or the payee's) reasonable needs and convenience. Usually the payments are made by credit transfer straight into a bank account or (increasingly rare) by cheque.

18.7   The council should not insist on paying you by credit transfer if:

(a) you do not have a bank account: R (Spiropoulos) v Brighton and Hove CC (see also GM para A6.120). But the council may be able to tell you which banks in your area offer basic accounts, and may give you a letter confirming your identity to help you open an account; or

(b) your bank is unlikely to let you take the money out because you have an overdraft. Although the 'right of first appropriation' in common law says you have the right to instruct your bank that the money will be used to pay your rent rather than reduce your overdraft, this right can be difficult to insist upon (for example, sometimes banks insist on a fresh instruction for each payment).

When rent allowances are paid

18.8   The first payment of your rent allowance should be within 14 days of your HB claim, or as soon as reasonably practicable after that. If the council cannot do this, it should make a payment on account: see paras 18.11-16.

18.9   The council decides how often payments are made after that, and should take into account how often and on what dates your rent is due. It can make:

(a) payments to you (or someone on your behalf):

- every two weeks – you can insist on this if your HB is more than £2 a week,
- every four weeks,
- every calendar month, or
- every week: see para 18.10;

(b) payments to your landlord or agent:

- every four weeks,
- every calendar month (but only if your rent is due calendar monthly).

The first payment to a landlord or agent can be for a shorter period if they have other tenants on HB. This is to allow all of the HB payments to them to be made on the same dates.

18.6   AA 134(1A),(1B); HB 91(1), 94; HB66+ 72(1),75; NIAA 126(1); NIHB 87(1), 91; NIHB66+ 68(1), 72

18.7   R (Spiropoulos) v Brighton and Hove CC [2007] EWHC 342 (Admin) www.bailii.org/ew/cases/EWHC/Admin/2007/342.html

18.8   HB 91(3); HB66+ 72(3); NIHB 87(3); NIHB66+ 68(3)

18.9   HB 92; HB66+ 73; NIHB 89; NIHB66+ 70

18.10   The council may pay you weekly if:

(a)   paying you over a longer period is likely to lead to an overpayment; or

(b)   your rent is due weekly and it is in your interests to be paid weekly.

For example, (b) could apply if you have difficulty budgeting. The council is not expected to check whether this is the case, but should take account of information provided by you or by someone on your behalf, including a social worker or key worker (GM para A6.143).

Payments on account

18.11   A 'payment on account' is an estimated amount of HB. The council must make a payment on account if:

(a)   your HB will be paid as a rent allowance (paras 18.2-3);

(b)   the council is unable to decide your claim within 14 days of getting it; and

(c)   this is not because you have failed to provide information and evidence: paras 18.12-13.

The rules about how and who it is paid to, are the same as for rent allowances (paras 18.6-7).

18.12   The council does not have to make a payment on account if:

(a)   it or the DWP has asked you to provide information or evidence reasonably required to decide your HB claim (see paras 16.22-30; and

(b)   you have failed without good cause to provide it.

18.13   But the council does have to make a payment on account if:

(a)   it has asked someone other than you for the information and evidence (GM para A6.161). For example it has asked:

- ▪ your landlord or agent for confirmation of your rent,

- ▪ the rent officer for a determination about your rent,

- ▪ the DWP for confirmation of your benefit entitlement, or

- ▪ the Home Office for confirmation of your conditions of entry or stay; or

(b)   you have not provided information or evidence because :

- ▪ you have not been asked for it, or

- ▪ you have good cause, for example it does not exist or you cannot get it.

18.14   Payments on account are not discretionary. If you meet the conditions (paras 18.11 and 18.13), the council:

(a)   must make a payment on account within 14 days of getting your claim, and should not wait to be asked: R v Haringey LBC ex parte Ayub (see also GM para A6.158); and

(b)   should continue making payments on account until your HB is decided.

You may need to remind the council to make a payment on account, or your landlord or agent can do this if your HB is likely to be paid to them. For delays, see also paras 20.11-15.

18.10   HB 92(6); HB66+ 73(6); NIHB 89(6); NIHB66+ 70(6)

18.11   HB 93(1); HB66+ 74(1); NIHB 90(1); NIHB66+ 71(1)

18.12   HB 93(1); HB66+ 74(1); NIHB 90(1); NIHB66+ 71(1)

18.14   R v Haringey LBC ex p Ayub 13/04/92 QBD 25 HLR 566 http://tinyurl.com/Ayub-Haringey

Payments on account amounts and adjustments

18.15   The amount of your payment on account is whatever the council decides is reasonable, based on the information available to it about your individual circumstances. It must notify you (or the payee) that if this turns out to be greater than your entitlement to HB, the overpayment will be recovered (para 19.9).

18.16   When the council decides your claim, the following rules apply. If your entitlement to HB is:

(a) greater than your payments on account, the council must pay the balance;

(b) less than your payments on account, the council must recover the overpayment by making deductions from your future payments of HB (para 19.40).

If you are not entitled to HB, the council recovers the overpayment from the person it was paid to (para 19.26).

Paying HB to someone on your behalf

18.17   This section explains when the council should pay your HB to someone on your behalf. It only applies if your HB is paid as a rent allowance (paras 18.2-3).

Attorneys, appointees, etc

18.18   If you are unable to act for yourself, the council can pay your HB to an attorney, appointee, etc, who claimed HB on your behalf (paras 16.5-7).

Nominees

18.19   If you want your council to pay your HB to someone else, the council can do this (but if you are unable to act, see instead para 18.18). They are usually called your nominee. You have to write to the council requesting this, and your nominee must either be:

(a) an individual aged 18 or more (for example an adult relative or friend); or

(b) a corporate body (for example a firm of solicitors).

18.20   The law does not stop your landlord or agent being your nominee. But:

(a) if you fall within the LHA scheme in England, Scotland or Wales, the council may not agree to this if it would undermine the main rules about paying HB to your landlord/ agent (paras 18.24-37);

(b) in all other rent allowance cases, it may be simpler to request payment to your landlord/agent using the main rule about this (see para 18.38).

18.15   HB 93(1),(2); HB66+ 74(1),(2); NIHB 90(1),(2); NIHB66+ 71(1),(2)

18.16   HB 93(3); HB66+ 74(3); NIHB 90(3); NIHB66+ 71(3)

18.18   HB 94(2); HB66+ 75(2); NIHB 91(2); NIHB66+ 68(2)

18.19   HB 94(3); HB66+ 75(3); NIHB 91(3); NIHB66+ 68(3)

Personal representatives and next of kin

18.21 If HB is due to you when you die, the council must pay it to your personal representative (i.e. the person responsible for settling your affairs, such as an executor), or (if you do not have a personal representative) your next of kin. Your next of kin is the first person in the following list who is aged 16 or more:

(a) your husband, wife or civil partner;

(b) your children or grandchildren;

(c) your parents, brothers or sisters, or their children.

This rule only applies if the executor or next of kin writes to the council requesting payment within one year of your death, or longer if the council agrees. But it does not apply to HB the council has to pay your landlord/agent: see para 18.29.

Paying HB to your landlord or their agent

18.22 This section explains when the council pays your HB to your landlord or their agent. It only applies if your HB is paid as a rent allowance (paras 18.2-3).

(a) The council must pay your HB to your landlord/agent if paras 18.24-29 apply to you.

(b) Otherwise, it may pay your HB to your landlord/agent if paras 18.30-41 apply to you.

(c) Otherwise, it must pay your HB to you, or to someone on your behalf (see paras 18.17-21).

Table 18.1 summarises these rules. There are exceptions if your landlord/agent is not a 'fit and proper person' (paras 18.42-44) or during the two weeks after you claim UC (para 17.23).

Table 18.1 **Paying HB to your landlord/agent**

This table summarises when your HB is paid to your landlord or their agent (see paras 18.22-23).

When the council must pay your landlord/agent

All rent allowance cases

In all rent allowance cases (paras 18.2-3), the council must pay your landlord/agent if:

(a) you have eight weeks or more rent arrears, unless it is in your overriding interests not to pay your landlord/agent: see paras 18.25-27;

(b) part of your DWP benefit is being paid to your landlord/agent: see para 18.28; or

(c) rent remains due to your landlord/agent when you die: see para 18.29.

18.21   HB 97(1)-(4); HB66+ 78(1)-(4); NIHB 94(1)-(4); NIHB66+ 75(1)-(4)

18.22   HB 94(1), 95, 96; HB66+ 75(1), 76, 77; NIHB 91(1), 92 ,93; NIHB66+ 68(1), 73, 74

T18.1   HB 95, 96, 97(5); HB66+ 76, 77, 78(5); NIHB 92, 93, 94(5); NIHB66+ 73, 74, 75(5)

When the council may pay your landlord/agent

LHA cases in England, Scotland or Wales

In LHA cases (para 9.3) in England, Scotland or Wales, the council may pay your landlord/agent if:

(d) your HB has previously been paid to your landlord/agent under the rules in (a) or (b) above: see para 18.33;

(e) paying your landlord/agent would help you secure or retain your tenancy: see para 18.34;

(f) you are likely to have difficulty managing your finances: see para 18.35;

(g) it is improbable that you will pay your rent: see para 18.36; or

(h) the council is considering whether the rules in (f) or (g) apply to you, but in this case only for up to eight weeks: see para 18.37.

See also (k) and (l) below.

Other rent allowance cases

In other rent allowance cases in England, Scotland and Wales which are not LHA cases, and in all rent allowance cases (including LHA cases) in Northern Ireland, the council/NIHE may pay your landlord/agent if:

(i) you have requested this or consented to it: see para 18.38; or

(j) it is in your and your family's interest: see para 18.39.

See also (k) and (l) below.

All rent allowance cases

In all rent allowance cases, the council may pay your landlord/agent if:

(k) you have not paid part or all of your rent, but this only applies to your first payment of HB (or first payment following a change to your HB): see para 18.40; or

(l) you have left your home and rent remains due to your landlord/agent: see para 18.41.

When the council must not pay your landlord/agent

All rent allowance cases

In all rent allowance cases, the council must not pay your landlord/agent if:

(m) your landlord/agent is not a 'fit and proper person', unless paying them is nonetheless in your and your family's best interests: see paras 18.42-44.

Landlord or agent

18.23 When your HB is payable to your landlord or agent, it is payable to:

(a) your landlord if your landlord collects your rent; but

(b) your landlord's agent if the agent collects your rent.

In the following paras, we use 'landlord/agent' to mean whichever of these applies.

18.23   HB 95(1), 96(4); HB66+ 76(1), 77(4); NIHB 92(1), 93(5); NIHB66+ 73(1), 74(5)

When HB must be paid to a landlord/agent

18.24   Paras 18.25-29 explain when the council must pay your HB to your landlord/agent. The rules about this apply in all rent allowance cases (paras 18.2-3). See also paras 18.42-54.

HB must be paid to landlord: eight weeks rent arrears

18.25   In all rent allowance cases, the council must pay your HB to your landlord/agent:

(a) if you have eight weeks or more rent arrears, counting arrears of eligible and ineligible service charges as well as arrears of rent: see para 18.26;

(b) unless it is in your overriding interests not to: see para 18.27.

This continues to apply until your rent arrears reduce below eight weeks (but see para 18.33).

18.26   Whether you have rent arrears (including arrears of service charges), and how much they are, are questions of fact (paras 20.19-21). The council is not expected to check this for every claim, but must consider any information you or your landlord/agent provide: R v Haringey LBC ex parte Ayub. It is clear that 'Rent is in arrears once the contractual date for payment has passed irrespective of whether the rent is due in advance or in arrears': [2019] UKUT 33 (AAC). In this case the rent was due two months in advance so there were at least eight weeks rent arrears at the outset and HB had to be paid to the landlord except as described in para 18.27.

> ### Example: Eight weeks rent arrears
>
> A private landlord lets a calendar-monthly tenancy from 1st July. She charges rent in advance on the 1st of each month. The tenant does not pay any rent.
>
> So by 2nd August, there are two calendar months of rent arrears. This is more than eight weeks of arrears, so the landlord is entitled to require the council to pay the tenant's HB to her.

18.27   If you have eight weeks or more rent arrears, your HB must be paid to your landlord/agent unless it is in your 'overriding interests' not to. It is up to you (or someone on your behalf) to give specific reasons about this: CH/3244/2007. If it is because your landlord/agent has not done essential repairs, you may be expected to have sent them a solicitor's letter with a schedule of disrepair prepared by a builder or surveyor: CH/3244/2007.

HB must be paid to landlord: deductions from DWP benefits

18.28   In all rent allowance cases, the council must pay your HB to your landlord/agent if, and for as long as, the DWP is paying part of your SPC, JSA, ESA or IS to them towards your rent arrears or hostel charges (para 23.38). The DWP should inform the council when this rule applies to you (GM para A6.188). But this rule doesn't apply when the DWP is paying part of your UC to your landlord/agent in supported or temporary accommodation (table 2.3), though in most of these cases the council can pay HB to your landlord/agent using the rules in paras 18.34-36.

18.25   HB 95(1)(b); HB66+ 76(1)(b); NIHB 92(1)(b); NIHB66+ 73(1)(b)

18.26   R v Haringey ex p Ayub: see footnote to para 18.14

18.28   HB 95(1)(a); HB66+ 76(1)(a); NIHB 92(1)(a); NIHB66+ 73(1)(a)

HB must be paid to landlord: rent due following death

18.29   In all rent allowance cases, the council must pay your HB to your landlord/agent if:

(a) HB remains due to you when you die, and rent remains due to your landlord/agent; and

(b) the council has already decided (before your death) to pay your landlord/agent.

But this is limited to the amount of rent remaining due at the date of your death. Any other HB due to you can be paid to your personal representative or next of kin (para 18.21).

When HB may be paid to a landlord/agent

18.30   Paras 18.33-41 explain when your HB may be paid to your landlord/agent.

(a) The rules in paras 18.33-37 and 18.40-41 apply if you fall within the LHA scheme (para 9.3) in England, Scotland or Wales.

(b) The rules in paragraphs 18.38-41 apply in:

   ▪ all other rent allowance cases in England, Scotland and Wales (for example housing association, exempt accommodation, rent referral and boarder cases), and

   ▪ all rent allowance cases in Northern Ireland.

See also paras 18.42-54. In England, Scotland and Wales, the overall effect of the rules is that HB is more likely to be paid to the landlord/agent in non-LHA cases than in LHA cases.

18.31   The rules in paras 18.33-41 are discretionary. If their conditions are met, the council may (but does not have to) pay your landlord/agent. The DWP has given councils extensive guidance about applying these rules in LHA cases (GLHA 4.00-6.102). But as with all discretions (para 20.24), the council must make its own decision. It should not have fixed rules or follow guidance without question: CH/2986/2005.

18.32   Some of the rules require the council to consider quite personal things about you, for example, your ability to manage your finances, the likelihood that you will pay your rent, and what your and your family's interests are (paras 18.35-36 and 18.39). In these cases, the DWP advises (HB/CTB A26/2009) that the council:

(a) can take account of information it already has, or gets from a home visit; and

(b) should also take account of information provided by you or by someone on your behalf, for example a relative or friend, a social worker or leaving care worker, or your landlord/agent.

Although this guidance is about LHA cases in England, Scotland and Wales, it is equally reasonable in other rent allowance cases.

HB may be paid to landlord: following a period when it must be

18.33   In LHA cases in England, Scotland and Wales, the council may pay your HB to your landlord/agent if it has previously done so under the rules in paras 18.25-28. It can do this as soon as your rent arrears reduce below eight weeks, or as soon as the DWP stops making direct payments, or (in either case) at a later date.

18.29   HB 97(5); HB66+ 78(5); NIHB 94(5); NIHB66+ 75(5)

18.33   HB 96(3A)(b)(iii); HB66+ 77(3A)(b)(iii)

HB may be paid to landlord: to secure or retain your tenancy

18.34   In LHA cases in England, Scotland and Wales, the council may pay your HB to your landlord/agent if this will assist you to secure or retain your tenancy (or other form of letting). This could encourage your landlord/agent to let to you (or continue to do so) while you are on HB. Some councils use this power to encourage the landlord to let at a lower rent (for example, a rent within the LHA figure).

HB may be paid to landlord: difficulty managing your finances

18.35   In LHA cases in England, Scotland and Wales, the council may pay your HB to your landlord/agent if you are likely to have difficulty managing your finances. For example, the DWP says (GLHA 5.070-074) this could be because you:

(a)   have difficulty budgeting, debt problems, or an undischarged bankruptcy;

(b)   are illiterate or unable to speak English;

(c)   are fleeing domestic violence;

(d)   are leaving care or prison; or

(e)   are getting Supporting People payments, or help from a charity.

See also paras 18.32 and 18.37.

HB may be paid to landlord: improbable you will pay rent

18.36   In LHA cases in England, Scotland and Wales, the council may pay your HB to your landlord/agent if it is improbable that you will pay your rent. This rule is about whether it is improbable you will pay rent in the future: CH/2986/2005. The DWP says this might be the case if you have regularly failed to pay rent (with no good reason) in the past (GLHA 6.063-064), for example if the council helped you get your tenancy for this reason (HB/CTB A26/2009). See also paras 18.32 and 18.37.

HB may be paid to landlord: while considering who to pay

18.37   In LHA cases in England, Scotland and Wales, the council may pay your HB to your landlord/agent while it is considering whether the rules in paragraphs 18.35-36 apply to you. The council can do this for up to eight weeks. Alternatively, it can pay you during this time. See also para 18.46.

HB may be paid to landlord: at your request or with your consent

18.38   In rent allowance cases in England, Scotland and Wales which are not LHA cases, and in all rent allowance cases in Northern Ireland, the council/NIHE may pay your HB to your landlord/agent if you request this or consent to it. The law does not require you to give a reason, but you can if you wish.

18.34   HB 96(3A)(b)(iv),(4); HB66+ 77(3A)(b)(iv),(4)

18.35   HB 96(3A)(b)(i); HB66+ 77(3A)(b)(i)

18.36   HB 96(3A)(b)(ii); HB66+ 77(3A)(b)(ii)

18.37   HB 96(3B); HB66+ 77(3B)

18.38   HB 96(1)(a),(3A)(a); HB66+ 77(1)(a),(3A)(a)

HB may be paid to landlord: your and your family's interests

18.39 In rent allowance cases in England, Scotland and Wales which are not LHA cases, and in all rent allowance cases in Northern Ireland, the council/NIHE may pay your HB to your landlord/agent if doing so would be in your and your family's interests. Although the rules in paras 18.33-37 do not apply in these cases, in practice the council is likely to take similar considerations into account. See also para 18.32.

HB may be paid to landlord: first payment after a claim or change

18.40 In all rent allowance cases, the council may pay your HB to your landlord/agent if you have not yet paid part or all of your rent for the period HB covers. But this is limited to the first payment following your claim for HB, or following a move or other change affecting your HB. And it only applies when paying your landlord/agent is 'in the interests of the efficient administration' of HB.

HB may be paid to your landlord: when you leave your home

18.41 In all rent allowance cases, the council may pay your HB to your landlord/agent if:

(a) you have left the accommodation the HB is paid for; and

(b) rent remains due to your landlord/agent there.

If your landlord/agent is not a fit and proper person

18.42 In all rent allowance cases, the council must not pay your HB to your landlord/agent:

(a) if your landlord/agent is not a 'fit and proper person' (paras 18.43-44);

(b) unless paying them is nonetheless in your and your family's 'best interests'.

This rule overrides the rules in paras 18.25-29 and 18.33-41. DWP guidance does not say what your and your family's best interests are, but see para 18.32 for information the council could reasonably take into account.

18.43 DWP guidance (GM A6.198) says the council should only consider whether the landlord/agent is or is not a fit and proper person if it is doubtful about [their] honesty in connection with HB. This could be because they are involved in fraudulent acts relating to HB. The DWP also suggests (GM A6.200) it could be because they have regularly failed to report changes they have a duty to report (para 17.2), or to repay overpayments which are recoverable from them (paras 19.23-26).

18.44 The following do not mean a landlord/agent is not a fit and proper person:

(a) their undesirable activity in non-HB matters, for example not paying parking fines (GM A6.197);

(b) using their right to request a reconsideration, or to appeal, before repaying an overpayment; or

(c) making complaints about maladministration, for example to the Ombudsman.

18.39   HB 96(1)(b),(3A)(a); HB66+ 77(1)(b),(3A)(a)

18.40   HB 96(2); HB66+ 77(2); NIHB 93(2); NIHB66+ 74(2)

18.41   HB 96(1)(c); HB66+ 77(1)(c); NIHB 93(1)(c); NIHB66+ 74(1)(c)

18.42   HB 95(3), 96(3),(4); HB66+ 76(3), 77(3),(4); NIHB 92(3), 93(3),(4); NIHB66+ 73(3), 74(3),(4)

Decisions about paying a landlord/agent

18.45   The council can make a decision about paying your HB to your landlord/agent:

(a) when you claim HB; and/or

(b) when there is a change in your or your landlord/agent's circumstances which affects this.

See paras 18.8-9 for when payments to a landlord/agent are made, and paras 18.11 and 18.14-16 about payments on account.

18.46   The council can suspend payments of HB (para 17.41) while it is deciding who to pay: CH/1821/2006. But the DWP has encouraged councils not to delay payments in this way (GLHA 5.111).

Decision notices about paying a landlord/agent

18.47   The council must issue two decision notices, one to your landlord/agent and one to you, when:

(a) it decides to pay your HB to them, or changes the amount of the payment (para 18.48); or

(b) they have asked the council to pay your HB to them, but the council has refused: CH/180/2006.

These must be in writing, and must be issued within 14 days of when the council makes the decision, or as soon as reasonably practicable after that.

18.48   When the council decides to pay your landlord/agent (or change the amount), the decision notice issued to them must contain:

(a) the amount of HB they will get for you, and when the payments start (or change);

(b) their duty to notify changes of circumstances, and examples of what they might be (para 17.2);

(c) an explanation about recovering overpaid HB from a blameless tenant (table 19.5(f)); and

(d) their rights in relation to the decision (para 18.49);

but it must not contain other information about your HB (for example personal or financial information about you or your household). The decision notice to you must contain the information in (a) to (c), and your rights in relation to the decision. In practice, this is sometimes instead included in the main decision notice about your HB (para 20.6).

Reconsiderations and appeals about paying a landlord/agent

18.49   When the council decides to pay, or not pay, your landlord/agent, both you and they are a 'person affected'. So both you and they have the right to obtain a statement of reasons, and to appeal if the right of appeal applies to the decision (para 20.42): CH/180/2006.

18.45   HB 89(1), 95, 96, 97(5); HB66+ 70(1), 76, 77, 78(5); NIHB 85(1), 92, 93, 94(5); NIHB66+ 66(1), 73, 74 ,75(5)

18.47   HB sch 9 paras 11,12; HB66+ sch 8 paras 11,12; NIHB sch 10 paras 11,12; NIHB66+ sch 9 paras 11,12

18.48   HB sch 9 paras 11,12; HB66+ sch 8 paras 11,12; NIHB sch 10 paras 11,12; NIHB66+ sch 9 paras 11,12

If the council pays the wrong person

18.50   If the council decided it had a duty to pay your landlord/agent (see para 18.22(a)) but paid you instead, the council must pay your landlord/agent: [2008] UKUT 31 (AAC). If the council fails to do this, your landlord/agent can appeal (para 20.41). What the council paid you is an overpayment which is likely to be recoverable from you (see para 19.23-26).

18.51   If the council decided it had a discretion to pay your landlord/agent (para 18.22(b)) but paid you instead, the council cannot pay your landlord/agent but they can seek compensation from the council: R(H) 2/08, [2010] UKUT 254 (AAC). If the council fails to do this, your landlord/agent can't appeal (para 19.66(b)) but can ask the Ombudsman to intervene (para 20.12) as in case nos. 17 012 147 and 18 017 737 [www].

18.52   It seems reasonable (following the reasoning in [2008] UKUT 31 (AAC)) that if the council decided it had a duty to pay you (para 18.22(c)) but paid your landlord/agent instead, the council must pay you. If the council fails to do this, you can appeal (para 20.41). What the council paid your landlord/agent is an overpayment which is likely to be recoverable from them (para 19.23-26).

How paying your landlord/agent affects your rent

18.53   When the council pays your HB to your landlord/agent, this discharges your liability to pay that amount of rent unless the council recovers it as an overpayment from your landlord/agent: see table 19.5.

If your landlord/agent refuses to accept your HB

18.54   A landlord/agent has the right to refuse payments of rent from someone who is not a party to the tenancy agreement: Bessa Plus Plc v Lancaster. Although this is uncommon, it could affect you if:

(a)   you are the HB claimant; but

(b)   your partner is the sole tenant of your home; and

(c)   your landlord/agent refuses to accept payment of your HB (because you are not on the tenancy agreement).

If this happens, you should be able to get the council to pay your HB to you (rather than your landlord/agent), or to your partner as your nominee (paras 18.19-20).

18.51   https://tinyurl.com/LGO-17-012-147
         https://tinyurl.com/LGO-18-017-737

18.53   HB 95(2), 96(4); HB66+ 76(2), 77(4); NIHB 92(2), 93(5); NIHB66+ 73(2), 74(5)

18.54   Bessa Plus plc v Lancaster 17/03/97 CA 30 HLR 48

Chapter 19 **Overpayments**

- Overpayment types and which are recoverable: see paras 19.1-11.
- The amount of an overpayment: see paras 19.12-22.
- Who to recover from: see paras 19.23-33.
- Methods of recovery: see paras 19.34-58.
- Decisions, notices and appeals: see paras 19.59-67.
- Fraud and penalties: see paras 19.68-79.

What is an overpayment

19.1   You are overpaid HB if you get more HB than you are entitled to. This is the case whether the HB is:

(a) paid to you or someone on your behalf; or

(b) paid to your landlord or their agent; or

(c) credited to your rent account (if you are a council tenant).

Table 19.1 summarises the types and causes of overpayments.

19.2   HB overpayments affect both claimants and landlords. Errors in overpayment decisions can worsen their debts, and also mean councils get the wrong amount of government subsidy (para 21.13). DWP guidance is in its HB Overpayments Guide 2020 (OG) and its good practice guide on recovering overpayments [www].

Table 19.1 **Overpayment types**

Official error overpayments (paras 19.4-7)

(a) Council (or NIHE) error overpayments – e.g. the council failed to act on information you provided, or delayed on acting on it, or made a duplicate payment (paid the same HB twice).

(b) DWP or HMRC error overpayments – e.g. the DWP wrongly awarded you a passport benefit, making your HB higher than it should have been.

Other overpayments (para 19.8)

(c) Claimant error overpayments – e.g. you gave the council incorrect information or failed to report a relevant change of circumstances.

19.1   AA 75(1), 134(2); HB 99; NIAA 73(1), 126(2); HB66+ 80; NIHB 96; NIHB66+ 77

19.2   https://www.gov.uk/government/publications/housing-benefit-overpayments-guide
https://www.gov.uk/government/publications/housing-benefit-overpayment-recovery-good-practice

(d) Landlord/agent error overpayments – e.g. your landlord (while receiving HB for you) gave the council incorrect information about a rent increase.

(e) No-one's fault overpayments – e.g. you were awarded backdated income, and this reduced your HB in the past.

Special cases (para 19.9)

(f) Payment on account overpayments – the council made a payment on account (para 18.11) that turned out to be too great.

(g) Future overpayments – you are a council tenant and HB that was credited to your rent account for a future period turned out to be too great.

(h) Migration overpayments – you transferred from HB to UC but the council continued to pay your HB beyond the two-week run on (paras 1.26-29).

Which overpayments are recoverable

19.3   HB overpayments are either:

(a) recoverable – councils can recover these but have discretion not to (para 19.10); or

(b) not recoverable – councils do not have the power to recover these under HB law.

Official error overpayments

19.4   An official error means an error by the council, the DWP or HMRC – or someone acting on their behalf (e.g. a contractor or partner organisation). But it doesn't include an error that you (the claimant) or the payee or someone acting on your or the payee's behalf 'materially contributed to'. Case law about this is in table 19.2.

19.5   For example, an official error can include:

(a) a mistake about what the facts are;

(b) an error in applying the law or case law;

(c) an accidental error; or

(d) a combination of the above (CH/943/2003).

19.6   An official error overpayment is only recoverable if at the time of receiving the payment decision notice:

(a) you (the claimant) or someone on your behalf could reasonably have been expected to realise it was an overpayment; or

(b) the payee or someone on their behalf could reasonably have been expected to realise it was an overpayment.

Case law about this is in table 19.3.

19.7   This rule protects a claimant who received and spent a payment innocently from having to repay money they can't afford (CH/1176/2003).

19.4   HB 100(3); HB66+ 81(3); NIHB 97(3); NIHB66+ 78(3)

19.6   AA 75(1); HB 100(1)-(3); HB66+ 81(1)-(3); NIAA 73(1); NIHB 97(1)-(3); NIHB66+ 78(1)-(3)

Other overpayments

19.8   All other overpayments are recoverable, including claimant error, landlord/agent error and no-one's fault overpayments (table 19.1(c)-(e)). In the law this is because they aren't due to official error.

Special cases

19.9   Payment on account, future and migration overpayments (table 19.1(f)-(h)) are recoverable however they were caused – even if they were due to official error. For migration overpayments see also para 19.46.

Council discretion not to recover

19.10   When an overpayment is recoverable, the council has discretion (para 20.24) about whether or not to recover it. So, the question of whether an overpayment is recoverable is separate from the question of whether to actually recover it.

19.11   You can ask the council to use this discretion if repaying the overpayment would cause you or your family hardship. The DWP says councils should have 'due regard' to your circumstances (OG 2.145-147). For appeals see para 19.66.

Table 19.2 **Official error overpayments: case law**

These cases were about whether an HB overpayment 'arose in consequence of an official error' (para 19.4).

(a)   How the council should make the decision

- The council should decide what is the substantial cause of the overpayment viewed in a commonsense way ([2010] UKUT 57 (AAC)), or who really caused the overpayment ([2011] UKUT 266 (AAC)). For this purpose:

- when an overpayment has more than one cause, they must be separated out. If the claimant delayed reporting a change and then the council delayed acting on it, only the second part is official error ([2016] UKUT 396 (AAC));

- when the facts are in dispute they are decided on the balance of probability (para 20.20). If the claimant says they reported a change but the council has no record of this, it can't be assumed that the council's procedures are infallible ([2014] UKUT 23 (AAC));

- for the overpayment not to count as official error, it is only necessary that the claimant contributed to the error, not necessarily the overpayment (CH/215/2008);

- terms like 'error' and 'mistake' are interchangeable (CH/943/2003).

19.8   AA 75(1); HB 100(1); HB66+ 81(1); NIAA 73(1); NIHB 97(1); NIHB66+ 78(1)

19.9   HB 93(3), 100(1),(4); HB66+ 74(3), 81(1),(4); UCTP 10; NIHB 90(3), 97(1),(4); NIHB66+ 71(3), 78(1),(4); NIUCTP 10

T19.2   R (Sier) v Cambridge CC HBRB [2001] EWCA Civ 1523
         www.bailii.org/ew/cases/EWCA/Civ/2001/1523.html

(b)   Overpayment was official error

The following were found to be council error:

- not asking the claimant fundamental questions about eligibility (CH/4228/2006);
- delays in applying to the rent officer (CH/361/2006);
- issuing an out-of-date application form ([2014] UKUT 201 (AAC));
- a mistake by another department that affected HB (CH/3586/2007);
- a failure by another department to pass information on to benefits staff or advise the claimant to do so (CH/2567/2007).

The following were found to be DWP error:

- telling the claimant it would pass on information to the council and not doing so (CH/3761/2005);
- a DWP decision that an appeal tribunal found to be an error of law ([2015] UKUT 197 (AAC)).

(c)   Overpayment wasn't official error

The following were found not to be council error:

- not cross-checking an HB claim form against information the claimant had given in a previous claim (R(H) 1/04);
- not asking follow-up questions that would have been prompted if the claimant had given accurate information ([2018] UKUT 418 (AAC));
- assessing benefit income wrongly, because the claimant hadn't understood which DWP figure to provide (CH/56/2008);
- not anticipating changes in the claimant's benefit income (CH/687/2006, R(H) 2/04), or earnings (CH/3/2008);
- a short delay (of 24 days) in acting on a change the claimant reported (CH/858/2006);
- having poor performance statistics which in any case weren't the cause of the overpayment ([2018] UKUT 433 (AAC)).

The following was found not to be DWP error:

- not notifying the council that a working age passport benefit had ceased – since this is the claimant's duty (table 17.1) not the DWP's (R (Sier) v Cambridge CC).

Table 19.3 **Realising there was an overpayment**

These cases – which were all official error overpayments – were about whether the claimant or payee 'could reasonably have been expected to realise' they were overpaid HB (para 19.6).

(a) How the council should make the decision

The council should decide whether the claimant or payee could have realised there 'was' an overpayment, not 'might be' (CH/858/2006). This includes considering:

- the claimant's knowledge, experience and capacity, generally and in relation to the HB scheme (R v Liverpool CC ex parte Griffiths);
- what the claimant could have realised from the decision notice they received at the time – not the overpayment notice (CH/1176/2003);
- what the claimant could have realised from the payment they received – or in rent rebate cases from the credit to their rent account (CH/1675/2005);
- when payment was to a landlord and the overpayment was due to the claimant moving out, whether the landlord knew they had left ([2013] UKUT 232 (AAC));
- when payment was to a landlord organisation, what the organisation as a whole could have realised (CH/4918/2003);
- when the decision depends on the burden of proof (para 20.21), this falls on the claimant or payee to show they couldn't have realised – not on the council to show they could (CH/4918/2003).

(b) Claimant could have realised

In these cases it was found that the claimant could reasonably have been expected to realise they were overpaid (so the official error overpayment was recoverable):

- the decision notice gave the basis of the HB calculation and this showed reasonably clearly that there was a mistake (CH/2409/2005);
- although the notice omitted the claimant's earnings, it listed their other income (CH/2554/2002);
- although the notice was wrong, the figures it gave were obviously different from the claimant's actual earnings (CH/2943/2007), or rent ([2008] UKUT 6 (AAC);
- although the notice was wrong, the claimant didn't attempt to reconcile it with their knowledge of their own situation (CH/2943/2007).

(c) Claimant couldn't have realised

In these cases it was found that the claimant couldn't reasonably have been expected to realise they were overpaid (so the official error overpayment wasn't recoverable):

- the decision notice was wrong, but was issued so late that the claimant wouldn't have realised it was wrong ([2016] UKUT 396 (AAC));
- the notice didn't explain that (or how) the claimant's earnings had been averaged ([2015] UKUT 237 (AAC));
- although the notice didn't include the claimant's retirement income, the claimant

might easily have assumed this was because everyone of his age received it (CH/2554/2002);

- the claimant thought the notice might be wrong so queried it more than once, but the council kept making payments, so the claimant assumed the council knew what it was doing (CH/3240/2007);

- the notice gave the wrong figure for income, but the council requested (and the claimant had given) details for the wrong period, so the claimant assumed it was right (CH/1780/2005);

- the notice gave the wrong figure for income, but the social security system in the claimant's home country had different assessment rules, so the claimant thought it was right (CH/858/2006);

- the claimant was not offered help understanding the notice, even though the council knew he had needed help with the claim form (CH/2935/2005).

The amount of an overpayment

19.12   The amount of an overpayment for a particular period is:

(a) what was actually paid for the period (including credited to your rent account if you are a council tenant);

(b) minus what you were entitled to for that period.

But the rules in this section can reduce this.

Diminishing capital

19.13   The diminishing capital rule applies when:

(a) a recoverable overpayment arose due to capital being wrongly taken into account (for whatever reason); and

(b) the overpayment period was longer than 13 weeks.

19.14   In these cases:

(a) at the end of the first 13 weeks of the overpayment period, the council must treat your capital as reduced by the amount that was overpaid during those 13 weeks;

(b) this gives an imaginary capital figure which is used to calculate your overpayment after that;

(c) the council repeats (a) and (b) at the end of each complete 13 weeks until the end of the overpayment period;

(d) but when the council calculates your HB after the end of the overpayment period, it uses your actual capital (not the imaginary amount).

T19.3   R v Liverpool CC ex parte Griffiths [1990] QBD
           www.rightsnet.org.uk/pdfs/liverpool_griffiths.pdf

19.12   HB 99; HB66+ 80; NIHB 96; NIHB66+ 77

19.13-15   HB 103; HB66+ 84; NIHB 100; NIHB66+ 81

19.15   This rule sometimes (but not always) reduces your overpayment. It reflects the fact that if the council had awarded you less HB due to taking the capital into account, you might have used some of the capital to pay your rent.

Example: Diminishing capital

James has been getting HB of £100 per week based on having no capital and a low retirement income. The council then finds he has had undeclared capital of £17,000 for the past 20 weeks.

- To begin with he had capital over the capital limit (para 15.4) so didn't qualify for HB. The overpayment for the first 13 weeks is (13 x £100 =) £1,300.

- His capital is then treated as reduced by £1,300 to £15,700.

- This is below the capital limit and gives him an assumed income of £12.00 per week (para 15.5). When this is added to his retirement income it turns out he would have qualified for HB of £92.20 per week. The overpayment for the remaining seven weeks is (7 x £7.80 =) £54.60.

- The total overpayment is £1,354.60.

- However, James's actual capital is still £17,000. So, he can't get HB until it reduces below £16,000 – which it will do if and when he repays the overpayment.

Underlying entitlement

19.16   The council must reduce your overpayment by any 'underlying entitlement' you have. This applies in all cases except overpayments (or any parts of an overpayment) caused by you moving home (in these cases the rule in para 19.20 may apply instead).

19.17   Underlying entitlement is HB that would have been awarded if:

(a) you kept the council fully and promptly informed of your true circumstances throughout the overpayment period, including all changes of circumstances no matter how frequent ([2015] UKUT 423 (AAC)); and

(b) in the case of a couple, your partner was the HB claimant rather than you, if this means you would have qualified for more HB ([2015] UKUT 460 (AAC)).

19.18   This rule undoes failures to report advantageous changes ([2019] UKUT 188 (AAC)) and undoes the effect of reporting them late (paras 17.13-15). But this is only for the purpose of calculating the overpayment so:

(a) all the underlying entitlement that falls within the overpayment period is used to reduce your overpayment, but not underlying entitlement falling outside it;

(b) the overpayment can be reduced as far as nil in some cases, but the balance can't be paid to you.

19.16-18   HB 104(1); HB66+ 85(1); NIHB 101(1); NIHB66+ 82(1)

19.19   The council should invite you to provide any information and evidence showing you have underlying entitlement. The onus is then on you to provide this (R(H) 1/05) and the council should allow you at least one month to do so. You can ask the council to reconsider decisions about underlying entitlement and appeal to a tribunal about it (para 19.65). But once the appeal time limit and any extended time limit has passed (paras 20.45-46) the council can't allow underlying entitlement based on new information or evidence (CH/360/2006).

Examples: Underlying entitlement

1. When there has been late notice of a change

Information: Blythe's non-dependant Gwenyth moved out six months ago, but Blythe did not tell her council until three months ago (and had no special circumstances for the late reporting of this change) so her council removed the non-dependant deduction from three months ago. Today the council discovered that Blythe has undeclared earnings from work over the previous nine months.

Assessment: The underlying entitlement rule mean the council must reduce the amount of the overpayment (due to Blythe's undeclared earnings from work) by the amount it could not award in relation to Gwenyth moving out. This results in a lower recoverable overpayment; it may even reduce the overpayment to nil, but in no circumstances can it result in Blythe getting more HB.

2. Calculation rules

Information: In William's case, there is a recoverable overpayment of £5 per week for weeks 1 to 20 inclusive (20 x £5 =£100), and underlying entitlement (because William did not tell the council about a beneficial change on time) in weeks 11 to 20 inclusive of £15 per week.

Assessment: The council uses William's underlying entitlement in weeks 11 to 20 inclusive (10 x £15 = £150) to reduce the overpayment (£100). This is enough to reduce the recoverable overpayment to nil but the council can't award the remainder of the underlying entitlement to William.

Moving home

19.20   When you move home, there is an overpayment if you are paid HB for longer than you were entitled to on your old home (para 3.29).

19.21   The council may reduce this overpayment by treating it as having been correctly paid for your new home, but only if:

(a)   you qualify for HB on your new home; and

(b)   the HB for your new home is:

    ■   administered by the same council, and

    ■   payable to the same person (you on both homes, or the same landlord/agent on both homes).

This rule can't be used for other moves (nor can the underlying entitlement rule in paras 19.16-19).

19.19   HB 86(1); HB66+ 67(1); NIHB 82(1); NIHB66+ 63(1)

19.21   HB 104A; HB66+ 85A; NIHB 101A; NIHB66+ 82A

Example: Calculating an overpayment when you move home

Bob gets rent allowance of £100 a week. He moves to a new home where he gets HB of £110 a week. Bob doesn't tell the council about the move for three weeks after leaving the earlier address. This results in an overpayment of £300 on the old address.

Bob is entitled to £110 a week on the new address for the same period (making £330 in total). The council may reduce the amount of the recoverable overpayment on Bob's old home by £300, reducing it to nil, and paying Bob the remaining £30 in relation to his new home.

Council tenants who paid more rent than required

19.22 If you are a council tenant and during the period of a recoverable overpayment you paid more rent than you were required to, the council may reduce your overpayment by these excess payments.

Example: A council tenant

Betty is a council tenant and is getting HB of £60 per week based on her state and private pensions. Her private pensions increase by £50 per week. She reports this promptly to the council, but the council doesn't reduce her HB for ten weeks.

However, Betty estimates she should pay an extra £35 per week towards her rent and does so for each of the ten weeks. When the council calculates her overpayment, it is £32.50 per week. Using the extra £35 per week she has paid, reduces her overpayment to nil (and leaves her £2.50 per week credit on her rent account).

Who to recover from

Overpayments due to official error

19.23 When an overpayment was due to official error (para 19.4), it is recoverable from:

(a) you – or someone acting on your behalf – if you/they could reasonably have been expected to realise it was an overpayment;

(b) the payee – or someone on their behalf – if they could reasonably have been expected to realise it was an overpayment;

(c) if both (a) and (b) apply – all of the above.

Overpayments due to claimant, appointee or landlord/agent error

19.24 When an overpayment was caused by you, someone acting on your behalf or your landlord/agent (para 19.25), it is recoverable from:

(a) you, or someone acting on your behalf if you or they caused the overpayment;

(b) the payee or agent if they caused the overpayment.

19.22   HB 104(2); HB66+ 85(2); NIHB 101(2); NIHB66+ 82(2)

19.23   AA 75(3); HB 101(2)(c),(3A); HB66+ 82(2)(c),(3A); NIAA 73(3); NIHB 98(2)(b),(4); NIHB66+ 79(2)(b),(4)

19.24   AA 75(3); HB 101(2)(b); HB66+ 82(2)(b); NIAA 73(3); NIHB 98(2)(b); NIHB66+ 79(2)(b)

19.25   For these purposes an overpayment is 'caused' by you or someone acting on your behalf or your landlord/agent if you or they misrepresented, or failed to disclose, a material fact when you claimed or when your circumstances changed. Disputes about this are uncommon, because the alternative (para 19.26) has a similar effect.

Other overpayments

19.26   Any other overpayment is recoverable from you or the payee. For example, this applies to an overpayment which is no-one's fault.

Recovery from you/your partner or someone acting on your behalf

19.27   When an overpayment is recoverable from you (paras 19.23-26) it is also recoverable from:

(a)   your partner if you are a couple (paras 19.28-29);

(b)   your partners in a polygamous marriage;

(c)   an attorney or someone acting on your behalf (para 16.5);

(d)   your estate if you die.

Couples

19.28   An overpayment recoverable from you is also recoverable from your partner if:

(a)   you were a couple at the time of the overpayment; and

(b)   you are a couple at the time of the recovery.

19.29   In these cases, your partner has the same rights as you to be notified about the overpayment and to ask for a reconsideration or appeal (CH/3622/2006). The council can't recover an overpayment from a former partner (if your relationship has ended, or if you die), or a new partner (if you became a couple after the overpayment period).

Recovery from your landlord or agent

19.30   When an overpayment is recoverable from the payee (paras 19.23-26), it is recoverable from:

(a)   your landlord if the HB was paid to them;

(b)   your landlord's agent if the HB was paid to them – this is the case even if the agent has already paid the money to the landlord (R(H) 10/07);

(c)   a third party who was wrongly paid HB if the overpayment was paid to the wrong person.

19.31   In these cases, the landlord, agent or third party has the same rights as you to be notified about the overpayment and to ask for a reconsideration or appeal. These rights are clearly set out in NSP v Stoke on Trent CC ([2020] UKUT 311 (AAC)).

19.25   HB 101(2)(b); HB66+ 82(2)(b); NIHB 98(2)(b); NIHB66+ 79(2)(b)

19.26   AA 75(3); HB 101(2)(a); HB66+ 82(2)(a); NIAA 73(3); NIHB 98(2)(a); NIHB66+ 79(2)(a)

19.27   AA 75(3); HB 102(1ZA); HB66+ 83(1ZA); NIAA 73(3); NIHB 99(1A); NIHB66+ 80(1A)

19.28   HB 102(1ZA); HB66+ 83(1ZA); NIHB 99(1A); NIHB66+ 80(1A)

19.30   HB 101(2)(b)(c); HB66+ 82(2)(b),(c); NIHB 98(2)(b),(c); NIHB66+ 79(2)(b),(c)

19.31   DAR 3(1)(d); NIDAR 3(1)(d)

Further rule for landlords and agents

19.32   The council must not recover overpaid HB from your landlord or agent if:

(a) you (the claimant) failed to disclose a material fact to the council when you claimed or when your circumstances changed;

(b) this failure could justify legal proceedings (para 19.68);

(c) the landlord/agent told the council or DWP in writing that they suspected there was an overpayment before the overpayment was identified (CH/2411/2006); and

(d) the landlord/agent did not collude in it or contribute to its period or amount.

A choice about who to recover from

19.33   When an overpayment is recoverable from two or more people (paras 19.23-26), each has a joint and several liability to repay the overpayment (R(H) 6/06). The council can choose which to recover from, and change the choice, but should not take steps to recover from both at the same time (CH/2583/2007). For appeals see paras 19.65-66.

Methods of recovery

19.34   This section explains the methods of recovery that are available when overpaid HB is recoverable from you or your landlord/agent, and how these affect your rent.

19.35   In this section, 'you' includes your partner and/or someone acting for you (para 19.27), and your 'landlord/agent' means whichever received the HB payment (para 19.30).

Methods of recovery from you

19.36   For both council and private tenants, when an HB overpayment is recoverable from you, it can be:

(a) deducted from your HB (paras 19.40-43);

(b) deducted from your DWP benefits (paras 19.44-46);

(c) deducted from your earnings (paras 19.47-49); or

(c) recovered by some other lawful method (para 19.50).

Methods of recovery from your landlord/agent

19.37   For private tenants, when an overpayment is recoverable from your landlord/agent, it can be:

(a) deducted from your HB, your landlord/agent's HB, or another (blameless) tenant's HB (paras 19.40-43);

(b) deducted from your landlord/agent's DWP benefits or earnings (paras 19.44-49); or

(c) recovered by some other lawful method (para 19.50).

19.32   HB 101(1),(3); HB66+ 82(1),(3); NIHB 98(1),(3); NIHB66+ 79(1),(3)

19.38   When an overpayment is recoverable from both you and your landlord/agent (para 19.33), it can be recovered by any of the methods in paras 19.36-37.

Overpayments and your rent

19.39   When overpayments are recovered this sometimes (but not always) means you need to pay more rent to avoid getting into arrears. Tables 19.4 and 19.5 explain this.

Table 19.4 **How overpayments affect your rent: council tenants**

Overpayments that are deducted from your on-going HB:

(a)   Because your HB is lower, you need to pay more towards your rent to avoid arrears.

Overpayments that are deducted from your DWP benefits or earnings, or that you repay from your own money:

(b)   These methods of recovery/repayment are mainly for people who are no longer on HB. They don't affect your rent.

Overpayments that are managed using your rent account:

(c)   When overpayments are managed using your rent account, they should be recorded separately so that your rent isn't affected. When you are making a payment you need to say whether you are putting it towards the overpayment or your rent, otherwise it is put towards the earliest debt first.

(d)   But if your tenancy agreement expressly allows this, the council can add HB overpayments to your rent account (as an extra rent charge), so you need to pay more towards your rent to avoid arrears.

Table 19.5 **How overpayments affect your rent: private tenants**

Overpayments that are deducted from your on-going HB:

(a)   Because your HB is lower, you need to pay more towards your rent to avoid arrears.

(b)   But if the overpayment was due to landlord/agent fraud (for which they have been convicted of an offence or agreed to pay a penalty: paras 19.74-77), the landlord/agent must treat you as having paid rent equal to the amount of the deductions so that your rent isn't affected.

T19.4(a),(b)   Direct consequences of method of recovery

T19.4(c)   R v Haringey LBC ex parte Ayub 13/04/92 QBD 25 HLR 566
                    www.rightsnet.org.uk/pdfs/R_V_Haringey_exp_Ayub.pdf

T19.4(d)   Additional rent clauses, typically to offset the landlord's expenses are a common feature in tenancy agreements.

T19.5(a),(c)   Direct consequences of method of recovery

T19.5(b)   AA 75(5)(b),(6); HB 106(3), 107(1),(2); HB66+ 87(3), 88(1),(2); NIAA 73(5)(b),(6); NIHB 103(3), 104(1),(2); NIHB66+ 84(3), 85(1),(2)

Overpayments that are deducted from your DWP benefits or earnings, or that you repay from your own money:

(c) These methods of recovery /repayment are mainly for people who are no longer on HB. They don't affect your rent.

Overpayments that are deducted from your landlord/agent's HB, DWP benefits or earnings, or that they repay from their own money:

(d) Your landlord/agent can add these amounts to your rent account (as an extra charge), so you need to pay more towards your rent to avoid arrears.

Overpayments that are deducted from a blameless tenant's HB:

(e) Your landlord/agent must treat the blameless tenant as having paid rent equal to the amount of the deduction so that their rent isn't affected.

(f) Your landlord/agent can add the amount of the deduction to your rent account (as an extra charge), so you need to pay more towards your rent to avoid arrears.

(g) The council's overpayment notice to the landlord/agent says who the blameless tenant is, but no notice is sent to the blameless tenant.

Deductions from HB

19.40 The council can recover an HB overpayment by taking deductions from your on-going HB, including transitional HB awarded to people migrating to UC (para 17.19).

19.41 When the overpayment is recoverable from you, the deductions can only be taken from your or your partner's HB.

19.42 But when the overpayment is recoverable from your landlord/agent, the deductions can be taken from:

(a) your or your partners HB; or

(b) your landlord/agent's own HB; or

(c) a 'blameless' tenant's HB – this means another tenant whose HB is paid to your landlord/agent.

19.43 Whenever deductions are taken from your or your partner's HB (paras 19.41, 19.42(a)), the deductions:

(a) must not reduce HB below 50p a week;

(b) must not exceed the maximum amount in table 19.6 except when they are taken from lump sum arrears of HB;

(c) can be reduced in cases of hardship.

T19.5(d),(f)   HB 95(2); HB66+ 76(2); NIHB 92(2); NIHB66+ 73(2)

T19.5(e)   AA 75(5)(c),(6); HB 106(3); HB66+ 87(3); NIAA 73(5)(b),(6); NIHB 103(3); NIHB66+ 84(3)

T19.5(g)   HB sch 9 para 15(2); HB66+ sch 8 para 15(2); NIHB sch 10 para 15(2); NIHB66+ sch 9 para 15(2)

19.40-42   AA 75(4),(5); HB 102, 106; HB66+ 83, 87; NIAA 73(4),(5); NIHB 99, 103; NIHB66+ 80, 84

19.43   HB 102(2)-(6); HB66+ 83(2)-(6); NIHB 99(3)-(7); NIHB66+ 80(3)-(7)

Table 19.6 **Maximum deductions from HB (2021-22)**

The maximum weekly deduction is:

- ■ £18.75 if you have been convicted of an offence or agreed to pay a penalty (para 19.68);
- ■ £11.25 in any other case.

Plus, in all cases, not more than half of:

- ■ any £5, £10, £20, £25 earned income and permitted work disregard (table 14.5);
- ■ any disregard of regular charitable or voluntary payments (para 13.30);
- ■ the £10 disregard of war pensions for bereavement or disablement (table 13.4).

Deductions from DWP benefits

19.44   If you aren't entitled to HB, the council can recover an overpayment by asking the DWP to take deductions from your on-going benefits.

19.45   When the overpayment is recoverable from you, the deductions can only be taken from your or your partner's DWP benefits. And when the overpayment is recoverable from your landlord/agent, the deductions can only be taken from their DWP benefits.

19.46   But this method of recovery can only be used for:

(a) overpayments caused by your or your landlord/agent's misrepresentation or failure to disclose – these can be recovered from the benefits in table 19.7; and

(b) migration overpayments (table 19.1(h)) – these are always recovered from your UC.

Table 19.7 **DWP benefits overpaid HB can be recovered from**

A recoverable overpayment of HB may be deducted from:

■ universal credit	■ state pension credit
■ JSA(IB)	■ ESA(IR)
■ income support	■ personal independence payment
■ retirement pension	■ incapacity benefit/SDA
■ maternity allowance	■ carer's allowance
■ industrial injuries benefits	■ disability living allowance
■ old style bereavement benefits	■ attendance allowance
■ 'new style' JSA/ESA	■ equivalent EU and Swiss benefits

All of these apply to recovery from a claimant or landlord/agent, but only the top three lines apply to recovery from a partner.

T19.6   HB 102(2)-(6); HB66+ 83(2)-(6); NIHB 99(3)-(5); NIHB66+ 80(3)-(5)

19.44-46   AA 75(4),(5); HB 102(1), 105, 106; HB66+ 83(1), 86, 87; NIAA 73(4),(5); NIHB 99(1), 102, 103; NIHB66+ 80(1), 83, 84

T19.7   HB 105, 106; HB66+ 86, 87; NIHB 102, 103; NIHB66+ 83, 84

Deductions from earnings

19.47   The council can recover an HB overpayment by requiring an employer to take deductions from future earnings. This is called a 'direct earnings attachment' (DEA) and is usually only used when deductions can't be taken from HB or DWP benefits.

19.48   When the overpayment is recoverable from you, the deductions can be taken from your earnings (but not your partner's as the DWP considers this would be inappropriate: LA Welfare Direct Bulletin 9/2019).

19.49   The main rules about deductions from your earnings are as follows (these also apply to deductions from a landlord/agent's earnings):

(a)   the council notifies your employer (and you);

(b)   the employer has ten days to confirm (or deny) you are an employee, and to claim exemption from making deductions if they are a new business or a micro business;

(c)   the employer calculates the deductions on a fixed scale and notifies you of the amount;

(d)   the employer pays the deducted amounts to the council and can take a further £1 per deduction for administrative expenses;

(e)   you and the employer must notify the council if you stop employment, and you must notify the council if you start new employment;

(f)   it is a criminal offence for the employer not to provide the information required or not to make deductions.

Full information is available online [www].

Other methods of recovery

19.50   The council can recover an HB overpayment by any other lawful method, including asking you to repay it from your own money, making payment arrangements with you, and as a last resort taking court action to enforce recovery of the debt (para 19.52).

Bankruptcy etc

19.51   An overpayment can't be recovered if:

(a)   the council made the overpayment decision (para 19.59) before you were granted a bankruptcy order; or

(b)   the overpayment was included in a debt relief order (DRO) in England and Wales or a sequestration order in Scotland.

But this doesn't apply (and therefore recovery can be made) if the overpayment was caused by fraud. While the order is in force and after it ends, the council can't recover the overpayment by any method (including by making deductions from your UC or other benefits): SSWP v Payne and Cooper; Re Nortel Companies [www].

19.47-48   AA 75(8)-(10); HB 106A; HB66+ 87A; NIAA 73(8)-(10); NIHB 103A; NIHB66+ 83A

19.49   Part 6 of the Social Security (Overpayments and Recovery) Regulations 2013 No 384 www.gov.uk/make-benefit-debt-deductions
            Part 6 of the Social Security (Overpayments and Recovery) Regulations (Northern Ireland) 2016 No 224

19.50   HB 102(1); HB66+ 83(1); NIHB 99(1); NIHB66+ 80(1)

19.51   SSWP v Payne & Cooper 14/12/11 UKSC [2011] UKSC 60 www.bailii.org/uk/cases/UKSC/2011/60.html
            Re Nortel Companies 24/07/13 UKSC [2013] UKSC 52 www.bailii.org/uk/cases/UKSC/2013/52.html

Court action

19.52   The DWP advises councils that legal proceedings should only be considered after attempts to recover by other means have failed and there is good reason to believe you can afford to make repayments (OG 7.23). Councils are told that before pursuing recovery through the courts they should allow your appeal period to run out, allow any outstanding appeal to be decided, send at least two letters requesting repayment and make sure that procedures are in place to check that you are getting all the HB and other benefits you may be entitled to (OG 7.20-22). But not all councils follow this guidance. Court action may take the form of civil proceedings for debt, but the following procedure (paras 19.53-58) is simpler.

The simplified debt recovery procedure

19.53   In England, Wales and Northern Ireland the council/DWP (NIHE/DFC) has the power to recover HB overpayments by execution in the County Court as if under a court order; and in Scotland (para 19.56) as if it were an extract registered decree arbitral (OG 7.24-38).

19.54   In England, Wales and Northern Ireland, the council/DWP can register an HB overpayment determination directly as an order of the County Court without the need to bring a separate action. The procedure is explained in DWP guidance (OG 7.24-38). The council/DWP applies to the court on form N322A [www], enclosing a copy of the overpayment notice and the relevant fee. The notice must include all the matters in para 19.61 (OG 5.07). An officer of the court then makes an order and a copy is sent to the council and to you. Once the order has been made, the council can use all the normal debt enforcement methods – a third party debt order allowing it to receive money owed to you by a third party; a warrant for the court bailiff to seize your goods; or a charging order against property/land you own.

19.55   You can't appeal against the order, but you or your landlord/agent may apply to the court to set it aside if the overpayment notice was defective or the council has ignored your HB appeal rights. For other kinds of disputes, you should ask the council to reconsider or appeal to a tribunal (Ghassemian v Borough of Kensington and Chelsea).

19.56   In Scotland, an HB overpayment determination is immediately enforceable by the council as if it were an extract registered decree arbitral (OG 7.24). The council/DWP doesn't need to register it with the Sheriff Court. The usual methods of enforcement are available.

19.53   AA 75(7); NIAA 73(7); NIAA 73(7)(a)

19.54   AA 75(7)(a)
          HB Overpayments Guide, Part 7 https://tinyurl.com/OPGuidePart7
          https://www.gov.uk/government/publications/form-n322a-application-to-enforce-an-award

19.55   Ghassemian v Kensington and Chelsea LBC [2009] EWCA Civ 743 www.bailii.org/ew/cases/EWCA/Civ/2009/743.html

19.56   AA 75(7)(b)

Time limits for court action

19.57　　In England, Wales and Northern Ireland the council/DWP must start any court enforcement action (paras 19.52-55) within six years. This limitation does not apply to any other method of recovery – such as deductions from future HB (OG 7.00-05). In Scotland your council cannot recover overpayments by any method after 20 years (OG 7.05).

19.58　　This time limit does not affect how far back an overpayment can go. But the further the overpayment goes back, the more difficult it may be for the council to provide the evidence needed to prove the overpayment to the court (OG 7.00).

Decisions, notices and appeals

Decisions and notices

19.59　　When the council decides you were overpaid, it should send you the following within 14 days or as soon as reasonably practicable:

(a) a decision notice about your corrected HB entitlement (paras 20.2-4) unless the overpayment was due to a duplicate payment (table 19.1(a)); and

(b) an overpayment notice (para 19.61).

These are sometimes combined in one notice.

19.60　　The council should also send the overpayment notice to each other 'person affected' (para 19.64). This includes every person from whom the overpayment is recoverable (paras 19.23-26) not just the person the council will actually recover it from (R(H) 6/06).

19.61　　The overpayment notice should contain the following information:

(a) the fact that there is a recoverable overpayment;

(b) the reason why there is a recoverable overpayment;

(c) the amount of the recoverable overpayment;

(d) how that amount was calculated;

(e) the benefit weeks to which the recoverable overpayment relates;

(f) if overpaid HB is to be deducted from future HB, the amount of the deduction;

(g) any other relevant matters;

(h) your rights to request a written statement, ask the council to reconsider, and to appeal to a tribunal, and how and when to do these (chapter 20).

19.62　　The council's notice should be clear about which 'revisions' and 'supersessions' the overpayment results from. These terms are explained in paras 20.31-32 but you are not expected to use them unless you wish to. Errors in a notice can affect the council's ability to recover the overpayment. Case law about this is in table 19.8.

19.57　s9, 38(1),(11), the Limitation Act 1980; s7, the Prescription and Limitation (Scotland) Act 1973; arts 2(1),(11), 6, the Limitation (Northern Ireland) Order 1989 No. 1339

19.59　HB 90(1); HB66+ 71(1); NIHB 86(1); NIHB66+ 67(1)

19.61　HB sch 9 para 15; HB66+ sch 8 para 15; NIHB sch 10 para 15; NIHB66+ sch 9 para 15

Table 19.8 **Notices and effect on recovery: case law**

This table is about the entitlement and overpayment notices the council should issue when there is an HB overpayment (para 19.59).

(a) The content of the notices

■ The notices must be clear and unambiguous, with proper use of statutory language and dates relevant to the revisions and supersessions that resulted in the overpayment (R(IS) 2/96; CH/3439/2004; C3/07-08 (IS); C2/10-11 (HB) [www]).

■ The overpayment notice must give the reason why there was an overpayment with enough detail to enable the recipient to judge whether to appeal. Just saying it was due to a 'change in circumstances' isn't enough (R v Thanet DC ex parte Warren Court Hotels Ltd).

■ The overpayment notice must name all the parties from whom the overpayment is recoverable. If it is recoverable from both claimant and landlord, naming just the landlord isn't enough (CH/3622/2005).

(b) The effect on recovery of the overpayment

■ If one or both notices are omitted, the overpayment is not recoverable ([2013] 208 UKUT (AAC)); R (Godwin) v Rossendale BC.

■ If one or both notices are incomplete, this can undermine recovery (Warwick DC v Freeman).

■ If a notice is incomprehensibly long (here, over 100 sheets with no summary) this can undermine recovery ([2019] UKUT 45 (AAC));

■ Trivial defects that cause no harm don't undermine recovery (Haringey LBC v Awaritefe).

■ If the council recovers HB from a landlord before issuing a valid notice, the landlord can apply to a court to get the money returned (Waveney DC v Jones).

■ If the landlord voluntarily repays HB before the council issues a valid notice, the landlord can't get the money returned (Norwich CC v Stringer).

T19.8   C3/ 07-08 (IS) and C2/ 10-11 (HB) are Northern Ireland Commissioners Decisions
         https://iaccess.communities-ni.gov.uk/NIDOC/users/internetsearchpage.aspx
         R v Thanet DC ex parte Warren Court Hotels Ltd 06/04/00 QBD https://tinyurl.com/Thanet-v-WCH
         R (Godwin) v Rossendale BC [2002] EWCA Civ 726 www.bailii.org/ew/cases/EWCA/Civ/2002/726.html
         Warwick DC v Freeman 31/10/94 CA www.rightsnet.org.uk/pdfs/warwick_v_Freeman.pdf
         Haringey LBC v Awaritefe [1999] EWCA Civ 1491 www.bailii.org/ew/cases/EWCA/Civ/1999/1491.html
         Waveney DC v Jones 01/12/99 CA www.rightsnet.org.uk/pdfs/Waveney_v_Jones.pdf
         Norwich CC v Stringer 03/05/00 www.ucc.ie/law/restitution/archive/englcases/norwich.htm

Reconsiderations and appeals

19.63 For all HB overpayments, each of the 'persons affected' (para 19.64) has the right:

(a) to ask the council to reconsider any matter relating to the overpayment; and

(b) to appeal to a tribunal about certain matters relating to the overpayment (para 19.65).

Chapter 20 explains how to do this.

Persons affected

19.64 When you are overpaid HB the persons affected are:

(a) you in all cases (whoever the overpayment is recoverable from);

(b) your partner if the overpayment is recoverable from them (para 19.28);

(c) your landlord/agent or anyone else if the overpayment is recoverable from them (para 19.30).

This means there are often two (or three) persons affected in the case of an overpayment appeal.

Appealable and non-appealable matters

19.65 You have the right to appeal about:

(a) your true HB entitlement during the HB overpayment period;

(b) whether the council has made the revisions and supersessions (paras 20.31-32) needed to establish that you have been overpaid (R(H) 3/04);

(c) the amount of the overpayment;

(d) whether the resulting overpayment is legally recoverable; and

(e) which person or persons it is recoverable from.

When your landlord/agent makes an appeal, (b) to (e) apply (CH/1129/2004; Wirral MBC v Salisbury Independent Living Ltd), but (a) does not (R(H) 7/04).

19.66 The tribunal doesn't have the power to decide:

(a) whether the council should use its discretion not to recover the overpayment ([2011] UKUT 266 (AAC)); and

(b) which person (if there is more than one) it should be recovered from (R(H) 6/06);

(c) what method the council should use to recover it (CH/2298/2007); or

(d) the rate of recovery (R(H) 7/04).

In some of these cases it may be possible to seek judicial review (para 20.53).

Recovery pending appeal

19.67 The DWP has advised councils that recovery of overpayments should in some cases be delayed in order to allow time to appeal, and that recovery action should be suspended from when an appeal is made to when it is decided (OG 4.240-241, 4.250).

19.63   HB sch 9 paras 2-5; HB66+ sch 8 paras 2-5; NIHB sch 10 paras 2-5; NIHB66+ sch 9 paras 2-5

19.64   HB 2(1) – definition: 'person affected'; HB66+ 2(1); DAR 3; NIHB 2(1); NIHB66+ 2(1); NIDAR 3

19.65-66 CPSA sch 7 para 6; NICPSA sch 7 para 6
          Wirral MBC v Salisbury Independent Living [2012] EWCA Civ 84 www.bailii.org/ew/cases/EWCA/Civ/2012/84.html

Fraud and penalties

19.68   The DWP's Counter Fraud and Compliance Directorate (CFCD) in Great Britain and the DFC's single Fraud Investigation Service in Northern Ireland are responsible for investigating fraud and related offences across all social security benefits, tax credits and HB. Prosecutions are conducted by the Crown Prosecution Service in England and Wales, the Procurator Fiscal in Scotland and the Public Prosecution Service in Northern Ireland. In some cases (usually less serious) you may be offered the chance to pay a penalty rather than face prosecution (paras 19.74-77).

Fraud offences by the claimant

19.69   You (the claimant) can be prosecuted under one of the social security fraud offences if you:

   (a)   make a false statement; or

   (b)   produce, provide or supply any document that is false in a material particular,

with the view to receiving HB (or other DWP benefit). You also commit an offence if you fail to promptly report a change of circumstances that you have a duty to notify (para 17.2) with the knowledge that it affects your award.

19.70   If you are convicted in the magistrates' court you are liable for an unlimited fine or up to three months in prison (or both), or up to six months in prison (and/or a fine) if the offence involved dishonesty. If you are convicted in the crown court for dishonestly making a false statement or failing to report a change, the maximum sentence is seven years in prison (and/or a fine). You are dishonest if you knew you were not telling the truth.

19.71   If you are convicted for fraud or agree to pay a penalty (paras 19.74-77) the council/ DWP can reduce your HB (or other benefits) for a fixed period.

Fraud offences by the landlord

19.72   If you are a landlord/agent you can be prosecuted for fraud (paras 19.69-70) if you assist the claimant by providing false information, etc. If you (the landlord/agent) receive HB on behalf of one (or more) of your tenants (paras 18.22-41) you can also be prosecuted if you fail to report a change of circumstances that you could reasonably be expected to know affects their HB. But in this case the only changes you must report to avoid prosecution are those that relate to your tenant's liability for rent (para 5.1) or their occupation of the dwelling.

19.73   If the landlord is a company, the company is liable for any offence (para 19.72) committed as well as any director, manager, secretary or officer of the company who consented to the act or omission from which the offence arose. If a landlord/agent is convicted of an offence or agrees to a pay a penalty (para 19.74) the council may decide that s/he is not a fit and proper person to receive HB payments (paras 18.42-44).

19.69   AA 111A, 112; NIAA 105A, 106

19.70   AA 111A(3), 112(2); NIAA 105A(3), 106(2)

19.71   The Social Security (Loss of Benefit) Regulations 2001 No. 4022; The Social Security (Loss of Benefit) Regulations (Northern Ireland) 2002 No.79

19.72   AA 111A(1C),(1F), 112(1C),(1E); NIAA 105A(1C),(1F), 106(1C),(1E)

19.73   AA 115; NIAA 109

Administrative penalties

19.74   The DWP (in consultation with the council) [www] may offer you the chance to pay an 'administrative penalty' rather than face prosecution, if:

(a)   the overpayment was caused by an 'act or omission' on your part; and

(b)   there are grounds for bringing a prosecution against you for an offence relating to that overpayment.

You do not have to agree to a penalty. You can opt for the possibility of prosecution instead. The DWP is expected to advise the council of the outcome of an administrative penalty offer [www].

19.75   The offer of a penalty must be in writing, explain that it is a way of avoiding prosecution, and give other information – including the fact that you can change your mind within 14 days (including the date of the agreement), and that the penalty will be repaid if you successfully challenge it by asking for a reconsideration or appeal. The DWP does not normally offer a penalty (but prosecutes instead) if an overpayment is substantial or there are other aggravating factors (such as you being in a position of trust).

19.76   The amount of the penalty is 50% of the recoverable overpayment. This is subject to a minimum of £350 and a maximum of £5,000 where your act or omission causing the overpayment occurred wholly on or after 1st April 2015. The maximum penalty where the relevant act or omission occurred before that date is £2,000. In Northern Ireland the maximum penalty is still set at £2,000.

19.77   The DWP may also make an offer of a penalty where your act or omission could have resulted in an overpayment and it thinks there are grounds for bringing a prosecution for a related offence. In these cases, the penalty is the fixed amount of £350.

Civil penalties

19.78   In Great Britain the council may impose a civil penalty of £50 on you if you:

(a)   negligently make an incorrect statement or representation or negligently give incorrect information or evidence relating to a claim or award and fail to take reasonable steps to correct the error; or

(b)   without reasonable excuse, fail to provide required information or evidence relating to a claim or award or fail to tell the council about a relevant change of circumstance; and

(c)   in any of these circumstances this results in the council making an overpayment; but

(d)   you have not been charged with an offence or cautioned.

19.79   The amount of the civil penalty is added to the amount of the recoverable overpayment. If you have been successfully prosecuted for fraud or offered an administrative penalty or caution, the council cannot issue you with a civil penalty for the same offence. If you want to appeal against a civil penalty you should appeal against the amount of the overpayment.

19.74   AA 115A(1),(1A),(7A)-(7B); NIAA 109A(1),(1A)

           DWP, Fraud Investigations: staff guide, May 2019 https://www.tinyurl.com/Fraud-Investigations

19.75   AA 115A(2),(4),(5); NIAA 109A(2),(4),(5)

19.76   AA 115A(3); NIAA 109A(3)

19.77   AA 115A(1A),(3A); NIAA 109A(1A),(3A)

19.78-79   AA 115-115D; The Social Security (Civil Penalties) Regulations 2012 No.1990

Chapter 20 **Decisions and appeals**

- Decision rights: see paras 20.1-4.
- Decisions, notices and reasons: see paras 20.5-24.
- Reconsiderations and when they take effect: see paras 20.25-40.
- Appeals to a tribunal and further appeals: see paras 20.41-53.
- Appeals about rent officer determinations: see paras 20.54-61.

Decision rights

20.1   This chapter explains the rights that go with HB decisions. The main ones are:

(a) getting reasons for the decision;

(b) asking the council to reconsider; and

(c) appealing to a tribunal.

Persons affected by decisions

20.2   These rights belong to:

(a) you (the HB claimant);

(b) someone acting for you if you are unable to act on your own behalf (for example an attorney or appointee: paras 16.5-7);

(c) your landlord or agent if the decision is about whether to pay your HB to them rather than you (paras 18.22-52);

(d) your landlord or agent or anyone else if the decision is about whether an overpayment is recoverable from them (paras 19.23-33).

The law calls these 'persons affected'. They can include individuals (e.g. you, your private landlord) and corporate bodies (e.g. a housing association, a firm of letting agents).

20.3   Others are not persons affected. For example, a landlord providing you with supported accommodation may be very concerned about how the authority decided the amount of your eligible rent, but they aren't a person affected in relation to that decision: Wirral MBC v Salisbury Independent Living Ltd.

Using your rights

20.4   You have to write requesting the rights in para 20.1 and sign your request. Or a solicitor or other representative aged 18 or over can write your request and sign it for you ([2015] UKUT 28 (AAC)). A non-legally qualified representative should have written authority from you to act on your behalf.

20.2   DAR 3; HB 2(1) definition: 'person affected'; HB66+ 2(1); NIDAR 3; NIHB 2(1); NIHB66+ 2(1)

20.3   Wirral MBC v Salisbury Independent Living Ltd [2012] EWCA Civ 84; www.bailii.org/ew/cases/EWCA/Civ/2012/84.html

Decisions, notices and reasons

Decisions

20.5   The council/NIHE makes decisions about your HB:

(a) when you make your claim (para 16.18);

(b) when your circumstances change (para 17.11);

(c) when your HB is overpaid (para 19.59); and

(d) when you ask for a reconsideration (paras 20.30).

Decision notices

20.6   The council/NIHE sends a decision notice to you (or someone acting for you: paras 16.5-7) and to each other person affected (para 20.2):

(a) when you make a claim, the notice must contain the information in table 20.1;

(b) when your HB changes, the notice must say what the change is (and can include the information in table 20.1);

(c) when you are overpaid, the notice must contain the information in para 19.61.

There are also rules for decision notices sent to landlords and agents about paying them HB (paras 18.47-48) or recovering overpayments (para 19.60).

20.7   Every decision notice (whoever it is issued to) must also contain information about the right to:

(a) get a statement of reasons (para 20.10);

(b) ask for a reconsideration (para 20.25);

(c) appeal, if the right to appeal applies to the decision (para 20.41);

and how to do these things.

Table 20.1 **Decision notices about claims**

When the council decides your claim for HB, it must issue a decision notice to you containing the following information.

If you are entitled to HB

(a) Your first day of entitlement.

(b) The normal weekly amount of your HB.

(c) If your HB is a rent allowance, when and how often it will be paid (and if it will be paid to your landlord/agent, see paras 18.47-48).

(d) Your duty to notify changes of circumstances, and examples of what these might be (para 17.2).

20.6   DAR 10; HB 90(1), sch 9 paras 1, 7, 8; HB66+ 71(1), sch 8 paras 1, 7, 8;
         NIDAR 10; NIHB 86(1), sch 10 paras 1, 7, 8; NIHB66+ 67(1), sch 9 paras 1, 7, 8

20.7   HB sch 9 paras 2-5; HB66+ sch 8 paras 2-5; NIHB sch 10 paras 2-5; NIHB66+ sch 9 paras 2-5

If you are not entitled to HB

(e)   The reason why you are not entitled.

(f)   If your HB is less than 50p a week, the amount and an explanation that this is below the minimum award (para 6.7).

All cases whether or not you are entitled

(g)   Your weekly eligible rent.

(h)   If standard deductions were made for fuel, how to change them (para 8.68).

(i)   The amount and category of non-dependant deductions.

(j)   Your applicable amount and how it was worked out (unless you are on a passport benefit).

(k)   Your weekly earned income and weekly unearned income (unless you are on a passport benefit or savings credit).

(l)   If you are on savings credit, the DWP's figures for your income and capital, any deductions from them, and the amount of your savings credit (para 13.15).

(m) Your rights in relation to the decision (para 20.7).

(n)   Any other information the council considers relevant.

Time limits for decisions and notices

20.8   When you make a claim for HB, the council/NIHE must:

(a)   make a decision within 14 days of getting the information and evidence it requires (para 16.22), or as soon as reasonably practicable;

(b)   send you a decision notice on the day it makes the decision, or as soon as reasonably practicable.

20.9   When the council/NIHE makes any other HB decision, it must send you a decision notice within 14 days or as soon as reasonably practicable.

Getting a written statement of reasons

20.10   You (or any other person affected) can request a statement of reasons about anything that wasn't explained in your decision. Your request should be in writing, signed (para 20.4), and made within one month of the date of the decision notice. The council/NIHE should provide the statement within 14 days so far as this is practicable. See paras 20.35 and 20.45 for how this affects the reconsideration and appeal time limits

T20.1   HB sch 9 paras 1-10, 13, 14; HB66+ sch 8 paras 1-10, 13, 14; NIHB sch 10 paras 1-10, 13, 14; NIHB66+ sch 9 paras 1-10, 13, 14

20.8-9   HB 89, 90(1)(a),(b); HB66+ 70, 71(1)(a),(b); NIHB 85, 86(1)(a),(b); NIHB66+ 66, 67(1)(a),(b)

20.10   DAR 10(2); HB 90(2),(4); HB66+ 71(2),(4); NIDAR 10(2); NIHB 86(2),(4); NIHB66+ 67(2),(4)

Delays

20.11   If the council/NIHE delays making a decision, issuing a notice or paying your HB, you can complain to the Ombudsman (para 20.12) normally after using the council's complaints procedure or failing to get a response in a reasonable time. In certain circumstances judicial review may provide an alternative remedy (para 20.53). If the council/NIHE has decided you are entitled to HB but delays paying it, you should get a payment on account if you are a private tenant (para 18.11). If that fails you may be able to get the county court or sheriff court to require it to pay: Waveney DC v Jones.

The Ombudsman

20.12   In cases of bad administration by the council/NIHE you can complain to the Ombudsman. Guidance on how to complain, what constitutes maladministration, and recent Ombudsman's reports are available online [www].

Delays and rent arrears

20.13   In England and Wales, the 'Pre-Action Protocol' [www] provides you with some protection against possession action if HB delays have caused your rent arrears. It applies to social renters and, from 25th June 2020, all renters.

20.14   Your landlord should not begin possession proceedings against you if:

(a)   you have provided all the information and evidence needed to decide your claim,

(b)   there is a reasonable expectation that you will qualify for HB, and

(c)   you have paid any rent which will not be met by HB.

20.15   If possession proceedings are begun, the council can be ordered to explain any delays and to pay costs if it caused them. On 27th March 2020, all possession actions were suspended for 90 days after which the protocol applies to all cases [www].

If you disagree with a decision

20.16   If you disagree with a decision about your HB, you can ask the council/NIHE to reconsider it (para 20.25); and/or appeal to a tribunal (para 20.41) if it is an appealable decision. See table 20.2 for a summary.

20.17   Many of the HB rules about reconsiderations and appeals are the same as in UC (volume 1 chapter 14). The main differences are:

(a)   in HB you can skip a reconsideration and go straight to an appeal, but in UC you can only appeal after a reconsideration;

(b)   in HB you send appeals to the council/NIHE which forwards them to the tribunal but in UC you send them straight to the tribunal.

20.11   Waveney DC v Jones 01/12/99 CA 33 HLR 3 www.rightsnet.org.uk/pdfs/Waveney_v_Jones.pdf

20.12   www.lgo.org.uk (England), www.ombudsman.wales (Wales)
www.spso.org.uk (Scotland), https://nipso.org.uk (Northern Ireland)

20.13   Pre-Action Protocol for Possession Claims by Social Landlords https://tinyurl.com/Rent-Protocol

20.15   Pre-Action Protocol, see 20.13

Table 20.2 **HB reconsiderations and appeals**

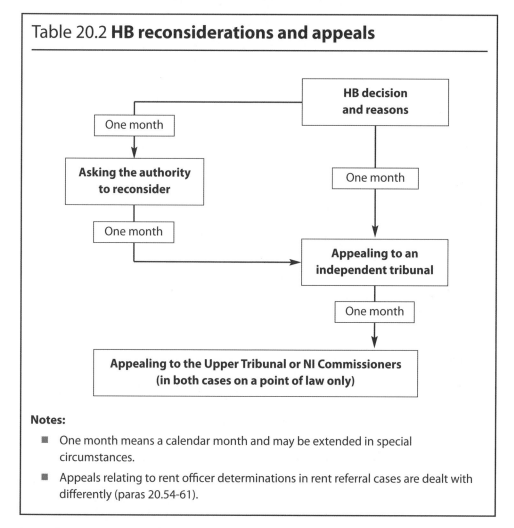

Notes:

- One month means a calendar month and may be extended in special circumstances.

- Appeals relating to rent officer determinations in rent referral cases are dealt with differently (paras 20.54-61).

How decisions are made

20.18 When the council/NIHE makes a decision about your HB, it should:

(a) identify the facts (paras 20.19-21); and

(b) apply the law to those facts (paras 20.22-24).

Deciding the facts

20.19 The council/NIHE should only take account of facts that are relevant to your HB. For example, who lives with you is normally relevant, but their personal characteristics are not.

Balance of probability

20.20 When there is a disagreement about the facts or the facts are uncertain, the council/NIHE should decide what they are based on the weight of evidence each way.

Burden of proof

20.21   When there is no evidence about the facts or where the evidence is balanced equally each way, the council/NIHE should decide who has to demonstrate what. For example:

(a) when you make a claim, it is up to you to demonstrate you are entitled;

(b) when you are told an overpayment is recoverable from you, it is up to the council/NIHE to demonstrate this.

Applying the law

20.22   The words of Acts of Parliament, regulations, orders, etc have their ordinary English meaning. But:

(a) some words or phrases are defined in the law – for example 'child' and 'young person' (paras 4.15-16);

(b) some law has been interpreted by Upper Tribunals and courts in case law (para 1.20) – for example deciding whether two people are a couple (para 4.10);

(c) the Supreme Court has decided that the council/NIHE or a tribunal may disapply a regulation, order, etc (but not an Act of Parliament) if it breaches the Human Rights Act 1998 (RR v SSWP).

The footnotes in this guide give the details of (a) and (b).

Judgment

20.23   The law uses terms like 'reasonable', 'appropriate', 'good cause' or 'special circumstances' to show that the council has to make a judgment. Examples include:

(a) whether it is 'reasonable' to award HB on two homes in the case of a person in fear of violence (para 3.14);

(b) how much it is 'appropriate' to restrict the rent in exempt accommodation (para 10.15);

(c) whether a claimant has 'good cause' for a late claim (para 16.44);

(d) whether a claimant has 'special circumstances' for their delay in notifying an advantageous change in circumstances (paras 17.15, 20.36, 20.46).

Discretion

20.24   A discretion differs from a judgment in the sense that the council/NIHE may choose what to do. The law usually says that it 'may' do something to show this. Examples include:

(a) whether to award discretionary housing payments (para 23.4);

(b) whether to recover a recoverable overpayment of HB (para 19.10);

(c) in some situations, whether to pay HB to a landlord (para 18.30).

20.22   RR v SSWP [2019] UKSC 52 www.bailii.org/uk/cases/UKSC/2019/52.html

Reconsiderations

20.25 You (or any other person affected) can ask the council/NIHE to reconsider any HB decision it has made.

20.26 The council/NIHE can also reconsider a decision without a request, for example because a case is being checked or there are new regulations or case law.

When you can request a reconsideration

20.27 You can request a reconsideration at any time, but if you don't meet the time limit (paras 20.35-36) you could get less HB (table 20.3(a)-(c)).

How to request a reconsideration

20.28 Requests for a reconsideration must be in writing. Some councils have a form you can use, or you can make the request in a letter or email.

Information and evidence

20.29 When you request a reconsideration you should provide any new information and evidence you have. If the council/NIHE needs information and evidence it should request this, and it must take it into account if you provide it within one month.

Reconsideration decisions and notices

20.30 The council/NIHE makes a decision about your request, and sends you a decision notice telling you:

    (a) whether it has altered your HB;

    (b) if it has, what it has altered and when from; and

    (c) your rights (para 20.1).

Revisions and supersessions

20.31 In the law, a changed decision is called a revision or supersession, but you don't have to use these terms when you request a reconsideration.

20.32 The terms have the following meanings:

    (a) a 'revision' alters your HB from the same date (in most cases) as the decision it is altering: you get arrears of HB back to then (or have been overpaid since then);

    (b) a 'supersession' alters your HB from a date later than the decision it is altering: you get arrears back to that later date (or have been overpaid since then);

    (c) a 'closed period supersession' is used when a change took place in the past and has already come to an end (CIS/2595/2003): you get arrears for that past fixed period (or have been overpaid during it).

20.25-28 CPSA sch 7 paras 3(1)(b), 4(1); DAR 4(1),(8),(9), 7(2),(6),(7); HB 89(1); HB66+ 70(1)
NICPSA sch 7 paras 3(1)(b), 4(1); NIDAR 4(1),(8),(9), 7(2),(6),(7); NIHB 85(1); NIHB66+ 66(1)

20.29-30 AA 5(1); DAR 4(5), 7(5), 10; HB 86(1),(3), sch 9; HB66+ 67(1),(3), sch 8
NIAA 5(1); NIDAR 4(4), 7(5), 10; NIHB 82(1),(3), sch 10; NIHB66+ 63(1),(3), sch 10

When reconsidered decisions take effect

20.33   When the council/NIHE changes a decision it has reconsidered, the change takes effect (alters your HB) from the date in table 20.3.

Table 20.3 **When reconsidered decisions take effect**

Type of reconsideration	When it takes effect
Decisions increasing or reinstating your UC	
(a) Reconsiderations requested or made within the time limit (one month or in some cases up to 13 months: para 20.36)	The date the original decision took effect (or should have)
(b) Requests made to correct an official error (at any time: para 20.37)	The date the original decision took effect (or should have)
(c) Other cases	The Monday of the benefit week in which the change is requested, or the council/NIHE first takes action to make it (if this is earlier)
Decisions reducing or ending your UC	
(d) All cases	The date the original decision took effect (or should have)

Notes:

- This table doesn't apply to decisions that are wrong due to change of circumstance where there is an equivalent rule (table 17.2).
- In the law, (a), (b) and (d) are revisions and (c) is a supersession (para 20.32).

Time limit for getting your arrears

20.34   Except for an official error (para 20.37), if you request a reconsideration that increases or reinstates your HB you only get all your arrears if you made your request (or your HB is altered) within the time limit. Table 20.3 shows how your request affects your arrears. A separate (but similar) rule applies instead if your circumstances have changed (paras 17.13-14).

20.35   Your request is within the time limit if it is received within one month of the council's decision notice (paras 20.8-9). But:

(a) any time is ignored from the date a statement of reasons was requested (para 20.10) to the date it was provided (both dates included);

(b) if an accidental error is corrected, any time before you were notified is ignored (para 20.40);

(c) if you have special circumstances the time limit can be extended (para 20.36).

T20.3   CPSA sch 7; DAR 1(2), 4(1),(2),(4), 7(2), 8(4),(5); NICPSA sch 7; NIDAR 1(2), 4(1),(2),(4), 7(2), 8(4),(5)

20.35   DAR 4(1),(4),10A(3); NIDAR 4(1),(4),10A(3)

Extending the time limit

20.36 The time limit for requesting a reconsideration is extended if:

(a) the council/NIHE receives your request within 13 months of the date of its decision notice;

(b) you say you are asking for it to be accepted late and give the reasons for the delay;

(c) your request 'has merit';

(d) there are special circumstances why it wasn't practicable for you to make the request earlier; and

(e) it is reasonable to accept your delay – the longer you delay the more compelling your special circumstances have to be.

When deciding this, the council/NIHE can't take account of ignorance or misunderstanding of the law or the time limits; or of an Upper Tribunal, the NI Commissioners or a court interpreting the law in a new way.

Official errors

20.37 In the case of official errors (paras 20.38-39), there is no time limit for changes. So your reconsideration request can be made at any time, and (if you are successful) you get arrears of HB back to the date the original decision took effect (or should have taken effect)

20.38 An 'official error' means an error by the council, the DWP or HMRC – or someone acting on their behalf (e.g. a contractor or a partner organisation). But it doesn't include an error that you (the claimant) or the payee or someone acting on your or the payee's behalf 'materially contributed to'.

20.39 For example, an official error can include:

(a) a mistake about what the facts are (e.g. because the council/NIHE failed to take account of information and evidence it had when the original decision was made);

(b) an error in applying the law or case law;

(c) an accidental error; or

(d) a combination of the above (CH/943/2003).

Accidental errors

20.40 There is an accidental error when the council fails to record, or to put into action its true intentions (e.g. by mis-entering data on a computer). The council/NIHE can correct an accidental error at any time. Any resulting change in your HB takes effect from the date the original decision took effect (or should have).

20.36   DAR 4(8), 5(1)-(6); NIDAR 4(7), 5(1)-(6)

20.37-38   DAR 1(2), 4(2); NIDAR 1(2), 4(2)

20.40   DAR 10A(1),(2); NIDAR 10A(1),(2)

Appeals to a tribunal

20.41   You (or any other person affected) can appeal about an HB decision to:

(a) a First-tier Tribunal in Great Britain; or

(b) an Appeal Tribunal in Northern Ireland.

These tribunals are independent of the council/NIHE. You can appeal to them either instead of or after asking the council/NIHE to reconsider its decision.

Which decisions can be appealed

20.42   Any HB decision can be appealed to a tribunal except those in table 20.4. If a decision is non-appealable, you can ask the council to reconsider it (para 20.25) or you may be able to apply for judicial review (para 20.53).

Table 20.4 **Non-appealable HB decisions**

(a) Whether or when you should be included in 'managed migration' to UC (para 1.28)

(b) LHA figures and areas (paras 9.21-28)

(c) The DWP's assessed income figure (table 13.3) – but deductions from it are appealable (table 13.3(a)-(f))

(d) Whether the council should run a local scheme for war disablement and bereavement pensions (paras 13.18)

(e) Which partner in a couple is to be the claimant (para 16.4)

(f) Who may claim on behalf of someone who is unable to act (para 16.5)

(g) Suspending or restoring HB (paras 17.41-42) – but terminating HB is appealable (para 17.44)

(h) When and how HB is paid (paras 18.2-8)

(i) The frequency of payment of a rent allowance (paras 18.9-10)

(j) Making a payment on account (paras 18.11-15)

(k) Paying outstanding HB after a death (para 18.21)

(l) Certain matters relating to overpayments (para 19.66)

(m) Rent determinations made by the rent officer in Great Britain (but see paras 20.55-56)

(n) Figures that are specified in the law (e.g. the capital limit, applicable amounts, or the benefit cap)

(o) Appeals in which the reconsideration was refused because it was outside the time limit and was not about official error (R(H) 8/05; [2018] UKUT 404 (AAC))

20.41   CPSA sch 7 para 6(3); NICPSA sch 7 para 6(3)

20.42   CPSA sch 7 para 6(1),(2),(4)-(6); DAR 16(1) and sch; NICPSA sch 7 para 6(1),(2),(4)-(6); NIDAR 16(1) and sch

T20.4   CPSA sch 7 para 6; DAR 16(1) and sch; NICPSA sch 7 para 6; NIDAR 16(1) and sch
         Beltekian v Westminster CC [2004] EWCA Civ 1784, reported as R(H) 8/05 www.bailii.org/ew/cases/EWCA/Civ/2004/1784.html

Appeals about overpayments

20.43   In relation to an overpayment appeal you are always a 'person affected'. If the council/ NIHE decides that the overpayment is recoverable from someone else (e.g. your landlord, their agent or your partner) or both of you, that other person is also always a 'person affected'. So there may be more than one person with the right to appeal or to take part in the appeal. Paras 19.65-66 explain which overpayment decisions are (or aren't) appealable.

How to appeal

20.44   Your appeal has to meet the tribunal requirements. It should:

(a) be in writing, signed (para 20.4) and sent to the council/NIHE;

(b) say what decision you are appealing about and why you consider it is wrong;

(c) give your name and address, and those of your representative if you have one;

(d) say which address you want documents about your appeal to be sent to; and

(e) be within the time limit (paras 20.45-46).

The council/NIHE can't insist on you using an official form so long as you meet these requirements. If you don't meet them, see para 20.47.

Time limit for appealing

20.45   Your appeal is within the time limit if the council/NIHE receives it within one month of its decision notice (paras 20.8-9) or, if you requested a reconsideration, within one month of its decision notice about that (para 20.30). But:

(a) if you requested a statement of reasons (para 20.10) within that month, the time limit is 14 days after the end of that month, or 14 days after the date the council provides the statement, whichever is later;

(b) if the time limit runs out on a non-working day it is extended to the next working day;

(c) if it is in the interests of justice the time limit can be extended (para 20.46).

Disputes about whether your appeal is within the time limit must be referred to the tribunal. And if the council's/NIHE's decision notice is invalid because it didn't meet the necessary requirements, the time limit doesn't start until the council/NIHE issues a valid notice (CH/1129/2004).

Extending the time limit

20.46   The time limit for appealing is extended if:

(a) the council/NIHE receives your appeal within 12 months of the end of the time limit described in para 20.45;

(b) you say why you are asking for it to be accepted late and give reasons for your delay;

20.43   Wirral MBC v Salisbury Independent Living Ltd [2012] EWCA Civ 84; [2012] H.L.R. 25; www.bailii.org/ew/cases/EWCA/Civ/2012/84.html

20.44   DAR 20(1); FTPR 23; NIDAR 20(1)

20.45   FTPR 12, 23, sch 1; NIDAR 18

(c) there are special circumstances why it wasn't practicable to make your appeal earlier – because you, your partner or a dependant have suffered a serious illness or died, or you aren't resident in the UK, or postal services were disrupted, or there were other 'wholly exceptional' special circumstances; and

(d) it is in the interests of justice to accept your delay – the longer your delay the more compelling your special circumstances have to be.

If the council/NIHE doesn't agree to extend the time limit, it must refer your request for an extension of time to the tribunal, and in some cases the tribunal has wider powers to accept this. But when deciding this, the council/NIHE and the tribunal can't take account of ignorance or misunderstanding of the law or the time limits; or of an Upper Tribunal, the NI Commissioners or a court interpreting the law in a new way.

Appeals that don't meet the requirements

20.47   If your appeal doesn't meet the requirements in para 20.44, the council/NIHE should write to you asking you to provide what is missing. For example, it might ask you to clarify which decision you are appealing or why you think the decision is wrong. The council/NIHE should allow you at least 14 days to do this and can allow longer. If you provide the information, it is treated as being part of your appeal. If you don't, the council/NIHE must send your appeal to the tribunal to decide whether it meets the requirements. The tribunal notifies you and the council/NIHE about this.

The council's/NIHE's appeal duties

20.48   When the council/NIHE receives your appeal, it has two choices:

(a) it can agree with your appeal (para 20.49); or

(b) it can send your appeal to the tribunal (para 20.50).

The council/NIHE must do one of these things unless the tribunal has decided your appeal doesn't meet the requirements (para 20.47), or you withdraw your appeal in writing.

Agreeing with your appeal and lapsing it

20.49   If the council/NIHE agrees with your appeal – either wholly or partly – it can treat it as a reconsideration. This means it must alter its decision, send you a decision notice about its new decision, and award any arrears of HB. It also means your appeal lapses and isn't sent to the tribunal. But you can make a fresh appeal if you still consider the council is wrong. For example, you could do this if the council/NIHE only partly agreed with your (lapsed) appeal.

Sending your appeal to the tribunal

20.50   When the council/NIHE sends your appeal to the tribunal, it must enclose a submission saying why it doesn't agree with it, along with any relevant documents. It must send a copy of these to you and any other person affected. The council should do this as soon as reasonably

---

20.46   DAR 19(5)-(9), 20(1); FTPR 2(1),(3), 5(3)(a), 7(2), 23(3)-(5),(8); NIDAR 19(3),(5)-(11), 20(1)

20.47   DAR 20(2)-(8); NIDAR 20(2)-(8)

20.48-50   CPSA sch 7 para 3(6); DAR 4(1),(6), 17(3),(4), 20(9); NICPSA sch 7 para 3(6); NIDAR 4(1),(6), 17(3),(4), 20(9)

practicable. The law does not give a fixed time limit, but four weeks is usually reasonable, unless your case is complex. If there is significant delay, you (or your representative) can make a written application direct to the tribunal asking it to issue a direction to the council/ NIHE to provide its submission, or asking the tribunal to issue a hearing date without waiting for the submission (R(H) 1/07).

Appeals and further appeals

20.51 The tribunal writes to you asking (among other things) whether you want there to be a hearing or if you want the appeal to be decided without one. The tribunal will keep you informed about what happens next. Once the tribunal has decided your appeal, it notifies its decision to you, the council/NIHE and any other person affected.

20.52 You can then make a further appeal, but only if you consider the tribunal has made a mistake about the law (and not about the facts), and only if you first ask the tribunal for a statement of its reasons within one month of receiving its decision. The council/NIHE can also do this. The further appeal goes to:

(a) an Upper Tribunal in Great Britain; or

(b) the NI Commissioners in Northern Ireland.

For more information about appeals and further appeals, see volume 1 chapter 14. You can also get details of tribunal procedures and rules online [www].

Judicial review

20.53 When using judgment or discretion, councils are bound by the principles of administrative law evolved by the courts. If they ignore these and the decision isn't appealable they can be challenged (as a last resort) by applying to the High Court (or in Scotland the Court of Session) for 'judicial review'. Examples of when a challenge may be successful are if the council:

(a) fails to consider each case on its merits, instead applying predetermined rules;

(b) takes into account matters which it ought not to consider;

(c) does not consider matters which it ought to take into account; or

(d) reaches a conclusion that no reasonable council could have come to (what is reasonable here means rational rather than what is the best decision).

A judicial review judgment can impose its own decision on the council/NIHE, or can tell the council what factors it should take into account in remaking its own decision (R v South Hams DC ex p Ash, which was about the discretion not to recover an overpayment).

20.52   FTPR 39; UTPR 21; NIDAR 23(1)-(4); NISR 1999/225 reg 9
www.gov.uk/appeal-benefit-decision
www.gov.uk/administrative-appeals-tribunal
www.gov.uk/government/publications/social-entitlement-chamber-tribunal-procedure-rules
www.justice-ni.gov.uk/articles/appeals-service
www.nihe.gov.uk/Housing-Help/Housing-Benefit/Appeals

20.53   R v South Hams DC ex p Ash 10/05/99 QBD [1999] EWHC Admin 418, 32 HLR 4055

Appeals about rent officer/NIHE rent determinations

20.54   This section explains how to appeal against rent determinations made by the rent officer in Great Britain or NIHE in Northern Ireland, and how errors in them are corrected. It applies to:

(a) any of the rent determinations made in rent referral cases (paras 10.28 and 10.40-51); and

(b) board and attendance determinations (paras 9.33-34).

See paras 20.55-60 in Great Britain and para 20.61 in Northern Ireland.

Rent officer re-determinations

20.55   In Great Britain, appeals against rent determinations are dealt with by the council making an application to the rent officer for a 're-determination'. The council:

(a) must make an application within seven days of receiving a valid request from you (para 20.56) – and must include a copy of your request and any information and evidence you provide;

(b) may choose to make an application at any time (with or without a request from you);

(c) can only make a maximum of two applications in the order (a) then (b), or three applications in the order (b) then (a) then (b).

The rules apply each time the rent officer makes a determination (paras 9.34 and 10.32).

20.56   Your request is valid if:

(a) it is sent to the council in writing and signed (para 20.4);

(b) it says you disagree with a rent determination, or raises matters which affect a rent determination; and

(c) you make it within one month of the date of a decision notice about your HB (paras 20.8-9).

20.57   The re-determination is made by the rent officer (known as a re-determination officer) with advice from one or two other rent officers. It covers all rent determinations that apply to you (paras 10.40-51), or if appropriate just the board and attendance determination (paras 9.33-34). The rent officer should send the redetermination to the council within 20 days of receiving the application for it or any further information they have requested from the council. They normally include their reasons and send a copy to you [www]. For changes to your HB, see para 20.59.

20.55-56   HB 15, 16; HB66+ 15, 16

20.57   DAR 4(3); ROO 4, sch 3
           Rent Officer Handbook: Redeterminations https://tinyurl.com/RO-Redetermination

Correcting errors

20.58   In Great Britain, the rent officer provides a substitute determination (or substitute re-determination) if:

(a) the council made an error in the information it gave them (e.g. about the occupiers of your home); or

(b) the rent officer discovers they made an error (e.g. in the data they used).

The council has to request this each time (a) applies, but not normally when (b) applies (DWP circular G5/2005).

Changes to your eligible rent

20.59   If the rent officer's new determination changes the amount of your eligible rent, the council must send you a decision notice about this. Your HB changes as follows:

(a) an increase in your eligible rent takes effect from the date the council's original decision took effect (or should have) – so you are awarded arrears of HB back to then; but

(b) a reduction in your eligible rent takes effect from the Monday following the date of the rent officer's new determination – so you haven't been overpaid HB before then.

Tribunal appeals

20.60   In Great Britain, you can't appeal to a tribunal about the rent officer's determinations or re-determinations, but you may be able to apply for judicial review (para 20.53). You can appeal to a tribunal (para 20.41) about whether you fall within the rent referral rules (table 10.3) and about the information the council provides to the rent officer ([2010] UKUT 79 (AAC); [2010] AACR 40).

Reconsiderations and appeals in Northern Ireland

20.61   In Northern Ireland, you can ask the NIHE to reconsider any rent determinations it has made and appeal to a tribunal about them (para 20.41). If your HB changes as a result:

(a) an increase in your eligible rent takes effect as described in table 20.3; but

(b) a reduction in your eligible rent normally takes effect from the Monday following the date of the NIHE's new rent determination.

20.58   ROO 4A, 7A; HB 17; HB66+ 17

20.59   CPSA sch 7 para 6(2)(c); DAR 4(3), 7(2)(c)

20.60   CSPA sch 7 para 6(2)(c)

20.61   NIDAR 4(1), sch para 1

Chapter 21 **Subsidy**

- General rules about subsidy for HB expenditure, local schemes, and administration: see paras 21.1-9.
- The effect of HB overpayments on subsidy: see paras 21.10-26.
- The effect of high rents etc on subsidy: see paras 21.27-43.

General rules

21.1   The councils in Great Britain that have a legal duty to administer and pay housing benefit are part reimbursed for this by the DWP. This reimbursement takes the form of subsidy payments which each council must claim. (For the separate rules about grants towards discretionary housing payments, see paras 23.18-19.)

21.2   The DWP pays councils subsidy for each financial year (1st April to 31st March) towards the:

(a)   actual HB paid (paras 21.3-4); and

(b)   HB administration costs (para 21.5).

The balance of the council's costs is met from the council's general fund in England and Scotland, or its council fund in Wales.

Subsidy for HB expenditure

21.3   The DWP pays each council subsidy towards the HB it pays in the financial year:

(a)   this equals 100% of all HB lawfully paid;

(b)   except that a lower amount (or no subsidy) is paid for:

- additional HB paid under a local scheme (para 21.4),
- some overpayments of HB (paras 21.10-26), and
- some payments of HB relating to high rents etc (paras 21.27-43).

Lawfully paid HB includes rebates, allowances, payments on account (chapter 18) and extended payments. It also includes payments made in the financial year for an earlier financial year. But each amount of HB can only get subsidy once.

21.3   AA 140A, 140B(1); SO 11(2),(3), 12(1)(a), 13, 14, 19(1)(h), 20

Subsidy towards local schemes

21.4   If the council runs a local scheme for war disablement and bereavement pensions (paras 13.18-19):

(a) first the council's annual subsidy is calculated (para 21.3), but including only the HB that would be awarded if it did not run a local scheme;

(b) then this is increased to take account of the local scheme. The increase equals the lower of:

  ■ 0.2% of the council's annual subsidy,

  ■ 75% of the additional HB awarded in the year as a result of the local scheme.

Subsidy for HB administration

21.5   The DWP also pays each council subsidy towards part of its HB administration costs in the financial year (for example staffing, accommodation, training and computers). The amounts for 2021-22 are in circular S1/2021. The DWP calls this a 'cash-limited specific grant'. It is separate from the grant for council tax rebate (CTR) administration, which is paid to councils by the MHCLG in England, or by the Scottish or Welsh Government.

New burdens funding

21.6   The government's 'new burdens doctrine' [www] says that the responsible central government department must assess and properly pay for all new burdens it places on councils. New burdens often arise in the administration of HB, for example, the carrying out of DWP welfare reforms (S2/2021). Other recent examples are set out in DWP subsidy circulars including S4/2020, S5/2020, S7/2020 and S9/2020.

Subsidy claims, payments and overpayments

21.7   To get subsidy, councils have to claim it from the DWP. They may not get their full amount of subsidy if they do not:

(a) claim it on time using the correct procedures;

(b) provide the information and evidence required by the DWP; and

(c) get their final subsidy claim assured/certified by their auditor by 30th November.

Subsidy is paid to the council in instalments throughout the year and a final (balancing) payment is made after the year for which subsidy is being claimed. The DWP has the power to recover subsidy which was overpaid, or was claimed in breach of the subsidy rules: R (Isle of Anglesey County Council) v SSWP, R (Lambeth LBC) v SSWP.

21.4   AA 134(8), SO 12(1)(d),(4)

21.5   AA 140B (4)(a), (4A), SO 12(1)(b), sch 1

21.6   New burdens doctrine: guidance for government departments: https://tinyurl.com/NewBurdens

21.7   SO part II
         R v Anglesey CC v SSWP 30/10/03 QBD [2003] EWHC 2518 Admin www.bailii.org/ew/cases/EWHC/Admin/2003/2518.html
         R (Lambeth LBC) v SSWP 20/04/05 QBD [2005] EWHC 637 Admin www.bailii.org/ew/cases/EWHC/Admin/2005/637.html

Subsidy law and guidance

21.8   The law about HB subsidy is in:

(a) sections 140A-140G of the Social Security Administration Act 1992 (which gives the legal framework); and

(b) the Income-related Benefits (Subsidy to Authorities) Order 1998, SI 1998 No.562 (which gives the detailed rules).

When the subsidy rules change for each financial year, the Order is usually amended at the end of that year, but advance warning is usually given in the *Subsidy Guidance Manual* and the 'S' series of circulars [www]. The DWP's *HB subsidy claims – local authority best practice guide* (June 2015) provides examples of how to complete subsidy claims [www]. In England the arrangements for the assurance of subsidy claims are set out in DWP circulars S1/2017, S7/2018 and S12/2018. The HB assurance process (HBAP) instructions for English councils and reporting accountants are available on gov.uk [www].

Subsidy and HB decision-making

21.9   When councils make decisions about awarding HB, or recovering overpaid HB, they have a duty to apply HB law fairly, objectively and impartially. If a decision means the council has to use its judgment (para 20.23), it must not allow the subsidy rules to affect this. But if a decision allows the council to use its discretion (para 20.24), it may take its own financial position (including the effect of the subsidy rules) into account as one factor: R v Brent LBC HBRB ex parte Connery. For examples see paras 10.27, 19.10-11 and 21.13.

Overpayments of HB

21.10   This section describes how much subsidy the DWP pays councils towards overpayments of HB.

Subsidy categories

21.11   For subsidy purposes, HB overpayments fall into the categories shown in table 21.1. The table also summarises the amounts of subsidy paid. The details for each category are in paras 21.14-26.

21.12   The rules about which HB overpayments are recoverable do not always correspond to the subsidy categories, but in broad terms:

(a) departmental error and authority error/administrative delay overpayments may or may not be recoverable: see the rules about official error overpayments in paras 19.4-7;

(b) other overpayments are usually recoverable: paras 19.8-9.

21.8   21.8 DWP Housing Benefit Subsidy Guidance Manual 2018 to 2019 https://tinyurl.com/SubsidyGuidance
        DWP Housing-Benefit-Subsidy Circulars https://tinyurl.com/SubsidyCirculars
        DWP's HB subsidy claims – local authority best practice guide (June 2015) https://tinyurl.com/DWPBestPractice
        HB Assurance Process documents https://tinyurl.com/HBAssurance

21.9   R v Brent LBC ex p Connery 20/10/89 QBD 22 HLR 40

Table 21.1 **Overpayments subsidy categories**

Subsidy category	Amount of subsidy
(a) Departmental error overpayments	100%
(b) Payment on account overpayments	100%
(c) Duplicate payment overpayments	25%
(d) Technical overpayments	Nil
(e) Authority error/administrative delay overpayments	100%, 40% or nil depending on certain thresholds
(f) Claimant error, fraudulent and other overpayments	40%

Notes

In broad terms:

- subsidy in (a) to (c) is paid only on unrecovered overpayments;
- subsidy in (e) and (f) is paid whether the overpayments are recovered or not.

Detailed rules about the subsidy categories, amounts, etc are in paras 21.14-26. Subsidy categories don't exactly match those in table 19.1.

Deciding subsidy categories

21.13   The council decides which subsidy category each HB overpayment falls into, but this is contentious because there is a strong financial incentive to misclassify: for example, to code a technical error (para 21.20) as a claimant error or not to code an error at all for administrative delay (para 21.21). This problem was recognised in old regulatory guidance for external auditors who were advised to test the classifications to provide assurance that they are correct and 'fairly stated'.

Departmental error overpayments

21.14   For subsidy purposes, a 'departmental error overpayment' means one caused by a mistake of fact or law (whether in the form of an act or omission):

(a) by the DWP or HMRC or someone providing services to them; or

(b) in a decision of a First-tier or Upper Tribunal.

This does not include an overpayment to which the claimant, or someone acting on the claimant's behalf, or the payee, materially contributed (para 21.25(c)). And it does not include an overpayment caused because a court interprets the law differently from how the DWP or HMRC or a tribunal interpreted it (para 21.25(d)).

T21.1   AA 140A; SO 11(2), 13, 18, 19(1)(e)-(i)

21.13   SO 18(4) Audit Commission, Certification Instruction BEN01 (06-07) para 35

21.14   SO 18(4)

21.15   Subsidy on these overpayments is 100% of:

(a) the total departmental error overpayments in the year;

(b) minus the total departmental error overpayments recovered in the year (whether they were overpaid in the year or in a previous year).

This means the council does not qualify for subsidy towards the amount it recovers.

Payment on account overpayments

21.16   A 'payment on account overpayment' means one caused when a payment on account is greater than the amount of HB a claimant qualifies for (paras 18.11-16).

21.17   Subsidy on these overpayments is 100% of:

(a) the total payment on account overpayments in the year;

(b) minus the total payment on account overpayments recovered in the year (whether they were overpaid in the year or in a previous year).

Duplicate payment overpayments

21.18   A 'duplicate payment overpayment' means one caused when:

(a) a duplicate payment of HB is issued because the first one was (or was alleged to have been) lost, stolen or not received; but

(b) the first one is in fact cashed.

21.19   Subsidy on these overpayments is 25% of:

(a) the total duplicate payment overpayments in the year;

(b) minus the total duplicate payments recovered in the year (whether they were issued in the year or in a previous year).

Technical overpayments

21.20   A 'technical overpayment' means one caused because:

(a) a council tenant's liability for rent ends (for example their tenancy ends) or reduces; but

(b) HB has already been credited to their rent account for a period after it ended or reduced.

No subsidy is paid on these overpayments.

21.15   SO 18(b)(i),(2),(3), 19(1)(e)

21.16   SO 18(7B)

21.17   SO 18(1)(f)

21.18   SO 18(1)(a)

21.19   SO 18(2)(b), (7)(7A)

21.20   SO 18(7),(7A)

Authority error/administrative delay overpayments

21.21   For subsidy purposes:

(a) an 'authority error overpayment' means one caused by a mistake of fact or law (whether in the form of an act or omission) by the council;

(b) an 'administrative delay overpayment' means one caused by a delay (rather than a mistake), but only when the council:

- is notified of a change of circumstances, and

- has the information and evidence it needs to make a decision on it, but

- fails to make the decision before the next HB payment date.

21.22   These do not include an overpayment to which the claimant, or someone acting on the claimant's behalf, or the payee, materially contributed (see para 21.25(c)). And they do not include an overpayment caused because a court interprets the law differently from how the council interpreted it (para 21.25(d)).

21.23   These overpayments are combined for subsidy purposes. The amount of subsidy (para 21.24) depends on:

(a) the total authority error and administrative delay overpayments in the year;

(b) as a percentage of the total HB paid in the year. (This means HB which qualifies for 100% subsidy: para 21.3.)

21.24   If the above percentage is:

(a) not more than 0.48% (the lower threshold), 100% subsidy is paid on all authority error and administrative delay overpayments in the year;

(b) more than 0.48% but not more than 0.54% (the higher threshold), 40% subsidy is paid on all these overpayments;

(c) more than 0.54%, no subsidy is paid on any of these overpayments.

In cases (a) and (b), the council qualifies for this subsidy even if it recovers some or all of these overpayments.

Example: Subsidy for authority error and administrative delay overpayments

A council's annual expenditure on correctly paid HB is £10,000,000.

So its lower threshold is £48,000 and its higher threshold is £54,000 for that year (see para 21.24).

If the total authority error and administrative delay overpayments in that year are:

- £45,000, the council gets subsidy of 100% of this, which is £45,000;

- £50,000, the council gets subsidy of 40% of this, which is £20,000;

- £55,000, the council gets no subsidy for this.

21.21-22   SO 18(6),(6ZA)

21.23   SO 18(1)(e),(6A)

21.24   SO 18(1)(e),(6A)

Claimant error, fraudulent and other overpayments

21.25 Any other overpayment qualifies for 40% subsidy, whether it is:

(a) a 'claimant error overpayment'. This means one caused by the claimant, or someone acting on the claimant's behalf, failing to provide required information or evidence;

(b) a 'fraudulent overpayment'. This means one where the claimant has been found guilty of an offence, made an admission under caution, or agreed to pay a penalty as an alternative to prosecution (para 19.74);

(c) an overpayment that would count as departmental error (para 21.14) or authority error/administrative delay, except that the claimant, someone acting on the claimant's behalf, or the payee, materially contributed to it (para 21.22);

(d) an overpayment caused because a court interprets the law differently from how the DWP, HMRC, a tribunal or the council interpreted it (paras 21.14 and 21.22);

(e) an overpayment caused by a third party, for example a landlord, whether or not they are the payee; or

(f) any other overpayment not included in paras 21.14-24.

21.26 Subsidy is 40% of the total of these overpayments in the year. The council qualifies for this subsidy even if it recovers some or all of these overpayments.

High rents etc

21.27 This section describes the subsidy limitations which apply when HB is paid for:

(a) exempt accommodation (paras 21.29-32);

(b) temporary accommodation for homeless people (paras 21.33-41);

(c) council tenants in certain circumstances (para 21.42); and

(d) rent referral cases which the council fails to refer to the rent officer (para 21.43).

21.28 The DWP pays councils 100% subsidy on all other payments of HB (para 21.3) regardless of how high the claimant's eligible rent is, so long as it is correctly assessed. In practice this applies in most HB cases, because most HB cases do not fall within any of the rules in para 21.27. In particular, local housing allowance (LHA) cases never fall within these rules. (For how eligible rent is assessed, see chapters 7 to 11.)

21.25(a)   SO 18(4A)

21.25(b)   SO 18(5),(5A)

21.25(c),(d) SO 18(4),(6)

21.25(e),(f) SO 18(1)(b)(iii),(2)

21.25   SO 18(1)(b)(iii),(c),(d),(2), 19(1)(ea),(f)

Exempt accommodation

21.29   'Exempt accommodation' is defined in paras 10.4-8. In exempt accommodation cases:

(a) details of the claimant's eligible rent are referred to the rent officer (paras 10.28-31);

(b) the rent officer's determinations are not binding on the assessment of the claimant's eligible rent (paras 10.37 and 21.9);

(c) but the subsidy limitations in paras 21.30-31 apply if:

  ■   the rent officer's determinations include a 'significantly high rent' or 'exceptionally high rent' determination (paras 10.42 and 10.44), and

  ■   the claimant's eligible rent is higher than these.

For exceptions for registered housing associations see para 21.32.

Subsidy limitations for exempt accommodation

21.30   The subsidy limitations for exempt accommodation apply to the part of the claimant's HB which is attributable to:

(a) the excess of the claimant's eligible rent;

(b) over the exceptionally high rent (EHR) determination (if there is one); or

(c) over the significantly high rent (SHR) determination (if there is no EHR).

21.31   Subsidy on HB attributable to this excess is:

(a) 100% when the claimant falls into the protected groups of people who:

  ■   could formerly afford their accommodation (paras 7.51-53), or

  ■   have had a death in their household (paras 7.54-56);

(b) 60% when:

  ■   the claimant or someone in their household is considered vulnerable (see para 10.23), and

  ■   there is no suitable cheaper alternative accommodation the claimant can reasonably be expected to move to (paras 10.24-25);

(c) nil in any other situation. For example, when there is no suitable alternative accommodation to make a comparison with (paras 10.17-20), or when the amount by which the council has restricted the claimant's eligible rent still leaves an excess (paras 10.15-16).

In all these cases, 100% subsidy is paid on HB not attributable to the excess. The example illustrates this.

21.29-32   SO 13, 16, sch 4

Example: Subsidy for exempt accommodation

A claimant is renting exempt accommodation. The rent officer has provided an exceptionally high rent (EHR) determination of £170 per week. But the council decides her eligible rent is £200 per week. This is because she falls into a vulnerable group and there is no suitable cheaper alternative accommodation she can move to. The claimant is not on a passport benefit and qualifies for HB of £80 per week.

Subsidy is calculated as follows (paras 21.30-31):

- the excess of her eligible rent over the EHR is £30 per week.

- First subsidy is calculated on the HB attributable
  to this excess: this is 60% of £30   £18 pw

- Then subsidy is calculated on the HB not attributable
  to the excess: this is 100% of £50   £50 pw

- Total subsidy   £68 pw

Note: If the landlord was a registered housing association and the council did not consider the rent unreasonably high, the council would get subsidy of 100% of the claimant's HB (para 21.32), which is £80 per week.

Registered housing association exempt accommodation

21.32   When the landlord of exempt accommodation is a registered housing association (para 7.14), the subsidy limitations in paras 21.30-31 only apply if the council considers:

(a) that the claimant's rent is unreasonably high; or

(b) in pension age HB claims, that the accommodation is unreasonably large.

This is because details of the claimant's rent can only be referred to the rent officer in these circumstances (table 10.3).

Temporary accommodation for homeless people

21.33   The subsidy limitations in paras 21.38-41 apply to accommodation:

(a) which is provided to prevent the claimant being or becoming homeless, or for the related purposes in part 7 of the Housing Act 1996, part 2 of the Housing (Wales) Act 2014 or part 2 of the Housing (Scotland) Act 1987;

(b) where the claimant's rent is payable to;

- an authority that administers HB ('an LA'), or
- a registered housing association (paras 7.13-15, 21.34) ('an HA');

(c) which falls within one of the descriptions in paras 21.35-37.

21.34   The subsidy limitations in paras 21.38-41 only apply to temporary accommodation, not the kinds of supported accommodation in table 2.3(a)-(d) and (f). And when temporary accommodation also meets the definition of exempt accommodation, the rules in paras 21.29-32 apply instead.

LA and HA board and lodging accommodation

21.35   For subsidy purposes this means accommodation:

(a) where the claimant's rent includes a charge for at least some meals which are cooked or prepared, and also consumed, in the accommodation or in associated premises; or

(b) which is in a hotel, guest house, lodging house or similar establishment.

But this doesn't include accommodation in a hostel (para 7.27) or care home (table 7.2).

LA and HA licensed accommodation

21.36   For subsidy purposes this means accommodation which the LA or HA rents from someone else other than under a lease (i.e. usually under a licence agreement). In this case, the subsidy rules depend on whether the accommodation is self-contained. 'Self contained' means the claimant's household doesn't have to share a kitchen, toilet or bathroom with another household.

LA and HA leased accommodation and HA owned accommodation

21.37   For subsidy purposes this means accommodation which:

(a) the LA or HA rents from someone else under a lease, but in the case of English LAs the lease must be for ten years or less and the accommodation must be outside the LA's Housing Revenue Account; or

(b) the HA owns.

But this doesn't include accommodation the LA owns.

Subsidy limitations for temporary accommodation

21.38   Subsidy on temporary accommodation (paras 21.33-37) is limited on a weekly basis to the lowest of:

(a) the claimant's entitlement to HB in the week;

(b) the 'maximum amount' (see para 21.40);

(c) the 'cap' figure of;

  ■   £500 if the accommodation is in one of the following London broad rental market areas: Central, Inner East, Inner North, Inner South East, Inner South West, Inner West and Outer South West;

  ■   £375 if the accommodation is elsewhere.

For further subsidy details, see circulars S1/2011, S5/2011 and G10/2012 [www].

21.34   SO 17(1), 17A(1), 17B(1), 17C(1)

21.35   SO 11(1), 17(1)(b)(i), 17B(1)(b)(i)

21.36   SO 17(1)(b)(ii),(4), 17A(1)(b)(i), 17B(1)(b)(ii), 17C(1)(b)(ii)

21.37   SO 17A(1)(b)(ii),(iii), 17C(1)(b)(i),(ii)

21.38   SO 13, 17(2),(5), 17A(2), 17B(2), 17C(2), sch 8
        https://tinyurl.com/HB-S5-2011
        https://tinyurl.com/HB-S1-2011
        https://tinyurl.com/Bulletin-G10-2012

21.39   Authorities also get grant funding towards the management costs of temporary accommodation in England through the Homelessness Prevention Grant [www] and in Scotland and Wales through block grants. The Homelessness Prevention Grant replaces MHCLG's flexible homelessness support grant and homelessness reduction grant from April 2021.

21.40   The 'maximum amount' (para 21.38(b)) is based on January 2011 local housing allowance (LHA) figures [www] for the broad rental market area the accommodation is in.

(a) For board and lodging accommodation (para 21.35) and non-self-contained licensed accommodation (para 21.36), the maximum amount is the January 2011 LHA figure for one-bedroom self-contained accommodation.

(b) For self contained licensed accommodation (para 21.36) and leased and HA-owned accommodation (para 21.37), the maximum amount is 90% of the January 2011 LHA figure [www] for the appropriate size of dwelling (para 21.41).

21.41   The appropriate size of dwelling (paras 21.40(b)) depends on the number of rooms, counting both bedrooms and living rooms, in the claimant's accommodation (not the size of their household). If their accommodation contains:

(a) one or two rooms, the appropriate size is one-bedroom self-contained accommodation;

(b) three rooms, the appropriate size is a two-bedroom dwelling

(c) four rooms, the appropriate size is a three-bedroom dwelling

(d) five or six rooms, the appropriate size is a four-bedroom dwelling

(e) seven or more rooms, the appropriate size is a five-bedroom dwelling (in January 2011 there were LHA figures for five-bedroom dwellings).

The law says this because other rooms in the claimant's accommodation must be regarded as living rooms (even if they are in fact bedrooms).

Example: subsidy for leased temporary accommodation

A London council houses a homeless family in a house outside London which it holds on a three year lease. The claimant's rent is payable to the London council and the claimant is entitled to HB of £260 per week. The house has three bedrooms and one living room, making four rooms in all. So the January 2011 LHA figure for a three-bedroom dwelling is used to calculate subsidy (paras 21.40-41). In the area the house is in, this figure is £180 per week.

Subsidy is therefore 90% of the January LHA figure, i.e. £162 per week.

21.39   www.gov.uk/government/publications/homelessness-prevention-grant-2021-to-2022

21.40-41   SO 17(3),(5), 17A(3),(4), 17B(3), 17C(3),(4)
            https://tinyurl.com/LHA-England-Jan-2011

Council tenants

21.42   The following subsidy limitations can apply to council tenants (para 7.11), but in practice they are rare. The DWP's *Subsidy Guidance Manual* [www] gives further details and exceptions:

(a) The 'rent rebate subsidy limitation scheme' applies in Wales only (section 9 of the manual). If a council increases its tenants' rents by more than its guideline rent increase, no subsidy is payable on the HB attributable to the excess (DWP circulars S8/2018 and S3/2019). The 'specified amounts' and 'guideline weekly rent increases' for 2021-22 are set out in circular S3/2021.

(b) The 'disproportionate rent increase rule' applies in Wales and Scotland only (see section 5 of the manual). If a council increases rents to its tenants on HB more than it increases its other rents, subsidy on the difference is restricted.

(c) Limitations on 'modular improvement schemes' apply throughout Great Britain (see section 8 of the manual). If a council offers its tenants the right to select optional services or facilities for an increase in rent, no subsidy is payable on the amount of HB attributable to these.

(d) Limitations on 'rent payment incentive schemes' apply throughout Great Britain (see section 8 of the manual). If a council makes payments (in cash or kind) to reward tenants for paying their rent on time, the total value of such payments is deducted from the amount of subsidy paid to the council

Failure to make a rent referral

21.43   'Rent referral cases' are described in paras 10.28-53. If the council:

(a) is required to refer an HB case to the rent officer during the year;

(b) but fails to do so before the date its final subsidy claim has to be submitted for that year,

no subsidy is paid for any of the HB awarded in the year for that case. In the past some councils have lost a significant amount of subsidy for this reason: R (Isle of Anglesey County Council) v SSWP, R (Lambeth LBC) v SSWP.

21.42   SO 11(2), 13, 15, 15A, 19(1)(a),(c),(2),(3), 20A, sch 4A
          DWP Housing Benefit Subsidy Guidance Manual 2018 to 2019 https://tinyurl.com/SubsidyGuidance

21.43   SO 13, 16, sch 4 para 6; R (Anglesey) v SSWP and R (Lambeth) v SSWP see footnote 21.7

Chapter 22 **State pension credit**

- Overview, basic conditions and how to claim state pension credit (SPC): see paras 22.1-9.
- Calculating SPC: see paras 22.10-21.
- Help with housing costs: basic conditions: see paras 22.22-25.
- Which housing costs are allowable: see paras 22.26-34.
- Calculating your housing costs: see paras 22.35-39.
- Other matters (payment and appeals): see paras 22.40-45.

Overview

22.1   This chapter describes who can get state pension credit (SPC) and which housing costs you can get help with in SPC.

22.2   SPC is for people on a low income who are aged at least 66 (pension age). It is administered in Great Britain by the DWP, and in Northern Ireland by the DFC. About 1.56 million people in the UK were getting SPC in August 2020 [www].

Guarantee credit and savings credit

22.3   There are two kinds of SPC:

(a) guarantee credit; and

(b) savings credit.

22.4   You can be awarded either kind or both, but savings credit is being phased out (para 22.8). Guarantee credit tops up your pension (and other) income to a minimum level (including if you have nil income). Savings credit provides an additional income if you have a modest pension and/or savings income above the amount of the basic state pension (as a 'reward' for saving).

Housing costs if you are on SPC

22.5   While you are on guarantee credit you can get:

(a) HB towards your rent and service charges (but see para 22.45 for future changes);

(b) SMI towards your mortgage interest (volume 1 chapter 8);

(c) SPC towards housing costs that aren't met by HB/SMI (table 22.3).

While you are on savings credit only (a) and (b) apply.

22.2   www.gov.uk/government/collections/dwp-statistical-summaries
www.communities-ni.gov.uk/topics/benefits-statistics

22.3-4   SPCA 1(3), 4(1),(1A),(2); NISPCA 1(3), 4(1),(1A),(2); SI 2019/37; NISR 2019/4

22.5   PC 6(6)(c); NIPC 6(6)(c)

Who can get SPC

22.6   You qualify for SPC if:

(a) you have made a claim for it (para 22.9);

(b) you and your partner (if you have one) are pension age or over;

(c) your partner (if you have one) doesn't get SPC;

(d) you aren't subject to 'immigration control' (or you meet one of the exceptions to this rule, e.g. if you are a refugee or have been granted humanitarian protection by the Home Office);

(e) you are present in Great Britain/Northern Ireland; and

   ■   you are 'habitually resident' in the Common Travel Area, and

   ■   you have a 'right to reside' in the UK;

(f) you meet the low-income condition (para 22.7) or the additional conditions for savings credit (para 22.21) (or both); and

(g) in the case of savings credit you meet the additional condition in para 22.8.

Pension age (for both men and women) is 66. For further details about what is meant by 'immigration control' (including exceptions), 'habitual residence' and 'right to reside', see volume 1 chapter 20.

The low income conditions

22.7   The low-income condition (para 22.6) for guarantee credit is:

(a) you have nil income; or

(b) your income is below the 'appropriate minimum guarantee'.

Your income includes any 'tariff income' from your savings and any income (and tariff income) of your partner. For savings credit you must have a 'qualifying income' that exceeds the savings credit threshold but is not so high that it results in a nil award (paras 22.19-21).

Savings credit: phasing out and restriction on new claims

22.8   Savings credit is being phased out, so you can now only get it:

(a) if you are single:

   ■   you are a woman and you were born before 6th April 1953, or

   ■   you are a man and you were born before 6th April 1951; or

(b) if you are a couple:

   ■   both of you would qualify had you been single, or

   ■   one of you qualified for savings credit before 6th April 2016 and has remained continuously entitled to it since.

22.6   SPCA 1(2),(3),(6), 2(1), 3(1),(2), 4; AA 1; Pensions Act 1995 sch 4 para 1; PC 2;
         NISPCA 1(2),(3),(6), 2(1), 3(1),(2), 4; NIAA 1; SI 1995/3213 sch 2; NIPC 2

22.7   SPCA 2(1)(a),(b); NISPCA 2(1),(a),(b)

22.8   SPCA 3(2)-(4), 3ZA; PC 7A; NISPCA 3(2)-(4), 3ZA; NIPC 7A

How to claim SPC

22.9   You claim SPC by telephone by calling 0800 991234 and your claim is complete if you provide your national insurance number and other information required during the call. You may also be asked to complete a written statement of your circumstances. Alternatively, you can make a claim in writing, but it is advisable to get someone to telephone for a form (such as an advisor or friend). If you complete and return the form within one month, the date of your claim is the date of the phone call. In Northern Ireland, you claim pension credit by calling 0808 1006165 or you can claim in writing by downloading the claim form [www]. For the time limit, backdating and making a claim in advance of your retirement, see paras 22.42-43.

Calculating SPC

How guarantee credit is calculated

22.10   The weekly amount of your guarantee credit equals:

(a)   your 'appropriate minimum guarantee' (para 22.11);

(b)   minus your weekly income (para 22.18).

If the result is between 1p and 9p, it isn't paid unless you get another benefit to pay it with (e.g. state pension). But if you don't, you count as having 'underlying entitlement' so you get 'passport' rights to other benefits (e.g. CTR, cold weather payments).

22.11   Your 'appropriate minimum guarantee' is made up of:

(a)   your 'standard minimum guarantee' (table 22.1); plus

(b)   in certain circumstances, additional amounts for:

■   each child or young person you or your partner is responsible for,

■   each child or young person (as above) who is disabled,

■   severe disability (of you/your partner),

■   a carer (for you/your partner), plus

(c)   your weekly eligible housing costs (para 22.37).

The weekly amounts for (a) and (b) are in table 22.1.

Standard minimum guarantee

22.12   Everyone qualifies for a standard minimum guarantee. You qualify for the appropriate rate depending on whether you are single or a couple (table 22.1).

22.9   C&P87 4D(3),(6A),(6B); NIC&P87 4C(3),(6A),(6B)
        https://www.nidirect.gov.uk/publications/pension-credit-application-form

22.10   SPCA 2(2); PC 13; NISPCA 2(2); NIPC 13

22.11   PC 6(1),(4),(5),(6)(a)-(d),(8), Sch 2A paras 9(1), 10; SI 2018/676; NIPC 6(1),(4),(5),(6)(a)-(d),(8), sch 2A paras 9(1), 10; NISR 2018/135

22.12   PC 6(1); NIPC 6(1)

Table 22.1 **Appropriate minimum guarantee: 2021-22**

Personal allowances

Single person	£177.10
Couple	£270.30
Each additional spouse in polygamous marriage	£93.20
First child or young person born before 6th April 2017	£65.10
Child or young person (each child/young person)	£54.60

Additional amounts

Disabled child (each child/young person)	lower rate	£29.66
	higher rate	£92.54
Severe disability	single rate	£67.30
	double rate	£134.60
Carer	claimant/partner/each	£37.70
Housing costs	Your weekly eligible housing costs (para 22.37)	

Additional amounts: children and young persons

22.13   You get an additional amount for each child and young person if:

(a) you or your partner do not get CTC for them; and

(b) you claimed SPC or your award is revised on or after 1st February 2019; and

(c) you or your partner are responsible for that child or young person.

The rules about whether you are responsible for a child/young person are the same as for HB (paras 4.14-19), including the rules about temporary absence (paras 4.24-25).

22.14   The amount is:

(a) if at least one child/young person was born before 6th April 2017, you get

■ the higher rate for one child/young person, and

■ the lower rate for each of the others;

(b) otherwise you get the lower rate for each child/young person.

But unlike HB or UC there is no two-child limit.

T22.1   PC 6(1),(5),(8), sch 2A paras 9(1), 10; SI 2019/480; NIPC 6(1),(5),(8), sch 2A paras 9(1), 10; SI 2019/46

22.13   PC 6(6)(d), sch 2A paras 1-7; SI 2018/676 reg 1; NIPC 6(6)(d), sch 2A paras 1-7; NISR 2018/135 reg 1

22.14   PC sch 2A paras 9(1), 10; NIPC sch 2A paras 9(1), 10

Additional amount(s): disabled child or young person

22.15   You qualify for a further additional amount for each child or young person you are responsible for who meets one of the following conditions:

(a)   you get the higher rate for each child/young person who is:

- ■   entitled to the highest rate of the care component of DLA, or

- ■   entitled to the enhanced rate of the daily living component of PIP, or

- ■   certified as blind or severely sight-impaired by a consultant ophthalmologist;

(b)   you get the lower rate for each child/young person who is entitled to disability living allowance or personal independence payment but does not meet the conditions in (a).

Additional amounts: severe disability and carer

22.16   You qualify for these additional amounts if you or you and your partner are severely disabled or a carer: the rules are the same as for HB (paras 12.25-33).

Additional amount: housing costs

22.17   Your weekly eligible housing costs (paras 22.22-39) are added to your standard minimum guarantee and any other additional amounts you qualify for (22.12-16). The total is your appropriate minimum guarantee (para 22.11).

Assessing income and capital for guarantee credit

22.18   Your and your partner's income and capital, including your pension income and most social security benefits, is treated in the same way as for pension age HB, except that:

(a)   there are some differences in the treatment of income; the main ones are:

- ■   there are no childcare or additional earnings disregards (paras 14.63-68),

- ■   the standard disregard for lone parents is £20 (table 14.5),

- ■   you can't qualify for a £20 disregard through having limited capability for work,

- ■   there is no carry-over of any unused earnings disregard to WTC (para 14.61), and

- ■   only £10 is disregarded from widowed parent's allowance (table 13.2);

(b)   you can get guarantee credit even if your capital is over £16,000 and if it is your tariff income (para 15.5) is calculated on all your assessed capital (not just the first £16,000);

(c)   your income is generally treated as being paid to you on the first day of your benefit week (para 22.41) in which it is due – or on the day it was due if this was before you made your claim; and

(d)   unlike HB, annual income is always converted into a weekly figure by dividing by 52 (there are no exceptions).

22.15   PC Sch 2A para 9(1)(b),(2),(3); NIPC Sch 2A para 9(1)(b),(2),(3)

22.16   PC 6(5),(6)(a), sch 1 paras 1-4; NIPC 6(5),(6)(a), sch 1 paras 1-4

22.17   PC 6(6)(c), sch 1 paras 1-15; NIPC 6(6)(c), sch 2 paras 1-15

22.18   SPCA 15, 16, 17(1) definition: 'social security benefits'; PC 14-16, sch 4, sch 5; NISPCA 15, 16, 17(1); NIPC 14-16, sch 4, sch 5

Examples: Eligible housing costs on guarantee credit

(a) A single pensioner with no income or capital, living in a leasehold flat

His eligible housing costs (towards service charges) are £30 per week.

His guarantee credit is calculated as follows:

- Appropriate minimum guarantee:

standard minimum guarantee	£177.10
eligible housing costs	£30.00

- He has no income to deduct

- Weekly amount of guarantee credit   £207.10

His guarantee credit meets the whole of his eligible housing costs. He also qualifies for maximum CTR.

(b) A non-dependant moves in with him

The adult daughter of the above leaseholder moves in and a non-dependant deduction of £102.85 applies for her. This reduces his eligible housing costs from £30 to nil (but is not used to reduce any other part of his applicable amount). His guarantee credit is now calculated as follows:

- Appropriate minimum guarantee:

standard minimum guarantee	£177.10
eligible housing costs	£0.00

- He has no income to deduct

- Weekly amount of guarantee credit   £177.10

His guarantee credit no longer meets any of his eligible housing costs. He still qualifies for maximum CTR but with a non-dependant deduction.

(c) A pensioner couple living in a leasehold flat

They have state and private pensions totalling £279.65 per week and have capital of £4,000. Their eligible housing costs (towards service charges) are £27.40 per week. Their guarantee credit is calculated as follows:

- Appropriate minimum guarantee:

standard minimum guarantee	£270.30
eligible housing costs	£27.40

- Minus their weekly income   – £279.65

- Weekly amount of guarantee credit   £18.05

Their guarantee credit meets only part of their eligible housing costs. But they still qualify for maximum CTR.

Calculating savings credit

22.19 The weekly amount of your savings credit depends on:

(a) the 'savings credit threshold' (table 22.2);

(b) the 'maximum savings credit' (table 22.2).

(c) your 'qualifying income' (para 22.20).

Table 22.2 **Savings credit threshold and maximum: 2021-22**	
Threshold	
Single	£153.70
Couple	£244.12
Maximum	
Single	£14.04
Couple	£15.71

22.20 Your total income is the same as calculated for guarantee credit (para 22.18). Your 'qualifying income' is the same as your total income but excluding: WTC, JSA(C), ESA(C), severe disablement allowance, maternity allowance and maintenance payments for you or your partner from a former spouse.

22.21 Your savings credit is worked out as follows:

(a) if your qualifying income is less than or equal to the threshold you don't get savings credit;

(b) if your qualifying income is greater than the threshold:

- your savings credit is 60% of the difference up to the maximum, but
- if your total income exceeds your 'appropriate minimum guarantee' (para 22.11) your savings credit is reduced by 40% of the excess (until it is reduced to nil).

22.19   SPCA 3(2)-(4),(6),(7); PC 7; NISPCA 3(2)-(4),(6),(7); NIPC 7

T22.2   SPCA 3(7); PC 7(2); SI 2019/480; NISPCA 3(7); NIPC 7(2); NISR 2019/46

22.20   SPCA 3(6); PC 9; NISPCA 3(6); NIPC 9

22.21   SPCA 3(2)-(4),(6),(7); PC 7; NISPCA 3(2)-(4),(6),(7); NIPC 7

Help with housing costs: basic conditions

22.22		Your housing costs are included as an additional amount in your appropriate minimum guarantee (para 22.17) only if:

(a)	your housing costs are the kind that are allowable (para 22.26); and

(b)	you or your partner:

- 	is liable for those costs (para 22.23), and

- 	occupy the home for which those costs are paid (para 22.24); and

(c)	the weekly amount of those costs is greater than any non-dependant deductions that apply in your case (para 22.37).

Liability for housing costs

22.23		You are liable for housing costs if you have a legal obligation or duty to pay them. You are treated as liable (whether you have actual liability or not) if:

(a)	your partner is liable for them; or

(b)	the liable person is not paying them; and

- 	you (the claimant) must pay them to continue living there, and

- 	it is reasonable in all the circumstances to treat you as liable for them; or

(c)	you share those costs with other members of the household none of whom is a close relative (para 5.18) of you or your partner, and

- 	one or more of those members is liable to meet those costs, and

- 	it is reasonable in the circumstances to treat you as sharing responsibility.

See example where (b) might apply.

Example: Claimant treated as liable because the liable person is not paying

Karl gets guarantee credit; it does not include an amount for housing costs because he lives with his sister in her flat. His sister is buying the lease with a mortgage; she also makes service charge payments to the landlord on which her right to occupy depends. His sister dies, and her estate becomes liable to meet the mortgage and service charge payments. But she did not leave a will and her estate is not making any payments. The building society cannot transfer the mortgage to Karl until his sister's estate is settled, but it agrees that if he pays the mortgage he can continue living there. The landlord also agrees to accept service charge payments from Karl.

It is reasonable to treat Karl as liable for mortgage interest payments, and because he gets SPC he can apply for a DWP loan to pay these (volume 1, chapter 8). His SPC is also revised to include an additional amount for his service charge payments.

- 	Adapted from DMG Volume 13 para 78215.

22.22	PC 6(6)(c), sch 2 para 1(1)(a),(b); NIPC 6(6)(c), sch 2 para 1(1)(a),(b)

22.23	PC sch 2 paras 1(1)(a),(b), 3; NIPC sch 2 paras 1(1)(a),(b), 3

Occupying the home

22.24 To get housing costs as an additional amount in your SPC you (the claimant) must be occupying the home for which those payments are made. You are treated as occupying the home if it is where you and your family normally live and this is decided in the same way as for HB (paras 3.2-4).

Moving home, two homes and temporary absence

22.25 As with HB, there are rules about when you can claim housing costs for two homes, during a temporary absence or if you move home. You are treated as occupying the home and can get a housing costs additional amount:

(a) if you are living in temporary accommodation while essential repairs are carried out, but only in respect of the dwelling you must make payments for, not both (para 3.13);

(b) during a period of temporary absence for up to 13 or, in some cases, 52 weeks (paras 3.5-12);

(c) on your new home for up to four weeks before you move if the delay is because you are:

- waiting for a disability adaptation (para 3.31), or
- waiting for local welfare assistance (para 3.33), or
- leaving care (para 3.35);

(d) on your previous home and your new home for up to four weeks if your liability for both is unavoidable (para 3.36);

(e) on your normal and your temporary home if your temporary absence:

- is due to fear of violence (para 3.14),
- because you are a student or trainee living at your term time address (para 2.28).

And in each case rules work in the same way as they do for HB but read as if 'housing costs' is substituted for rent (and the law is in the footnote for that para).

Allowable housing costs

22.26 Your housing costs are allowable if:

(a) they are one or more of the type of costs in table 22.3; and

(b) the charge (or part of it) isn't an excluded cost (para 22.29).

If you are a homeowner (including a long leaseholder or a shared owner) and make interest payments on a mortgage or loan secured on your home these costs aren't allowable, but you may be able to get a DWP loan towards these if you still qualify for guarantee credit: see volume 1, chapter 8.

22.24 PC sch 2 paras 1(1)(a),(b), 4(1),(2); NIPC sch 2 paras 1(1)(a),(b), 4(1),(2)

22.25 PC sch 2 para 4(3)-(13); NIPC sch 2 para 4(3)-(13)

22.26 PC sch 2 paras 1(1)(b), 5(1), 10, 13(1),(2); NIPC sch 2 paras 1(1)(b), 5(1), 10, 13(1),(2)

Table 22.3 **Allowable housing costs**

The following kinds of housing cost are allowable, to the extent that they aren't excluded (para 22.29). They are included as an additional amount in your 'appropriate minimum guarantee' (para 22.11):

(a) Rent or ground rent on a long tenancy

■ A long tenancy is one where the lease is made by deed registered with the land registry and granted for a specified number of years, exceeding 21, or for a fixed term with a promise in the agreement for perpetual renewal (unless it is sub-let, and the original lease was for less than 21 years). It includes a lease granted for life because the law treats these as a 90-year agreement.

(b) Service charges if you are a homeowner or long leaseholder

■ A service charge is eligible if it isn't excluded (para 22.29) and your right to occupy is conditional on you paying it (see also para 22.29 if you are a shared owner).

(c) Payments under a co-ownership scheme

■ You are a co-owner if your home is let by a housing association (para 7.13) and under the terms of the agreement you are entitled to a payment based on the value of your home when you cease to be a member of the scheme. (See notes for the co-owner/shared owner distinction).

(d) Payments relating to a Crown tenancy or licence

■ You are a Crown tenant/licensee if your landlord is the Crown or a government department, except if your home is managed by the Crown Estates Commission or the landlord is the Duchy of Cornwall or Lancaster (in which case you are eligible for HB: table 7.2).

(e) Rentcharges

■ A rentcharge (or chief rent) is an annual fee paid by a freehold homeowner to a third party who has no other interest in the property. They are part of an historic system whereby the former land owner is entitled to a fee as a condition of them agreeing to release the land for development. No new rentcharges can be created after 21st July 1977.

(f) Payments for a tent and site fee

■ If the dwelling you occupy as your home is a tent, housing costs are allowed for the tent and the pitch on which it stands.

Notes:

■ A shared owner means someone who owns a fixed share in their home (typically 25, 50 or 75 per cent) and who rents the remaining share from their landlord (usually a housing association). A shared owner (unlike a co-owner) gets help with their service charges in HB instead of SPC (para 22.29).

■ If you are a homeowner, long leaseholder or shared owner with a mortgage or loan secured on your home see para 22.5.

T22.3   PC sch 2 para 13(1)(a)-(f),(6)(a)-(d); NIPC sch 2 para 13(1)(a)-(f),(6)(a)-(d)

Service charges, estimated bills and final adjustments

22.27   Most service charges for long-leases/owner occupied dwellings are based on the landlord/managing agent's actual costs so the charge for each period is variable rather than a fixed amount. The usual practice is for the landlord/managing agent to send a bill based on the estimated costs with final adjustments being made some time after the end of the accounting period.

Length of award and how charges are attributed

22.28   Your housing costs are attributed to a fixed 52-week period from the date your liability first arose. At any one time your award may therefore be made up of housing costs arising from different liabilities notified at different times (para 22.27 and see example).

Example: Attribution of service charge award based on estimated and final bills

A claimant claims SPC on 1st April 2020. Their SPC includes a weekly amount of £8.31 for housing costs arising from estimated service charges of £432.00 based on the landlord's estimated bill for the period 1st April 2020 to 31st March 2021 (£432.00 ÷ 52 = £8.31 rounded up to the nearest penny: para 22.38). The last day of their housing costs award is 30th March 2021 (exactly 52 weeks from 1st April 2020).

In March 2021, the claimant sends the DWP the landlord's (estimated) service charge bill of £565.00 for the financial year 1st April 2021 to 31st March 2022. The award is superseded on the grounds of an anticipated change of circumstances with a housing costs award of £10.87 per week for the 52-week period 31st March 2021 to 29th March 2022.

On 8th September 2021 the claimant receives an invoice from their landlord for £243.85, being the balance of the finalised service charges for the year ending on 31st March 2021. The DWP supersedes the decision of March 2021 to award housing costs of £10.87 and £4.69 for the period 8th September 2021 to 29th March 2022 and £4.69 for the period 30th March 2022 to 6th September 2022, the balance for the year 2020-21 being paid over 52 weeks.

If a further estimate for charges for the year 2021-22 is received, the September 2021 decision would be superseded.

■   Adapted from DMG Volume 13 para 78487.

22.28   PC sch 2 para 13(3); NIPC sch 2 para 13(3)

Excluded housing costs

22.29   Even if your housing costs are of the kind in table 22.3 they are nevertheless excluded from help if:

(a) they relate to a service charge that is eligible for HB (table 7.1). So, you can't get help with your service charges in your SPC if you are a shared owner (unless you are a co-owner), but you get help in your HB instead (para 7.24);

(b) any part of a charge that relates to business use (para 22.30) if the dwelling is part of a building that is partly residential and partly business;

(c) any charge for 'repairs and improvements' (para 22.31);

(d) any charge or part of a charge that relates to an ineligible service (para 22.32);

(e) any housing cost to the extent that it is considered excessive (paras 22.33-34).

Apportionment for business use

22.30   If your home forms part of a building that is liable for both business rates and council tax, your housing costs are in proportion to the residential part of the building only. That fraction is the current market value of the residential part of the building divided by the combined market values of the business and residential parts. If the building was built or converted before 1st April 1990 the rateable values (as at 31st March 1990) are used instead.

Repairs and improvements

22.31   Any charge that relates to 'repairs or improvements' is excluded from SPC. This includes a wide range of measures undertaken to maintain the fitness of the building for human habitation such as:

(a) provision of washing or sanitary facilities (bath, shower, lavatory) and drainage facilities;

(b) repairs to the heating system;

(c) provision of damp proof measures or insulation;

(d) provision of ventilation or natural lighting;

(e) provision of lighting or power sockets;

(f) repairs of unsafe structural defects;

(g) adapting the dwelling for the needs of a disabled person, or to provide additional bedrooms so that children or young persons of the opposite sex can sleep separately.

But if you are a homeowner or long leaseholder and have taken out a mortgage or secured loan for these you might be able to get DWP loan payments: see volume 1, chapter 8.

22.29   PC sch 2 paras 5(1), 10, 13(2)(a)-(c); NIPC sch 2 paras 5(1), 10, 13(2)(a)-(c)

22.30   PC sch 2 para 6(1)-(3); NIPC sch 2 para 6(1)-(3)

22.31   PC sch 2 paras 12(2), 13(2)(c); NIPC sch 2 paras 12(2), 13(2)(c)

Ineligible service charges

22.32   Any part of your housing costs for services that wouldn't be eligible for HB (table 8.3 and para 8.59) – including any service charge that isn't related to the provision of adequate accommodation: para 8.51 – is deducted from your weekly housing costs as follows:

(a) if you are a Crown tenant and your rent includes a charge for water, that amount is deducted if it is known, or in any other case the likely amount;

(b) if the charge includes an amount for fuel that isn't separately identified:

- the standard amount as for HB (table 8.4) is deducted, unless

- you provide evidence of the actual or approximate amount that allows the charge to be estimated, in which case the deduction is that estimated amount;

(c) in any other case:

- if the charge is separately identified, that amount is deducted, otherwise

- the part of that payment that is 'fairly attributable' to the cost of providing that service having regard to the costs of comparable services.

Excessive housing costs

22.33   If your allowable housing costs are considered excessive, the DWP will decide how much would be reasonable and deducts the excess. Your housing costs may be considered excessive if:

(a) the dwelling you occupy is larger than is required by you, your partner, any person aged under 20, and any other non-dependant, having regard to suitable alternative accommodation occupied by a similar sized household;

(b) the immediate area in which your home is located is more expensive than other areas where suitable alternative accommodation exits;

(c) the costs being met are higher than those of suitable alternative accommodation in the area.

But in certain circumstances you can be protected from a deduction or it can be delayed (para 22.34).

22.34   No deduction is made from your housing costs (para 22.33):

(a) if it is unreasonable to expect you to seek cheaper suitable alternative accommodation, considering:

- the availability of suitable accommodation and the level of housing costs in the area, and

- the circumstances of the occupiers in para 22.33(a), including their state of health, employment prospects and whether it will result in a change of school; or

---

22.32   PC sch 2 para 13(2)(a),(b),(5); NIPC sch 2 para 13(2)(a),(b),(5)

22.33   PC sch 2 para 10(1)(a)-(c); NIPC sch 2 para 10(1)(a)-(c)

22.34   PC sch 2 para 10(4)-(10); NIPC sch 2 para 10(4)-(10)

(b) in any other case, for up to 26 weeks immediately following the date on which the matters in 22.33(a)-(c) first began to apply, if you could meet those costs (without SPC) when you first entered into them (and for a further 26 after that if you use your 'best endeavours' to find cheaper accommodation).

In calculating the 26 weeks, any period on IS/JSA(IB)/ESA(IR) is treated as being a period on SPC, as well as any gaps in your award of 12 weeks or less.

Calculating your housing costs

22.35   Your housing costs are part of your minimum income guarantee (para 22.11). Because SPC is a weekly benefit your housing costs are converted to a weekly figure, even if you pay them over a different cycle (four-weekly, monthly, quarterly, etc).

Conversion to weekly figures

22.36   Where your housing costs are paid other than weekly, the weekly figure is calculated by dividing the yearly amount by 52. It is always 52 weeks, even in a year that is treated as having 53 weeks, or if there are period(s) in the year where no payment is due ('rent-free').

Calculating your weekly housing costs

22.37   To calculate your weekly housing costs work through the following steps:
  (a) start with the gross weekly figure and deduct the amount amount of ineligible charges;
  (b) if part of building is used for business calculate the proportion of those costs that is attributable to residential use;
  (c) if you are jointly responsible for payments, your eligible housing costs is the proportion (of (a) or (b)) that you are responsible for (but if a person you share liability with isn't paying you are treated as responsible for their share: para 22.23);
  (d) deduct the appropriate weekly amount that applies for each non-dependant (para 22.39).

If the result from (d) is nil (or negative), then your appropriate minimum guarantee (para 22.11) doesn't include an amount for housing costs.

22.38   Where any part of the calculation (para 22.37) results in a fraction of a penny, that figure is rounded up to next whole penny, unless it involves the apportionment of a non-dependant charge (para 6.19(c)) in which case it is rounded (up or down) to the nearest penny.

22.35   PC sch 2 para 13(1); NIPC sch 2 para 13(1)

22.36   PC sch 2 para 13(3); NIPC sch 2 para 13(3)

22.37   PC sch 2 paras 5(1), 6(2),(3),(5), 10(1), 11(2),(5), 14; NIPC sch 2 paras 5(1), 6(2),(3),(5), 10(1), 11(2),(5), 14

22.38   PC sch 2 paras 13(5), 15; NIPC sch 2 paras 13(5), 15

Non-dependant deductions

22.39 All the rules about non-dependants that apply to pension age HB also apply to SPC. This includes the rules about: who 'resides with you' (paras 4.29-31), the situations when a deduction doesn't apply and the amount of the weekly deduction (tables 6.2 and 6.3). The only differences to HB are:

(a) if you are a shared owner and a deduction has been made from your HB no deduction is made from your SPC housing costs in respect of the same non-dependant;

(b) the following aren't counted as non-dependants:

- anyone aged under 20 and who you are responsible for,
- anyone who isn't a close relative (para 5.18) of you/your partner and who makes payments to you/your partner on a commercial basis (such as rent),
- anyone jointly liable for housing costs or a co-owner with you/your partner.

In the case of (b), in most situations the outcome is the same as for HB but there are very slight differences.

Other matters

When your SPC is paid

22.40 SPC is usually paid fortnightly or four weekly in arrears on the same day as your state pension, according to the last two digits of your national insurance number as follows:

(a) 00 to 19 – Monday

(b) 20 to 39 – Tuesday

(c) 40 to 59 – Wednesday

(d) 60 to 79 – Thursday

(e) 80 to 99 – Friday

But there are some exceptions to this, the main one being that if your SPC award started before 6th April 2010, it is usually paid weekly in advance on a Monday.

Your benefit week

22.41 Your benefit week is the seven days ending on your pay day if it is paid in arrears or starting on your pay day if it is paid in advance.

Time limit for claiming and backdating

22.42 The time limit for claiming SPC is three months from the date you first became entitled to it. If you claim within the time limit you get all the arrears: there are no further conditions, so you do not need to show 'good cause'. If you claim after the time limit you only get three months arrears. The time limit cannot be extended for any reason.

22.39   PC sch 2 para 14; NIPC sch 2 para 14

22.40   C&P87 22C, 22CA, 26B, 26BA; NIC&P87 22C, 22CA, 26B, 26BA

22.41   PC 1(1) – definition 'benefit week'; NIPC 1(1)

22.42   C&P87 19(2),(3)(i); NIC&P87 19(2),(3)(i)

Advance claims: reaching pension age

22.43   You can make an advance claim for SPC up to four months before the date you reach pension age (and also for state pension). If you are on UC you can get an overlapping payment of your UC and SPC (volume 1, chapter 3).

Appeals about SPC

22.44   Most decisions about your pension credit – including any additional amount for your housing costs – can be reconsidered and then appealed to a tribunal. The rules are similar to UC: the time limit is one month, and you must go through a mandatory reconsideration before you can appeal to a tribunal: see volume 1, chapter 14.

Planned changes

22.45   The government plans that payments that are eligible for pension age HB (typically rent: table 7.1) will become part of your eligible housing costs (table 22.3) when pension age HB is abolished; although this isn't expected to happen until 2023 or 2024 after all existing working age HB claims have been transferred to UC (HM Treasury, Budget Red Book 2018, para 5.39) [www].

22.43   C&P87 4E(2); NIC&P87 4D(2)

22.44   SI 1999/991 reg 3ZA; FTPR 22(2)-(4); NISR 1999/162 regs 3ZA, 31, 33

22.46   https://www.tinyurl.com/Red-Book

Chapter 23 **Other help with housing costs**

- ■ Discretionary housing payments (DHPs) towards your rent or service charges: see paras 23.1-19.
- ■ Welfare supplementary payments in Northern Ireland: see paras 23.20-34.
- ■ Local welfare assistance schemes: see paras 23.35-37.
- ■ Direct payments to your landlord from your SPC or legacy benefits for rent arrears or hostel charges: see paras 23.38-56.

Discretionary housing payments

23.1   This section describes how the council/NIHE can award you a discretionary housing payment (DHP) if you are entitled to HB or a UC housing costs element and need further help towards your rent or related housing costs. DHPs are not part of HB, but are administered by the same councils/NIHE as HB.

23.2   The DHPs in this section are separate from the (similarly named) discretionary hardship payments which the DWP can award to people whose legacy benefits end as a result of managed migration to UC (para 1.28).

The law and guidance on DHPs

23.3   The Acts of Parliament governing DHPs are the Child Support, Pensions and Social Security Act 2000 and its Northern Ireland equivalent. The details of the DHP scheme are in the Discretionary Financial Assistance Regulations 2001 and its Northern Ireland equivalent (see appendix 1). DWP guidance for councils is in its Discretionary Housing Payments Guidance manual (DHPGM) [www]. In Scotland, the Scottish Government is responsible for DHPs.

Who can get DHPs

23.4   To get a DHP you must meet the conditions in paras 23.5-6. DHPs are discretionary: the council doesn't have to award you a DHP even if you meet the conditions so you shouldn't rely on getting one. (But see para 23.9 in Scotland.)

Basic conditions

23.5   The basic conditions for getting a DHP are:

(a) you are entitled to HB or a UC housing costs element;

(b) you are liable for rent (in any kind of social or private sector letting); and

(c) you 'appear… to require further financial assistance… in order to meet housing costs'.

There are also some restrictions on what a DHP can be used for (paras 23.10-11).

23.3   CPSA 69,70; Scotland Act 2016 s25 SI 2016/759 reg 3; NICPSA 60,61; SI 2001/1167; NISR 2001/216
www.gov.uk/government/publications/discretionary-housing-payments-guidance-manual

23.5   DFA 2(1); NIDFA 2(1)

Requiring financial assistance

23.6   DHP law doesn't define what requiring 'some further financial assistance' means. The DWP says you usually need to demonstrate you 'are unable to meet housing costs from [your] available income' or 'have a shortfall as a result of the welfare reforms' (DHPGM 1.18-19). But your (and your family's) circumstances don't have to be 'exceptional' or causing you 'hardship'. And the council/NIHE shouldn't take account of any DLA mobility component you or your partner receive, or have a fixed rule or policy that it always takes account of any DLA care component or equivalent PIP component (Hardy v Sandwell MBC).

Housing costs

23.7   DHP law doesn't list which 'housing costs' you can get help with. They clearly include rent and any eligible service charges you pay (para 8.42). The DWP says (DHPGM 1.16, 4.1-18) they can also include rent in advance; deposits; and other lump sum costs associated with a housing need such as removal costs. But see para 23.11 for items that are excluded.

Uses for DHPs: Great Britain

23.8   In Great Britain DHPs can be used to help with:

(a)   reductions in your HB due to the following:

- the benefit cap (para 6.21),
- the social renter size criteria (para 8.9) (and this is nearly always the case in Scotland: para 23.9),
- the private renter LHA rules (para 9.4),
- the social or private renter rent referral rules (para 10.39),
- the income taper (para 6.6),
- non-dependant deductions (para 6.9);

(b)   similar reductions in your UC (DWP circular G8/2016);

(c)   a shortfall in your rent to prevent your household becoming homeless while the housing authority explores other options;

(d)   a rent deposit or rent in advance if you are getting HB/UC on your present home and are waiting to move into a new home;

(e)   the gap between the end of your UC for housing costs and the start of your HB when you move into supported or temporary accommodation (table 17.3).

These are examples, and DHPs can be used in other situations. Examples (a) to (d) are based on DWP guidance (DHPGM 3.2) and for (e) see para 23.15.

23.7   R (Hardy) v Sandwell MBC [2015] EWHC 890 (Admin); www.bailii.org/ew/cases/EWHC/Admin/2015/890.html

Social renter size criteria in Scotland

23.9 In Scotland you get a DHP regardless of your circumstances to cover the full reduction due to the social renter size criteria (paras 8.9-16). The only exception is if you don't meet the basic conditions because your HB is reduced to nil after the reduction is applied. Apart from that, all the possibilities in para 23.8 apply.

Uses for DHPs: Northern Ireland

23.10 In Northern Ireland you can only get a DHP to help with:

(a) a shortfall between your eligible rent and your actual rent due to the LHA or rent referral rules (paras 9.4 and 10.39);

(b) the loss of the family premium (para 12.24); or

(c) a reduction due to the benefit cap (to the extent that the reduction is not met by a WSP: para 23.23-28).

Exceptions

23.11 You can't get a DHP to help with any of the following:

(a) service charges that are ineligible for HB (para 8.57) or (if you aren't on HB) for UC;

(b) any charges for water, sewerage or allied environmental services;

(c) any liability for council tax, or in Northern Ireland rates;

(d) increases to cover rent arrears which are not eligible for HB (para 8.79);

(e) reductions in any benefit due to the recovery of an overpayment of HB/UC, or to sanctions relating to jobseekers, child support or benefit offences.

DHP claims

23.12 You can make your DHP claim in any way the council/NIHE agrees to (e.g. in writing or by telephone) or someone can claim on your behalf if this is reasonable. Some councils have a special DHP form you can use. You should provide information and evidence you are asked for when you claim. And if your circumstance change in a way that could affect your DHPs, you (and the person they are paid to if this is different) should tell the council/NIHE about this. In Scotland you can use the Scottish Government website to apply online [www].

DHP awards

23.13 DHPs can be awarded for a fixed period, an open-ended period or as a lump sum, but see paras 23.14-15 for limits. The council/NIHE can start or stop your award when it thinks fit. This means you may have to reclaim, possibly several times, if you need DHPs for more than a short period.

23.9   www.gov.scot/policies/social-security/support-with-housing-costs/

23.10   NIDFA 2(1)(a)-(d)

23.11   DFA 3(a),(aa),(b),(c),(f)-(p); NIDFA 3(a).(aa),(ab),(b)-(m)

23.12   DFA 5, 6; NIDFA 5, 6
https://www.mygov.scot/discretionary-housing-payment/

23.13   DFA 5; NIDFA 5

DHP amounts and limits

23.14   When DHPs are awarded for a period, the following limits apply:

(a) if you are on HB, the weekly total of your HB and DHP must not be greater than:

  ▪ your actual rent,

  ▪ minus any service/support charges that are ineligible for HB (para 8.57);

(b) if you are on UC, the monthly amount of your DHP must not be greater than your UC housing costs element. In other words, not greater than the monthly amount of:

  ▪ your actual rent,

  ▪ minus any service/support charges that are ineligible for UC (volume 1, chapter 6).

If you are on HB in supported or temporary accommodation (table 2.3) the limit (a) applies, but the law is not completely clear about this if you are also on UC.

23.15   The above limits don't apply when DHPs are awarded:

(a) as a lump sum (e.g. towards a deposit or rent in advance); or

(b) 'for past housing costs (arrears of rent) on the ground that [you are] currently receiving full housing benefit' (Gargett v Lambeth LBC) (and see DHPGM 4.1-4, 4.20).

Payments and overpayments

23.16   The council/NHE can pay your DHP to you, or to someone else if appropriate (e.g. someone acting on your behalf or your landlord). It also has a discretion to recover overpayments of DHPs that are due to you (or someone else) not giving correct information, or due to an error it has made.

Decisions, notifications and appeals

23.17   When you claim a DHP the council/NIHE must decide whether or not to award you one. It must give you written notice of its decision, including reasons, as soon as reasonably practicable. You can ask the council/NIHE to review its decision if you disagree with it, but the detailed rules about reconsiderations don't apply. You can't appeal to a tribunal, but in limited circumstances you may be able to apply for judicial review (para 20.53).

DHP expenditure: government grants and limits

23.18   In England and Wales the DWP makes grants to councils towards their expenditure on DHPs. This is separate from HB subsidy. The details are in the Discretionary Housing Payments (Grants) Order SI 2001/2340. In 2021-22 the amounts for each English and Welsh council are in circular S4/2021 and the total is £140 million. The council has to claim this grant by 30th April in the following financial year, but doesn't have to submit audited accounts. In Scotland, grants to Scottish authorities are allocated by the Scottish Government. The total allocation for 2021-22 is £83.1 million (Scottish Budget 2020-21, table 5.14 [www]).

23.14   DFA 4(1),(2); NIDFA 4(1),(2)

23.15   R (Gargett) v Lambeth LBC [2008] EWCA Civ 1450; www.bailii.org/ew/cases/EWCA/Civ/2008/1450.htm

23.16   DFA 8; NIDFA 8

23.18-19 CPSA 70; SI 2001/2340; SI 2014/2918; SSI 2014/298; http://tinyurl.com/Scot-Budget-2021-22

23.19   The council doesn't have to spend the exact amount of its grant on DHPs; it can spend less or more. In England and Wales the maximum it can spend in any year is two and a half times the amount of its grant for that year. This limit doesn't apply in Scotland, and the Scottish Government provides funding to councils for the additional expenditure on the social renter size criteria (para 23.9).

Welfare supplementary payments in Northern Ireland

23.20   In Northern Ireland, welfare supplementary payments (WSPs) can help people affected by recent changes in HB and other social security benefits. This section describes how WSPs can help with your rent if your HB is reduced as a result of the benefit cap or the social renter size criteria ('bedroom tax').

23.21   WSPs are not part of the HB scheme and are administered by the DFC in conjunction with the NIHE.

The law and guidance on WSPs

23.22   The primary legislation governing WSPs is the Welfare Reform (Northern Ireland) Order SI 2015/2006. Relevant details are in the Welfare Supplementary Payments Regulations (Northern Ireland) 2016 NISR 2016/178, the Welfare Supplementary Payment (Amendment) Regulations (Northern Ireland) 2017 NISR 2017/28, and the Housing Benefit (Welfare Supplementary Payment) Regulations (Northern Ireland) 2017 NISR 2017/35.

WSPs for the benefit cap

23.23   The benefit cap is explained in paras 6.21-33. It was introduced in Northern Ireland on 31st May 2016 (the 'old' benefit cap) and reduced on 7th November 2016 (the 'new' benefit cap). But in each case, this usually started affecting your HB from a later date (para 6.31). WSPs can be awarded for the old benefit cap, the new benefit cap, or both (paras 23.24-28).

23.24   You qualify for benefit cap WSPs if:

(a) you are a lone parent or couple with at least one child or young person in your family (para 4.14);

(b) your HB is reduced as a result of the benefit cap;

(c) you have been entitled to 'welfare benefits' since 31st May 2016 or 7th November 2016 (para 23.25); and

(d) your home is in Northern Ireland (para 23.26).

23.25   'Welfare benefits' means any of the benefits in table 6.4(a). If you were a couple who separated on or after 31st May 2016 and met condition (a) or (b) when you separated, you continue to meet condition (a) and/or (b) whenever your former partner does.

23.21   SI 2015/2006 arts 137, 137A; NISR 2016/178 (as amended by NISR 2016/389); NISR 2017/28 part 2; NISR 2017/35

23.22-27   NISR 2016/178 regs 1-4A, 13-16

23.26   You can only get benefit cap WSPs if you are present and normally resident in Northern Ireland. But during a temporary absence from Northern Ireland you can get them for:

(a)   up to 13 weeks if your absence is to receive medical treatment; or

(b)   up to four weeks if your absence is for any other reasons;

so long as your absence is unlikely to exceed 52 weeks. And you can only get them for the first four weeks you are in prison (in Northern Ireland or elsewhere).

23.27   WSPs for the benefit cap are awarded from the first day your HB is reduced as a result of it. To begin with, they equal the amount of your benefit cap reduction (table 6.4), so you don't lose any money. After that, they go down if your benefit cap reduction goes down, but can never go up.

23.28   WSPs end when your HB ends or (if earlier) if your benefit cap reduction ends or (in all cases) on 31st March 2020, and can never start again.

WSPs for the social renter size criteria

23.29   The social renter size criteria are explained in paras 8.9-16. They were introduced on 20th February 2017. WSPs can be awarded whenever your HB is affected by size criteria (paras 23.30-32).

23.30   You qualify for size criteria WSPs if:

(a)   you rent from the NIHE or a registered housing association;

(b)   your HB is reduced because your home has more bedrooms than the size criteria allow (table 11.1); and

(c)   your home is in Northern Ireland (the rules about temporary absence are the same as for HB: para 3.5).

You can't get size criteria WSPs if you rent from any other landlord.

23.31   Size criteria WSPs are awarded from the first day your HB is reduced as a result of the size criteria. They equal the amount of the reduction in your HB (paras 8.12-13), so you don't lose any money. Whenever the reduction in your HB goes up or down, your size criteria WSPs go up or down by the same amount. With one exception (para 23.32), they continue for as long as you qualify for them, and start again whenever you qualify for them again.

23.32   Size criteria WSPs end if:

(a)   you move to another home rented from the NIHE or a registered housing association;

(b)   your move is not a 'management transfer' arranged by your landlord(s); and

(c)   your new home has even more bedrooms (compared with what you are allowed following your move) than your old home did (compared with what you were allowed before your move).

23.29-32   NISR 2017/28 regs 1-7, 14

23.33   NISR 2016/178 reg 2; NISR 2017/28 regs 2(1),(5), 7, 15

WSP awards and appeals

23.33   You are awarded WSPs without having to make a claim. The DFC uses information provided by the NIHE, and by your landlord if you rent from a registered housing association. You can ask the DFC to review your award if you think it is wrong. You can't appeal to a tribunal but may be able to apply for judicial review (para 20.53).

WSP payments and overpayments

23.34   WSPs are paid four weekly in arrears. They are paid to you (or someone on your behalf) or to your landlord or agent if your HB is paid to them (but not a private landlord/agent unless they are registered with the Landlord Registration Scheme). Overpayments of WSPs are nearly always recoverable – from you and/or the person they were paid to. The methods include making deductions from future payments of WSPs, HB, some other social security benefits, or earnings.

Local welfare assistance/discretionary support

23.35   You may be able to get help from:

(a) a local welfare assistance scheme in England;

(b) the Welsh Discretionary Assistance Fund;

(c) the Scottish Welfare Fund; or

(d) discretionary support in Northern Ireland.

These are not part of the HB scheme. In England they are administered by local councils under their general power to promote well-being. In Scotland, local councils administer the funds according to national rules and guidance. In Wales and Northern Ireland the funds are administered by the national government or their agents.

23.36   To get help you normally have to be 'in need' and without the money to meet the need. But the schemes and funds are discretionary, so you have no right to help. Payments can be a grant or a loan but many councils provide help only (or mainly) on a non-cash basis.

23.37   In general terms you may be able to get help to:

(a) avoid becoming homeless;

(b) avoid entering institutional care (e.g. residential care, hospital or prison);

(c) set up home after leaving institutional care; or

(d) meet a crisis and avoid harm.

In Scotland you cannot get a grant or loan for rent or mortgage payments, rent in advance, repair costs or any housing costs that could be covered by a DHP. Similar exclusions apply in Northern Ireland but you may get a loan for rent in advance to secure a tenancy. In England local councils set their own rules but in practice similar exclusions are likely to apply.

23.34   NISR 2016/178 regs 4(7)-(9), 11; NISR 2017/28 regs 4-13, schs 1, 2; NISR 2017/35 regs 4-13, schs 1, 2

23.35   England: Localism Act 2011, s1;   Scotland: The Welfare Funds (Scotland) Act 2015; SSI 2016/107
          Wales: Government of Wales Act 2006, s70;   Northern Ireland: NIWRO 135; NISR 2016/270

23.37   Scotland: https//www.mygov.scot/scottish-welfare-fund/
          Wales: https://gov.wales/discretionary-assistance-fund-daf
          Northern Ireland: https://www.nidirect.gov.uk/articles/extra-financial-support

Direct payments from DWP benefits

23.38   This section describes how the DWP can make deductions from your SPC/JSA/ESA/IS and pay them direct to your landlord to cover your rent arrears and/or any hostel charges not covered by your HB. It gives the rules for Great Britain. Similar rules apply in Northern Ireland but some of the details differ.

23.39   Direct payments are not part of the HB scheme, but are administered by the DWP, and in Northern Ireland by the DFC. The DWP/DFC call them 'third party payments'.

The law and guidance on direct payments

23.40   The law about direct payments is in schedule 9 of the Social Security (Claims and Payments) Regulations SI 1987/1968 and schedule 8A of its Northern Ireland equivalent (see appendix 1). DWP guidance for landlords and mortgage lenders is in *How to Apply for Third Party Payments* and the *Third Party Payments Creditor/Supplier Handbook* [www]. Guidance for councils is in GM D1.570-689.

What direct payments can be used for

23.41   The DWP can make direct payments:

(a) to your landlord towards arrears of rent including service charges;

(b) to your landlord, if you live in a hostel, towards essential services that are not eligible for HB;

(c) to your utility supplier to cover fuel and/or water charges and certain other debts.

They are designed to encourage your landlord to let you stay in your home rather than evict you because of arrears. They cannot be used to repay rent arrears on your former home. This guide does not give the rules about direct payments for utility bills and other debts, except to the extent that these charges are included in your rent, but these are listed in para 23.56).

When direct payments can be made

23.42   The basic conditions for making direct payments are in para 23.43 and further details are in the rest of this section. But direct payments are discretionary. This means the DWP doesn't have to make them even if all the conditions are met, though in practice it usually does.

Basic conditions

23.43   The DWP can only make direct payments if:

(a) you or your partner get a qualifying benefit (para 23.44);

(b) you or your partner also get HB (or you live in a hostel and have made a claim for HB); and

(c) the direct payments are for the dwelling you occupy as your home.

There are also further conditions for each kind of direct payment: see paras 23.46-49.

23.40   C&P87 35(1) and sch 9; NIC&P87 34A(1) and sch 8A
         tinyurl.com/creditordeductions

23.43   C&P87 sch 9; NIC&P87 sch 8A

Qualifying benefits

23.44 Direct payments can only be made if you or your partner are:

(a) on state pension credit (SPC) – whether this is guarantee credit or savings credit or both;

(b) on income support (IS);

(c) on income-based JSA;

(d) on income-related ESA;

(e) on contribution-based JSA and are also entitled to JSA(IB) at the same rate; or

(f) on contributory ESA and are also entitled to ESA(IR) at the same rate.

The last two apply because in these circumstances you are paid JSA(C)/ESA(C) rather than JSA(IB)/ESA(IR).

Direct payments if you get universal credit

23.45 The rules in this section (paras 23.38-56) don't apply if you are on UC, including if you are on UC and HB because you live in supported or temporary accommodation (table 2.3); the UC direct payment rules apply instead (volume 1, chapter 12).

Benefits from which deductions can be made

23.46 When the DWP makes a direct payment, it deducts the same amount from your qualifying benefit (para 23.44). But if the amount of your SPC, IS or JSA(IB) is insufficient to make the deduction, the DWP can make it from any retirement pension, JSA(C), incapacity benefit or severe disablement allowance you or your partner get (whether this is paid separately or together with your SPC/IS/JSA(IB)).

Direct payments for rent arrears

23.47 The DWP can make direct payments to your landlord for rent arrears if:

(a) you meet the basic conditions (para 23.43);

(b) you have rent arrears (para 23.48) of:

- at least four times your weekly rent, or
- if you live in a hostel (para 7.27) at least £100; and

(c) either:

- the arrears have accrued or persisted over at least eight weeks and your landlord has requested direct payments, or
- they have accrued or persisted over less than eight weeks and the DWP considers it is in your and your family's overriding interests to make direct payments, or
- you live in a hostel and are eligible for direct payments of service charges (para 23.49).

When this applies to you, your HB must also be paid to your landlord (para 18.28).

23.43-44   C&P87 sch 9 para 1(1) definition: 'specified benefit', (2),(3); NIC&P87 para 1(1)-(3)

23.45   C&P87 1(3); NIC&P87 1(3)

23.46   C&P87 sch 9 para 5(1),(1A),(2); NIC&P87 para 5(1)(1A),(2)

23.47   C&P87 sch 9 paras 1(1) definition: 'rent', 5(7); NIC&P87 para 5(7)

23.48	For the above purposes (para 23.47), both 'rent' (also called 'gross rent') and 'rent arrears':

(a)	include all the following (whether or not they are eligible for HB):

- your rent (or licence fee, etc: table 7.1),
- any service or other charges included in your rent, and
- any separate charge made by your landlord for water or services;

(b)	but do not include:

- any fuel charge that is not eligible for HB and varies more than twice a year,
- any unpaid non-dependant charge, or
- any unpaid amount relating to a former home.

The amounts in (b) are also ignored when calculating the period over which your rent arrears have accrued or persisted.

Direct payments for hostel charges

23.49	The DWP can make direct payments to your landlord for hostel charges if:

(a)	you meet the basic conditions (para 23.43) – but see para 23.45 if you live in supported or temporary accommodation;

(b)	you live in a hostel (para 7.27); and

(c)	your hostel charges include an amount for fuel, meals, laundry and/or cleaning (other than communal areas).

This can apply whether or not you have arrears of rent or other charges. When it does apply, your HB must also be paid to your landlord (para 18.28).

Amounts deducted from your benefits

23.50	Paras 23.51-53 explain how much is deducted from your social security benefit and paid to your landlord as a direct payment. Paras 23.54-56 give the limits that can affect this.

23.51	All the amounts in the rest of this section are given as weekly figures. The standard amount of £3.75 (para 23.52) is 5% of the personal allowance for a single person aged 25-plus (table 12.1) rounded up to the next multiple of 5p. It only changes when the personal allowance changes.

Amount for rent arrears

23.52	The amount deducted as a direct payment for rent or mortgage arrears is:

(a)	the standard amount of £3.75; plus

(b)	(in rent arrears cases) the amount of any fuel and/or water charges that are included in your rent and that aren't eligible for HB.

Once all your rent arrears are cleared, the amount in (b) can continue to be deducted as a direct payment if this is in the 'interests of [your] family'.

23.48	C&P87 sch 9 para 5(1),(1A),(2); NIC&P87 sch 8A para 5(1),(1A),(2)

23.49	C&P87 SI 1987/1968 sch 9 para 4A; NIC&P87 sch 8A para 4A

23.51	C&P87 sch 9 paras 1(1) definition: '5%', 3(2),5(6); NIC&P87 sch 8A paras 1(1),3(2),5(6)

23.52	C&P87 sch 9 paras 2,5(6),(7); NIC&P87 sch 8A paras 2,5(6),(7)

Amount for hostel charges

23.53   The amount deducted as a direct payment for hostel charges equals the amount of your charges for fuel, meals, laundry and/or cleaning (other than communal areas). This is calculated as described in paras 8.22 and 10.51 or, if your HB hasn't yet been awarded, the DWP should estimate it.

Limits to amounts for rent arrears

23.54   Once the amount for rent arrears has been calculated (para 23.52):

(a) it is reduced whenever necessary to leave you receiving 10p a week of your qualifying benefit (para 23.44);

(b) if it is higher than 25% of:

  ▪ your qualifying benefit's applicable amount,

  ▪ plus (if you are on CTC) your CTC and child benefit,

  it is reduced to that 25% unless you consent to a higher amount.

Limits when there is more than one direct payment

23.55   Amounts can be deducted from your DWP benefits to make direct payments for other purposes, and in many cases they equal or include a standard amount of £3.75. If more than one direct payment applies to you:

(a) the maximum deduction for standard amounts is £11.25 (3 x £3.75);

(b) the total deduction is reduced whenever necessary to leave you receiving 10p a week of your qualifying benefit (para 23.44).

23.56   If the above limits mean that only some direct payments can be made, they are made in the following order of priority:

(a) rent or mortgage arrears;

(b) fuel;

(c) water;

(d) council tax;

(e) unpaid fines;

(f) child support;

(g) repayments of refugee integration loan;

(h) loan repayments to certain affordable credit lenders (credit unions);

(i) tax credit overpayment debts and self assessment debts.

23.53   C&P87 sch 9 para 4A(3); NIC&P87 sch 8A para 4A(3)

23.54   C&P87 sch 9 para 2(2); NIC&P87 sch 8A para 2(2)

23.55-56   C&P87 sch 9 paras 8,9; NIC&P87 sch 8A paras 8,9

Appendix 1 **Legislation**

England, Wales and Scotland

Main primary legislation (Acts)

The Social Security Contributions and Benefits Act 1992

The Social Security Administration Act 1992

The Child Support, Pensions and Social Security Act 2000

The Welfare Reform Act 2007

The Welfare Reform Act 2012

The Welfare Reform and Work Act 2016

Main secondary legislation (Regulations and Orders)

SI 2006/213	The Housing Benefit Regulations 2006
SI 2006/214	The Housing Benefit (Persons who have attained the qualifying age for state pension credit) Regulations 2006
SI 2006/217	The Housing Benefit and Council Tax Benefit (Consequential Provisions) Regulations 2006
SI 1997/1984	The Rent Officers (Housing Benefit Functions) Order
SI 1997/1995	The Rent Officers (Housing Benefit Functions) (Scotland) Order
SI 1998/562	The Income-related Benefits (Subsidy to Authorities) Order 1998
SI 2001/1002	The Housing Benefit and Council Tax Benefit (Decisions and Appeals) Regulations
SI 2001/1167	The Discretionary Financial Assistance Regulations
SI 2014/1230	The Universal Credit (Transitional Provisions) Regulations 2014

Recent secondary legislation: housing benefit

The following is a list of amendments etc (or otherwise relevant) to the main regulations from 6th April 2020. This list is up to date as at 5th April 2021.

SI 2020/618	The Social Security (Income and Capital) (Miscellaneous Amendments) Regulations 2020
SI 2020/655	The Universal Credit (Persons who have attained state pension credit qualifying age) (Amendment) Regulations 2020
SI 2020/683	The Social Security (Income-Related Benefits) (Persons of Northern Ireland – Family Members) (Amendment) Regulations 2020
SI 2020/989	The Social Security (Scotland) Act 2018 (Young Carer Grants, Short-Term Assistance and Winter Heating Assistance) (Consequential Provision and Modifications) Order 2020
SI 2020/1156	The Social Security (Coronavirus) (Prisoners) Amendment Regulations 2020
SI 2020/1201	The Social Security (Coronavirus) (Further Measures) (Amendment) and Miscellaneous Amendment Regulations 2020
SI 2020/1209	The Citizens' Rights (Application Deadline and Temporary Protection) (EU Exit) Regulations 2020
SI 2020/1309	The Immigration and Social Security Co-ordination (EU Withdrawal) Act 2020 (Consequential, Saving, Transitional and Transitory Provisions) (EU Exit) Regulations 2020
SI 2020/1372	The Immigration (Citizens' Rights etc.) (EU Exit) Regulations 2020
SI 2020/1519	The Rent Officers (Housing Benefit and Universal Credit Functions) (Modification) Order 2020
SI 2021/162	The Social Security Benefits Up-rating Order 2021
SI 2021/188	The Housing Benefit (Persons who have attained the qualifying age for state pension credit) (Amendment) Regulations 2021
SI 2021/476	The Social Security (Coronavirus) (Miscellaneous Amendments) Regulations 2021

Recent transitional regulations and commencement orders: universal credit

The following is a list of commencement orders from 6th April 2020 affecting the roll-out of universal credit full service and consequent phasing out of housing benefit for new working age claims. This list is up to date as at 5th April 2021.

SI 2019/1152	The Universal Credit (Managed Migration Pilot and Miscellaneous Amendments) Regulations 2019
SI 2021/4	The Universal Credit (Transitional Provisions) (Claimants previously entitled to a severe disability premium) Amendment Regulations 2021

Northern Ireland

Main primary legislation (Acts and Acts of Northern Ireland Assembly)

The Social Security Contributions and Benefits (Northern Ireland) Act 1992

The Social Security Administration (Northern Ireland) Act 1992

The Child Support, Pensions and Social Security Act (Northern Ireland) 2000

The Welfare Reform Act (Northern Ireland) 2007

The Welfare Reform Act (Northern Ireland) 2015

The Welfare Reform (Northern Ireland) Order SI 2015/2006

The Welfare Reform and Work (Northern Ireland) Order 2016 SI 2016/999

Main secondary legislation (Statutory Rules and Orders)

NISR 2006/405	The Housing Benefit Regulations (Northern Ireland) 2006
NISR 2006/406	The Housing Benefit (Persons who have attained the qualifying age for state pension credit) Regulations (Northern Ireland) 2006
NISR 2006/407	The Housing Benefit (Consequential Provisions) Regulations (Northern Ireland) 2006
NISR 2008/100	The Housing Benefit (Executive Determinations) Regulations (Northern Ireland) 2008
NISR 2001/213	The Housing Benefit (Decisions and Appeals) Regulations (Northern Ireland) 2001
NISR 2001/216	The Discretionary Financial Assistance Regulations (Northern Ireland) 2001
NISR 2016/226	The Universal Credit (Transitional Provisions) Regulations (Northern Ireland) 2016

Recent secondary legislation: housing benefit

The following is a list of amendments etc (or otherwise relevant) to the main regulations from 6th April 2020. This list is up to date as at 5th April 2021.

SI 2019/129   The Social Security (Amendment) (Northern Ireland) (EU Exit) Regulations 2019

NISR 2020/108   The Social Security (Income and Capital) (Miscellaneous Amendments) Regulations (Northern Ireland) 2020

NISR 2020/119   The Universal Credit (Persons who have attained state pension credit qualifying age) (Amendment) Regulations (Northern Ireland) 2020

NISR 2020/149   The Social Security (Income-related Benefits) (Persons of Northern Ireland – Family Members) (Amendment) Regulations (Northern Ireland) 2020

NISR 2020 227   The Social Security (Coronavirus) (Prisoners) (Amendment) Regulations (Northern Ireland) 2020

NISR 2020/242   The Social Security (Coronavirus) (Further Measures) (Amendment) and Miscellaneous Amendment Regulations (Northern Ireland) 2020

SI 2020/1209   The Citizens' Rights (Application Deadline and Temporary Protection) (EU Exit) Regulations 2020

SI 2020/1309   The Immigration and Social Security Co-ordination (EU Withdrawal) Act 2020 (Consequential, Saving, Transitional and Transitory Provisions) (EU Exit) Regulations 2020

SI 2020/1372   The Immigration (Citizens' Rights etc) (EU Exit) Regulations 2020

NISR 2021/14   The Housing Benefit and Universal Credit Housing Costs (Executive Determinations) (Modification) Regulations (Northern Ireland) 2021

NISR 2021/70   The Housing Benefit (Persons who have attained the qualifying age for state pension credit) (Amendment) Regulations (Northern Ireland) 2021

NISR 2021/82   The Social Security Benefits Up-rating Order (Northern Ireland) 2021

NISR 2021/105   The Social Security (Coronavirus) (Miscellaneous Amendments) Regulations (Northern Ireland) 2021

Recent transitional regulations and commencement orders: universal credit

The following is a list of commencement orders and other secondary legislation from 6th April 2020 relating to housing benefit. This list is up to date as at 5th April 2021.

NISR 2019/152   The Universal Credit (Managed Migration and Miscellaneous Amendments) Regulations (Northern Ireland) 2019

NISR 2021/2   The Universal Credit (Transitional Provisions) (Claimants previously entitled to a severe disability premium) (Amendment) Regulations (Northern Ireland) 2021

Appendix 2 **Selected weekly benefit rates from April 2021**

	£
Attendance allowance	
Higher rate	89.60
Lower rate	60.00
Bereavement support payment	
(higher rate)	80.77
(standard rate)	23.08
Child benefit	
Only or older/oldest child	21.15
Each other child	14.00
Carer's allowance	
Claimant	67.60
Disability living allowance	
Care component	
Highest rate	89.60
Middle rate	60.00
Lowest rate	23.70
Mobility component	
Higher rate	62.55
Lower rate	23.70
Employment and support allowance (new style)	
Personal allowances	
Aged under 25	59.20
Aged 25 or over	74.70
Components	
Work-related activity	29.70
Support	39.40
Guardian's allowance	18.00

£

Industrial disablement pension

20% disabled	36.58
For each further 10% disability up to 100%	18.29
100% disabled	182.90

Jobseeker's allowance (new style)

Aged under 25	59.20
Aged 25 or over	74.70

Maternity and paternity pay and allowance

Statutory maternity, paternity and adoption pay	151.97
Maternity allowance	151.97

Personal independence payment

Daily living component	
Enhanced rate	89.60
Standard rate	60.00
Mobility component	
Enhanced rate	62.55
Standard rate	23.70

Retirement pension

New state pension (flat rate)	179.60
Old state pension (basic pension)	137.60
Old state pension spouse or civil partner's insurance (basic pension)	82.45

Severe disablement allowance

Basic rate	81.25
Age-related addition	
Higher rate	12.15
Middle and lower rate	6.75

Statutory sick pay

Standard rate	96.35

Widow's/widower's benefits (for deaths before 6th April 2017)

Widowed parent's allowance (standard rate)	122.55
Widow's pension (standard rate)	122.55

For details of other benefit rates from April 2021 (including means-tested benefits, tax credits and war pensions) see Circulars A1/2021 and A2/2021.

Appendix 3 **Equivalent CTR footnote references**

Table A: England

This table shows the equivalent footnote references for the law on council tax rebates in England for chapters 12-15 of this guide

	Prescribed Requirements (SI 2012 No. 2885)	**Default Scheme (SI 2012 No. 2886)**
12.5	sch 1 para 6(1)(a), sch 2 para 1	25(1)(a), 26(1)(a), sch 2 para 1, sch 3 para 1
12.6	sch 2 para 1; SI 2018/1346 reg 4	sch 2 para 1(1)(b),(2)(b)
12.7	–	26(1)(a), sch 3 para 1(1)(a),(b),(2),(3)
12.8	–	26(1)(a), sch 3 para 1(1)(c)
12.9	sch 1 para 6(1)(b), sch 2 para 2(1)	25(1)(b), 26(1)(b), sch 2 para 2(1), sch 3 para 3(1)
12.10-11	sch 1 para 6(1)(b); SI 2017/1305 reg 7	25(1)(b), 26(1)(b)
12.12	sch 1 para 6(1C); SI 2017/1305 reg 17	–
12.13	sch 1 para 6(1A)-(1C)	–
12.14	sch 1 para 6(1B),(1C)	–
12.17	SI 2017/1305 reg 17	–
12.18	SI 2017/1305 reg 17(4)-(9)	–
12.19	sch 1 para 6(1)(c),(d), sch 2 paras 3, 6-9	25(1)(c),(d), 26(1)(c),(d), sch 2 paras 3, 6-9, sch 3 paras 4, 11-14
12.22	sch 2 paras 8, 12(3)	sch 2 paras 8, 12(3), sch 3 para 13, 17(3)
12.23	sch 2 paras 7, 12(2)	sch 2 paras 7, 12,(2), sch 3 para 12, 17(5)
12.24	sch 1 para 6(1)(c), sch 2 para 3; SI 2015/2041 regs 2(4)(b), 3	25(1)(c), 26(1)(c), sch 2 para 3, sch 3 para 4
12.25	sch 2 para 6	sch 2 para 6, sch 3 para 11
12.26	sch 2 para 12(1)(a)	sch 2 para 12(1)(a), sch 3 para 17(2)(a)
12.27	sch 2 para 12(1)(b)	sch 2 para 12(1)(b), sch 3 para 17(2)(b)
12.28	sch 2 para 6(7)(d),(8)	sch 2 para 6(7)(d),(8), sch 3 para 11(5)(b),(6),(7)
12.29-31	sch 2 para 9(1),(2)	sch 2 para 9(1),(2), sch 3 para 14(1),(2)
12.30	sch 2 para 12(4)	sch 2 para 12(4), sch 3 para 17(4)
12.32	sch 2 para 11	sch 2 para 11, sch 3 para 16
12.33	sch 2 para 11	sch 2 para 11, sch 3 para 16
12.37	–	sch 3 paras 9, 10(8)
12.38	–	sch 3 para 17(1)
12.39	–	sch 3 para 10(1)(a)
12.40	–	sch 3 para 12(1)(a)-(c)
12.41	–	sch 3 para 12(1)(b)-(c)
12.42	–	sch 3 paras 18, 21, 22

12.43	–	sch 3 paras 18, 19
12.44	–	sch 3 paras 20(2), 23, 24
12.46	–	sch 3 paras 2, 18, 19
12.50	–	sch 3 paras 25, 26, 28
12.52	8(1)	8(1)
12.53	sch 2 paras 7(2), 8(c)	sch 2 paras 7(2), 8(c), sch 3 paras 12(2), 13(c)
12.54	sch 2 para 6(4),(5)	sch 2 para 6(4),(5), sch 3 para 10(1)(a)(vii),(2)
T12.2(a)	sch 2 paras 6(7)(a)-(c), 12(1)(b)(i)	sch 2 paras 6(7)(a)-(c), 12(1)(b)(i), sch 3 paras 10(1)(a)(iii)-(v), 11(5)(a), 12(1)(b),(c),(3), 17(2)(b)
T12.2(b)	sch 2 paras 7(1)(a),(b), 8(a)	sch 2 paras 7(1)(a),(b), 8(a), sch 7 paras 12(1)(b),(c), 13(a)
T12.2(c)	sch 2 para 9(2)(b)	sch 2 para 9(2)(b), sch 7 para 14(2)(b),(4)(b)
12.55	sch 2 para 10	sch 2 para 10, sch 3 para 15
13.1	sch 1 paras 16(1),(2), 24(1)(a),(b)	39(1),(2), 57(1)(a),(b)
13.2	sch 1 para 11	33, sch 8 para 25
13.3	sch 1 para 13	38, sch 7 para 14, sch 8 paras 8, 9
13.4	sch 1 para 17(9)-(11), sch 4, sch 5	40(9)-(11), 52(2), 54(2), 61(2), sch 5, sch 6, sch 7, sch 8
13.5	sch 1 para 13	35, sch 7 para 14, sch 8 paras 8, 9
13.6	sch 1 paras 17(1),(7), 24(1)	40(1),(7), 49(1),(2), 57(1)
13.7	sch 1 paras 17(1),(7), 24(1)	40(1),(7), 49(1),(2), 57(1)
13.8	sch 1 paras 17(1), 24(1)	40(1), 47-49, 57(1)
T13.1	sch 1 paras 16(1), 17(11), sch 5	39(1), 40(11), 54(2), sch 6, sch 8
T13.1(a)-(c)	sch 1 paras 13,16(1)(j)(zi)	35, 37, sch 8 paras 8, 9
T13.1(d)-(f)	sch 1 para 16(1)(j)(i)-(v)	39(1)(j)(i)-(v), sch 8 paras 11,14
T13.1(g)	sch 1 para 16(1)(j)(xiii)	39(1)(j)(xiii)
T13.1(h)	sch 1 para 16(1)	39(1)
T13.1(i)	sch 1 para 16(1)(j)(vi)	39(1)(j)(vi), sch 8 para 66
T13.1(j)	sch 1 para 16(j)(vii)	39(1)(j)(vii), sch 8 para 52
T13.1(k)	sch 1 para 16(1)(j)(x)	39(1)(j)(x), sch 8 para 38
T13.1(l)	sch 1 para 16(j)(ix)	39(1)(j)(ix), sch 8 para 37(a), sch 10 para 25(a)
T13.1(n)	sch 1 para 16(1)(j)(xx)-(xxvii)	No equivalent
T13.1(o)	sch 1 para 16(1)	39(1), sch 8 para 51, sch 10 paras 47, 48
T13.1(p)	sch 1 para 16(1)	2(1), 39(1), sch 8 paras 2, 3, 18, 52, 63
T13.1(q)	sch 1 para 16(1)(u)	2(1), 39(1)(u), sch 8 para 12
T13.2(a)-(m)	sch 1 para 16(1)(b),(c),(j)	39(1)(b),(c),(j), 49(1),(3), 54(1)
T13.2(n)	sch 5 paras 7, 8	sch 6 paras 7, 8, sch 8 para 21
T13.2(o)	sch 1 para16(1)(j)(v),(n), sch 5 para 2	2(1), 39(1)(j)(v),(n), sch 6 para 2, sch 8 para 14
13.11	sch 1 paras 16(1)(j), 17(7)	39(1)(j), 40(7), 49(1),(2), 54(1)

13.12	sch 1 paras 16(1)(b), 24	39(1)(b),(3), 49(1), 54(1),(5), 59, 64(10), 67(4)(g),(h)
13.13	sch 6 para 28	sch 9 para 28
13.14	sch 1 paras 14(2)(a), 17(7)	36(2)(a), 40(7)
13.15	sch 1 para 14(1)	36(1)
T13.3	sch 1 para 14(2)-(5)	36(2)-(5)
13.16	sch 1 para 16(1)(e)-(h),(l)-(m), sch 5 para 1	39(1)(e)-(h),(l)-(m), sch 6 para 1, sch 8 para 20
13.18	See Volume 1 para 16.9	See Volume 1 para 16.9
T13.4	2(1), sch 1 paras 16(1)(e)-(h),(l)-(m), 24(1)(a), sch 5 paras 1-6	2(1), 39(1)(e)-(h),(l)-(m), 49(1), 54(1), 57(1)(a), sch 6 paras 1-6, sch 8 paras 13, 14, 20, 54-56
13.20	sch 1 paras 16(1)(j)(viii), 24(1)(a), sch 5 para 13	39(1)(j)(viii), 54(1), 57(1)(a), sch 6 para 13, sch 8 para 53
13.21	sch 1 paras 16(2)-(4), 24(1)(a)	39(2)-(4), 54(1),(4),(5), 57(1)(a)
13.22	sch 1 para 16(3)	39(2), 54(1),(4),(5)
13.25	sch 1 para 16(1)	2(1), 39(1), sch 8 paras 30-34, 59
T13.5(a)-(f)	sch 1 para 16(1)	2(1), 39(1), sch 8 paras 30-34, 59
T13.5(g)-(h)	sch 1 para 16(1)	39(1), sch 8 para 59
T13.5(i)	sch 1 para 16(1)	39(1), sch 8 para 65
T13.5(j)	sch 1 para 16(1)	2(1) definition 'occasional assistance', 39(1)(j)(ix), sch 8 para 37(b)
T13.5(k)	sch 1 para 16(1)	39(1), sch 8 para 64
T13.5(l)	sch 1 para 16(1)	39(1), sch 8 para 45
13.27	2(1), sch 1 paras 16(1)(c),(d),(t),(x), 17(13), 18(2), 24(1)(a)	2(1), 39(1)(c),(d),(t),(x), 40(13), 41(2), 49(1), 51(2), 57(1)(a), sch 8 para 4
13.29	sch 1 para 24(1)	49(1), 57(1)
T13.6	sch 1 para 16(1)(o), sch 5 para 20	39(1)(o), 49(1), sch 6 para 20, sch 8 paras 49, 50
13.30	sch 1 para 16(1)	39(1), sch 8 para 19(1)(a),(b),(2)
T13.7(a)	sch 1 para 16(1)	39(1), sch 8 para 25
T13.7(b)	2(1), sch 1 para 16(1)(p), sch 5 para 9	2(1), 39(1)(p), sch 6 para 9, sch 8 para 27
T13.7(c)	sch 1 para 16(1)(v), sch 5 para 10	39(1)(v), sch 6 para 10, sch 8 para 26
T13.8(a)	Not PA	sch 8 paras 4, 22(2),(3)
T13.8(b)	sch 1 para 16(1), sch 5 para 23	39(1), 64(5), sch 6 para 23, sch 8 paras 4, 22(1)
13.32	sch 1 paras 16(1)(d), 17(13)	39(1)(d), 40(13), 55(2), sch 8 para 4
13.33	sch 1 paras 16(1)(d), 17(13), sch 5 para 11,	39(1)(d), 40(13), 55(2), sch 6 para 11, sch 8 para 4
13.34	sch 1 para 16(1)(w),(5)	39(1)(w),(5)
13.35	sch 1 para 16(1)	39(1), sch 8 para 35
13.36(c)	sch 1 para 16(1)(i), sch 5 para 12	39(1)(i), 49(1), sch 6 para 12, sch 8 para 19(1)(c)
13.37	sch 1 para 16(1)	39(1), 74
13.38	—	20, 24, 73(1), 75(1),(4),(6), 81(1),(6)
13.39	—	73(1), 81(1)(a)(ii),(b)(ii), 83, 84
T13.9	—	54(6)-(9), 73(1), 81

T13.10	—	54(6)-(9), 73(1), 76
13.40	—	80
13.41	—	73(1), 82, 85(2)
13.43	—	2(1), sch 8 para 61, sch 10 para 54
13.44	sch 1 para 16(1)	39(1), 49(1), sch 8 para 4
T13.11(a)	sch 1 para 16(1)	39(1), sch 8 para 5
T13.11(b)	sch 1 paras 16(1), 18(2)(f)	2(1), 41(2)(f), 51(2)(d), sch 8 para 6
T13.11(c)	sch 1 paras 16(1), 18(2)(b)	39(1), 41(2)(b), 51(2)(b), sch 8 para 7
T13.11(d)	sch 1 para 16(1)	39(1), sch 8 para 17
T13.11(e),(f)	sch 1 para 16(1)	39(1), sch 8 para 46
T13.11(g),(h)	sch 1 para 16(1)	39(1), sch 8 para 47
T13.11(i)	sch 1 para 16(1)	39(1), sch 8 para 48
T13.11(j)	sch 1 para 16(1)	39(1), sch 8 para 15
T13.11(k)	sch 1 para 16(1)	39(1), 51(2)(a), sch 8 para 28
T13.11(l)	sch 1 para 16(1)	39(1)
T13.11(m)	sch 1 para 16(1)	39(1), sch 8 para 44
T13.11(n)	sch 1 para 16(1)	39(1), 55(4), sch 8 para 18(1)(c)
13.46	sch 1 para 17(13)	40(13), sch 8 para 4
13.47	sch 4 para 7, sch 6 paras 18, 19	sch 5 para 7, sch 6 paras 18, 19, sch 7 para 13, sch 8 paras 23, 24
13.48	sch 1 para 16(1)(k), 40(8), sch 4 para 11, sch 5 paras 16, 17	39(1)(k), 40(8), sch 5 para 11, sch 6 paras 16, 17, sch 7 paras 15, 16, sch 8 paras 29, 39
13.49	sch 5 para 12(3)(b),(c)	sch 6 para 12(3)(b),(c), sch 8 para 40
13.53	sch 1 para 11(1)	33(1), 56(9),(10)
13.54	sch 1 para 22(1),(4)	45(1),(4), 56(2), 67(4)
13.55	sch 1 para 22(1)-(8)	45(1)-(8)
13.56	—	56(2),(11), 67(4)
13.57	—	56(3)(c), 67(5)(c)
13.58	sch 1 para 23(1)	46(1), 56(3)(a),(b), 67(5)(a),(b), sch 8 para 28(2)
13.59	sch 1 paras 16(1), 23(2),(3)	39(1), 46(2),(3), 56(4),(11), 67(6)
13.60	sch 1 para 22(9)-(12),(15),(16)	45(9)-(12),(15),(16), 56(1),(13)
13.61	sch 1 paras 12, 14(2)(f)	34, 36(2)(f)
14.4	2(1), sch 1 para 17(9)(a), 19(1), 29(1)	40(9)(a), 42(1), 52(1),(2), 61(1),(2)
14.6	2(1), sch 1 para 16(1)(a)	2(1), 39(1)(a)
14.7	sch 1 para 18	41, 51
T14.1(a)	sch 1 para 18(1)	41(1), 51(1)
T14.1(b)	sch 1 para 17(5)	40(5), 55(3)
T14.1(c)	sch 1 para 18(1)(m)	41(1)(m), 51(1)(k)
T14.1(d)	sch 1 para 18(1)(h)-(l)	41(1)(h)-(l), 51(1)(j)
T14.1(e)	sch 1 para 18(1)(d)	41(1)(d), 51(1)(d)

T14.1(f)	sch 1 para 18(1)(e)	41(1)(e), 51(1)(e)
T14.1(g)	sch 1 para 18(1)(a)	41(1)(a), 51(1)(a)
T14.1(h)	sch 1 para 18(1)	41(1), 51(1)
T14.1(i)	sch 1 para 18(1)(c)	41(1)(c), 51(1)(c)
T14.1(j)	sch 1 para 18(1)(b)	41(1)(b), 51(1)(b)
T14.1(k)	sch 1 para 18(1)(g)	41(1)(g), 51(1)(l)
T14.1(l)	sch 1 para 18(1)	41(1), 51(1)
T14.1(m)	sch 1 para 18(1)	41(1), 51(1)
T14.1(n)	sch 1 para 18(1)(f),(2)(b)	41(1)(f),(2)(b), 51(1)(f),(2)(b)
T14.1(o)	2(8), sch 1 para 18(2)(f)	41(2)(f), 51(2)(d)
T14.1(p)	sch 1 para 18(2)(e)	41(2)(e), 51(1)(g)-(i)
T14.1(q)	sch 1 paras 18(1)(b), 31(1)	41(1)(b), 51, 63(1)
T14.1(r)	sch 1 para 18(2)(a),(3)	41(2)(a),(3)
T14.1(s)	—	64(2)
T14.1(t)	—	64(6)
T14.1(u)	—	64(3)
T14.1(v)	sch 1 para 18(2)(c)	41(2)(c), 51(1)(c)
T14.1(w)	sch 1 para 16(1)	39(1), 51(1)
14.8	sch 1 paras 17(2),(3A),(4),(4A) 24(1)(a)	40(2),(4), 47(1)-(3), 57(1)(a)
14.9		2(1), 47(1)-(3)
14.10	2(1), sch 1 para 17(2)-(4)	2(1), 40(2)-(4)
14.12	sch 1 para 17(3A),(4A)	No equivalent
14.13	—	51(1)(d), 64(4)
14.14	sch 4 para 9	sch 5 para 9, sch 7 paras 1(a),(b), 2(a),(b),(i), 19
14.15	—	51(1)(d), 64(4)
14.16	—	sch 7 paras 1(c), 2(a),(b),(ii), 19
14.17	2(1), sch 1 paras 15, 19	2(1), 38, 42, 47(4), 52
14.18	sch 1 para 18	41, 51
14.19	sch 1 para 19(2)(a),(d)	42(2)(a),(d), 52(3)(a),(d)
14.20	2(1), sch 1 para 19(5),(a),(b)	2(1), 42(5)(a),(b), 52(6),(a),(b), 56(10)(a),(b)
14.22	sch 1 para 19(2)(b),(c),(3),(4),(5)(c)	42(3)(b),(c),(4),(5),(6)(c), 52(2)(b),(c),(3),(4),(5)(c), 56(10)(c)
14.23	2(1), sch 1 paras 15, 19	2(1), 38, 42, 47(4), 52
14.24		56(6),(10)
14.25		56(6),(7),(8),(11)
14.27	2(1), sch 1 para 21(1)	2(1), 44(1), 53(1)
14.28	sch 1 para 21(1)	44(1), 53(1)
T14.2	sch 1 para 21(2)	44(2), 53(2)
14.29	sch 1 paras 20, 24(1)(a)	43, 48(1), 57(1)(a)
14.30	2(1), sch 1 para 20	2(1), 43, 48(1)

14.34		sch 7 para 3
14.36	2(1), sch 1 paras 15, 29	2(1), 38, 48(2), 61
14.37	sch 1 para 21(1)	44(1), 53(1)
14.38	sch 1 para 29(2)(a),(3),(6)	61(3)(a),(4),(7)
T14.3(a)-(e)	sch 1 para 29(5),(7)(b)	61(6),(8)(b)
T14.3(f)	sch 1 para 29(2)(a),(3),(6)	61(3)(a),(4),(7)
T14.3(g)-(n)	sch 1 para 29(4),(7)(a)	61(5),(8)(a)
14.40	sch 1 para 29(2)(a),(3)	61(3)(a),(4)
14.45	sch 1 para 29(6)	61(7)
14.46	sch 1 para 29(3)(a)	61(3)(a)
14.47	sch 1 para 29(1)(b)	61(1)(b)
14.50	sch 1 para 29(9)	61(10)
14.52	sch 1 para 30(4)(b)	62(4)(b)
14.53	sch 1 para 29(1)(b)(i),(2)(b),(8)(a)	61(1)(b)(i),(2)(b),(9)(a), 62
14.54	sch 1 para 28, 30(1)-(3)	2(1), 60, 62(1)-(3)
14.55	NI Only	NI Only
T14.4	2(1), sch 1 para 30	2(1), 62
14.56	2(1), sch 1 para 29(1)(b)(ii),(2)(c), (8)(b),(10),(11)	2(1), 61(1)(b)(ii),(3)(c),(9)(b),(11),(12)
14.57	2(1), sch 1 paras 15, 29	2(1), 38, 48(2), 61
14.58	sch 1 paras 16(1)(q),(r), 17(9)(b),(10)	39(1)(q),(r), 40(6),(9)(b),(10), 53(3)
14.59	sch 1 para 17(5)	40(5), 53(4)
14.61	2(1), sch 1 paras 17(9), 24(1)(c),(2), sch 4 paras 1-6, 8, 10(1),(3), sch 5 para 21	2(1), 40(9), 52(2), 57(1)(c),(2), 61(2), sch 5 paras 1-6, 8, 10(1),(3), sch 6 para 21, sch 7 paras 4-12, sch 8 para 58
14.62	sch 4 paras 1-6, 8	sch 5 paras 1-6, 8, sch 7 paras 4-12
T14.5(a)	sch 4 para 6	sch 5 para 6, sch 7 para 12
T14.5(b)	sch 4 paras 1(a), 2	sch 5 paras 1(a), 2, sch 7 para 5
T14.5(c)		sch 7 para 4
T14.5(d)	2(1) sch 4 para 5	sch 5 para 5
T14.5(e)	sch 4 paras 1(b), 4	sch 5 paras 1(b), 4, sch 7 paras 6, 7
T14.5(f)	sch 4 paras 1(b), 3	sch 5 paras 1(b), 4, sch 7 paras 9, 10
T14.5(g)	sch 4 para 8(b)	sch 5 para 8(b), sch 7 para 8
T14.5(h)	sch 4 para 8(a)	sch 5 para 8(a), sch 7 para 11
14.63	sch 1 para 25(1)	58(1)
14.64	sch 1 para 24(3)	57(3)
14.65	sch 1 para 25(5),(9)	58(5),(10)
T14.6	sch 1 para 25(5),(7)-(8),(17)	58(5),(7)-(9)
14.66	sch 1 para 25(6),(13),(17)	58(6),(9),(14)
14.67	sch 1 para 25(1)(c),(10)	58(1)(c),(11)

14.67(a)	sch 1 para 25(11)(b),(c)	58(11)(b)-(e)
14.67(b),(c)	sch 1 para 25(10)(f),(g),(k)	58(11)(h),(i),(m)
14.67(d)	sch 1 para 25(11)(d),(e),(11),(12)	58(11)(f),(g),(12),(13)
14.67(e)	2(1), sch 1 para 25(11)(g)	58(11)(n)
14.67(f)	sch 1 para 25(10)(l)	58(11)(a)
14.67(g),(h)	sch 1 para 25(1)(c)	58(1)(c)
14.68	sch 4 para 10	sch 5 para 10, sch 7 para 18
14.69	2(1), 10(1)	2(1), 10(1)
14.70	10(2)-(4)	10(2)-(4)
T14.7	sch 4 para 10(2)	sch 5 para 10(2), sch 7 para 18(2)
14.71-72	2(1), 10(1),(5)-(8), sch 1 para 25(2)-(4),(14)-(16)	2(1), 10(1),(5)-(8), 58(2)-(4),(15)-(17)
14.73	sch 4 para 10(4)	sch 5 para 10(4), sch 7 para 18(4)
15.1	sch 1 para 31(1)	63(1)
15.2	sch 1 para 11	33, 63(4)
15.3	sch 1 para 13	35, sch 10 paras 8, 9
15.4	11(2), sch 1 paras 15, 24(1)(b), 31, 37, sch 6	23, 38, 57(1)(b), 63(2), 71, 72, sch 9, sch 10
15.5	sch 1 paras 24(1)(b), 37	57(1)(b), 71, 72
15.10-11	See text	See text
15.11	sch 1 paras 17(1),(7),(12), 24(1), 31(1)	40(1),(7),(12), 49(1),(2), 57(1), 63(1)
15.12	sch 1 para 31(1)	63(1)
15.14	sch 1 para 32	65
15.15	sch 1 para 32	65
15.16	sch 1 para 32(a)	65(a)
15.17	sch 1 para 32(b)	65(b)
15.18	sch 1 para 36	70
15.19	sch 1 para 33	66
15.20	sch 6 para 23	sch 9 para 23, sch 10 para 28
15.22	sch 1 para 31(1)	63(1)
15.23	sch 1 para 31(1)	63(1)
15.24	sch 1 paras 31(1), 32(a)	63(1), 65(a)
15.25	2(1), sch 6 paras 11, 12, 24, 28, 29A, 32	2(1), sch 9 paras 11, 12, 24, 32, sch 10 paras 16, 21, 35, 36
15.26	sch 1 para 16(1)(i), sch 5 paras 22, 23	39(1)(i), 64(5), sch 6 paras 22, 23, sch 8 para 36
15.27	sch 6 paras 5, 31	sch 9 paras 5, 31, sch 10 paras 10, 37
15.29	sch 1 para 31(1),(2), sch 6	63(1),(2), sch 9, sch 10
T15.1	sch 1 para 31(2), sch 6	63(1),(2), sch 9, sch 10
T15.1(a)	sch 6 para 26	sch 9 para 26, sch 10 para 4
T15.1(b)	sch 6 para 4(a)	sch 9 para 4(a), sch 10 para 7(a)
T15.1(c)	sch 6 para 4(b)	sch 9 para 4(b), sch 10 para 7(b)

T15.1(d)	sch 6 paras 1-3	sch 9 paras 1-3, sch 10 paras 5, 32, 33
T15.1(e)	sch 6 para 6	sch 9 para 6, sch 10 para 30
T15.1(f)	sch 6 para 7	sch 9 para 7, sch 10 para 31
T15.1(g)	sch 6 para 5	sch 9 para 5, sch 10 para 10
T15.1(h)	—	2(1), sch 10 paras 6, 14(b)
T15.1(i)	—	sch 10 para 41
T15.1(j)	—	sch 10 para 13(a)
T15.1(k)	—	sch 10 para 13(b)
T15.1(l)	—	2(1), sch 10 para 14(a)
T15.1(m)	—	sch 10 para 26
T15.1(n)	sch 6 paras 18, 20(a)	sch 9 paras 18, 20(a)
T15.1(o)	sch 6 paras 18, 19	sch 9 paras 18, 19
T15.1(p)	sch 6 paras 18, 20(b)	sch 9 paras 18, 20(a)
15.30	sch 6	sch 9, sch 10
15.31	sch 1 para 31(1)	63(1)
15.32	sch 6 para 8	sch 9 para 8, sch 10 para 15
15.33	sch 6 paras 9, 10	sch 9 paras 9, 10, sch 10 para 11
15.34-35	sch 1 para 34(3),(4)	67(7),(8)
15.38	sch 1 para 31(1)	63(1)
15.39	sch 6 para 33	sch 9 para 33, sch 10 paras 10, 17
15.40	sch 1 para 31(1),(2)	63(1),(2)
15.42	2(1), sch 1 para 16(1), sch 6 paras 14, 16, 16A	2(1), 39(1), sch 8 para 41, sch 9 paras 14, 16, sch 10 paras 29, 38, 59
15.43	sch 6 para 17	sch 9 para 17, sch 10 para 50
15.44	sch 5 paras 14, 15	sch 6 paras 14, 15, sch 8 para 19(1)(c)-(e)
15.45	—	sch 10 paras 50, 51
15.46	sch 6 paras 13, 15	sch 9 paras 13, 15, sch 10 paras 58, 60
15.48	sch 1 para 16(1)	39(1), sch 8 para 15, sch 10 para 52
15.50(a)	—	sch 10 paras 47, 48
15.50(b)	—	64(8),(9), sch 10 paras 2, 3, 11(3),(4), 39, 53, 56
15.50(c)	—	sch 10 paras 23, 24, 63, 64
15.50(d),(e)	sch 6 paras 29, 29B	sch 9 para 29, sch 10 para 62
15.50(f)	sch 6 paras 18, 21(1)(e)	sch 9 paras 18, 21(1)(e), sch 10 para 61
15.50(g)	sch 6 paras 18, 21(1)(f)	sch 10 para 25(b)
T15.2	sch 1 para 31(3), sch 6 paras 18, 21(a)-(d),(2), 22	63(3), 64(10), sch 9 paras 18, 21(a)-(d),(2), 22, sch 10 para 12
15.51	sch 1 paras 16(1)(j)(xiii); 31(1),	39(1)(j)(xiii), 63(3), sch 10 para 25
15.53	sch 1 para 31(1)	63(1), 64(7), sch 10 para 38
15.55	sch 1 para 31(1)	63(1)
15.59	sch 1 para 34(5)	67(9)

15.60	sch 1 para 34(1)	67(1)
15.62	sch 1 para 34(2)	67(2)
15.63	sch 1 paras 31(1),(2), 34(1),(2)	63(1),(2), 67(1),(2), sch 10 para 15
15.65	sch 1 paras 34(1), 35	67(1), 68, 69
15.66	sch 1 para 35(1)-(4),(5),(10)	68(1)-(5),(10), 69(1)-(5),(10)
15.67	sch 1 para 35(1)(a),(2),(3),(10)	68(1)(a),(2),(3),(10), 69(1)(a),(2),(3),(10)
15.69	sch 1 para 35(1)(b),(4),(5),(10)	68(1)(b),(4),(5),(10), 69(1)(b),(4),(5),(10)
15.70	sch 1 para 35(1)(b),(7)-(10)	68(1)(b),(7)-(10), 69(1)(b),(7)-(10)

Table B: Scotland and Wales

This table shows the equivalent footnote references for the law on council tax rebates in Scotland and Wales for chapters 12-15 of this guide

	CTR Regulations Scotland		CTR Regulations Wales	
	Working age SSI 2012 No. 303	**Pension age** SSI 2012 No. 319	**Prescribed Requirements** SI 2013 No.3029	**Default Scheme** SI 2013 No. 3035
12.5	21(1)(a), sch 1 para 1	20(1)(a), sch 1 para 2	sch 1 para 1(1)(a), sch 2 para 1, sch 6 para 1(1)(a), sch 7 para 1	23(1)(a), 24(1)(a), sch 2 para 1, sch 3 para 1
12.6	sch 1 para 1	sch 1 para 2	sch 2 para 1	sch 2 para 1
12.7	sch 1 para 1(a),(b),(2),(3)	–	sch 7 para 1(a),(b),(2),(3)	sch 3 para 1(a),(b),(2),(3)
12.8	sch 1 para 1(1)(c)	–	sch 7 para 1(1)(c)	sch 3 para 1(1)(c)
12.9	sch 1 para 3	sch 1 para 3	sch 2 para 2, sch 7 para 3	sch 2 para 2, sch 3 para 3
12.10-11	21(1)(b),(c)	20(1)(b)	sch 1 para 1(1)(b), sch 6 para 1(1)(b)	23(1)(b), 24(1)(b)
12.12-18	Not Scotland	Not Scotland	Not Wales	Not Wales
12.19	21(1)(c)-(d), sch 2 paras 4, 11-14	20(1)(c),(d), sch 1 paras 4, 7-10	sch 1 para 1(1)(c),(d), sch 2 paras 3, 6-9, sch 6 para 1(1)(c),(d), sch 7 paras 4, 11-14	23(1)(c),(d), 24(1)(c),(d), sch 2 paras 3, 6-9, sch 3 paras 4, 11-14
12.22	sch 1 paras 13, 17	sch 1 paras 9, 13(3)	sch 2 paras 8, 12(3), sch 7 paras 13, 17(3)	sch 2 paras 8, 12(3), sch 3 paras 13, 17(3)
12.23	sch 1 paras 12(1)(b),(c), 17	sch 1 paras 8, 13(2)	sch 2 paras 7, 12(2), sch 7 paras 12(1)(b),(c), 17(5)(a)	sch 2 paras 7,12(2), sch 3 paras 12(1)(b),(c), 17(5)(a)
12.24	21(1)(c), 22A, sch 1 para 4; SSI 2016/81, reg 2; SSI 2020/25, reg 5	20(1)(c), sch 1 para 4; SSI 2016/81, reg 18	sch 1 para 1(1)(c), sch 2 para 3, sch 6 para 1(1)(c), sch 7 para 4	23(1)(c), 24(1)(c), sch 2 para 3, sch 3 para 4
12.25	2(1), sch 1 para 11(2)	2(1), sch 1 para 7(2)	2(1), sch 2 para 6(2), sch 7 para 11(2)	2(1), sch 2 para 6(2), sch 3 para 11(2)
12.26	sch 1 para 17	sch 1 para 13(1)(a)	sch 2 para 12(1)(a), sch 7 para 17(2)(a)	sch 2 para 12(1)(a), sch 3 para 17(2)(a)
12.27	sch 1 para 17	sch 1 para 13(1)(b)	sch 2 para 12(1)(b), sch 7 para 17(2)(b)	sch 2 para 12(1)(b), sch 3 para 17(2)(b)
12.28	sch 1 para 11(5)(b),(6),(7)	sch 1 para 7(7)(b),(8)	sch 2 para 6(7)(d),(8), sch 7 para 11(5)(b),(6),(7)	sch 2 para 6(7)(d),(8), sch 3 para 11(5)(b),(6),(7)
12.29	sch 1 para 14	sch 1 para 10	sch 2 para 9, sch 7 para 14	sch 2 para 9, sch 3 para 14
12.30	—	sch 1 para 13(4)	sch 2 para 12(4), sch 7 para 17(4)	sch 2 para 12(4), sch 3 para 17(4)
12.33	sch 1 para 16	sch 1 para 12	sch 2 para 11, sch 7 para 16	sch 2 para 11, sch 3 para 16
12.37	sch 1 paras 9, 10(9)	–	sch 7 paras 9, 10(8)	sch 3 paras 9, 10(8)
12.38	sch 1 para 17	–	sch 7 para 17(1)	sch 3 para 17(1)
12.39	2(1), sch 1 para 10(1)(a)	–	2(1), sch 7 para 10(1)(a)	2(1), sch 3 para 10(1)(a)
12.40-41	sch 1 para 12(1)(a)-(c)	–	sch 7 para 12(1)(a)-(d)	sch 3 para 12(1)(a)-(d)
12.41	sch 1 para 12(1)(b)-(c)	–	sch 7 para 12(1)(b)-(d)	sch 3 para 12(1)(b)-(d)
12.42	sch 1 paras 18, 21, 22	–	sch 7 paras 18, 21, 22	sch 3 paras 18, 21, 22
12.43	sch 1 paras 18, 19	–	sch 7 paras 18, 19	sch 3 paras 18, 19

12.44	sch 1 paras 20(2), 23, 24	–	sch 7 paras 20(2), 23, 24	sch 3 paras 20(2), 23, 24
12.46	sch 1 paras 2, 18, 19	–	sch 7 paras 2, 18, 19	sch 3 paras 2, 18, 19
12.50	sch 1 paras 25, 26, 28	–	sch 7 paras 25, 26, 28	sch 3 paras 25, 26, 28
12.52	11(1)	11(1)	8(1)	8(1)
12.53	sch 1 paras 12(2), 13(c)	sch 1 paras 8(2), 9(c)	sch 2 paras 7(2), 8(c), sch 7 paras 12(2), 13(c)	sch 2 paras 7(2), 8(c), sch 3 paras 12(2), 13(c)
12.54	sch 1 para 10(1)(a)(v),(2)	sch 1 paras 7(4),(5)	sch 2 paras 6(4),(5), sch 7 para 10(1)(a)(vii),(2)	sch 2 paras 6(4),(5), sch 3 para 10(1)(a)(vii),(2)
T12.2(a)	sch 1 paras 10(1)(a)(iii), 11(5)(a), 12(1)(b),(c),(3), 17	sch 1 paras 7(7)(a), 13(1)(b)(i)	sch 2 paras 6(7), 12(1)(b)(i), sch 7 paras 10(1)(a)(iii)-(v), 11(5)(a), 12(1)(b)-(d),(3), 17(6)(b	sch 2 paras 6(7), 12(1)(b)(i), sch 3 paras 10(1)(a)(iii)-(v), 11(5), 12(1)(b)-(d),(3), 17(2)(b)
T12.2(b)	sch 1 paras 12(1)(b),(c), 13(a)	sch 1 paras 8(1)(a),(b), 9(a)	sch 2 paras 7(1)(a),(b), 8(a), sch 7 paras 12(1)(b),(c), 13(a)	sch 2 paras 7(1)(a),(b), 8(a), sch 3 paras 12(1)(b),(c), 13(a)
T12.2(c)	sch 1 para 14(2)(b),(4)(b)	sch 1 para 10(2)(b)	sch 2 para 9(2)(b), sch 7 para 14(2)(b),(4)(b)	sch 2 para 9(2)(b), sch 3 para 14(2)(b),(4)(b)
12.55	sch 1 para 15	sch 1 para 11	sch 2 para 10, sch 7 para 15	sch 2 para 10, sch 3 para 15
13.1	27(1)(a),(b),(4)	27(1),(2), 28(1),(a),(b)	sch 1 paras 5(1), 8(1),(2), 18(1)(a),(b), sch 6 para 20(1)(a),(b)	30(1), 33(1),(2), 54(1)(a),(b)
13.2	24, sch 4 para 24	2	sch 1 para 5(1), sch 6 para 7, sch 9 para 25	30, sch 7 para 25
13.3	sch 4 paras 7, 8	26	sch 1 para 9, sch 8 para 14, sch 9 paras 8, 9	35, sch 6 para 14, sch 7 paras 8, 9
13.4	35(2), 37(2), 39(2), sch 3, sch 4	31(8)-(10), sch 2, sch 3	sch 1 para 11(9)-(11), sch 3, sch 4, sch 6 paras 15(2), 17(2), 24(2), sch 8, sch 9	37(9)-(11), 49(2), 51(2), 58(2), sch 4, sch 5, sch 6, sch 7
13.5	sch 3 para 14, sch 4 paras 7, 8	24	sch 1 para 7, sch 8 para 14, sch 9 paras 8, 9	32, sch 6 para 14, sch 7 paras 8, 9
13.6	27(1), 31(1),(2)	28(1), 31(1),(6)	sch 1 paras 11(1),(7), 18(1), sch 6 paras 12(1),(2), 20(1)	37(1),(7), 46(1),(2), 54(1)
13.7	27(1), 31(1),(2)	28(1), 31(1),(6)	sch 1 paras 11(1),(7), 18(1), sch 6 paras 12(1),(2), 20(1)	37(1),(7), 46(1),(2), 54(1)
13.8	27(1), 29-31	28(1), 31(1)	sch 1 paras 11(1), 18(1), sch 6 paras 10-12, 20(1)	37(1), 44-46, 54(1)
T13.1	39(2), sch 4	27(1), 31(10), sch 3	sch 1 paras 10(1), 11(11), sch 4, sch 6 para 17(2), sch 9	36(1), 37(11), 51(2), sch 5, sch 7
T13.1 (a)-(c)	26, sch 4 paras 7, 8	24, 27(1)(j)(xxvi)	sch 1 para 7, sch 6 para 9, sch 9 paras 8, 9	32, 34, sch 7 paras 8, 9
T13.1 (d)-(e)	sch 4 para 10	27(1)(j)(ii),(iii)	sch 1 para 10(1)(j)(i),(ii), sch 9 para 11	36(1)(j)(i),(ii), sch 7 para 11
T13.1(f)	2(1), sch 4 para 13	2(1), 27(1)(j)(iv)-(vi)	2(1), sch 1 para 10(1)(j)(iii)-(v), sch 9 para 14	2(1), 36(1)(j)(iii)-(v), sch 7 para 14
T13.1(g)	sch 4 para 20A	27(1)(j)(xva)	sch 1 para 10(1)(j)(xiii)	36(1)(j)(xiii)
T13.1(h)	—	27(1)	sch 1 para 10(1)	36(1)
T13.1(i)	sch 4 para 64	27(1)(j)(vii)	sch 1 para 10(1)(j)(vi), sch 9 para 66	36(1)(j)(vi), sch 7 para 66
T13.1(j)	sch 4 para 51	27(1)(j)(viii)	sch 1 para 10(1)(j)(vii), sch 9 para 52	36(1)(j)(vii), sch 7 para 52
T13.1(k)	sch 4 para 38	27(1)(j)(xii)	sch 1 para 10(1)(j)(x), sch 9 para 38	36(1)(j)(x), sch 7 para 38

	Working age SSI 2012 No. 303	Pension age SSI 2012 No. 319	Prescribed Requirements SI 2013 No.3029	Default Scheme SI 2013 No. 3035
T13.1(l)	sch 4 para 36, sch 5 para 24	27(1)(j)(x)	sch 1 para 10(1)(j)(ix), sch 9 para 31, sch 10 para 25	36(1)(j)(ix), sch 7 para 31, sch 9 para 25
T13.1(n)	sch 4 para 66	27(1)(j)(xxii)	No equivalent	
T13.1(o)	sch 4 para 50, sch 5 paras 47, 48	27(1)	sch 1 para 10(1), sch 9 para 51, sch 10 paras 46, 47	36(1), sch 7 para 51, sch 9 paras 46, 47
T13.1(p)	2(1), sch 4 paras 1, 2, 17, 51, 61	2(1), 27(1),	2(1), sch 1 para 10(1), sch 9 paras 2, 3, 18, 52, 63	2(1), 36(1), sch 7 paras 2, 3, 18, 52, 63
T13.1(q)	2(1), sch 4 para 11	2(1), 27(1)(u)	2(1), sch 1 para 10(1)(u), sch 9 para 12	2(1), 36(1)(u), sch 7 para 12
T13.2 (a)-(m)	31(1),(3), 39(1)	27(1)(b),(c),(j)	sch 1 para 10(1)(b),(c),(j), sch 6 paras 12(1),(3), 17(1)	36(1)(b),(c),(j), 46(1),(3), 51(1)
T13.2(n)	sch 4 para 20	–	sch 4 paras 7, 8, sch 9 para 21	sch 5 paras 7, 8, sch 7 para 21
T13.2(o)	2(1), sch 4 para 13	2(1), 27(1)(j)(v),(n)	2(1), sch 1 para 10(1)(j)(v),(n), sch 4 para 2, sch 9 para 14	2(1), 36(1)(j)(v),(n), sch 5 para 2, sch 7 para 14
13.11	31(1),(2), 39(1)	27(1)(j), 31(6)	sch 1 paras 10(1)(j), 11(7), sch 6 paras 12(1),(2), 17(1)	36(1)(j), 37(7), 46(1),(2), 51(1)
13.12	31(1), 32, 39(1),(5), 45(9)	27(1)(b),(4)	sch 1 paras 10(1)(b),(3) 21, sch 6 paras 12(1), 17(1),(5), 27(10)	36(1)(b),(3), 46(1), 51(1),(5), 56, 61(10)
13.13	–	sch 4 para 30A	sch 5 para 27	sch 8 para 27
13.14	–	25(2)(a), 31(6)	sch 1 paras 8(2)(a), 11(7)	33(2)(a), 37(7)
13.15	–	25(1)	sch 1 para 8(1)	33(1)
T13.3	–	25(2)-(6)	sch 1 para 8(2)-(5)	33(2)-(5)
13.16	sch 4 para 19	27(1)(e)-(h),(l)-(m), sch 3 para 1	sch 1 para 10(1)(e)-(h),(l)-(m), sch 4 para 1, sch 9 para 20	36(1)(e)-(h),(l)-(m), sch 6 para 1, sch 7 para 20
13.18	See volume 1 para 16.6	See volume 1 para 16.6	See volume 1 para 16.7	See volume 1 para 16.7
T13.4	27(1)(a), 31(1), 39(1), sch 4 paras 12, 13, 19, 53-55	2(1), 27(1)(e)-(h), (l)-(m), 28(1)(a), sch 6 paras 1-5	2(1), sch 1 paras 10(1)(e)-(h), (l)-(m),18(1)(a), sch 4 paras 1-6, sch 6 paras 12(1), 17(1), 20(1)(a), sch 9 paras 13, 14, 20, 54-56	2(1), 36(1)(e)-(h),(l)-(m), 46(1), 51(1), 54(1)(a), sch 5 paras 1-6, sch 7 paras 13, 14, 20, 54-56
13.20	27(1)(a), sch 4 para 52	27(1)(j)(ix), 28(1)(a), sch 3 para 12	sch 1 paras 10(1)(j)(viii), 18(1)(a), sch 4 para 13, sch 6 paras 17(1), 20(1)(a), sch 9 para 53	36(1)(j)(viii), 51(1), 54(1)(a), sch 5 para 13, sch 7 para 53
13.21	27(1)(a), 39(1),(4),(5)	27(3)-(5), 28(1)(a)	sch 1 paras 10(2)-(4), 18(1)(a), sch 6 paras 17(1),(4),(5), 20(1)(a)	36(2)-(4), 51(1),(4),(5), 54(1)(a)
13.22	39(1),(4),(5)	27(3)	sch 1 paras 10(2), sch 6 para 17(1),(4),(5)	36(2), 51(1),(4),(5)
13.25	2(1), sch 4 paras 29-33, 57	2(1), 27(1)	2(1), sch para 10(1), sch 9 paras 30-34, 59	2(1), 36(1), sch 7 paras 30-34, 59
T13.5 (a)-(f)	2(1), sch 4 paras 29-33, 57	2(1), 27(1)	2(1), sch para 10(1), sch 9 paras 30-34, 59	2(1), 36(1), sch 7 paras 30-34, 59
T13.5 (g)-(h)	sch 4 para 57	27(1)	sch para 10(1), sch 9 para 59	36(1), sch 7 para 59
T13.5(i)	sch 4 para 63	27(1)	sch para 10(1), sch 9 para 65	36(1), sch 7 para 65

T13.5(j)	sch 4 para 37	27(1)(j)(xi)	2(1) definition 'occasional assistance', sch 1 para 10(1), sch 9 para 37(b)	2(1), 36(1), sch 7 para 37(b)
T13.5(k)	sch 4 para 62	27(1)	sch para 10(1), sch 9 para 64	36(1), sch 7 para 64
T13.5(l)	sch 4 para 44	27(1)	sch para 10(1), sch 9 para 45	36(1), sch 7 para 45
13.27	2(1), 27(1)(a), 31(1), 34(2), sch 4 para 3	2(1), 27(1)(c),(d),(t),(x), 28(1)(a), 31(12), 32(2)	2(1), sch 1 paras 10(1)(c),(d),(t),(x), 11(13), 12(2), 18(1)(a), sch 6 paras 2(1), 36(1)(c),(d),(t),(x), 37(13), 12(1), 14(2), 20(1)(a), sch 9 para 4	38(2), 46(1), 48(2), 54(1)(a), sch 7 para 4
13.29	27(1), 31(1)	28(1)	sch 6 paras 12(1), 20(1)	46(1), 54(1)
T13.6	31(1), sch 4 paras 48, 49	27(1)(o), sch 3 para 19	sch 1 para 10(1)(o), sch 4 para 20, sch 6 para 12(1), sch 9 paras 49, 50	36(1)(o), 46(1), sch 5 para 20, sch 7 paras 49, 50
13.30	sch 4 para 18(1)(a),(b),(2)	27(1)	sch 1 para 10(1), sch 9 para 19(1)(a),(b),(2)	36(1), sch 7 para 19(1)(a),(b),(2)
T13.7(a)	sch 4 para 24	27(1)	sch 1 para 10(1), sch 9 para 25	36(1), sch 7 para 25
T13.7(b)	sch 4 para 26	2(1), 27(1)(p), 8 sch 3 para	2(1), sch 1 para 10(1)(p), sch 4 para 9, sch 9 para 27	2(1), 36(1)(p), sch 5 para 9, sch 7 para 27
T13.7(c)	sch 4 para 25	27(1)(v), sch 3 para 9	sch 1 para 10(1)(v), sch 4 para 10, sch 9 para 26	36(1)(v), sch 5 para 10, sch 7 para 26
T13.8(a)	sch 4 paras 3, 21(2),(3)	–	sch 9 paras 4, 22(2),(3)	sch 7 paras 4, 22(2),(3)
T13.8(b)	45(4), sch 4 paras 3, 21(1)	–	sch 1 para 10(1), sch 4 para 23, sch 6 para 27(5), sch 9 paras 4, 22(1)	36(1), 61(5), sch 5 para 23, sch 7 paras 4, 22(1)
13.32	40(2), sch 4 para 3	27(1)(d), 31(12),	sch 1 paras 10(1)(d), 11(13), sch 6 para 18(2), sch 9 para 4	36(1)(d), 37(13), 52(2), sch 7 para 4
13.33	40(2), sch 4 para 3	27(1)(d), 31(12), sch 3 para 10	sch 1 paras 10(1)(d), 11(13), sch 4 para 11, sch 6 para 18(2), sch 9 para 4	36(1)(d), 37(13), 52(2), sch 5 para 11, sch 7 para 4
13.34	Not WA	27(1)(w),(6)	sch 1 para 10(1)(w),(5)	36(1)(w),(5)
13.35	sch 4 para 34	27(1)	sch 1 para 10(1), sch 9 para 35	36(1), sch 7 para 35
13.36(c)	31(1), sch 4 para 18(1)(c)	27(1)(i), sch 3 para 11	sch 1 para 10(1)(i), sch 4 para 12, sch 6 para 12(1), sch 9 para 19(1)(c)	36(1)(i), 46(1), sch 5 para 12, sch 7 para 19(1)(c)
13.37	53	39(1)	sch 1 para 10(1), sch 11 para 2	36(1), 71
13.38	20(2),(4),(6), 52(1), 59(1), 60	–	sch 11 paras 1(1), 3(1),(4),(6), 9(1), 10	70(1), 72(1),(4),(6), 78(1), 79
13.39	52(1), 59(1)(a)(ii),(b)(ii), 62, 63	–	sch 11 paras 1(1), 9(1)(a)(ii),(b)(ii), 12, 13	70(1), 78(1)(a)(ii),(b)(ii), 81, 82
T13.9	39(7)-(10), 52(1), 59	–	sch 6 para 17(6)-(9), sch 11 paras 1(1), 9	51(6)-(9), 70(1), 78
T13.10	39(7)-(10), 52(1), 54	–	sch 6 para 17(6)-(9), sch 11 paras 1(1), 4	51(6)-(9), 70(1), 73
13.40	58	–	sch 11 para 8	77
13.41	52(1), 61, 64(2)	–	sch 11 paras 1(1), 11, 14(2)	70(1), 80, 83(2)
13.43	2(1), sch 4 para 59, sch 5 para 54	–	2(1), sch 9 para 61, sch 10 para 52	2(1), sch 7 para 61, sch 9 para 52
13.44	31(1), sch 4 para 3	27(1)	sch 1 para 10(1), sch 6 para 12(1), sch 9 para 4	36(1), 46(1), sch 7 para 4
T13.11(a)	sch 4 para 4	27(1)	sch 1 para 10(1), sch 9 para 5	36(1), sch 7 para 5

	Working age SSI 2012 No. 303	Pension age SSI 2012 No. 319	Prescribed Requirements SI 2013 No.3029	Default Scheme SI 2013 No. 3035
T13.11(b)	2(1), 34(2)(d), sch 4 para 5	2(1), 32(2)(f)	2(1), sch 1 para 12(2)(f), sch 6 para 14(2)(d), sch 9 para 6	2(1), 38(2)(f), 48(2)(d), sch 7 para 6
T13.11(c)	34(2)(b), sch 4 para 6	27(1), 32(2)(b)	sch 1 paras 10(1), 12(2)(b), sch 6 para 14(2)(b), sch 8 para 7	36(1), 38(2)(b), 48(2)(b), sch 7 para 7
T13.11(d)	sch 4 para 16	27(1)	sch 1 para 10(1), sch 9 para 17	36(1), sch 7 para 17
T13.11 (e),(f)	sch 4 para 45	27(1)	sch 1 para 10(1), sch 9 para 46	36(1), sch 7 para 46
T13.11 (g),(h)	sch 4 para 46	27(1)	sch 1 para 10(1), sch 9 para 47	36(1), sch 7 para 47
T13.11(i)	sch 4 para 47	27(1)	sch 1 para 10(1), sch 9 para 48	36(1), sch 7 para 48
T13.11(j)	sch 4 para 14	27(1)	sch 1 para 10(1), sch 9 para 15	36(1), sch 7 para 15
T13.11(k)	34(2)(a), sch 4 para 27	27(1)	sch 1 para 10(1), sch 6 para 14(2)(a), sch 9 para 28	36(1), 48(2)(a), sch 7 para 28
T13.11(l)	—	27(1)	sch 1 para 10(1)	36(1)
T13.11(m)	—	27(1)	sch 1 para 10(1), sch 9 para 44	36(1), sch 7 para 44
T13.11(n)	40(4), sch 4 para 17(1)(c)	27(1)	sch 1 para 10(1), sch 6 para 18(4), sch 9 para 18(1)(c)	36(1), 52(4), sch 7 para 18(1)(c)
13.46	sch 4 para 3	31(12)	sch 1 para 11(13), sch 9 para 4	37(13), sch 7 para 4
13.47	sch 3 para 13, sch 4 paras 22, 23	sch 2 para 7, sch 3 paras 17, 18	sch 3 para 7, sch 4 paras 18, 19, sch 8 para 13, sch 9 paras 23, 24	sch 4 para 7, sch 5 paras 18, 19, sch 6 para 13, sch 7 paras 23, 24
13.48	sch 3 paras 15, 16, sch 4 paras 28, 39	27(1)(k), 31(7), sch 2 para 11, sch 3 paras 15, 16	sch 1 paras 10(1)(k), 11(8), sch 3 para 11, sch 4 paras 16, 17, sch 8 paras 15, 16, sch 9 paras 29, 39	36(1)(k), 37(8), sch 4 para 11, sch 5 paras 16, 17,sch 6 paras 15, 16, sch 7 paras 29, 39
13.49	sch 4 para 40	sch 3 para 11(3)(b),(c),	sch 4 para 12(3)(b),(c), sch 9 para 40	sch 5 para 12(3)(b),(c), sch 7 para 40
13.53	41(9),(10)	21(1)	sch 1 para 5(1), sch 6 para 19(9),(10)	30(1), 53(9),(10)
13.54	41(2), 48(2)	41(1),(4)	sch 1 para 16(1),(4), sch 6 paras 19(2), 30(2)	42(1),(4), 53(2), 64(2)
13.55	–	38(1)-(7),(14)(a)	sch 1 para 16(1)-(8)	42(1)-(8)
13.56	41(2),(11), 48(2)	–	sch 6 paras 19(2),(11), 30(2)	53(2),(11), 64(2)
13.57	41(3)(c), 48(3)(c)	–	sch 6 paras 19(3)(c), 30(3)(c)	53(3)(c), 64(3)(c)
13.58	41(3)(a),(b), 48(5)(a),(b), sch 4 para 27(2)	39(1)	sch 1 para 17(1), sch 6 paras 19(3)(a),(b), 30(3)(a),(b), sch 9 para 28(2)	43(1), 53(3)(a),(b), 64(3)(a),(b), sch 7 para 28(2)
13.59	41(4),(11), 48(4)	27(1), 39(2),(3)	sch 1 paras 10(1), 17(2),(3), sch 6 paras 19(4),(11), 30(4)	36(1), 43(2),(3), 53(4),(11), 64(4)
13.60	41(1),(13)	38(8)-(10),(13),(14)(b)	sch 1 para 16(9)-(12),(15),(16), sch 6 paras 19(1),(13)	42(9)-(12),(15),(16), 53(1),(13)
13.61	25	25(2)(f)	sch 1 para 8(2)(f), sch 6 para 8	31, 33(2)(f)
14.4	35(1),(2), 37(1),(2)	31(8)(a), 33(1), 36(1)	sch 1 paras 11(9)(a), 12(1), sch 6 para 14(1),(2), sch 6 para 24(1),(2)	37(9)(a), 39(1), 49(1),(2), 58(1),(2)
14.6	2(1)	2(1), 27(1)(a)	2(1), sch 1 para 10(1)(a)	2(1), 36(1)(a)

14.7	34	32	sch 1 para 12, sch 6 para 14	38, 48
T14.1(a)	34(1)	32(1)	sch 1 para 12(1) sch 6 para 14(1)	38(1), 48(1)
T14.1(b)	40(3)	31(4)	sch 1 para 11(5) sch 6 para 18(3)	37(5), 52(3)
T14.1(c)	34(1)(k)	32(1)(m)	sch 1 para 12(1)(m), sch 6 para 14(1)(k)	38(1)(m), 48(1)(k)
T14.1(d)	34(1)(j)	32(1)(h)-(l)	sch 1 para 12(1)(h)-(l), sch 6 para 14(1)(j)	38(1)(h)-(l), 48(1)(j)
T14.1(e)	34(1)(d)	32(1)(d)	sch 1 para 12(1)(d), sch 6 para 14(1)(d)	38(1)(d), 48(1)(d)
T14.1(f)	34(1)(e)	32(1)(e)	sch 1 para 12(1)(e), sch 6 para 14(1)(e)	38(1)(e), 48(1)(e)
T14.1(g)	34(1)(a)	32(1)(a)	sch 1 para 12(1)(a), sch 6 para 14(1)(a)	38(1)(a), 48(1)(a)
T14.1(h)	34(1)	32(1)	sch 1 para 12(1), sch 6 para 14(1)	38(1), 48(1)
T14.1(i)	34(1)(c)	32(1)(c)	sch 1 para 12(1)(c), sch 6 para 14(1)(c)	38(1)(c), 48(1)(c)
T14.1(j)	34(1)(b)	32(1)(b)	sch 1 para 12(1)(b), sch 6 para 14(1)(b)	38(1)(b), 48(1)(b)
T14.1(k)	34(1)(l)	32(1)(g)	sch 1 para 12(1)(g), sch 6 para 14(1)(l)	38(1)(g), 48(1)(l)
T14.1(l)	34(1)	32(1)	sch 1 para 12(1), sch 6 para 14(1)	38(1), 48(1)
T14.1(m)	34(1)	32(1)	sch 1 para 12(1), sch 6 para 14(1)	38(1), 48(1)
T14.1(n)	34(1)(f),(2)(b)	32(1)(f),(2)(b)	sch 1 para 12(1)(f),(2)(b), sch 6 para 14(1)(f),(2)(b)	38(1)(f),(2)(b), 48(1)(f),(2)(b)
T14.1(o)	34(2)(d)	32(2)(f)	sch 1 para 12(2)(f), sch 6 para 14(2)(d)	38(2)(f), 48(2)(d)
T14.1(p)	34(1)(g)-(i)	32(2)(e)	sch 1 para 12(2)(e), sch 6 para 14(1)(g)-(i)	38(2)(e), 48(1)(g)-(i)
T14.1(q)	34, 43(1)	32(1)(b), 41(1)	sch 1 para 12(1)(b), sch 6 para 14	38(1)(b), 48, 60(1)
T14.1(r)	Not WA	32(2)(a),(3)	sch 1 para 12(2)(a),(3)	38(2)(a),(3)
T14.1(s)	45(1)	–	sch 6 para 27(2)	61(2)
T14.1(t)	45(5)	–	sch 6 para 27(6)	61(6)
T14.1(u)	45(2)	–	sch 6 para 27(3)	61(3)
T14.1(v)	34(1)(c)	32(2)(c)	sch 1 para 12(2)(c), sch 6 para 14(1)(c)	38(2)(c), 48(1)(c)
T14.1(w)	34(1)	27(1)	sch 1 para 10(1), sch 6 para 14(1)	36(1), 48(1)
14.8	27(1)(a), 29(1)-(3)	31(3), 28(1)(a)	sch 1 paras 11(2),(4), 18(1)(a), sch 6 paras 10(1)-(3), 20(1)(a)	37(2),(4), 44(1)-(3), 54(1)(a)
14.9	2(1), 29(1)-(3)	–	2(1), sch 6 paras 10(1)-(3)	2(1), 44(1)-(3)
14.10	–	2(1), 31(2),(3)	2(1), sch 1 paras 11(2)-(4)	2(1), 37(2)-(4)
14.12	No equivalent	No equivalent	sch 1 paras 11(2),(4), 18(1)(a), sch 6 paras 10(1)-(3), 20(1)(a)	No equivalent
14.13	34(1)(d), 45(3)	–	sch 6 paras 14(1)(d), 27(4)	48(1)(d), 61(4)
14.14	sch 3 paras 1(a),(b), 2(a),(b),(i), 19	sch 2 para 9	sch 3 para 9, sch 8 paras 1(a),(b), 2(a),(b),(i), 19	sch 4 para 9, sch 6 paras 1(a),(b), 2(a),(b),(i), 19

	Working age SSI 2012 No. 303	Pension age SSI 2012 No. 319	Prescribed Requirements SI 2013 No.3029	Default Scheme SI 2013 No. 3035
14.15	34(1)(d), 45(3)	–	sch 6 paras 14(1)(d), 27(4)	48(1)(d), 61(4)
14.16	sch 3 paras 1(c), 2(a),(b),(ii), 19	–	sch 8 paras 1(c), 2(a),(b),(ii), 19	sch 6 paras 1(c), 2(a),(b),(ii), 19
14.17	2(1), 29(4), 35	2(1), 26, 33	2(1), sch 1 paras 9, 13, sch 6 paras 10(4), 15	2(1), 35, 39, 44(4), 49
14.18	34	32	sch 1 para 10, sch 6 para 14	38, 48
14.19	35(3)(a),(d)	33(2)(a),(d)	sch 1 para 13(2)(a),(d), sch 6 paras 15(3)(a),(d)	39(2)(a),(d), 49(3)(a),(d)
14.20	2(1), 35(6),(a),(b), 41(10)(a),(b)	2(1), 33(4)(a),(b)	2(1), sch 1 para 13(5)(a),(b), sch 6 paras 15(6)(a),(b), 19(10)(a),(b)	2(1), 39(5),(a),(b), 49(6),(a),(b), 53(10)(a),(b)
14.21	Not Scoland	Not Scotland	Not Wales	Not Wales
14.22	35(2)(b),(c),(3),(4),(5)(c), 41(10)(c)	33(2)(b),(c),(3),(4)(c)	sch 1 para 13(3)(b),(c),(4), (5),(6)(c), sch 6 paras 15(2)(b),(c), (3),(4),(5)(c), 19(10)(c)	39(3)(b),(c),(4),(5),(6)(c), 49(2)(b),(c),(3),(4),(5)(c), 53(10)(c)
14.23	2(1), 29(4), 35	2(1), 26, 33	2(1), sch 1 paras 9, 13, sch 6 paras 10(4), 15	2(1), 35, 39, 44(4), 49
14.24	41(6),(10)	–	sch 6 para 19(6),(10)	53(6),(10)
14.25	41(6),(7),(8),(11)	–	sch 6 para 19 (6),(7),(8),(11)	53(6),(7),(8),(11)
14.27	2(1), 36(1)	2(1), 35(1)	2(1), sch 1 para 15(1), sch 6 para 16(1)	2(1), 41(1), 50(1)
14.28	36(1)	35(1)	sch 1 para 15(1), sch 6 para 16(1)	41(1), 50(1)
T14.2	36(2)	35(2)	sch 1 para 15(2), sch 6 para 16(2)	41(2), 50(2)
14.29	27(1)(a), 30(1)	28(1)(a), 34	sch 1 paras 14, 18(1)(a), sch 6 paras 11(1), 20(1)(a)	40, 45(1), 54(1)(a)
14.30	2(1), 30(1)	2(1), 34	2(1), sch 1 para 14, sch 6 paras 11(1),	2(1), 40, 45(1)
14.34	sch 3 para 3	–	sch 8 para 3	sch 6 para 3
14.36	2(1), 30(2), 37	2(1), 26, 36	2(1), sch 1 paras 9, 23, sch 6 paras 11(2), 24	2(1), 35, 45(2), 58
14.37	36(1)	35(1)	sch 1 para 15(1), sch 6 para 16(1)	41(1), 50(1)
14.38	37(3)(a),(4),(7)	36(2)(a),(3),(6)	sch 1 para 23(2)(a),(3),(6), sch 6 para 24(3)(a),(4),(7)	58(3)(a),(4),(7)
T14.3 (a)-(e)	37(6),(8)(b)	36(5),(7)(b)	sch 1 para 23(5),(7)(b), sch 6 para 24(6),(8)(b)	58(6),(8)(b)
T14.3(f)	37(3)(a),(4),(7)	36(2)(a),(3),(6)	sch 1 para 23(2)(a),(3),(6), sch 6 para 24(3)(a),(4),(7)	58(3)(a),(4),(7)
T14.3 (g)-(n)	37(5),(8)(a)	36(4),(7)(a)	sch 1 para 23(4),(7)(a), sch 6 para 24(5),(8)(a)	58(5),(8)(a)
14.40	37(3)(a),(4)	36(2)(a),(3)	sch 1 para 23(2)(a),(3), sch 6 para 24(3)(a),(4)	58(3)(a),(4)
14.45	37(7)	36(6)	sch 1 para 23(6), sch 6 para 24(7)	58(7)
14.46	37(3)(a)	36(2)(a)	sch 1 para 23(2)(a), sch 6 para 24(3)(a)	58(3)(a)
14.47	37(1)(b)	36(1)(b)	sch 1 para 23(1)(b), sch 6 para 24(1)(b)	58(1)(b)

14.50	37(10)	36(9)	sch 1 para 23(9), sch 6 para 24(10)	58(10)
14.52	38(3)(b)	37(3)(b)	sch 1 para 24(4)(b), sch 6 para 25(4)(b)	59(4)(b)
14.53	37(1)(b)(i), (2)(b),(9)(a), 38	36(1)(b)(i),(8)(a), 37	sch 1 paras 23(1)(b)(i), (2)(b),(8)(a), 24, sch 6 paras 24(1)(b)(i),(3)(b),(9)(a), 25	58(1)(b)(i),(2)(b),(9)(a), 59
14.54	2(1), 38(1)-(2)	2(1), 37(1),(2)	2(1), sch 1 paras 22, 24(1)-(3), sch 6 paras 23, 25(1)-(3)	2(1), 57, 59(1)-(3)
14.55	Not Scotland	Not Scotland	Not Wales	Not Wales
T14.4	2(1), 38	2(1), 37	2(1), sch 1 para 24, sch 6 para 25	2(1), 59
14.56	2(1), 37(1)(b)(ii), (3)(c),(9)(b),(11),(12)	2(1), 36(1)(b)(ii), (2)(c),(8)(b),(10),(11)	2(1), sch 1 para 23 (1)(b)(ii),(2)(c), (8)(b),(10),(11); sch 6 para 24(1)(b)(ii),(3)(c),(9)(b),(11),(12)	2(1),58(1)(b)(ii),(3)(c), (9)(b),(11),(12)
14.57	2(1), 30(2), 37	2(1), 26, 36	2(1), sch 1 paras 9, 23, sch 6 paras 11(2), 24	2(1), 35, 45(2), 58
14.58	36(3)	27(1)(q),(r), 31(5),(8)(b),(9)	sch 1 paras 39(1)(q),(r), 11(6), (9)(b),(10), sch 6 para 16(3)	36(1)(q),(r), 37(6),(9)(b),(10), 50(3)
14.59	36(4)	31(4)	sch 1 para 11(5), sch 6 para 16(4)	37(5), 50(4)
14.61	2(1), 27(1)(c),(2), 35(2), 37(2), sch 4 paras 1-6, 8, 10(1),(3), sch 3 paras 4-12, sch 4 para 56	2(1), 28(1)(c),(2), 31(8), sch 4 paras 1-6, 8, 10(1),(3), sch 5 para 21	2(1), sch 1 paras 11(9), 18(1)(c),(2), sch 6 paras 15(2), 20(1)(c),(2), 24(2), sch 3 paras 1-6, 8, 10(1),(3), sch 4 para 21, sch 8 paras 4-12, sch 9 para 58	2(1), 37(9), 49(2), 54(1)(c),(2), 58(2), sch 4 paras 1-6, 8, 10(1),(3), sch 5 para 21, sch 6 paras 4-12, sch 7 para 58
14.62	sch 3 paras 4-12	sch 2 paras 1-6, 8	sch 3 paras 1-6, 8, sch 8 paras 4-12	sch 4 paras 1-6, 8, sch 6 paras 4-12
T14.5(a)	sch 3 para 12	sch 2 para 6	sch 3 para 6, sch 8 para 12	sch 4 para 6, sch 6 para 12
T14.5(b)	sch 3 para 5	sch 2 paras 1(a), 2	sch 3 paras 1(a), 2, sch 8 para 5	sch 4 paras 1(a), 2, sch 6 para 5
T14.5(c)	sch 3 para 4	–	sch 8 para 4	sch 6 para 4
T14.5(d)	Not PA	sch 2 para 5	sch 3 para 5	sch 4 para 5
T14.5(e)	sch 3 paras 6, 7	sch 2 paras 1(b), 4	sch 3 paras 1(b), 4, sch 8 paras 6, 7	sch 4 paras 1(b), 4, sch 6 paras 6, 7
T14.5(f)	sch 3 paras 9, 10	sch 2 paras 1(b), 4	sch 3 paras 1(b), 4, sch 8 paras 9, 10	sch 4 paras 1(b), 4, sch 6 paras 9, 10
T14.5(g)	sch 3 para 8	sch 2 para 8(b)	sch 3 para 8(b), sch 8 para 8	sch 4 para 8(b), sch 6 para 8
T14.5(h)	sch 3 para 11	sch 2 para 8(a)	sch 3 para 8(a), sch 8 para 11	sch 4 para 8(a), sch 6 para 11
14.63	28(1)	29(1)	sch 1 para 19(1), sch 6 para 21(1)	55(1)
14.64	27(3)	28(3)	sch 1 para 18(3), sch 6 para 20(3)	54(3)
14.65	28(5),(10)	29(5),(10)	sch 1 para 19(5),(10), sch 6 para 21(5),(10)	55(5),(10)
T14.6	28(5),(7)-(9)	29(5),(7)-(9)	sch 1 para 19(5),(7)-(9), sch 6 para 21(5),(7)-(9)	55(5),(7)-(9)
14.66	28(6),(9),(14)	29(6),(9),(14)	sch 1 para 19(6),(9),(14), sch 6 para 21(6),(9),(14)	55(6),(9),(14)
14.67	28(1)(c),(11)	29(1)(c),(11)	sch 1 para 19(1)(c),(11), sch 6 para 21(1)(c),(11)	55(1)(c),(11)
14.67(a)	28(11)(b)-(e)	29(11)(b)-(e)	sch 1 para 19(11)(b),(c), sch 6 para 21(11) (11)(a)-(c)	55(11)(b)-(e)

	Working age SSI 2012 No. 303	Pension age SSI 2012 No. 319	Prescribed Requirements SI 2013 No.3029	Default Scheme SI 2013 No. 3035
14.67 (b),(c)	28(11)(h),(i),(m)	29(11)(h),(i),(m)	sch 1 para 19(11)(f)-(j), sch 6 para 21(11) (11)(f)-(j)	55(11)(h)-(l)
14.67(d)	28(11)(f),(g),(12),(13)	29(11)(f),(g),(12),(13)	sch 1 para 19(11)(d),(e),(12),(13), sch 6 para 21(11) (11)(f),(g),(12),(13)	55(11)(f),(g),(12),(13)
14.67(e)	28(11)(n)	29(11)(n)	sch 1 para 19(11)(l), sch 6 para 21(11)(l)	55(11)(n)
14.67(f)	28(11)(a)	29(11)(a)	sch 1 para 19(11)(a)	55(11)(a)
14.67 (g),(h)	28(1)(c)	29(1)(c)	sch 1 para 19(1)(c), sch 6 para 21(1)(c)	55(1)(c)
14.68	sch 3 para 18	sch 2 para 10	sch 3 para 10, sch 8 para 18	sch 4 para 10, sch 6 para 18
14.69	2(1), 6(1)	2(1), 6(1)	2(1), 10(1)	2(1), 10(1)
14.70	6(2)-(4)	6(2)-(4)	10(2)-(4)	10(2)-(4)
T14.7	sch 3 para 18(2)	sch 2 para 10(2)	sch 3 para 10(2), sch 8 para 18(2)	sch 4 para 10(2), sch 6 para 18(2)
14.71-72	2(1), 6(1),(5)-(8), 28(2)-(4),(15)-(17)	2(1), 6(1),(5)-(8), 29(2)-(4),(15)-(17)	2(1), 10(1),(5)-(8), sch 6 para 19(2)-(4),(15)-(17), sch 6 para 21(2)-(4),(15)-(17)	2(1), 10(1),(5)-(8), 55(2)-(4),(15)-(17)
14.73	sch 3 para 18(4)	sch 2 para 10(4)	sch 3 para 10(4), sch 8 para 18(4)	sch 4 para 10(4), sch 6 para 18(4)
15.1	43(1)	41(1)	sch 1 para 25(1), sch 6 para 26(1)	60(1)
15.2	24, 44	21	sch 1 para 5, sch 6 paras 7, 26(3)	30(4), 60(4)
15.3	sch 5 paras 7, 8	24	sch 1 para 7, sch 6 paras 8, 9	32, sch 8 paras 8, 9
15.4	27(1)(b), 42, 43, 51, sch 5	27(2), 28(1)(b), 40, 41(2), sch 4	27, 30, sch 1 paras 18(1)(b), 25(2), 31, sch 5, sch 6 paras 20(1)(b), 26(2), 33, sch 10	21, 35, 54(1)(b), 60(2), 68, 69, sch 8, sch 9
15.5	27(1)(b), 51	27(2), 28(1)(b)	sch 1 paras 18(1)(b), 31, sch 6 paras 20(1)(b), 33	54(1)(b), 68, 69
15.10-11				
15.11	27(1), 31(1),(2), 43(1)	28(1), 31(1), (6),(11), 41(1)	sch 1 paras 11(1),(7),(12), 18(1), 25(1), sch 6 paras 12(1),(2), , 20(1) 26(1)	37(1),(7),(12), 46(1),(2), 54(1), 60(1)
15.12	43(1)	41(1)	sch 1 para 25(1), sch 6 para 26(1)	60(1)
15.14	46	42	sch 1 para 26, sch 6 para 28	62
15.15	46	42	sch 1 para 26, sch 6 para 28	62
15.16	46(a)	42(a)	sch 1 para 26(a), sch 6 para 28(a)	62(a)
15.17	46(b)	42(b)	sch 1 para 26(b), sch 6 para 28(b)	62(b)
15.18	50	46	sch 1 para 30, sch 6 para 32	67
15.19	47	43	sch 1 para 27, sch 6 para 29	63
15.20	sch 9 para 28	sch 4 para 23	sch 5 para 23, sch 10 para 28	sch 8 para 23, sch 9 para 28
15.22	43(1)	41(1)	sch 1 para 25(1), sch 6 para 26(1)	60(1)
15.23	43(1)	41(1)	sch 1 para 25(1), sch 6 para 26(1)	60(1)
15.24	43(1), 46(a)	41(1), 42(a)	sch 1 paras 25(1), 26(a), sch 6 paras 26(1), 28(a)	60(1), 62(a)

15.25	2(1), sch 5 paras 15, 20, 35, 36	2(1), sch 4 paras 11, 12, 24, 33	2(1), sch 5 paras 11, 12, 24, 31, 33, sch 10 paras 16, 21, 35, 36, 63	2(1), sch 8 paras 11, 12, 24, 31, 33, sch 9 paras 16, 21, 35, 36, 63
15.26	37(5), sch 4 para 35	27(1)(i), 36(4), sch 3 para 22	sch 1 para 10(1)(i), sch 4 paras 22, 23, sch 6 para 27(5), sch 9 para 36	36(1)(i), 61(5), sch 5 paras 22, 23, sch 7 para 36
15.27	sch 5 paras 9, 37	sch 4 paras 5, 32	sch 9 paras 5, 30, sch 10 paras 10, 37	sch 8 paras 5, 30, sch 9 paras 10, 37
15.29	43(1),(2), sch 5	41(1),(2), sch 4	sch 1 para 25(1),(2), sch 6 para 26(1),(2), sch 5, sch 10	60(1),(2), sch 8, sch 9
T15.1	43(1),(2), sch 5	41(1),(2), sch 4	sch 1 para 25(1),(2), sch 6 para 26(1),(2), sch 5, sch 10	60(1),(2), sch 8, sch 9
T15.1(a)	sch 5 para 3	sch 4 para 26	sch 5 para 26, sch 10 para 4	sch 8 para 26, sch 9 para 4
T15.1(b)	sch 5 para 6(a)	sch 4 para 4(a)	sch 5 para 4(a), sch 10 para 7(a)	sch 8 para 4(a), sch 9 para 7(a)
T15.1(c)	sch 5 para 6(b)	sch 4 para 4(b)	sch 5 para 4(b), sch 10 para 7(b)	sch 9 para 7(b)
T15.1(d)	sch 5 paras 4, 32, 33	sch 4 paras 1-3	sch 5 paras 1-3, sch 10 paras 5, 32, 33	sch 8 paras 1-3, sch 9 paras 5, 32, 33
T15.1(e)	sch 5 para 30	sch 4 para 6	sch 5 para 6, sch 10 para 30	sch 8 para 6, sch 9 para 30
T15.1(f)	sch 5 para 31	sch 4 para 7	sch 5 para 7, sch 10 para 31	sch 8 para 7, sch 9 para 31
T15.1(g)	sch 5 para 10	sch 8 para 5	sch 5 para 5, sch 10 para 10	sch 8 para 5, sch 9 para 10
T15.1(h)	2(1), sch 5 paras 5, 13(b)	–	2(1), sch 10 paras 6, 14(b)	2(1), sch 9 paras 6, 14(b)
T15.1(i)	sch 5 para 41		sch 10 para 41	sch 9 para 41
T15.1(j)	sch 5 para 12(a)	–	sch 10 para 13(a)	sch 9 para 13(a)
T15.1(k)	sch 5 para 12(b)	–	sch 10 para 13(b)	sch 9 para 13(b)
T15.1(l)	2(1), sch 5 para 13(a)	–	2(1), sch 10 para 14(a)	2(1), sch 9 para 14(a)
T15.1(m)	sch 5 para 26	–	sch 10 para 26	sch 9 para 26
T15.1(n)	–	sch 4 paras 18, 20(a)	sch 5 paras 18, 20(a)	sch 8 paras 18, 20(a)
T15.1(o)	–	sch 4 paras 18, 19	sch 5 paras 18, 19	sch 8 paras 18, 19
T15.1(p)	–	sch 4 paras 18, 20(a)	sch 5 paras 18, 20(a)	sch 8 paras 18, 20(a)
15.30	sch 5	sch 4	sch 5, sch 10	sch 8, sch 9
15.31	43(1)	41(1)	sch 1 para 25(1), sch 6 para 26(1)	60(1)
15.32	sch 5 para 14	sch 4 para 8	sch 5 para 8, sch 10 para 15	sch 8 para 8, sch 9 para 15
15.33	sch 5 para 10	sch 4 paras 9, 10	sch 5 paras 9, 10, sch 10 para 11	sch 8 paras 9, 10, sch 9 para 11
15.34-35	48(5),(6)	44(3),(4)	sch 1 para 28(3),(4), sch 6 para 30(5),(6)	64(7),(8)
15.38	43(1)	41(1)	sch 1 para 25(1), sch 6 para 26(1)	60(1)
15.39	sch 5 paras 9, 16	sch 4 para 34	sch 5 para 32, sch 10 paras 10, 17	sch 8 para 32, sch 9 paras 10, 17
15.40	43(1),(2)	41(1),(2)	sch 1 para 25(1),(2), sch 6 para 26(1),(2)	60(1),(2)
15.42	2(1), sch 4 para 41, sch 5 paras 29, 38, 59	2(1), 27(1), sch 4 paras 14, 16	2(1), sch 1 para 10(1), sch 5 paras 14, 16, sch 9 para 41, sch 10 paras 29, 38, 57	2(1), 36(1), sch 7 para 41, sch 8 paras 14, 16, sch 9 paras 29, 38, 57
15.43	sch 5 para 51	sch 4 para 17	sch 5 para 17, sch 10 para 48	sch 8 para 17, sch 9 para 48
15.44	sch 4 para 18(1)(c)-(e)	sch 3 paras 13, 14	sch 4 paras 14, 15, sch 9 para 19(1)(c)-(e)	sch 5 paras 14, 15, sch 7 para 19(1)(c)-(e)
15.45	sch 5 paras 50, 51		sch 10 paras 48, 49	sch 9 paras 48, 49
15.46	sch 5 paras 58, 60	sch 4 paras 13, 15	sch 5 paras 13, 15, sch 10 paras 56, 58	sch 8 paras 13, 15, sch 9 paras 56, 58

	Working age SSI 2012 No. 303	Pension age SSI 2012 No. 319	Prescribed Requirements SI 2013 No.3029	Default Scheme SI 2013 No. 3035
15.48	sch 5 para 52	27(1), sch 4 para 15	sch 1 para 10(1), sch 9 para 15, sch 10 para 50	36(1), sch 8 para 15, sch 9 para 50
15.50(a)	sch 5 paras 47, 48	–	sch 10 paras 46, 47	sch 9 paras 46, 47
15.50(b)	45(7),(8), sch 5 paras 1, 2, 10(3),(4), 39, 53, 56	–	sch 6 para 27(8),(9), sch 10 paras 2, 3, 11(3),(4), 39, 51, 54	61(8),(9), sch 9 paras 2, 3, 11(3),(4), 39, 51, 54
15.50(c)	sch 5 paras 22, 23, 63, 64	–	sch 10 paras 23, 24, 61, 62	sch 9 paras 23, 24, 61, 62
15.50 (d),(e)	sch 5 para 62	sch 4 para 29	sch 5 para 28, sch 10 para 60	sch 8 para 28, sch 9 para 60
15.50(f)	sch 5 para 61	41(1)	sch 5 paras 18, 21(1)(e), sch 10 para 59	sch 8 paras 18, 21(1)(e), sch 9 para 59
15.50(g)	sch 5 para 25	41(1)	sch 5 paras 18, 21(1)(f), sch 10 para 25(b)	sch 8 paras 18, 21(1)(f), sch 9 para 25(b)
T15.2	45(9), sch 5 paras 11, 40, 42	41(3), sch 4 paras 18, 21(a)-(d),(2), 22, 25	sch 1 para 25(3), sch 5 paras 18, 21(a)-(d),(2), 22, 25, sch 6 para 27(10), sch 10 paras 12, 40, 42	60(3), 61(10), sch 8 paras 18, 21(a)-(d),(2), 22, 25, sch 9 paras 12, 40, 42
15.51	43(1), sch 5 paras 65, 67, 68, 72	27(1)(j)(xva), 41(1), sch 4 paras 30B, 30D, 30E, 30G	sch 1 paras 10(1)(j)(xiii), 25(1); sch 5 para 28C, sch 6 para 26(1), sch 10 para 65	36(1)(j)(xiii), 60(1), sch 8 para 28C, sch 9 para 65
15.53	43(1), 45(6), sch 5 para 38	41(1)	sch 1 para 25(1), sch 6 paras 26(1), 27(7), sch 10 para 38	60(1), 61(7), sch 9 para 38
15.55	43(1)	41(1)	sch 1 para 25(1), sch 6 para 26(1)	60(1)
15.59	48(7)	44(5)	sch 1 para 28(5), sch 6 para 30(7)	64(9)
15.60	48(1)	44(1)	sch 1 para 28(1), sch 6 para 30(1)	64(1)
15.62	–	44(2)	sch 1 para 28(2)	64(2)
15.63	43(1),(2), sch 5 para 14	41(1),(2)	sch 1 paras 25(1),(2), 28(1),(2), sch 6 paras 26(1),(2), 30(1), sch 10 para 15	60(1),(2), 64(1),(2), sch 9 para 15
15.65	48(1)	44(1)	sch 1 paras 28(1), 29, sch 6 paras 30(1), 31	64(1), 65, 66
15.66	49(1)-(4),(8)	45(1)-(4),(8)	sch 1 para 29(1)-(5),(10), sch 6 para 31(1)-(5),(10)	65(1)-(5),(10), 66(1)-(5),(10)
15.67	49(1)(a),(2),(3),(8)	45(1)(a),(2),(3),(8)	sch 1 para 29(1)(a),(2),(3),(10), sch 6 para 31(1)(a),(2),(3),(10)	65(1)(a),(2),(3),(10), 66(1)(a),(2),(3),(10
15.69	49(1)(b),(4),(8)	45(1)(b),(4),(8)	sch 1 para 29(1)(b),(4),(5),(10), sch 6 para 31(1)(b),(4),(5),(10)	65(1)(b),(4),(5),(10), 66(1)(b),(4),(5),(10)
15.70	49(1)(b),(5)-(8)	45(1)(b),(5)-(8)	sch 1 para 29(1)(b),(7)-(10), sch 6 para 31(1)(b),(7)-(10)	65(1)(b),(7)-(10), 66(1)(b),(7)-(10)

Index

References in the index are to paragraph numbers (not page numbers), except that 'A' refers to appendices, 'T' refers to tables in the text and 'Ch' refers to a chapter.